# Teaching in Secondary School

## Meeting the Challenges of Today's Adolescents

# Teaching in Secondary Schools

## Meeting the Challenges of Today's Adolescents


**Mark D. Baldwin**
California State University San Marcos

**Joseph F. Keating**
California State University San Marcos

**Kathryn J. Bachman**
University of California, San Diego

Upper Saddle River, New Jersey
Columbus, Ohio

**Library of Congress Cataloging-in-Publication Data**

Baldwin, Mark D.
Teaching in secondary schools: meeting the challenges of today's adolescent/Mark D. Baldwin, Joseph F. Keating, Kathryn J. Bachman.
p. cm.
Includes bibliographical references and index.
ISBN 0-13-042223-1
1. High school teaching. I. Keating, Joseph F. II. Bachman, Kathryn J. III. Title.

LB1737.A3B35 2006
373.1102–dc22

2005045890

**Vice President and Executive Publisher:** Jeffery W. Johnston
**Executive Editor:** Debra A. Stollenwerk
**Senior Editorial Assistant**: Mary Morrill
**Production Editor:** Kris Roach
**Production Coordination:** Bookworks
**Design Coordinator:** Diane C. Lorenzo
**Cover Designer:** Terry Rohrbach
**Cover Image:** Corbis
**Photo Coordinator:** Sandy Schaefer
**Production Manager:** Susan Hannahs
**Director of Marketing:** Ann Castel Davis
**Marketing Manager:** Darcy Betts Prybella
**Marketing Coordinator:** Tyra Poole

This book was set in Palatino by TechBooks/GTS York, PA Campus. It was printed and bound by Hamilton Printing. The cover was printed by Phoenix Color Corp.

**Photo Credits:** Marc Anderson/PH College, p. 35; Scott Cunningham/Merrill, pp. 182, 198; Kathy Kirtland/Merrill, p. 251; David Mager/Pearson Learning Photo Studio, p. 223; Anthony Magnacca/Merrill, pp. 116, 164; Tim McCabe/USDA Natural Resources Conservation Service, p. 232; Liz Moore/Merrill, pp. 27, 108; Pearson Learning Photo Studio, p. 79; SuperStock/PictureQuest, p. 228; Anne Vega/Merrill, pp. 52, 205; Tom Watson/Merrill, p. 144; Shirley Zeiberg/PH College, p. 2.

---



Pearson Education Ltd.
Pearson Education Singapore Pte. Ltd.
Pearson Education Canada, Ltd.
Pearson Education—Japan
Pearson Education Australia Pty. Limited
Pearson Education North Asia Ltd.
Pearson Educación de Mexico, S.A. de C.V.
Pearson Education Malaysia Pte. Ltd.

10 9 8 7 6 5 4 3 2 1
ISBN: 0-13-042223-1

*This book is dedicated to Josephine Melenchek Keating, who passed away in March 2004 after a long and courageous battle with breast cancer. Josephine personally and professionally consistently exemplified the guiding theme of this book, "The Circle of Courage." The four main tenets of this model (Belonging, Mastery, Independence, and Generosity) guided her life's work as a teacher and writer. Her students, friends, and family will dearly miss her, but her legacy and example will continue to live on in the lives of those she influenced. Thank you, Josephine, for that legacy.*

# Foreword

There is no question that secondary schools differ from elementary schools in many ways. We further acknowledge the perception that structuring effective educational experiences is more difficult with adolescents in secondary settings. Underlying this perception is an assumption that the secondary schools of the future will have the same organizational structures and curricular, instructional, and assessment practices to which we have become accustomed.

Those of us who have attended and taught in public high schools in North America share a particular view, a paradigm (Kuhn, 1970), of a "typical" secondary school. This paradigm includes teachers working alone in their select content areas of expertise; lock-step, grade-by-grade curriculum; an emphasis on individualistic and competitive student outputs and grading; classes scheduled in 50-minute time blocks; students tracked by academic ability; learning that occurs only within classroom walls for most students or in vocationally oriented sites for others; and separation of students who do not have English as a primary language and special education–eligible students and their teachers into their own tracks or classes.

As Kuhn (1970) described in his observation of scientific revolutions, individuals who hold a particular view or paradigm can become blind to evidence that suggests that this view no longer works, rings true, or is necessary. The paradigm can actually block people from seeing an emerging new view, in the context of this discussion, of a student-centered, inclusive secondary educational experience. Fortunately, the introduction to and elaboration of an alternative paradigm can overcome this blockage or paradigm paralysis.

## *The Circle of Courage: A Paradigm for Effective Secondary Education*

Over the past two decades, the authors of this foreword have been questioning community members around the world about what they value as priority educational outcomes for the students they teach, are responsible for, or care about. We have asked many thousands of citizens across North and Central America and Western and Eastern Europe as well as Russia, China, Vietnam, Laos, and Micronesia the question, "What outcomes, attitudes, dispositions, and skills do you want schooling to develop in youth by the time they leave high school? In other words, what are critical goals of education for the youth you educate and care about?" Regardless of the divergent perspectives, vested interests, or locale of the respondents, their answers are strikingly similar and tend to fall into one or more of four categories borrowed from Native American culture: Belonging, Mastery, Independence, Generosity. Furthermore, no distinction exists between what is important for youth with identified learning needs (e.g., students with disabilities, students considered gifted, students who are English language learners, students eligible for special education) and those without similar needs.

In traditional Native American societies, the main purpose for existence as a society was to produce courageous youth by fostering their development in the four dimensions of Belonging, Mastery, Independence, and Generosity, which together are referred to as the "Circle of Courage" (Brendtro, Brokenleg, & Bockern, 2002). Examples of frequently identified outcomes that represent each of the four sections of the Circle of Courage follow:

1. **Belonging:** experiencing *personal development,* achieving social competence, having friends, forming and maintaining relationships, getting along with others, and being part of a community.
2. **Mastery:** being able to *communicate,* becoming competent in something, and reaching one's potential.
3. **Independence:** engaging in *problem solving,* assuming personal responsibility and accountability for decisions, having confidence to take risks, and being a lifelong learner.
4. **Generosity:** exercising *social responsibility,* being a contributing member of society, valuing diversity, being empathetic, and being a global steward.

If you examine the outcomes for each Circle of Courage dimension, it becomes clear that most people believe that the curriculum must not only include but also go far beyond traditional academic domains.

Many educators acknowledge the pressure they feel to facilitate Mastery outcomes (e.g., standards and high-stakes testing) for their students, but this often occurs at the expense of other areas of the Circle of Courage (i.e., Belonging and Generosity). Native Americans purposely represented all of the dimensions in a circle, as a medicine wheel, to remind us that if one or more of the dimensions are missing or compromised the circle may collapse and the youth's development put at risk. Although we support accountability and mastery, we believe that a danger exists to any society that emphasizes academics only, at the cost and expense of the other dimensions of the Circle of Courage.

## *Translating the Circle of Courage Paradigm into Practice in Secondary Schools*

A basic premise of this book is that in effective secondary schools all students are welcomed, valued, supported, empowered, and are learning together through common, yet fluid, activities and environments. Certain schools not only value the goals of education of Belonging, Mastery, Independence, and Generosity but also use them to structure student learning opportunities. If we adopt the Circle of Courage goals of Belonging, Mastery, Independence, and Generosity as valid and valuable goals of secondary education, then we should assess everything we do in school (e.g., curriculum, instruction, assessment, discipline, staffing patterns, educating students in inclusive versus segregated environments) to see whether these practices facilitate or thwart the attainment of these goals.

The national secondary reform movement documents, such as *Second to None* (1992), *Breaking Ranks* (1996), and *What Matters Most* (1996), and the ideals they espouse very much align with the Circle of Courage goals and thus with the concepts described in this text. All of these documents in one way or another advocate a rigorous yet adaptable curriculum in which students learn to collaborate effectively with others in the context of cooperative settings (Belonging); have opportunities through multiple teaching strategies to learn and apply knowledge (Mastery); are able to individually demonstrate this knowledge through a variety of authentic assessments (Independence); and have opportunities for personal interaction, giving, and learning with the larger community outside the school (Generosity).

This book describes some of the emerging trends and best practices that help secondary educators implement the paradigm represented by the Circle of Courage. The authors translate this paradigm into approaches for altering curriculum, instruction, assessment, discipline procedures; promoting positive student social interaction on campus and service in the community; and crafting the needed supports for individual students. Training new teachers in the approaches presented in this textbook will equip them well to meet the challenges in today's schools.

## References


Brendtro, L. K., Brokenleg, M., & Bockern, S. V. (2002). *Reclaiming youth at risk: Our hope for the future.* Bloomington, IN: National Education Service.

California Task Force (1992). *Second to none.* Sacramento, CA: Department of Education.

Kuhn, T. S. (1970) . *The structure of scientific revolutions.* Chicago, IL: University of Chicago Press.

National Association of Secondary School Principals (1996). *Breaking ranks: Changing an American institution.* Reston, VA: NASSP.

National Commission on Teaching and America's Future (1996). *What matters most.* New York: NCTAF.



Jacqueline S. Thousand, PhD
Professor, College of Education
California State University San Marcos

Richard A. Villa, EdD
President, Bayridge Consortium, Inc.

# Preface

*Teaching in Secondary Schools: Meeting the Challenges of Today's Adolescents* has been designed to help the preservice teacher build a strong knowledge base, firm foundations of practice, and a range of skills to successfully teach in today's secondary schools.

The text material covers a range of core topics focused on the essential background knowledge and skills needed to enter the profession. This is a starting point for a professional educator's career. Further exploration of ideas, instructional strategies, and assessment techniques will be necessary to become a powerful educator.

*Teaching in Secondary Schools: Meeting the Challenges of Today's Adolescents* primarily focuses on the preparation of high school teachers. The guidance provided by documents concerning the preparation of high school teachers, such as *Second to None* and *Breaking Ranks,* makes it clear the teacher's focus must first and foremost be on the student. As a result, teachers may apply the ideas presented in this textbook, whether in planning, instructional strategies, assessment, or classroom environment, to middle school contexts as well as high school settings.

## Conceptual Framework

We have selected the Circle of Courage as a guiding theme to frame the entire textbook (Brendtro et al., 2002). In use for centuries as a framework for educating youth, this model is grounded in Native American traditional approaches to guiding children and adolescents into their place in society. Developmental research, aligned with the ideas of such researchers as William Glasser, Abraham Maslow, and Rudolph Dreikurs, also supports this model.

The Circle of Courage model involves four key components: *Belonging, Mastery, Generosity,* and *Independence*. Graphically represented as a circle with four sections (illustrated in Chapter 1, Figure 1.1), the Circle of Courage reminds educators that we must always focus on all aspects of student's development if we hope to help them develop as adults who engage in healthy and productive lives. In contrast, absence or underdevelopment of any one or more of the sections of the circle will likely indicate emotional or behavioral difficulties in a student. As the reader proceeds through the text, reference to the four aspects of the Circle of Courage will continue. As an integral part of the text, we have woven them throughout each chapter accordingly.

A second anchor integrated throughout *Teaching in Secondary Schools: Meeting the Challenges of Today's Adolescents* is the use of teacher standards prepared by the Interstate New Teacher Assessment and Support Consortium (INTASC). This consortium—dedicated to reforming education, licensing, and professional development of teachers—believes evidence of competency in each of the standards indicates a new teacher's readiness to enter the profession.

We have chosen to highlight the INTASC standards because they represent the "best practice" of those hoping to enter the teaching profession. Each chapter begins with one or more INTASC principles aligned with the material that follows and additionally presents key dispositions from that principle. We believe the key dispositions identified by INTASC make a significant difference in the preparation of teachers, offering guidance to a new professional beyond knowledge and skills by suggesting attitudes and behaviors needed to become a competent teacher. New teachers who shape their professional stance around the key dispositions enhance their opportunity to remain successful for many years.

The three aspects of the INTASC standards—knowledge, dispositions, and performances—provide a benchmark for those entering the world of a teacher. At any point during their preparation, preservice teachers will be able to conduct a self-analysis to determine how to focus their energies to continue to move toward accomplishing their ultimate goals. The book contains several activities designed to assist preservice teachers in self-assessing professional growth.

## Organization of the Text

The book is divided into five units. Unit I provides a foundation for the teaching profession itself, addressing today's schools and today's learners. It introduces both the Circle of Courage and INTASC standards. Unit II builds upon the previous unit with specifics on planning instruction and ties them appropriately to assessment. The unit begins with a chapter on assessment in accordance with the work of Wiggins and McTighe (1998), who believe that curriculum should be "designed backward," identifying desired results first. Assessment tools needed to determine student understanding should drive the learning experiences and instruction. The next chapters focus on instructional strategies and the development of the unit and lesson plans.

Unit III addresses approaches for engaging learners, delving into a more sophisticated level of planning, such as strategies for integrating cooperative learning and interdisciplinary connections. Unit IV deals with creating supportive environments for learning, including a chapter on diverse inclusive classrooms and a chapter on classroom management. Unit V focuses on challenges extending beyond the classroom, beginning with a chapter on collaboration between schools and communities. The final chapter addresses issues of professionalism, revisiting and culminating prior discussion of teacher dispositions and delving further into the attributes of successful teachers. Professionalism is tied together with student focus, as illustrated by the Circle of Courage.

We hope that the arrangement of the chapters works in a logical fashion for the best use of the instructor and preservice teacher. Recognizing there is no one best sequence to prepare a teacher, the chapters also allow for flexibility in their application. Faculty guiding teacher preparation will be able to determine the most effective way to use the textbook in their courses.

## Special Features

- *INTASC Principles and Key Dispositions.* Each chapter begins with the appropriate INTASC standards and key dispositions it is aligned with. Instructional Resource A contains a complete set of all 10 standards. Each standard includes the knowledge, dispositions, and performances INTASC identifies. Each chapter contains specific standards to assist preservice teachers in assessing their readiness to enter the profession during various stages of their preparation program. This allows preservice teachers to compare their knowledge, dispositions, and performances to important benchmarks.

- *"A Closer Look."* Throughout the textbook, the use of a magnifying glass icon alerts the reader to additional material that is available within the text, as well as at the end of the text in the Instructional Resources section. "A Closer Look" helps link ideas to provide the reader with examples of concepts presented and how to apply them in everyday practice.
- *Putting It Into Practice Activities.* The intent of each "Putting It Into Practice" assignment is to provide practical application of the ideas presented in the chapter. We believe that research and theoretical understanding are only part of the preparation for the profession. Teachers must be able not only to understand the ideas but also to transfer ideas into effective practice. Putting It Into Practice provides the reader the opportunity to move ideas into application.
- *Applying Technology Activities.* The need to include technology as a part of teacher preparation is a critical component of training as education moves through the twenty-first century. Technology should not be in addition to what teachers do in the classroom; instead it must be infused as an aspect of effective practice. As is true with instructional strategies, technology must be included only when it enhances learning. Accordingly, "Applying Technology" activities enhance the material being covered only in the sections that meet these criteria.
- *Chapter Summaries.* The chapter summary and reflection at the end of each chapter reviews the points presented, clarifies the overall purpose, and ties concepts together. Additionally, this section includes a reflection on the overall framework of the book and the relationship to practice utilizing the Circle of Courage concept as well as student self-reflection on teacher dispositions as related to the chapter.
- *Instructional Resources.* Numerous Instructional Resources at the end of the textbook allow preservice teachers the opportunity to extend their understanding of the material in a specific chapter. Instructional Resources include the complete INTASC standards, action research examples, service-learning projects, sample unit and lesson plans, examples of cooperative learning strategies applied in a classroom setting, as well as examples of strategies used to connect parents and community with secondary schools.


## ACKNOWLEDGMENTS

| Contributing Writers | Areas of Contribution |
|---|---|
| Katherine Hayden, EdD | Education technology |
| Toni Hood, EdD | Service-learning<br>Community connections |
| Jennifer Jeffries, EdD | Culture and climate<br>Professional development<br>Administration |
| James Keating | Classroom management |
| Michelle Mullen | Literacy<br>Assessment<br>Unit and lesson planning |
| Alice Quiocho, EdD | Second-language learners<br>Culture and diversity<br>Differentiated instruction |

(*continued*)

| Contributing Writers | Areas of Contribution |
|---|---|
| Francisco Rios, PhD | Culture and diversity<br>Second-language learners<br>Adolescent development |
| Pat Stall, EdD | Literacy<br>Assessment |
| Rene Townsend, EdD | Tenure and promotion<br>Administration |

We also want to thank the reviewers for their valuable comments. They are Jeri Jo Alexander, Auburn University Montgomery; Janet Boyle, Indiana University—Purdue University at Indianapolis; Wendy Burke, Eastern Michigan University; Leigh Chiarelott, Bowling Green State University; Judith Costello, Regis College; Barbara Kacer, Western Kentucky University; Todd Kenreich, Towson University; Cynthia G. Kruger, University of Massachusettes—Dartmouth; Stephen Lafer, University of Nevada, Reno; Marie Lassmann, Texas A&M University, Kingsville; William R. Martin, George Mason University; Joyce C. Ragland, Eureka College; Angelia J. Ridgway, University of Indianapolis; and Patricia Ryan, Otterbein College.

## References

Brendtro, L. K., Brokenleg, M., & Bockern, S. V. (2002). *Reclaiming youth at risk: Our hope for the future.* Bloomington, IN: National Education Service.

California Task Force (1992). *Second to none.* Sacramento, CA: Department of Education.

Council of Chief State School Officers (1992). Model standards for beginning teacher licensing, assessment, and development: A resource for state dialogue. Washington, DC: Author. www.ccsso.org/content/pdfs/corestrd.pdf

Dreikurs, R. (1982). *Maintaining sanity in the classroom.* New York: Harper and Row.

Glasser, W. (1969). *Schools without failure.* New York: Harper and Row.

Maslow, A. H., Frager, R. & Fadiman, J. (1987). *Motivation and personality* (3rd ed.). New York: Addison-Wesley.

National Association of Secondary School Principals (1996). *Breaking ranks: Changing an American institution.* Reston, VA: NASSP.

National Commission on Teaching and America's Future (1996). *What matters most.* New York: NCTAF.

Wiggins, G., & McTighe, J. (1988). *Understanding by design.* Alexandria, VA: Association for Supervision and Curriculum Development.

# Educator Learning Center: An Invaluable Online Resource

Merrill Education and the Association for Supervision and Curriculum Development (ASCD) invite you to take advantage of a new online resource, one that provides access to the top research and proven strategies associated with ASCD and Merrill—the Educator Learning Center. At www.educatorlearningcenter.com, you will find resources that will enhance your students' understanding of course topics and of current educational issues, in addition to being invaluable for further research.

### How the Educator Learning Center Will Help Your Students Become Better Teachers

With the combined resources of Merrill Education and ASCD, you and your students will find a wealth of tools and materials to better prepare them for the classroom.

*Research*

- More than 600 articles from the ASCD journal *Educational Leadership* discuss everyday issues faced by practicing teachers.
- A direct link on the site to Research Navigator™ gives students access to many of the leading education journals, as well as extensive content detailing the research process.
- Excerpts from Merrill Education texts give your students insights on important topics of instructional methods, diverse populations, assessment, classroom management, technology, and refining classroom practice.

*Classroom Practice*

- Hundreds of lesson plans and teaching strategies are categorized by content area and age range.
- Case studies and classroom video footage provide virtual field experience for student reflection.
- Computer simulations and other electronic tools keep your students abreast of today's classrooms and current technologies.

### Look Into the Value of Educator Learning Center Yourself

A four-month subscription to Educator Learning Center is $25 but is **FREE** when packaged with any Merrill Education text. In order for your students to have access to this site, you must use this special value-pack ISBN number **WHEN** placing your textbook order with the bookstore: 0-13-168662-3. Your students will then receive a copy of the text packaged with a free ASCD pincode. To preview the value of this web site to you and your students, please go to www.educatorlearningcenter.com and click on "Demo."

# Brief Contents

# Contents

## *List of Instructional Resources*

# Unit I

## Foundational Issues

### An Overview of the Profession

# Chapter 1

# Today's Secondary Schools

## INTRODUCTION TO THE CHAPTER

Welcome to the profession. Many of you have made a firm decision to prepare yourselves to become the next generation of teachers who will influence the lives of hundreds of students. In preparing to take on the responsibilities of the profession, you will need to be well grounded in your practice and develop guidelines that will allow you to make sound decisions. One significant strategy this book uses to get you started in the right direction has been the inclusion of two key strands woven into the chapters. We believe that these strands—(1) the Circle of Courage model and (2) the Interstate New Teacher Assessment and Support Consortium (INTASC) standards developed by the Council of Chief State School Officers (1992), including the dispositions of successful teachers—will help guide your practice with students. The INTASC standards will also assist you in understanding your own strengths and growth areas as you prepare for a successful career. We will develop both strands in more detail in this chapter.

The primary goals of Chapter 1 are to review the history of secondary schools and current reform movements, overview the philosophies that have had significant influence on educational practice, describe some of the challenges new teachers will encounter on their paths to working with students, and provide a framework for thinking about your practice as it develops. Section 1 of Chapter 1 reviews the models of schooling from past to present. Although school structures have changed over the years, many practices remain similar to those one might find in the early twentieth century. These patterns will be discussed and analyzed to determine their impact on the work of teachers today.

Section 2 of this chapter provides an overview of four educational philosophies that have greatly influenced the work of teachers in their classrooms, the way that curriculum is developed, and the efforts to reform schools. You can use the activities to help clarify your own educational philosophy. Though most of you will have taken separate courses dealing specifically with these ideas and practices, they are well worth reviewing in the context of your preservice teaching experience. It is important to be constantly mindful of the forces that operate on your teaching practices and exert continuous influence on your work and your students' learning.

Section 3 guides your professional development as it introduces the Circle of Courage model, designed to assist a professional's work with students by using a powerful approach to practice. This section also overviews INTASC standards and teacher dispositions to help you assess your own development as a teaching professional. The INTASC standards act as a benchmark of the knowledge, dispositions, and performances used to assess effective teacher preparation. An additional piece identifies specific personal behaviors or attributes of those who desire to become and remain powerful, effective teachers. We have adapted these seven attributes to target preservice teachers as they engage in preservice study.

You can use each section in this chapter, as well as every section in the book, as a means to actively engage your thinking about your preparation and assist you in identifying targeted areas for growth as you prepare for your own classroom. Each section affords you opportunities to put what you are reading into practice, ideas of where to go for additional study should you wish to explore topics further, and up-to-date references for your own research. The work you do in schools will build on this foundation as you evolve professionally into the teacher you want to become.

## SECTION 1: HISTORICAL OVERVIEW OF SECONDARY SCHOOLS

Today's practice in secondary schools is firmly grounded in practices that have evolved over the past two centuries. Although looking at past practice does not provide specific ideas for today's classroom practice, it does serve as a reminder of previous strategies that have succeeded or failed. Many of today's current practices or new innovations have a long historical record. For example, progressive educators in the 1930s tried individualization, team teaching, open classrooms, alternative schools, work-study programs, nongraded schools, and competency-based programs in one form or another (Pulliam, 1995). As educators help transform secondary schools to meet the demands of today's schools, they can use such information to help inform changes. Additionally, if teachers are going to become change agents and proponents of reform, they need to understand the culture in which today's schools operate.

### Early Schools

As you might expect, the ideas of European educational thinking have strongly influenced the development of educational practice in the United States. Early philosophers, such as Czech John Amos Comenius (1592–1670), believed the purpose of education was to help improve all of society. Comenius envisioned a system in which well-trained teachers would teach all children. John Locke (1632–1704) theorized that students should do more than learn to read in school. He believed that education should be individualized, encourage creativity, and engage all five senses in the discovery of ideas. Other early philosophers—Jean-Jacques Rousseau (1712–1778), Johann Heinrich Pestalozzi (1746–1827), and Johann Friedrich Herbart (1776–1841)—were also instrumental in presenting ideas that focused on child-centered education with students participating in their own learning. These ideas would, over time, find root in the American educational system.

The belief in the value of formal education existed early in the development of the nation. Even in colonial times, education provided opportunities for a limited number of students, primarily white males of wealth and power. Not long after the establishment of the new nation, many recognized the importance of literacy for all citizens as a key to sustaining and safeguarding this grand experiment of democracy and liberty. The earliest public schools, known as common schools, were tax supported, and their curriculum focused on reading, writing, arithmetic, and history. Children could attend these schools for the first three years free and then had to pay a fee for further schooling.

### Birth of the Modern High School

In the early 1820s, public high schools began to emerge in the Boston area as an alternative to Latin grammar schools and English academies. However, high schools had no significant impact on American education until the late 1800s. High schools then began providing advanced education, previously available only at expensive boarding schools, to many students at a modest cost (Cremin, 1980).

As the public began to focus more on secondary schools, they widely debated the primary purposes of high schools. Should schooling emphasize preparation for life and occupation, or formal instruction to form a well-disciplined mind and wisdom to ponder the larger questions about life and happiness? In the end, the curriculum that began to dominate secondary schools centered on advanced science, math, English, history, and the political economy. Even though the forces of the Industrial Revolution led to an increasing focus on practical rather than theoretical learning, the curriculum would not change significantly over the next two centuries. The public viewed the modern high school, together with vocational guidance, as one of the primary means of sorting individuals to meet the needs of the labor market.

The importance of a secondary education grew rapidly. Whereas in 1890 only about 6% (300,000) of the potential school-age population, students ages 14 to 17, attended either a public or private high school, by 1900 this number had risen to 519,000 and by 1940 to 66% (6,546,000) of the eligible student population. The growth of secondary schools continues and an estimated 16 million or more students will be enrolled in public high schools by 2008 (Spring, 2001; Wirt et al., 1998).

***Reactions to Public Schools.*** As noted earlier, a tax-supported universal free school system developed from the 1830s to the 1860s. One underlying goal of the educational system was to socialize young students coming into its classrooms. In public schools, this process was primarily grounded in the Puritan heritage and ideas of the nation. Ideas such as respect for authority, postponement of immediate gratification, neatness, punctuality, responsibility for one's own work, and obeying rules, began to be infused into instruction. Teaching of the dominant culture's values created continuing issues in a multicultural society.

Initially advocates designed the public school movement to protect the ideology of an American Protestant culture, creating cultural and political values centering on Protestantism, republicanism, and capitalism. As a result the common schools were never truly common to all students even in the nineteenth century. Critics charged that the use of state educational funds to promote Protestant religious values was inappropriate. This approach caused problems such as the hostility that developed between Catholics and Protestants. So strong were their feelings of exclusion, Catholics found it necessary to establish their own system of independent parochial schools (Kaestle & Vinorskis, 1980).

***Desegregating Schools.*** From the onset of public schools, groups of students have been excluded from the evolving educational system. Because the system was developed for the dominant culture, it did not necessarily incorporate those of African, Native American, or Hispanic decent. For example, struggles of African Americans for equal educational opportunities can be identified as early as the beginning of the nineteenth century. Though legally permitted to go to school, few black children actually attended. Both the hostile reception given black children in public schools, and the poor economic conditions of the black population, resulted in low attendance rates, making it necessary for most members of these families to work in order to provide life's basic necessities.

Segregated schools did not provide solid educations to those groups not being served by traditional public schools. Even as early as the 1820s, the African American community realized that the result of segregated education was an inferior education for their children. Segregated schools provided nothing on an equal basis, including the employment of inferior teachers sent to work in these schools. The landmark *Brown v. Board of Education* of

*Box 1.1*

**Brown v. Board of Education**

On May 17, 1954, the U.S. Supreme Court unanimously struck down the legal justification for segregation, which had been based on an 1896 court ruling that public accommodations segregated by race were legal as long as they were "separate but equal." The court ruled that to separate black students "from others of similar age and qualifications solely because of their race generates a feeling of inferiority as to their status in the community that may affect their hearts and minds in a way unlikely ever to be undone." The court concluded that in public education separate educational facilities were "inherently unequal."

Topeka, Kansas, in 1954 forced the courts to recognize the inherent inequality of segregated schools (see Box 1.1). Although it accomplished recognition, the ruling did not put an end to an educational system that provided a varying range of educational experience to students of color. Patterns of discrimination against minority students continue to plague schools in the twenty-first century.

## Educational Reform Movements

A Massachusetts educator, Horace Mann, initiated many of the sweeping changes that transformed the system of public schools between 1837 and 1848. Examples were a shift of financial support of schools from parents to the state, the establishment of grade levels based on age and performance, the extension of school terms from commonly 2 to 3 months to up to 10 months, the introduction of standardized textbooks, and mandatory attendance laws (Boyer et al., 2000).

Reformers enacted other changes to the structure of schools, making them more hierarchical, bringing together several small districts to form larger ones, standardizing educational methods and curriculum, as well as developing more formal teacher training (Kaestle, 1983). Additionally, effort increased to enroll more nonattendees, particularly those children living in urban slums, factory tenements, and families of free black citizens. Despite this development in thinking, these efforts were not particularly successful at that time.

Beginning in the 1920s, critics began to attack the public school system as inadequate. Social reformers, known as *muckrakers,* criticized the use of mechanical teaching and learning techniques, the inept nature of school administrations, and the lack of parental concern and involvement. Many of these same issues identified in the early 1900s continue to be targets of criticism today.

During the 1990s, researchers formed a number of committees or task forces to study the perceived shortcomings of secondary schools. Several key documents addressing the issues of reforming secondary education resulted from these efforts. Among the most widely cited by secondary educators have been *Second to None* (California Task Force, 1992), *Breaking Ranks: Changing an American Institution* (National Association of Secondary School Principals, 1996), and *What Matters Most* (National Commission on Teaching and America's Future, 1996). Although unique in some aspects of their focus, these documents share common themes throughout their recommendations.

The National Association of Secondary School Principals reported a good summary of the shared view of the status of today's secondary schools:

> High schools have continued to go about their business in ways that sometimes bear startling resemblance to the flawed practices of the past. Students pursue their education largely in traditional classroom settings, taught by teachers who stand before row upon row of desks. Mostly, these teachers lecture at students, whose main participation in class is limited to terse answers to fact-seeking questions. High schools persist in organizing instruction subject by subject with little effort to integrate knowledge. (*Breaking Ranks,* 1996, p. 4)

The reform documents challenged secondary educators to develop powerful teaching and learning opportunities; to create accountability and assessment systems to guide practice; and to provide comprehensive support for all students. The reports called for providing competent, caring, and qualified teachers in every classroom. In addition to identifying needed changes, these documents provide blueprints for correcting them: making high schools into smaller units; personalizing instruction; connecting learning to the world beyond the classroom walls; as well as identifying rationale for more interactive, collaborative pedagogy in interdisciplinary curricula.

Despite these calls for reform, a great deal of uniformity continues in today's high schools. Most require students to attend similar hours each day, roughly the same number of days each year, award credits known as Carnegie units for courses completed, and require the same number of credits for graduation. As educational researcher Larry Cuban noted in his 1984 study on secondary schools, instructional practices had changed little from the 1800s to then. The same observations could be made for schools in the first decade of the twenty-first century.

You will face a major challenge as a new teacher helping transform high schools: Secondary schools are complex organizations that take considerable coordination to run effectively. Any change to one part of the system impacts many aspects of the school. Unless reformers look at the entire secondary system, efforts for change will continue to be ineffective.

As you work through this text, you will have the opportunity to reexamine many of the early patterns established in our public secondary schools. Keep in mind, as similar as our high schools are to each other in curriculum and structure, each has its own unique culture and environment. In determining your own ideas and visions of secondary schools, it can be helpful to remember how patterns were developed in the past so that you are better able to clearly understand the challenges you will face in helping provide meaningful educational experiences for all students.

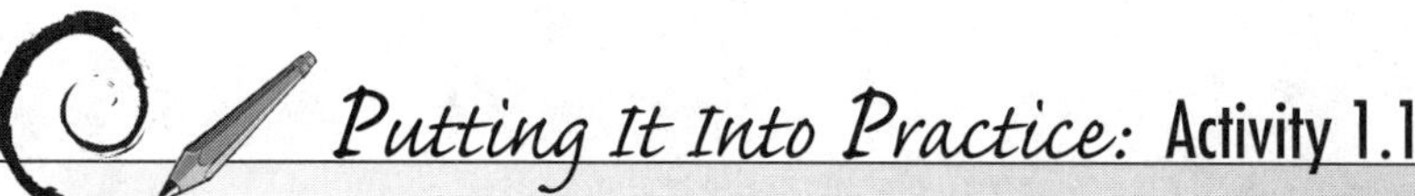

### *Putting It Into Practice:* Activity 1.1

In small teams, select one of the three reform documents written in the 1990s and develop a short executive summary to present in class. As part of the presentation, identify three recommendations or ideas in your document that the team considers most important in reforming secondary schools. Explain your rationale for selecting these ideas as well as the challenges of implementing such changes into today's high schools.

### *Putting It Into Practice:* Activity 1.2

Assume the role of an interested observer of secondary schools and visit a local high school. Based on your own experience and your knowledge of the reform documents, try to identify elements of the school that you believe could be long-established patterns. Report your findings in a short paper. Include in the paper your thoughts on the effectiveness of the organization of class periods, teaching techniques, class management practices, and any other elements you deem important. Finally, using the reform documents as resources, conclude your paper with ideas on how, given the opportunity, you would change the current system to meet the needs of all students more effectively.

## SECTION 2: PROFESSIONAL PRACTICE

In observing any classroom in which powerful teaching and learning are happening, you will see a teacher who has designed a purposeful lesson for students. If you were to explore with that teacher the rationale for the lesson, how it connects to previous work, how it leads to further lessons, and why the teacher selected certain instructional and assessment strategies, you would begin to understand that teacher's educational philosophy. Such a belief foundation is essential for every teacher who wants to work purposefully in a classroom. Unfortunately, we have all seen the teacher who seems only to be filling a class period with activities, often with little connection to each other or previous lessons. These ineffective teachers haven't grounded their practice in their own well-thought-out philosophy.

### Educational Belief Foundations

Because many of you have already completed courses that focus much of the curriculum on educational philosophies, Section 2 of this chapter will provide only a review of four influential educational philosophies while presenting ideas on how to begin determining your own educational foundation. By the conclusion of this section, each of you should have begun to identify your own beliefs concerning the role of schools in today's society, as well as the roles you believe teachers, students, parents, and communities play in educating all students. A well-thought-out educational philosophy can help guide you in making teaching decisions: designing engaging lessons, addressing class management issues, and determining what to include in your classroom curriculum.

### *Putting It Into Practice:* Activity 1.3

Prepare and be ready to share a short paper on your current educational beliefs. Your paper should discuss each of the following elements:

- *The primary purpose of today's schools.* For example, do you believe schools serve primarily to prepare students for the workforce? Do they serve to pass along the dominant culture's beliefs? Do you believe they serve to provide preparation for college?
- *Curriculum to be taught.* Should schools teach just the core subjects? What about the arts or vocational courses?
- *The role of the teacher.* Are teachers the sole source of knowledge in the classroom? Are they guides? Are they facilitators?
- *The role of the student.* Are they active participants in their own education? Are they vessels to be filled with knowledge?
- *The role of administrators.* Are they managers of big organizations? Are they instructional leaders?
- *The role of parents.* Are they coeducators, or outside observers?
- *The role of the community.* Should the community have a say in what should be taught? Should it decide on the resources to be used? Should the community be a partner in the process of education?

## Overview of Educational Philosophies

Though there are many educational philosophies, four seem to have had significant and consistent impact on American schools. The following pages of this section provide an overview of perennialism, progressivism, essentialism, and existentialism: the major tenets, primary proponents as well as criticisms of each philosophy, and the roles of teachers and students in the context of each philosophy.

***Perennialism.*** Perennialism as an educational philosophy had a considerable impact on secondary schools in the twentieth century. Today its influence is still visible in many public schools. Perennialist educators believe that nature, human nature in particular, has a constant quality. Two major proponents of this philosophy, Robert M. Hutchins (1899–1977) and Mortimer Adler (1902–2001), both believed in the similarity of all people, regardless of who they were, where they lived, or where they came from. For these educators, human characteristics have changed little from century to century. Their central premise was that we are all, in the end, rational creatures. Based on these ideas, Hutchins and Adler believed that everyone in American schools needed a similar education.

They insisted the goal of education and schools was to develop rationality in students and to nourish the intellect. Hutchins and Adler believed that through the acquisition of the timeless principles of reality, truth, and values, students would indeed become educated members of society. Perennialists see the students' primary role as learning for the sake of learning.

Perennialists suggest that truth is constant and changeless over time and can best be revealed through the enduring classics of Western culture. As a result of this belief, perennialists insist on a curriculum that emphasizes the traditional subjects: history, language, math, science, and the arts. Additionally, they place particular emphasis on literature and the humanities because they believe these subjects can best reveal to students insights into the human condition.

Proponents of this philosophy believe that education should be a rigorous and demanding undertaking. Even though education is preparation for life, it doesn't need to be lifelike at this point. The role of the school is to develop the intellectual capabilities of students. The role of the teacher is to guide students and direct their intellectual and emotional levels toward higher purposes. Teachers focus students on the classics and instruct them in the basic skills of reading, writing, and mathematics. The most frequent form of instructional strategy in a perennialist school is teacher-centered, direct instruction. The perennialist teacher acts as the dispenser of knowledge. The teacher functions to help students reach their own conclusions about the consistent underlying principles of humankind.

The perennialist's educational approach to learning has an authoritarian nature; students must never undermine the authority of the teacher. The students function as the receivers of knowledge and academic skills. The teacher instructs them in how to reason logically and ethically.

Criticisms of the perennialist philosophy include suggestions that the curriculum is far too Eurocentric and ignores all thinkers and writers except those who are white males. Critics insist on a more inclusive curriculum that addresses contributions by women, minorities, and other cultures. Those who disagree with the perennialist philosophy also note that perennialists do not believe vocational and academic specializations should be a goal of formal study, nor are extracurricular activities important because they create a diversion from the main goals of education and scholarship. Critics of the perennialists suggest that variety in the curriculum and inclusion of extracurricular activities in fact help engage students in their own learning process and promote the school's connections with a wider range of the student population.

***Progressivism.*** An educational philosophy known as progressivism caused a tremendous impact on the educational system in the 1920s and 1930s. The father of this movement was American philosopher John Dewey (1859–1952). Grounded in the philosophy of pragmatism, progressives believe that for ideas to be of any worth, they must have a practical value. In the mid-1940s, the strong influence of this philosophy led to attacks by critics that this educational approach caused declines in student test scores. Nonetheless, progressivism has had significant impact on schools. Many of the curricular and instructional approaches advocated by its proponents are still evidenced in today's classrooms.

Unlike the perennialist philosophy that perceives truth and knowledge as fixed and knowable, progressives view the world and nature as being in constant flux. Progressives consider change to be the one constant. Adherents to this philosophy believe that knowledge must continually be redefined and rediscovered. Progressives believe not only that students should solve their own problems but also that their education should help develop their disposition toward the idea that they can and should be involved in community problem solving.

Progressive educators perceive problem solving to be the primary function of the mind. As such, the goal of education should be to develop this problem-solving ability. To accomplish this, the school and the teachers need to design and provide experiences for students that enable the further development of problem-solving skills. Progressivists believe this focus allows for continued intellectual growth in students. Such educators value knowledge only for its ability to help individuals solve human problems.

The role of progressive teachers is to help students develop problem-solving abilities and strategies. They begin with the introduction of simple projects, gradually helping students learn systematic ways to investigate problems, until students have fully mastered the scientific method. In short, the teacher helps students learn how to think, not what to think. The teacher focuses on equipping the student with the ability and skills to cope with change.

A progressive classroom would be unlikely to utilize drills, memorization, or authoritarian power. The expectation is that teachers and students learn together in their studies. Rather than being a presenter of knowledge, the progressive teacher functions as an intellectual guide in the problem-solving process. The teacher first focuses on students, helping them identify their own questions on a topic or issue. Next, the teacher assists the students in shaping a hypothesis concerning the questions, as well as possible ways to test for an answer. Teachers then guide students to ask the right questions and find the appropriate resources needed to solve the problem.

As you might expect, curriculum in the progressive school can vary widely. The problem-solving strategy can be learned in a variety of subjects, including those that are traditional. Instructional strategies are student-centered group activities and group problem solving. As previously noted, students exercise a strong voice in the development and path of the curriculum.

The impact of the progressive movement has been significant. The movement broadened thinking about the function of schools, incorporating the importance of concern for family and community life. The movement also expanded instructional strategies to include group work, collaborative problem solving, and the interdisciplinary approach. Educators began looking at students more holistically, a whole-child approach, as well as focusing on making the curriculum useful for all students in the public schools, not just a privileged few. They saw schools as small democratic societies and as places not only to prepare for life but also to learn to live it in a democratic way (Cremin, 1980).

Some critics of progressive education blamed this movement for a decline in student learning as judged by test scores. Progressive educators were also criticized for being too permissive with students and not providing them with enough content knowledge to be successful in their academic pursuits. In response, these critics developed the essentialist educational philosophy.

***Essentialism.*** In the late 1930s, headed by William Bagley (1874–1946), the Essentialistic Education Society began advocating for an intellectual curriculum in public schools. Viewed largely as a reaction to progressive education—which many perceived as failing American youth by encouraging academic mediocrity and being excessively concerned with student needs or interests—the essentialists advocated for the role of education as a transmitter of essential core knowledge common to all students. They believed the role of the school was to equip students to help solve contemporary problems.

Conservative educators did not consider this educational philosophy radically new. They had always believed the intent of formal education was to transmit the accumulated knowledge of the past in order to make students literate. The philosophy itself draws from two older philosophies: idealism, in which the mind is the central element of reality and the tool for learning core knowledge in order to live well; and realism, which suggests that learning occurs best through contact with the physical world.

Similarities also exist between essentialist philosophy and perennialist philosophy. Both agree about the existence of a body of knowledge all people must learn in order to function effectively in society, though they don't necessarily agree on what this core knowledge should be. Unlike the perennialists, the essentialists do not emphasize the truths or the classics but focus instead more on current reality. If, for example, the culture widely holds that students need computer literacy to be successful in society, then there should be a place for it in the curriculum. The essentialists believe their approach is more fluid, congruent with the idea that knowledge can and will change as information changes.

The curriculum of the essentialist is grounded in the belief that human nature is essentially the same everywhere: same needs, wants, and issues. Essentialists believe that the curriculum must focus on a strong liberal education with emphasis on science and language. The curriculum should work to hone the intellectual abilities of students so that they can become rational, active members of society. In a school system that adheres to this philosophy, you would most likely find an emphasis on reading, writing, and mathematics. Once these are mastered, students follow a curriculum of foreign language, fine arts, history, science, and social science. Unlike in perennialist schools, the essentialist curriculum would also include industrial arts and health. The essentialist curriculum received renewed attention in the late 1970s and early 1980s because the back-to-basics movement, stressing reading, writing, and mathematics, resurfaced.

The teacher's role in an essentialist school is to instill in students the old-fashioned values of discipline, self-control, and hard work. Essentialists believe students are not prepared to direct their own learning, as in the progressive philosophy. Instead, the teacher must direct learning by creating a structure and time frame to assist students in mastering subject matter. Practical hands-on problem solving, learning by doing, has no part in the essentialist teacher's repertoire, because essentialist educators believe so much knowledge is abstract.

Essentialist teachers emphasize the teaching of facts and so design a highly structured curriculum with few frills. Lecture will be the predominant mode of instruction. Few classroom discussions take place, drill and memorization predominate, and exams are used for assessment. The student's role in school is to learn from the teacher, who believes students require discipline and pressure to keep learning. Teachers provide this guidance as the authority figure, with the philosophy that students are there to listen and learn.

Critics maintain two primary concerns with essentialism. First, only Western history and culture support the basic tenets of this belief system. The primary focus on Eurocentric perspectives discourages discussion about social, economic, and educational discrimination as experienced by minority and low-socioeconomic students. Second, critics are concerned that because students' passivity in the learning process rarely causes them to explore concepts or engage in issues in ways that connect them personally to the learning.

***Existentialism.*** The last of the four philosophies explored in this section, existentialism, most recently emerged in public schools. Existentialism, as an educational philosophy, had an impact on American schools in the 1960s and 1970s, not under its own name, but rather through several different movements. It is more familiar to some as the human potential movement, which stressed the development of all aspects of a person, or the values clarification approach to moral education, whereby students had to discover their own values. Each of these approaches has roots in existential philosophy.

Developed in the early 1800s by Danish theologian Søren Kierkegaard (1813–1855) and modernized by French philosopher Jean-Paul Sartre (1905–1980), this philosophy emphasizes the subjective nature of the human experience, the importance of individual creativity, and choice in an otherwise nonrational world. For the existentialist, life has no absolute meaning; therefore, an individual must find meaning in his or her life.

Choice is the critical concept for the existentialist educator. Individuals will choose who they will be. Even those who allow others to make those decisions have, in fact, made a choice. As a result, existentialism encourages students, when confronted with conflicting values, to look inward at their own situation and choose what is right for them. This helps students evaluate their own decisions and assume responsibility for their actions. This way, students do not simply rely on faith-based directives or what they are told to do. The goal of existentialist education is for students to learn that they are free to choose their own paths.

The existentialist teacher encourages students to reflect on and explore life. Teachers guide students to use individual experiences as a basis for their decision-making processes. Teachers create an environment for independent action, enabling students to make choices and accept responsibility for their behavior. For example, an existentialist teacher would not assign a detention or study hall for a student who is wasting time in class. Instead the teacher would just lower the student's grade. The existentialist believes that in time, the student will realize the teacher doesn't give grades; students earn them by their individual choices and actions. In effect, the teacher helps students make good choices in the future by allowing them freedom to make poor choices now in order to learn.

Because existentialism is individual-focused, a prescribed curriculum does not exist. In general, existentialists believe that students should be allowed to take a wide range of electives to encourage self-expression. Classes should be thought provoking. The teacher should help design activities relevant to each student. Student experiences help create the direction for learning. In general, existentialists consider the humanities and arts excellent areas for student exploration.

The teacher and student in an existentialist school must develop an honest and open relationship. Instead of authoritarian figures in the classroom and the imposition of group rules, a great deal of freedom is provided with the intent of developing the self as well as directing the student. According to the existentialist educator, the first step in education is to understand oneself. Only then can students become who they are to be. Existentialist teachers help students explore the world and open up possibilities for them.

The existentialist school helps students become intellectually equipped to hone a deep commitment to helping create a better society. Content and activities helping students confront their own freedom are the essence of an existential school. Choice and responsibility are the key learnings in this type of school.

Critics note the individual nature of this educational approach. The existentialist educator does not use the instructional strategies of collaboration and group work, and yet many educators believe these skills are essential for students to function effectively in modern society. Critics also cite the lack of a uniform curriculum. Other than for self-knowledge, students will not be held accountable for any common outcomes. This makes it difficult to assess the quality of the education.

Table 1.1 provides a condensed overview of the four educational philosophies discussed in this section. The table is divided into sections for each philosophy to help you review: basic tenets, goals of education, curriculum, role of teachers, role of students, and criticisms.

## Your Educational Philosophy

Teachers who continue to reflect on their own educational philosophy will be influenced by continued professional development opportunities, the stage of their teaching career, the community in which they serve, as well as new educational research, which may point the way toward a new direction. As you continue your credential program and after you become a classroom teacher, remain open to the possibility that your educational philosophy may continue to evolve.

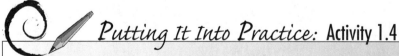

### *Putting It Into Practice:* Activity 1.4

After reading Section 2 to refresh your thoughts regarding the influence of educational philosophy on today's schools, make a list of the ideas that match your own beliefs (review your ideas from Activity 1.3). You should draw concepts from as many of the four philosophies as align with your own thoughts. Next, draw a pie chart and divide it into pieces, allotting percentages to those philosophies from which you have drawn your ideas. For example, you may believe that you are 50% progressive, 20% essentialist, 25% existentialist, and 5% perennialist. Code each section of the pie chart to the corresponding philosophy. Finally, write a paragraph explaining your decisions. This activity will help you clearly identify and articulate your own, possibly eclectic, educational philosophy.

**TABLE 1.1** *Overview of Educational Philosophies*

| | Perennialism | Progressivism | Essentialism | Existentialism |
|---|---|---|---|---|
| Basic Tenets | • Truth is constant and changeless over time.<br>• Human nature has a constant quality.<br>• All people are basically the same: rational creatures. | • Ideas must have practical value.<br>• World and nature are in constant flux.<br>• Change is constant.<br>• Value of knowledge is its ability to help solve human problems. | • Human nature is essentially the same everywhere.<br>• All people must learn a body of knowledge in order to function effectively in society.<br>• Knowledge can and will change as information changes.<br>• Learning occurs best through contact with the physical world. | • Human experience is subjective.<br>• Individual creativity is important.<br>• Life has no absolute meaning; finding meaning is an individual choice. |
| Goals of Education | • Develop rational ability in students.<br>• Nourish the intellect.<br>• Provide similar education for all.<br>• Encourage students to become rational active members of society. | • Continually redefine knowledge.<br>• Help resolve community issues.<br>• Have schools function as small democratic societies. | • Transmit knowledge of the past.<br>• Equip students to solve contemporary problems.<br>• Make students more literate. | • Assist students to look at their own experiences and make choices.<br>• Teach that students are free to choose their own path.<br>• Help students become intellectually equipped to have a deep commitment to helping create a better society. |
| Curriculum | • Emphasis is on the enduring Western classics.<br>• Courses should be rigorous and demanding.<br>• Instruction is direct/teacher-centered. | • Content varies widely, because problem solving can be learned in many subjects.<br>• Instruction uses student-centered and group problem-solving strategies. | • Knowledge is abstract; therefore, there is little hands-on teaching.<br>• The intellectual abilities of students should be challenged.<br>• The emphasis is on reading, writing, and mathematics. | • Curriculum is not prescribed.<br>• Students should take a wide range of electives.<br>• Classes should be thought provoking.<br>• Humanities and arts are excellent areas for student exploration. |

| | | | | |
|---|---|---|---|---|
| | • Traditional subjects covered: history, language, math, science, and the arts. | | • Advanced students will work on foreign language, fine arts, history, science, and social science. | |
| Role of Teachers | • Dispense knowledge.<br>• Emphasize the basic skills of reading, writing, and math.<br>• Focus instruction on the classics.<br>• Help students reach their own conclusions about the consistent underlying principles of humankind. | • Design and provide experiences for students that help them learn to think critically and develop problem-solving abilities and strategies.<br>• Help students learn how to think, not what to think.<br>• Act as an intellectual guide.<br>• Use a broad range of instructional strategies. | • Instill in students the old-fashioned values of discipline, self-control, and hard work.<br>• Direct student knowing.<br>• Use lecture as the predominate mode of instruction.<br>• Use drill, memorization, and exams for assessment. | • Help students evaluate their own decisions and assume responsibility for their actions.<br>• Encourage student reflection on and exploration of life.<br>• Guide students to use individual experiences as a basis for decision making.<br>• Create an environment for independent action.<br>• Design experiences relevant to each student. |
| Role of Students | • Never undermine the authority of the teacher.<br>• Be the receiver of knowledge and academic skills.<br>• Learn to reason logically and ethically. | • Learn to be problem solvers.<br>• Learn together with the teacher.<br>• Have a strong voice in the development and path of curriculum. | • Need constant discipline and pressure to study.<br>• Listen to and learn from the teacher. | • Develop open and honest relationships with the teacher.<br>• Have considerable freedom to determine their own areas of explanation. |
| Criticisms | • The approach is too Eurocentric.<br>• Student engagement in the learning process is lacking.<br>• The positive effects of extracurricular activities are overlooked. | • Failing to emphasize the "basics" caused decline in student test scores.<br>• Society's youth were failed by encouraging mediocrity.<br>• The approach is too student centered. | • Essentials of this system are found only in Western culture and history.<br>• Some view this as discriminating against nonwhite students.<br>• Students are passive in the learning process. | • The individual nature of this approach lacks collaboration or group work, not preparing students to work with others in a modern society.<br>• Uniform curriculum and common outcomes are lacking. |

## SECTION 3: PROFESSIONAL DEVELOPMENT

In choosing to become a secondary educator, you have probably weighed the wide range of societal problems that confront any teacher. If you have read the results of the U.S. Census 2000, it will come as no surprise that the United States is becoming more and more a multiracial, multi-ethnic, and multiclass society. The complex societal influences on a student's life can create a myriad of challenges inside the classroom. A basic question to ask oneself is whether schools are succeeding in creating opportunities for all students; or whether large numbers of poor and nondominant-culture students are leaving schools without the knowledge and skills necessary to function in today's society.

As a future teacher, you need to raise your awareness of the problems and begin to examine the role a teacher might play in advocating for all students. Most of the issues today are not new to secondary schools: poverty, homelessness, teenage pregnancy, abuse, neglect, substance abuse, violence, suicide, and gender issues. However, increasing numbers of school incidences related to these societal issues make it clear that today's teachers must address these problems much more frequently than in the past.

This section introduces you to the Circle of Courage model, intended to guide your overall thinking in working with young adolescents. It also introduces you to the INTASC standards intended to create a benchmark for effective teachers. The Circle of Courage model and INTASC standards are two significant strands woven throughout the chapters of this book.

### Circle of Courage

The first strand—the Circle of Courage model, developed by Larry Brendtro, Martin Brokenleg, and Steve Van Bockern (2002)—provides guidance on both the reasons adolescents behave as they do as well as ideas on how to best educate them. Brendtro et al. developed the Circle of Courage model around an approach toward life that Native Americans have used for centuries. The model's approach toward educating youth is well grounded in developmental research, aligned with the ideas of such researchers as William Glasser, Abraham Maslow, and Rudolph Dreikurs.

The Circle of Courage model involves four key components: Belonging, Mastery, Generosity, and Independence, graphically represented as a circle with four sections in Figure 1.1. The circle illustrates the necessity of developing all four sections in order for an adult to be engaged in a healthy and productive life. By contrast, absence of or underdevelopment in any one or more of the sections of the circle will likely indicate emotional or behavioral difficulties in a student.

We concur with the core ideas presented in the Circle of Courage and have used them as a guide in the preparation of teachers in our own credential programs. You can greatly enhance helping today's students learn in your classrooms by following the guidelines the Circle of Courage offers.

***Belonging.*** The model suggests that inorder to be successful students must connect with their peers, their classes, their schools, and, importantly, their teachers. This sense of *Belonging* must be present if teachers are to provide guidance in developing the other three sections of the circle. For example, without a sense of Belonging students have difficulty developing a strong sense of Generosity.

Students who feel a sense of segregation within a school or classroom lack this sense of Belonging. In the 1960s and 1970s, many school systems in the United States

**FIGURE 1.1** The Circle of Courage

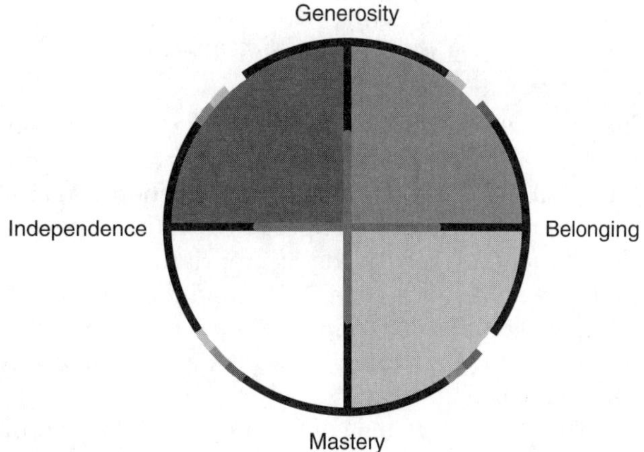


Note: From *Reclaiming Youth at Risk: Our Hope for the Future* by Larry K. Brendtro et al., 2002, Bloomington, Indiana. Used with permission. Artist: George Blue Bird. The Circle of Courage is a Trademark of Circle of Courage, Inc. For more information: Web site www.reclaiming.com or E-mail courage@reclaiming.com.

made efforts to remedy this situation by attempting to change an existing de facto pattern of segregation. However, even in more-integrated schools second-generation segregation has also taken its toll. Second-generation segregation refers to forms of racial segregation that result from practices in schools such as tracking, ability grouping, and misplacement of students in special education classes (Spring, 1996).

This indicates a critical role for teachers and schools in today's pluralistic society. Educators must work for the elimination of prejudices and stereotypes and build classroom communities that offer all students the opportunity to belong and access the skills and knowledge needed to be productive members of society.

Students lacking a connection to their learning community will likely behave in nonresponsive, resistant, or even antagonistic ways toward the efforts of teachers. They may even drop out of school. These students believe school is a place they are coerced into attending rather than one they desire to be a part of. As teachers, therefore, ideas of connecting with students in every aspect of the learning process must be foremost in our minds. Planning lessons, selecting instructional strategies, and creating our classroom environments should include elements that foster a sense of Belonging.

***Mastery.*** Once a sense of Belonging is established, students' opportunities for *Mastery* will be increased. They will be able to master the knowledge and skills necessary to lead productive lives in today's world. For teachers to help students acquire these important core elements, all parts of the lesson, including instructional techniques and assessment strategies, must allow students the opportunity to demonstrate competence in their learning. Chapters 3, 4, and 5 explore techniques to equip you with the necessary skills to provide all students with an opportunity to master your course goals and objectives. Without Mastery, students become frustrated, behave in inappropriate ways, and develop a sense of worthlessness.

***Generosity.*** Students who achieve Mastery will begin to feel successful and then should be given opportunities to share their skills and ideas with others. Whether it is through cooperative work in classrooms or by being involved with service-learning projects, this spirit of *Generosity* can help build a student's self-worth. Students quickly learn they have a responsibility to become active participants in their communities. Yet, without opportunities to share their talents, students find it difficult to become caring, responsible adults.

***Independence.*** The final section of the Circle of Courage is that of *Independence*. One primary aim of education is to help prepare responsible adults, who can assume responsibility for their own lives and actions. Again, the teacher selects strategies to create powerful learning experiences in the classroom to help students in developing their Independence. In the appropriate environment, learning becomes more and more the student's responsibility, and the learning strategies of the teacher evolve to allow students to take control of their own learning and lives. In classrooms such as these, assessment strategies become appropriate ways to hold students accountable for their learning.

The use of the Circle of Courage model in guiding your approach to planning a classroom environment as well as instructional and assessment strategies can assist you in providing all students the opportunity to learn. Thinking through your teaching approaches in this way also provides guidance in connecting with students who, as Brendtro et al. have stated, may need to mend their broken circles (2002). In guiding practice in this manner, you provide students with more opportunities to rebuild their lost confidence and be successful in your classroom.

## INTASC Core Teaching Standards

Now we introduce you to the second strand woven throughout the book as an important tool for developing and maintaining your professional practice. Utilizing an external benchmark with which to compare yourself can be very helpful in gauging your professional growth. We believe an excellent resource to use in this endeavor is the core teaching standards developed by the Council of Chief State School Officers, called the Interstate New Teacher Assessment and Support Consortium (INTASC) standards (1992). See Box 1.2.

The work on the INTASC standards directly connects to the reform efforts discussed in Section 1. As secondary schools began to restructure approaches to teaching students, it became evident that new roles for teachers needed to be clarified. Because the educational community now expects schools to facilitate all students to learn and perform at high levels, teachers can no longer be satisfied with simply covering the material. Instead, more and more, they need to use strategies that support the needs of all learners. As a result, INTASC has focused on the new demands of schools and new requirements of teachers by setting the goal to identify core standards required in learner-centered approaches. In doing so, the task force identified a common core of teaching knowledge and skills necessary for a new generation of teachers.

*Box 1.2*

### Interstate New Teacher Assessment and Support Consortium

INTASC is a consortium dedicated to reforming education, licensing, and professional development of teachers. The standards were developed by the Council of Chief State School officers and member States. This consortium includes institutions of higher education, state education departments, and national education organizations. The team of educators developed standards representing a common core of teaching knowledge, dispositions, and performances necessary for a twenty-first-century educator.

Council of Chief State School Officers (1992). Model Standards for beginning teacher licensing, assessment, and development: A resource for state dialogue. Washington, DC: Author. www.ccsso.org/content/pdfs/corestrd.pdf

The standards for beginning teachers are organized into 10 principles; each includes an explanation of the knowledge, dispositions, and performances that characterize the principle. The 10 principles state that new teachers should:

1. understand the discipline they teach and how to teach it to students;
2. know how children learn and develop, and can provide learning opportunities that support their development;
3. understand that students learn differently, and adapt their instruction to diverse learners;
4. use a variety of instructional strategies to encourage critical thinking, problem solving, and performance skills;
5. create environments that encourage positive social interaction, active learning, and self-motivation;
6. understand effective communication techniques and use them in the classroom;
7. plan instruction based on knowledge of subjects, students, the community, and curriculum goals;
8. use formal and informal assessment strategies to evaluate and ensure the continuous development of the learner;
9. continually evaluate their own practices and seek opportunities to grow professionally; and
10. foster relationships with colleagues, parents, and community agencies to support students' learning and well-being.

## Professional Teacher Dispositions

A significant piece of the INTASC standards are the dispositions: those personal behaviors that are considered appropriate to maximize student affect and learning in a classroom situation. As a new teacher, by knowing, valuing, and observing these qualities in practicing teachers, you can begin to evaluate your own behaviors in your teaching practice. We introduce teacher dispositions in the first chapter because we believe the overall quality of a new teacher's performance is likely to increase by becoming aware of these characteristics early on in his or her training.

One example to help illustrate the importance of teacher dispositions comes from Principle 4 of the INTASC standards (Instructional Resource A): "The teacher understands and uses a variety of instructional strategies to encourage students' development of critical thinking, problem solving, and performance skills." This principle includes the dispositions of (1) valuing the development of students' critical thinking, independent problem solving, and performance capabilities; and (2) flexibility and reciprocity in the teaching process as necessary for adapting instruction to student responses, ideas, and needs.

### A Closer Look

All 10 INTASC core standards can be read in their entirety in **Instructional Resource A. Instructional Resource A** includes the key principles, as well as a complete breakdown of the respective knowledge, dispositions, and performances used to assess a new teacher's competence in relation to a standard.

The teacher dispositions in Principle 4, as in each of the INTASC standards' principles, can help guide you as a teacher in the way you apply professional knowledge and skills in undertaking your work. The dispositions serve as an important source to help teachers plan, teach, and respond within the classroom to best meet the needs of all students. A teacher guided by the teacher dispositions just listed would likely plan for an interactive classroom, crafting activities that encourage students to perform at higher levels of thinking. The teacher would also maintain a constant awareness of the lesson as it unfolded, adapting rather than sticking rigidly to a preplanned lesson. How and what dispositions a teacher exhibits is probably one of the most important factors in determining the success of an individual teacher.

Another reason we present dispositions here is to ensure that a new professional striving to acquire the knowledge and skills necessary to be successful in the classroom does not overlook them. All three aspects of becoming a teacher—knowledge, dispositions, and performances—must be part of your training. Success in the classroom does not occur without attention to the ways teachers approach their work. We highlight INTASC teacher dispositions throughout each chapter as a continuous reminder of their importance.

With the INTASC standards, teachers entering the profession should be able to assess their own practice in relation to any given standard. At the beginning of each chapter of this textbook is a list of the key standards most closely aligned with the ideas, strategies, and activities that follow. We suggest you keep the specific INTASC principles in mind as you read the material presented and think about their application. We also recommend that prior to beginning a chapter you read each identified standard in its entirety as provided in Instructional Resource A. As you study the material in the chapter and complete the activities, we believe each preservice teacher can then begin to both self-assess readiness to meet the standard as well as gain a broader understanding of the expectations for teachers entering the profession in this era of educational reform.

## Attributes of Successful Preservice Teachers

To help you further in identifying certain professional benchmarks as you proceed with your coursework and field experiences, we now introduce you to another tool that may precede the use of INTASC dispositions. Through our own practice in teacher education, we have identified seven personal attributes of successful teachers and have adapted them to target preservice teachers. The distinction between these seven attributes, as presented, and the INTASC dispositions is that the former consist of those behaviors necessary to be successful while engaging in preservice study, whereas the latter are to be used as a tool to assess professional readiness for stepping into the classroom as a teacher.

Some teachers (as the saying goes) are "born" with these qualities but most individuals require at least some assistance. Strategies to assist the development of these personal attributes include recognizing the manifestation of the behavior in a classroom setting through observations, seeking feedback from peers or teachers on your teaching practice through guided experience, and initiating more practice through modification and adaptation based on feedback. These teacher attributes should be identified early so that you as a future teacher have the opportunity to observe others and can model and evaluate your own personal behaviors in teaching practices. Figure 1.2 summarizes the seven personal attributes of successful preservice teachers.

**FIGURE 1.2** Seven Personal Attributes of Successful Preservice Teachers

| Attribute | Descriptor |
|---|---|
| 1. General classroom attendance, promptness, and participation | The preservice teacher:<br>• is on time and respects time boundaries (breaks, etc.)<br>• regularly attends class<br>• actively participates |
| 2. Attention to classroom discussion protocols | The preservice teacher:<br>• respects time limitations<br>• recognizes and respects the perspectives of fellow classmates<br>• gives wait time<br>• listens actively<br>• uses noninterruptive skills<br>• mediates disagreements by working to understand others' perspectives and finding common ground<br>• genuinely encourages all to participate |
| 3. Social and cooperative skills (as illustrated in cooperative projects) | The preservice teacher:<br>• assumes responsibility of one's roles<br>• is open to consensus and mediation<br>• effectively communicates ideas<br>• attends group meetings<br>• is dependable<br>• respects others' ideas<br>• expects quality work from self and colleagues<br>• manages time effectively<br>• uses organizational skills and leadership skills<br>• is assertive but not aggressive<br>• uses reflection as a means of evaluation<br>• motivates and offers positive reinforcement to others |
| 4. Attention to assignments | The preservice teacher:<br>• meets time deadlines<br>• produces quality products<br>• responds cooperatively to constructive criticism<br>• uses rubrics or other stipulated criteria to shape an assignment<br>• prioritizes tasks and performs/supervises several tasks at once |
| 5. General classroom demeanor | The preservice teacher:<br>• is professional, creative, kind, sensitive, respectful, has a sense of humor, is supportive of fellow classmates and instructors<br>• recognizes others' perspectives as valid and works to include all "voices" in the classroom<br>• is aware of and responsive to issues and behaviors that might marginalize colleagues in the classroom |

FIGURE 1.2 *(continued)*

| Attribute | Descriptor |
|---|---|
| 6. Flexibility | The preservice teacher:<br>• is responsive when reasonable adjustments to the syllabus, curriculum, schedule, and school site assignments become necessary (common to the educational arena)<br>• can work through frustrations by problem solving with others and not letting emotional responses dominate or impair thinking ("bounces" back easily)<br>• can work calmly under stress |
| 7. Openness to and enthusiasm for learning | The preservice teacher:<br>• can engage with a variety of educational ideas with an open mind and a sense of exploration<br>• demonstrates passion for and metacognition of learning across the curriculum and within discipline areas<br>• takes advantage of learning opportunities and seeks out additional opportunities for learning |

You may want to complete Putting It Into Practice: Activity 1.5 several times during various stages of your professional preparation program. Applied in this way, you can measure personal growth throughout your credential program. Later on the activity may also provide a strategy to self-evaluate against the INTASC standards. Undertaking this reflective analysis can be a beginning effort in assisting your preparation to step into your own classroom with a sense of professional confidence.

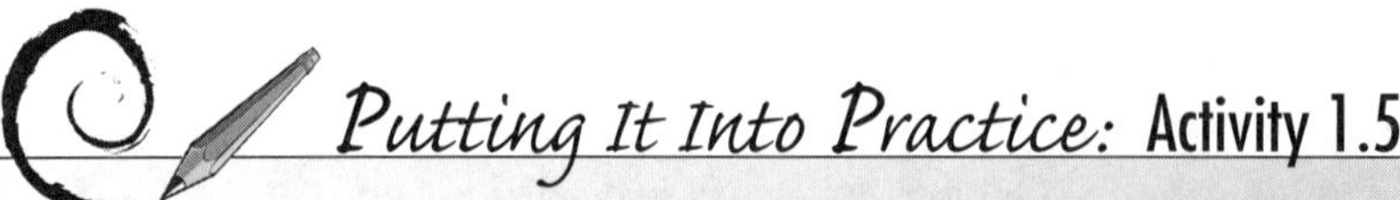

## *Putting It Into Practice:* Activity 1.5

Use the scoring criteria for teacher attributes (rubric) provided in Figure 1.3 to rate yourself on the seven personal attributes of successful preservice teachers in the courses you are currently taking. When you have completed the self-assessment, identify at least three growth areas you will focus on for improvement, set target goals for each, and detail specific strategies you will develop to meet these goals. Work with a partner to discuss your self-analysis as well as your action plans. Keep your action plan where you can refer to it frequently and monitor your success in moving toward your goals. Teacher attribute example activity in Figure 1.4 provides an example of a completed questionnaire.

**FIGURE 1.3** Scoring Criteria for Teacher Attributes

**Score each of the seven attributes on a 5-point rubric.**

5 Excellent qualities demonstrated for this attribute as noted with justification (no evidence of subpar descriptors)
4 Above average qualities demonstrated for this attribute as noted with justification (few or no subpar descriptors)
3 Average qualities demonstrated for this attribute as noted with justification (some limitations of descriptors noted)
2 Below average qualities demonstrated for this attribute (numerous limitations of descriptors noted)
1 Well below average qualities demonstrated for this attribute (serious overall limitations noted in this area)

**FIGURE 1.4** Teacher Attributes Example Activity

| Attribute | Self-Rating/Justification |
|---|---|
| 1. General classroom attendance, promptness, and participation | 3: In recent years, I have become more comfortable actively participating in class. I continually engage in the discussion or task at hand, and rarely mentally or physically stray from the topic at hand. On occasion, I have been tardy to class due to work or other considerations, but rarely. I am conscientious of time and seek to maintain a perfect (or near perfect) attendance record, missing class only under pressing circumstances (if ever). |
| 2. Attention to classroom discussion protocols | 3+: I have worked to become an active class participant in recent years (as opposed to high school, when I did not feel as comfortable taking on this role). I notice when students have not yet spoken and encourage them to do so. When waiting to share my perspective, I do not raise my hand while others are speaking. Rather, I listen to what they are saying. This sometimes means I forget what I was going to say, but that is better than shutting out someone else's views. In small group discussions, I ask lots of questions, especially of those who are not as actively participating. I don't feel the need to dominate the discussion, but I do speak up if I feel I have something worthwhile to say. |
| 3. Social and cooperative skills (as illustrated in cooperative projects) | 3: The process of working cooperatively within a group is a dynamic one. No two groups, even successful ones, function in exactly the same way. I have become more comfortable "going with the flow" with these groups. I have had to unlearn many poor experiences and coping mechanisms from past group work adventures. I stick to my role in the group as we have assigned it and actively help others when I can. I speak up if I feel the group is not functioning and try to come up with positive solutions that will accommodate everyone's schedules and skills. I am engaged in an ongoing process of discovery and am continually learning. |
| 4. Attention to assignments | 4: After years and years of practice, I have become adept at producing quality work as requested by my teachers. I work diligently on assignments, adhering to protocols and conscientiously putting my best foot forward. When I don't understand the requirements for a particular assignment, I am not shy about asking questions. I proofread my work and usually feel confident about my efforts when I submit assignments. When I fall short of requirements or am not successful for some reason, I speak with the instructor for feedback and suggestions for the future. I take my work seriously and attempt to balance quality work with all the other demands of school and work. |

FIGURE 1.4 *(continued)*

| Attribute | Self-Rating/Justification |
|---|---|
| 5. General classroom demeanor | 3+: Although this depends largely on the class, in general I have a positive classroom demeanor. When the instructor encourages it, I take time to get to know my classmates and enjoy listening to them. My sense of humor about myself helps me to take risks. This was not always true. As I have grown older, I have become more comfortable with myself, which translates to an easier, more relaxed attitude in the face of challenges or thoughtful discussion. Although some topics ignite my passions, I still maintain perspective and get along well with others. Finally, I am conscientious of my statements in class, realizing that my statements do have an impact on those around me. I am cautious and thoughtful about what I say and am ready to admit when I am wrong. |
| 6. Flexibility | 3: I continue to try to work calmly under stress. Working in the high-pressure environment of the legal field has helped me buckle down when needed and work with others in tight, stressful circumstances. I have also learned to produce good work under such circumstances. Mostly, I have learned to adapt to circumstances beyond my control, keeping my sense of humor along the way. Sometimes this is much tougher than at other times, but I continue to try to ride the waves of change with a positive attitude. |
| 7. Openness to and enthusiasm for learning | 4: I love school and always have. I love learning, thinking about learning, and engaging in dialogue about learning. I find it exciting to pick up a new skill or learn a new concept and can't wait to share it with others. Teachers rarely have to drag me to a new concept. Rather, I intuitively know that even if I may not like a particular book or lesson, I can always gain something from it. Mostly, I love listening to my peers. I have learned a tremendous amount from my classmates over the years, sometimes more than from any textbook I have read. |

| Growth Areas | Target Goals |
|---|---|
| 1. Attribute 1: Active participation | 1. Be more engaged in class discussions. |
| 2. Attribute 3: Working in groups, collaboration | 2. Work in groups with a more positive attitude. |
| 3. Attribute 6: Time management and flexibility | 3. Remain open to shifting plans and time frames. |
| SPECIFIC STRATEGIES | 1. Come to class with brief notes concerning what I have determined important to contribute to the discussion concerning the assigned topic. In class, become more assertive in sharing my ideas, not always waiting to hear the ideas of others first.<br>2. When assigned to a group project be aware of the "old tapes" my mind plays based on previous group work experiences. Work actively to help the group organize, set clear goals, and establish time lines. Be willing to work toward consensus on issues when the group is stuck.<br>3. Accept the fact that the teaching and learning process is a dynamic one and that a flexible approach toward shifting priorities is important. Create time lines to meet assignment deadlines but stay open to shifting the priorities as new tasks are assigned. Always build in time to exercise as these breaks will both help me stay balanced in my approach to school and work as well as to "recharge" my thinking to meet deadlines with a clear mind. |

## SECTION 4: CHAPTER SUMMARY AND REFLECTION

This chapter provides you with a starting point for your training as a teacher. We developed each section to help you create a strong understanding of the profession you are moving into, as well as to assist in creating a professional foundation on which to build your practice. In Section 1 you read how secondary schools slowly evolved into the institutions we see today. You also read about some early patterns of development that continue to present challenges to educating all students. This section concluded with an overview of important reform documents that provide insight on addressing the issues confronting secondary education. Section 2 provided a brief review of four influential educational philosophies. You should note how each of these philosophies continues to influence how teachers develop and present curriculum as well as the roles teachers and students are expected to perform to meet the goals of schooling in the United States. The section also provided opportunities to explore your own educational beliefs and develop your educational philosophy.

The final section of this chapter, guiding your professional development, included the Circle of Courage model, which offers an effective holistic approach to guide your work with students and standards of teaching to gauge your own professional development and readiness to enter the teaching profession. The component sections of Belonging, Mastery, Generosity, and Independence provide teachers with a framework to approach the difficult task of educating all adolescents and helping them prepare for their adult lives. The INTASC standards and teacher attributes focus on you as a preservice teacher and as a new teacher. Both set high standards for those interested in the challenging task of teaching in today's secondary schools. You can use both the INTASC standards and the seven personal attributes of successful preservice teachers to identify your own strengths in the classroom as well as target growth areas to improve your practice. If you choose to use them in this way, you will be taking the first steps to becoming a reflective practitioner.

## References


Boyer, P. S., Clark, C. E., Kett, J. F., Salisbury, N., Sitkoff, H., & Woloch, N. (2000). *The enduring vision: A history of the American people.* (4th ed.). Boston: Houghton Mifflin.

Brendtro, L. K., Brokenleg, M., & Bockern, S. V. (2002). *Reclaiming youth at risk: Our hope for the future.* Bloomington, IN: National Education Service.

California Task Force (1992). *Second to none.* Sacramento, CA: Department of Education.

Campbell, P. B. (1986). What's a nice girl like you doing in a math class? *Phi Delta Kappan, 67,* 516–520.

Council of Chief State School Officers (1992). Model standards for beginning teacher licensing, assessment, and development: A resource for state dialogue. Washington, DC: Author. www.ccsso.org/content/pdfs/corestrd.pdf

Cremin, L. A. (1980). *American education: The national experience 1783–1976.* New York: Harper and Row.

Cuban, L. (1984). *How teachers taught: Constancy and change in American Classrooms 1890–1980.* New York: Longman.

Jomills, H. B., II, Crain, R. L., & McPartland, J. M. (1984). A long-term view of school desegregation: Some recent studies of graduates as adults. *Phi Delta Kappan, 66,* 259–264.

Kaestle, C. (1983). *Pillars of the republic: Common schools and American Society, 1780–1860.* New York: Hill and Wang.

Kaestle, C., & Vinorskis, M. (1980). *Education and social change in nineteenth century Massachusetts*. New York: Cambridge University Press.

National Association of Secondary School Principals (1996). *Breaking ranks: Changing an American institution*. Reston, VA: NASSP.

National Commission on Teaching and America's Future (1996). *What matters most*. New York: NCTAF.

Pulliam, J. D., & Patten, J. V. (1995). *History of education in America*. Upper Saddle River, NJ: Prentice Hall.

Reese, W. (1995). *The origins of the American high school*. New Haven: Yale University Press.

Sadker, M., Sadker, D., & Klein, S. (1991). The issue of gender in elementary and secondary education. In G. Grant (Ed.), *Review of research in education* (pp. 272–273). Washington DC: American Educational Research Association.

Spring, J. (1996). *American education* (7th ed.). New York: McGraw-Hill.

Spring, J. (2001). *The American school: 1642–2000* (5th ed.). New York: McGraw-Hill.

Tyack, D. (1978). *The one best system. A history of American urban education*. Cambridge, MA: Harvard University Press.

Wirt, J., Snyder, T., Sable, J., Choy, S. P., Bae, Y., Stewart, J., Gruner, A., & Perie, M. (1998). *The condition of education 1998* (NCES 98-013). Washington, DC: U.S. Department of Education, Office of Educational Research and Improvement.

# Chapter 2

## Today's Learners

**INTASC Principle 2:** The teacher understands how children learn and develop, and can provide learning opportunities that support their intellectual, social, and personal development.

**Key Disposition**

- The teacher appreciates individual variation within each area of development, shows respect for the diverse talents of all learners, and is committed to help them develop self-confidence and competence.

**INTASC Principle 6:** The teacher uses knowledge of effective verbal, nonverbal, and media communication techniques to foster active inquiry, collaboration, and supportive interaction in the classroom.

**Key Dispositions**

- The teacher recognizes the power of language for fostering self-expression, identity development, and learning.
- The teacher appreciates the cultural dimension of communication, responds appropriately, and seeks to foster culturally sensitive communication by and among all students in the class.

## Introduction to the Chapter

Adolescents are still children in the process of growing physically, psychologically (including developing a sense of identity), cognitively, socially, and morally. Adolescents also stand at the door of adulthood, making decisions about drug use, sexual activity, career options, and friendships that will play pivotal roles in their lives.

This chapter covers being responsive to the needs of adolescent learners. With that idea in mind, much of the chapter focuses on adolescent development as informed by the broader academic field of educational psychology. Section 1 introduces the major theories around development. This section examines models of learning and development along with the major theorists who have influenced educational thinking in this area.

Section 2 presents the issues, theories, and thoughts regarding cognitive development. Intellectual development theory, which is a particular concern of teachers, is also explored, including an approach for teachers to enhance the cognitive and intellectual development of students. This section also provides a description of first- and second-language development as well as its implications for teachers. Section 3 looks at biological and psychological development with special focus on identity development. Section 4 addresses social and ethical development with an emphasis on relationships and moral development, ending with Carl Rogers's humanist perspective and suggestions for teachers.

Although the discussion here attempts to describe each of these developmental domains differently, you should understand that they are interrelated and often overlap. Consider the example of the female student who, in comparison to her peers, is an "early maturer" in terms of her physical development. How she thinks (cognitive) about her early development (physical) is intertwined with how she sees her herself in terms of her identity (personality). In addition, how others treat her (social) and her earlier decisions about sexual relations with others (moral–ethical) all come into play.

Adolescence focuses on people from the ages of 10 to 20, with a significant range of differences among students in this age group (consider the differences between a 10-year-old and an 18-year-old). It is helpful to consider adolescence as comprising three distinct stages: early adolescence, middle adolescence, and late adolescence. We have aimed this chapter at development of middle adolescents during the high school years, the main focus of this textbook.

Professional education organizations try to cultivate a developmental framework for teachers who work with adolescents. As noted previously, we consider the framework the Circle of Courage model provides as the most appropriate to meet the needs of adolescents. All four parts of an individual's "circle" (Belonging, Mastery, Generosity, and Independence) must be intact in order to develop a self-secure, prosocial approach to life (Brendtro et al., 2002). This matches up with many traditional developmental views. No one aspect of the whole student should be ignored. Consider the summary statements from the National Association for Secondary School Principals, the organization notes that high schools should "get students ready for the next stage of life" and "play a role in the personal development of young people as social beings" (National Association for Secondary School Principals, 1996). Schools must address the concepts of Belonging and Generosity in order to build on self-esteem and promote learning at the appropriate developmental levels. State credentialing agencies have a keen interest in ensuring that teachers recognize developmental theories and their applications to the classroom. For example, California requires that individuals interested in teaching should be oriented to the common traits and individual differences that characterize children and adolescents (California Task Force, 1992). Clearly, the developmental needs of students matter. We believe that adolescents learn best when material is presented and teaching is engaging in ways that are both appropriate and challenging given students' developmental levels.

## SECTION 1: THEORIES OF LEARNING AND DEVELOPMENT

Before describing the specific developmental theories, you need to understand several hypotheses on which theories of development rely. Most developmental theories rest on the hypothesis that certain specific, observable fixed stages mark growth and development. Consider the differences between an infant, a child, an early adolescent, an adolescent, and an adult. Significant differences obviously exist in their intellectual, social, physical and moral–ethical worlds. Developmental theorists believe that these differences can be specifically identified and appear in fixed, predictable stages. These stages, many theorists argue, qualitatively differ from each other. The difference across age groups is not in *how much* but in *what kind*. The rings in the cross section of a tree provide a helpful analogy. Each distinct ring marks an important period of time. The rings, though, build on each other.

A second hypothesis upon which developmental theories rest is that these stages are hierarchical. This means that what happens at one stage builds on what has happened at earlier stages. For example, we believe that an infant's ability to stand without holding on to other things sets the stage for learning to walk. Similarly, learning to think critically about concrete things (things in the here and now, such as the characteristics of a good teacher) sets the stage for thinking critically about abstract things (things beyond the here and now, such as the characteristics of a good theory).

A third hypothesis is that the differences between students of similar chronological age are a matter of speed. That is, some adolescents progress through certain stages more quickly, or more slowly, than others. Eventually, however, all will progress through the stages identified, given healthy life circumstances. According to this hypothesis about one third will be progressing slower than average, one third will be average, and one third will be faster than average.

The third hypothesis complicates the developmental picture and warns us to be careful of sweeping generalizations about all adolescents. Individual experiences and the influence of others can either hinder or foster developmental growth. A person's values, life experiences, coping skills, and knowledge base all profoundly affect his or her place along a developmental continuum. It is important to get to know our students as individuals. Rarely is an individual fully in one stage. Although the individual tends to do most things, in most situations, from one developmental stage, evidence exists of previous stages as well as moments of trying out future roles and stages.

We must consider that many of the theories of development have been constructed as a result of working with students from the majority Euro American population. When applying developmental theories to minority groups, including those outside the United States, and when these groups do not fit the Euro American model, educators have tended to suppose developmental deficiencies. This perpetuates a belief in racial or ethnic superiority when, instead, it should represent the narrow range of the developmental domain when applied in cross-cultural contexts. For example, the early work done on adolescent identity development focused on the demands associated with choosing a career. The groups used were Euro American male college students, making the career-choice demand seem logical. However, as will be discussed later in this chapter, other developmental demands around adolescent identity present themselves to females and ethnic minority populations. It is important to keep in mind that the Mastery section of the Circle of Courage recognizes that all students can learn and each student must be given the opportunity to demonstrate competence, and this may be exhibited in a variety of ways.

Awareness of differences in developmental needs among all adolescents is a key aspect of facilitating mastery in cognitive, physical, and social competence. The following are different theorists' models of learning and development that highlight important differences in how we believe growth and development progress.

## Scheme Development

Jean Piaget (1928) advanced one of the best known of the developmental theories. He developed his theory of development by observing his own children. One of Piaget's strongest advocates, Eleanor Duckworth (1987), has argued that knowing Jean Piaget's theories is less helpful than knowing how to be a keen observer (like Jean Piaget) of our own students.

Piaget (Wadsworth, 1996) developed a scheme theory of development. In an effort to organize the world, people develop schemata (plural of *scheme*), defined as a systematic pattern of thinking around objects (such as characteristics of hamburgers), around actions (such as characteristics of a serve in tennis), and eventually around abstractions (such as characteristics of democracy). Piaget argued that as humans develop, these schemes become more and more complex. Two processes moderate scheme development: *assimilation* (fitting an experience into a preexisting scheme) and *accommodation* (creating a new scheme to understand an event). Both are critical and knowing when to assimilate and when to accommodate helps people adapt to their world. By adolescence, students have developed many schemes, some of which are complex. Assessing students' preexisting schemes will help in planning how to modify or build new schemes based on even greater sophistication in thinking.

Piaget argued that several variables foster development. Chief among these is experience. A student's encounter with the environment, including reflecting back on the encounter, fosters growth and development. A second critical variable that fosters development is the physical and physiological maturation of the person. Piaget placed less importance on *social transmission* (telling others) and the social and cultural context in which the child grows up. Piaget was not interested in forcing growth and development; rather, he believed it should happen naturally. To him, the goal of education is not to increase the amount of knowledge, but to create the possibilities for a child to invent and discover. He believed teaching too fast keeps children from inventing and discovering on their own. According to Piaget (1973), teaching involves creating situations in which children can discover structures instead of transmitting structures that they may assimilate on only a verbal level.

One final mechanism of development is worth noting in Piagetian thinking. People seek *equilibrium* in their thinking. Piaget defines this as knowing when to assimilate new information into an existing scheme and when to accommodate that information by creating a new scheme. Equilibrium is also the process of being aware of, and then dealing with, conflicting thoughts. As we mature and develop, we become better able to detect contradictions in our own thinking, and equilibrium requires that we work to resolve these cognitive discrepancies. Introducing *disequilibrium* (presence of cognitive contradictions) constructively fosters learning because students, to resolve contradictions, must refine their thinking.

While Piaget's work was well known around the world, the Russian psychologist Lev Vygotsky was working to provide an alternative model known as social cultural development. Although Vygotsky's model did not become known to many in the West until recently, it has since become one of the most important models guiding our thinking about development.

## Social–Cultural Contexts of Learning

Vygotsky (1978, 1986) argued that children develop in the context of working or living with more competent others. Similarly Brendtro et al. (2002) have suggested the spirit of Belonging is essential to cognitive development, noting, "The presence of a strong sense of belonging makes young people more receptive to guidance from other community members" (p. 47). For Vygotsky, the social and cultural contexts of learning are paramount in understanding the kinds of development that occur. As young people observe those at upper levels of growth and development, they attempt new levels of growth themselves. When the models provide assistance, they substantially help learners meet these new developmental demands. Over time, these individuals internalize the assistance and then can master the development task. This would explain, for example, how Brazilian children selling candy often develop sophisticated mathematical abilities at an early age, before having been taught mathematics.

Consider development happening at three levels (Vygotsky, 1978): those developmental tasks that can be done alone (*mastery*) and that indicate a person's actual developmental level; those that can be done with assistance from others (*zone of proximal,* or *potential, development*) and that indicate a person's emerging developmental abilities; and those that are clearly beyond any developmental ability at the time (*undeveloped capacities*). The following example illustrates these points.

Consider your own apprenticeship experience as a preservice teacher. You can probably do some tasks on your own, such as taking roll and making announcements. You can probably do some other tasks if provided assistance in the form of support, advice, or models, such as developing a lesson plan. You may be able to complete the task after reviewing a model lesson plan, having each part of the plan explained, and defining the difference between objectives and activities. You may simply not be aware of still other tasks, such as unobtrusive ways to get a class back on task: looking directly at or standing close to students who are not paying attention. Ultimately, you hopefully will internalize the support, advice, or model, which will become part of your thoughts, and you will gain the ability to complete the task of lesson planning, in this example, on your own.

Learning occurs first on an interpersonal level between people and then on a psychological level inside the person's head. The educational community has more fully embraced Vygotsky's work because it describes the significant role that the teacher, as the more expert "other" capable of providing helpful assistance, can play in the growth and development of students. The type of assistance through support, advice, or modeling is referred to as scaffolding. More specific techniques of scaffolding will be described in depth in Chapter 5, Section 3, Unit and Lesson Plans.

In contrast to Piaget, Vygotsky (1978, 1986) claims that what the child can do in cooperation today, can be done alone tomorrow. The best instruction marches ahead of development and leads it. It is still necessary to determine the lowest threshold at which instruction may begin, but we must consider the upper threshold as well: Instruction must be oriented toward the future, not the past. Vygotsky's work argues in favor of heterogeneous cooperative learning. Students need to see those at advanced stages of thinking because the more advanced thinkers can better recall the kinds of scaffolds helpful to them. These models also help identify the kinds of assistance teachers can provide to students so that they can succeed at developmental tasks just beyond their range of individual ability.

## The Constructivists

Vygotsky's work would not have received such a warm reception in the United States had it not been for prior acceptance of several major theories of learning set under the umbrella of cognitive psychology. Two distinct theories of cognition fit under this umbrella. One line of thinking focuses on how information is processed in the brain: New information is taken in and worked on in the short-term memory; then it is mixed with long-term knowledge, stored in long-term memory, and later recalled. Gagne (1977) has identified how lessons can be developed in a way that mirrors our understanding of how the brain processes information (events of a lesson). Another theorist, David Ausubel, and his colleagues (Ausubel, Novack, & Hanesian, 1978), using this same information-processing model, have spoken for the need to purposefully access prior knowledge and previously mastered ideas and concepts, so that new knowledge can be anchored to the existing knowledge via the use of advanced organizers. Chapter 4, Section 1, Instructional Strategies, describes the use of advanced organizers further.

## *Putting It Into Practice:* Activity 2.1

Develop a list of local community-based organizations (CBOs) that serve adolescents. Volunteer in after-school activities at one of these organizations. Be sure to spend time working with adolescents and learning what you can about them and their world. Your key objectives include learning how adolescents act differently and similarly out of school as they do in school, about the kinds of services that these agencies provide, as well as understanding the way the CBO works to solve issues that affect adolescents. Be sure to interview a variety of staff members of the CBO about what they see as critical issues affecting adolescents and developmental trends. Document your observations, interview data, and reflections.

A second focus of constructivism is not connected to models of how information is processed, but instead emphasizes the active construction of knowledge on the part of learners, both on their own and in their interactions with others. Constructivist theorists promote the idea that learners are constantly trying to make sense of their world. Learners bring their own unique experiences and understandings to the learning task. Building on these previous experiences and understandings, students construct new understandings, sometimes requiring the reconstruction of previously held learning. According to constructivists, students not only process information but also act as active thinkers, explainers, interpreters, and questioners. The construction of knowledge helps to explain why students in the same classroom do not always learn the same thing.

One constructivist, Jerome Bruner (1960), believes that all students are capable of grappling with any complex thoughts and ideas and will develop some level of sophisticated thought about how things work. Teachers, however, do not always know how to present these ideas in a helpful way, given the learners' developmental levels. Bruner recommends the use of discovery learning, wherein students can uncover concepts for themselves. In essence, the *how* of learning is more important than the *what* of learning.

## SECTION 2: COGNITIVE DEVELOPMENT

Section 1 described the relationship between learning and development. This section examines various perspectives of cognitive and intellectual development. First, we explore Piaget's stages regarding cognitive development. Then we look at the theory of multiple intelligence with special attention to the work of Harvard professor Howard Gardner. We then examine *epistemological* stages of development: how students come to *know* something. Finally, we address language acquisition related to stages of learning. Note that all of these theories—whether focused on cognitive development, multiple intelligence, or epistemological sophistication, or levels of learning—concern adolescents' overall intellectual growth.

### Stages of Cognitive Development

Jean Piaget posits that students move through four stages of cognitive development. Cognitive development is marked by the degree to which individuals can think logically and scientifically about the world.

***Sensorimotor.*** The first stage is knowledge that comes from *sensorimotor* activity and occurs from birth to 2 years of age. Children come to know by way of movement and what they experience through the senses. At this stage, when something is hidden from view, a child thinks the object has disappeared. For example, the child does not even look for a favorite toy hidden under a blanket because, in the child's thinking, it is no longer there.

***Preoperational.*** A second stage, covering 2 to 7 years of age, is called *preoperational* or prelogical. This stage is characterized most by how students cannot think. A classic activity marking the characteristics of this stage involves showing students how water from a tall, thin cylinder can be poured into a short, wide cylinder. When asked if there is more, less, or the same amount of water in the new cylinder, the students will likely answer, "less," even though they just saw you pour the water from the old into the new cylinder. Piaget suggests that students do not sense it is the same amount because they cannot reverse the action by mentally pouring it back into the tall cylinder. Nor can they concentrate on more than one thing; these students focus only on height, not width. They are incapable of *conservation*, knowing that objects stay the same regardless of changes in their properties.

***Concrete Operations.*** The third stage, from approximately ages 7 to 12, is characterized by an ability to reverse thinking, to concentrate on more than one element, and to appreciate the principle of conservation in thinking about concrete objects. This stage, called *concrete operations,* indicates logical mental thinking about concrete objects, actions, and observable properties. Besides the ability to think logically about concrete things, such as the characteristics of a car, this stage demonstrates an inability to think logically about abstract things, such as the characteristics of liberal politics, or to respond to hypothetical situations. The other characteristic of concrete operational thought is an inability to be aware of their own thinking and reasoning; students do not see inconsistencies in their own thinking.

***Formal Operations.*** The final stage, and the one of most interest to secondary school teachers, is *formal operations,* logical mental thinking about concepts, rules, laws, and abstract properties, the world in the abstract. Here, students show the ability to develop theories, form hypotheses, test these hypotheses in their heads, consider multiple causes and consequences, control variables, and systematically think through problems and possible solutions. Equally important, students demonstrate being aware of their own thinking, being critical of their own reasoning, and checking with outside sources of information for confirmation of their thinking.

We hope you understand how important it is to understand these latter stages when considering what you can expect of an adolescent learner. It is equally important to recognize that you need to cultivate, nurture, and develop this last stage. The speculation is that few adults are capable of thinking consistently in a world of formal operations. Most of the everyday thinking required of adults centers around the concrete world, figuring out why the car engine is making a strange noise, how to balance the checkbook, or where to go on the next family vacation. Because most of our reasoning focuses naturally on the concrete world, educators must take care to continually develop the abstract reasoning and self-reflection skills marked by this stage of cognitive growth and development. Rather than presupposing, for example, that students know the stages of problem resolution, you need to remind them, model problem solving for them, and monitor its use.

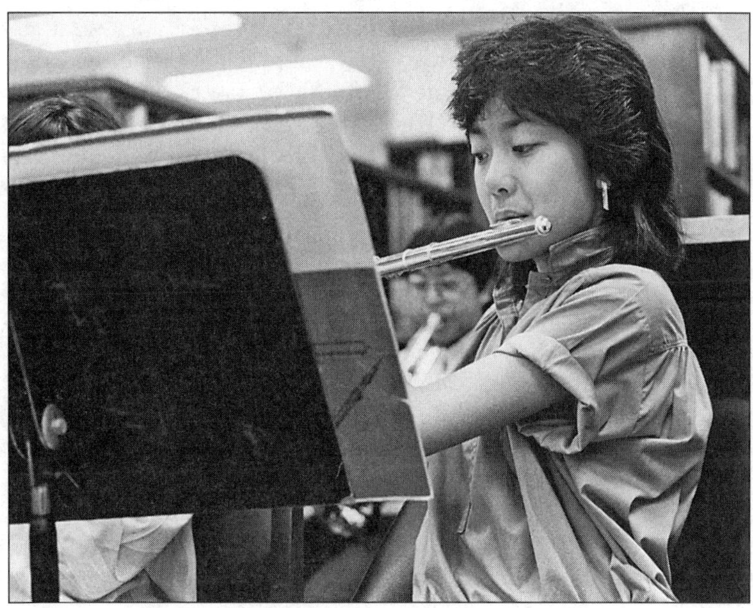

## Multiple Intelligence Theory

As Bruner (1960) suggests, people may engage in different kinds of thinking. It seems obvious, of course, that a connection between thinking and intelligence exists. Intelligence is generally assumed to be a form of thinking.

Howard Gardner (1983, 2000) has emerged as the most prominent spokesperson on multiple kinds of intelligence. His book *Frames of Mind* (1983) has appealed to a widespread audience for several reasons. First, it challenges traditional views of intelligence, which Gardner argues have centered on only two of the kinds of intelligence he identifies: linguistic and logical–mathematical, such as the Piagetian model previously described. Second, it enjoys cross-cultural appeal because other kinds of intelligence more valued in other cultures are now recognized within the United States. Finally, applications to classroom learning, teaching, and assessment can be easily made. Gardner argues that real people have a blend of intelligences and that teachers should consider instruction that uses all the intelligences. Nonetheless, most students will be strong in at least one of the intelligence areas.

Gardner argues that there are several kinds of intelligence. Initially he explored seven:

- *Musical intelligence:* the near-natural ability expressed by some to create, perform, and comprehend sound, especially as embodied in music.
- *Bodily kinesthetic intelligence:* the ability to control movement with balance, agility, and grace; especially embodied in athletic activities.
- *Logical–mathematical intelligence:* the ability to mentally process logical problems and equations, most often those associated with standardized tests.
- *Linguistic intelligence:* the ability to learn, construct, and comprehend languages, including one's primary language, with grace and ease; especially seen in people who have an ear for learning languages.
- *Spatial intelligence:* the ability to comprehend (perceive and interpret) shapes and images in three dimensions, both when the image can be physically seen (such as the shapes of buildings) and when it cannot (mentally rotating an image in your mind, such as a model of DNA).

- *Interpersonal intelligence:* the ability to interact with others, understand and be sensitive to them, and interpret their behaviors, all of which are instrumental in being able to influence others.
- *Intrapersonal intelligence:* the ability to understand and sense one's own being, to tap into who one is, how one feels, and why one acts in certain ways; especially seen in people keenly attuned to their own thoughts and feelings.

Most recently, Gardner (2000) has advanced an eighth intelligence:

- *Naturalist intelligence:* the ability to identify and classify patterns in nature, to relate to their surroundings; especially seen in people who are sensitive to their place within any given context.

Gardner suggests that although we have, historically, privileged one kind of intelligence, all forms of intelligence are of equal utility. Consider the student learning English as a second language or Spanish as a foreign language and the teacher willing to look beyond the value of linguistic and logical–mathematical intelligence, which have traditionally been the focus. People with musical intelligence will be acutely aware of the sounds of new language. Those demonstrating bodily kinesthetic intelligence will be especially cognizant of the movement of the mouth and tongue when pronouncing new words or making new sounds. People with interpersonal intelligence will be aware of modifications in language use depending on those with whom they interact. People with intrapersonal intelligence will be attuned to their own ability to learn languages and to the strategies they use to do so. It could even be argued that people with spatial, naturalist, or both kinds of intelligence will be especially adept at helping students recognize the environmental features whereby new language learning is taking place as well as their orientation to this new space.

As mentioned earlier, the theory of multiple intelligence has appealed to a wide audience because of its ease of application to teaching and learning. Teachers can help students gain a sense of Mastery, one of the four sections of the Circle of Courage, by recognizing students feel successful when they can adjust a basic framework for learning that fits with their own individual learning style or multiple intelligences. Consider all the various ways you can teach a lesson as prompted by thinking about these multiple intelligences. You can likewise use these ways of teaching as alternative forms of assessment. We have started a list for you in Figure 2.1, to which you can add ideas of your own.

## Epistemological Frameworks

Another category of cognitive growth and development centers on our epistemologies. *Epistemology* is the philosophy concerned with the nature and justification of human knowledge: how we come to know, what we believe about knowing, and how these beliefs influence our thinking and reasoning processes. Epistemological orientations guide teacher behavior and allow teachers to observe students' own epistemological development. Students move from an absolute understanding of things as right or wrong, black or white, and based in authority, to the contextual understanding of things based on knowledge as created by people who see things as right or wrong given their specific situation, and based in the self.

Work by Baxter Magolda (1992), building on the work of others, most notably Perry (1970) and Belenky, Clinchy, Goldberger, and Tarule (1986), identified four

**FIGURE 2.1** Application of Multiple Intelligences

| | |
|---|---|
| Musical intelligence | Sing a song, write a poem, or do a rap about what they are learning. |
| Bodily kinesthetic intelligence | Do a role-play, perform a pantomime or charades, or create a game designed to demonstrate what they are learning. |
| Logical–mathematical intelligence | Construct an outline, create syllogisms, or problem solve a dilemma evident in what they are learning. |
| Linguistic intelligence | Keep a journal, tell a story, give a speech, or stage a debate about something related to what they are learning. |
| Spatial intelligence | Create an artistic expression using collage or diorama, use guided mental imagery, or cut out pictures that speak to what they are learning. |
| Interpersonal intelligence | Work in cooperative groups, focus on how people are feeling, or develop person-to-person communication activities based on what they are learning. |
| Intrapersonal intelligence | Have students identify helpful thinking and learning strategies, self-evaluate their understandings, or think about their reactions to what they are learning. |

stages of epistemological growth. Each stage leads to particular expectations of learners, peers, teachers, teaching, assessment, and educational decision making.

***Absolute Stage.*** In the first stage, the *absolute stage*, students hold that absolute truth exists and that those with authority hold this truth. Thus, a student studying the Mexican-American War in history will view one side as being right and one side as being wrong, because the textbook or teacher says so.

***Transitional Stage.*** In the second stage, the *transitional stage*, students come to see that one side was not all right nor was one side all wrong and, as important, that authorities are not all knowing. The same student now comes to see that each side had some justification, and perhaps the student will conclude that one side was more justified than the other. Likewise, the student comes to believe that there is more to the Mexican-American War than was written in a particular textbook.

***Independent Stage.*** In the third stage, the independent stage, students begin to question authority and to believe that their own opinions are equally valuable. Thus, history students begin to actively critique what they read in the textbook and believe that their own understandings of the Mexican-American War are just as valid as what is written in the textbook.

***Contextual Stage.*** In the final stage, the *contextual stage*, students come to know by judging evidence available, given a specific context, and to realize that some people have more expertise than others. Students come to believe that knowledge evolves and is reconstructed on the basis of new evidence and new contexts. The student studying the Mexican-American War comes to value certain people's expertise, such as the expertise of a Mexican historian who had access to primary sources not available to the U.S. historian. The student may recognize the complexity of the Mexican-American War with political implications related to slavery, as well as to manifest destiny. The student may see that a difference in perspective could describe the motives for the war either as freedom for a new state or as an invasion of one nation by another. The student remains open to how people might interpret this same event differently as new evidence about the causes and implications of the Mexican-American War come to light in the future.

With respect to their cognitive development, we would expect that as students learn more, they would come to see greater complexity. This complexity includes recognition that more causes and effects exist than we normally understand at first glance. The complexity is extended with students' exposure to multiple perspectives because these offer alternative explanations for similar events. All this complexity leads students to understand that a simple understanding of ideas and events is rare.

## Language Acquisition

Due to the increase in the numbers of second-language learners enrolling in schools across this nation, teachers today must be aware of the language development needs of English language learners. As with other developmental domains, we can provide only the briefest sketch here and so encourage further study on this important topic.

The mind unconsciously hypothesizes the rules of the language that the child hears and then applies these rules in speech interactions. Based on feedback from others, including the gentle corrections from more experienced speakers, these rules become gradually clarified and correctly applied. For example, at earlier stages of learning English, learners gather that adding *-ed* to a word moves it from the present to the past tense (such as going from *play* to *played*). This rule applies to and is evident in children's speech even when it is inappropriately applied ("I *goed* to the museum"). Gradually, the language learner hypothesizes, from the gentle correction of others ("You *went* to the museum?"), that *-ed* works for most verbs in the past tense but there are exceptions. Most of this happens in meaningful speech situations; rarely are people explicitly taught language rules. By age 5, children have a vocabulary of over 10,000 words and speak grammatically correct English, even if they cannot articulate the rules.

Language develops in specific phases. The *receptive skills* (listening and reading) precede the *productive skills* (speaking and writing). People often understand more than they can say. It takes about 2 years to develop *basic interpersonal communication skills* (BICS): speech about easy content, often in the here and now, and with lots of clues, such as "how is the weather?" spoken outside while pointing to the sky. It takes 5 to 7 years to develop *cognitive academic language proficiency skills* (CALPS): speech about difficult content, beyond the here and now, and with few clues, no visuals, no realia (real things), and no linguistic support, such as listening to a lecture on the balance of power between the judicial, executive, and legislative branches of government. CALPS language, not BICS language, characterizes most secondary education classes (Cummins, 1981).

***Stages of Language Development.*** Krashen and Terrell (1983) suggest five stages of language development. In the *preproduction stage,* students understand spoken language and react to simple language requests. Being in a silent period, they need to hear the language spoken. They may be able to use *yes, no,* and other one-word responses. Again, not expressing belies the fact that they understand more than they can demonstrate. In the *early speech production stage,* students can produce a few words or short phrases as well as recognize the written version of their oral vocabulary. In the *speech emergence stage,* students speak in longer phrases and complete sentences. Students can also read and write simple text in the target language. Students in the *intermediate fluency stage* can engage in conversation and produce connected narrative. Involvement in lessons that develop higher levels of language use in content areas serves students best in this stage of language development. The final stage is full English-language proficiency.

***First- and Second-Language Acquisition (L1 and L2).*** So far, we have made little distinction between learning a first language (L1) and acquiring a second language (L2). In fact, important similarities exist between learning L1 and L2. These include the fact that both:

- require meaning-laden environments for maximum development;
- are influenced by a multitude of cognitive, social, and affective factors;
- require understandable speech from language speakers;
- exhibit a silent period and predictable errors during different stages of language development; and
- demand that attention be placed on motivation.

Important differences between L1 and L2 need to be understood as well. Some of these differences are listed below.

- Motivation differs and is typically less for the L2, because learners can already move about in the world in one language.
- Students usually have less exposure to, especially to the variety of, second-language speech, and spend less time in the L2.
- The L1 can both interfere with and facilitate development of the L2.
- Educators place more unrealistic and different expectations on L2 learners, including more focus on grammar and assumptions of quicker language acquisition, often with concomitant negative attitudes toward the L2 learner's language and culture.
- Schools require L2 learners to develop oral, narrative-written, and expository-written language at the same time, and they often exclude students from the core curriculum until students can demonstrate certain levels of language proficiency.

We hope it is evident that teachers of students for whom English is a second language have a considerable task on their hands: how to teach academic content in a way that facilitates the acquisition of the English language. Motivation as an important concern must be consistently addressed. Schools need to offer positive opportunities to hear and practice the language with native English speakers, especially those speakers who are respectful and empathetic of learning a second language. Educators must make the academic content that is taught understandable, by way of lots of clues, including gestures, props, drawings, and real things. Finally, helping students see connections between what they already know, including what they learned in their L1 and what they are learning, will greatly facilitate both academic and language development. Chapter 4, Instructional Strategies, provides a number of strategies to help you meet the goals of working with students whose second language is English.

## *Putting It Into Practice:* Activity 2.2

Sections 1 and 2 contain many major theories and models. In small teams of three or four students, select one of the learning theories or models. Your team will develop graphics and visuals on your selected topic. Each team will present a "Poster Session" that involves using your visuals and teaching a 20- to 25-minute minilesson explaining the theory and highlighting the main concepts. Each team will also address any aspects of the theory/model your team may question. As part of the lesson, each team must identify how its theory/model can be useful to a classroom teacher to help reach all students. For example, describe how you would modify a lesson to make it more engaging based on the theory's ideas.

## SECTION 3: BIOLOGICAL AND PSYCHOLOGICAL DEVELOPMENT

The physical and psychological development of adolescents are intertwined. First, however, it is important to note that adolescence is the second greatest physical growth stage in our lives, second only to prenatal development to early childhood. During adolescence, *puberty*, the growth to physical adulthood and sexual maturity, marks physical development. Some, including Rousseau and Freud, have argued that these physical changes cause the great turbulence many adolescents experience. Others, most notably the anthropologist Margaret Mead, have argued that the social environment—how parents, peers, siblings, teachers, and society respond to the adolescent in particular cultural contexts—more fully explains whether this experience will be positive or negative. Most developmental psychologists today take a balanced view in noting the importance of both biological and environmental factors, in interaction, in determining the adolescent experience.

### Physical Growth

The first of two central elements of physical growth during adolescence is development into adult body size, weight, shape, and muscle-to-fat makeup. The second of these central elements is sexual maturity, most evident in those sexual characteristics that are either visible or not visible. Certain interactive effects exist between the social and the physical dimensions of development. Early maturing boys, for example, tend to have an advantage in the United States, especially when physical prowess channeled into athletic activity can take place. Conversely, for girls, slender body frames tend to be more valued (note the images portrayed of young women in advertising). For girls, maturing later seems to be of greater advantage. This relates partly to the society's cultural ideals of beauty and partly to peer response and the need to fit in. However, some believe the long-term effects of not fitting in comes back as an advantage to late-maturing boys and early-maturing girls. The hypothesis states that the stress of not fitting in and having a body image different from the social ideal develops coping skills in these students that will benefit them well into adulthood.

While biological changes, especially the production of sex hormones, influence physical development and sexual maturation, they also influence adolescents emotionally. Hormonal production does affect emotional reactions. In boys, this manifests as anger and irritability and in girls, anger and depression. This moodiness must also be understood in terms of environmental and social factors. For example, adolescents experience more negative life events, such as dating difficulties or challenges with more difficult school content, than they did in childhood. Likewise, the change in moods also relates to the fact that adolescents move in and out of different situations, from home to school or to friends' homes, more frequently than do children or adults. Interestingly, Chikszentmihalyi and Larson (1984) found that emotional lows more likely occurred in adult-controlled situations, such as classrooms, and emotional highs when spending time with friends and in free-choice types of activities, such as in pursuing hobbies.

Adolescents also experience the conflicting challenge of needing the advice and counsel of adults while desiring to break away from them. Psychologists suggest that the conflict experienced with parents is psychological preparation for adolescents' eventual moving out on their own. Heightened cognitive, moral, and identity development also present a challenge as adolescents can sense conflicts in the behavior and teachings of adults.

## Personality and Identity

The work of developmental psychologist Erik Erikson has influenced the psychological domain most strongly. His eight-stage psychosocial theory of personality development spans from infancy to late adulthood. Erikson (1963) suggests that psychological development depends on the quality of relationships with others. He also contends that each stage brings with it some developmental task. Due to the comprehensive nature of his theory of development, we will restrict our discussion to the chief developmental challenge associated with adolescence: identity development. Keep in mind, however, that earlier stages of development also affect identity development. The ability to trust others or the ability to develop a sense of independence, characteristic of earlier stages of development, exerts an important influence on the development of identity.

***Erikson's Identity Development Theory.*** Erikson suggests that adolescents often experience an identity crisis as they move into and through this developmental stage. Indeed, adolescence is a time of soul searching and inner exploration. Adolescents must decide on the values and beliefs that will mark their existence. They also must make life choices about vocation, politics, and religion. For Erikson, this search for self is critical to identity development, whereas the lack of direction or not accepting direction provided by others leads to *identity diffusion*. Recently, the psychological community has called into question the use of the term *identity crisis,* instead favoring the term *identity exploration.* More than simply a change of words, it acknowledges that this stage of identity development is not always one of great negativity or one marked by the suddenness evident in most life crises. Identity develops in the context of day-to-day decisions and their gradual incorporation into a holistic image of who adolescents want to be.

Identity formation advances first with the incorporation of a holistic sense of identity, away from the singular descriptions of childhood, such as "I'm good in math," with an understanding of the changes that often take place in this identity as time and place change. Adolescents qualify self-descriptions with statements such as "I'm almost always happy," or "With my friends, I'm very honest." A second advancement in identity formation during adolescence is an increase in the importance paid to the social dimension of identity: friendliness and the ability to develop intimacy with others.

***Marcia's Identity Development Theory.*** Marcia (1980) has been instrumental in describing how adolescents move toward identity development. He suggests four different stages of identity development dependent on the degree of exploration and the degree of commitment to an identity. *Identity diffusion* is marked by a lack of exploration of identity and a lack of commitment to an identity. *Identity foreclosure* is characterized by the acceptance, without exploration, of the identity others provide. For example, a teenager decides to become a lawyer because the teenager's parents have told their child that it is the appropriate career. The child adopts a high commitment to that identity without questioning it. *Identity moratorium* is evident by high degrees of exploration without solid commitments. Finally, *identity achievement* is marked by exploration of identity choices and commitment to some specific choices.

Marcia's work focused primarily on only a few dimensions of identity: vocational, political, and religious in particular. More recently, other scholars have advanced another dimension of identity: ethnic identity development (Cross, 1991; Helms, 1990). Early efforts suggested that, in a society in which Euro Americans hold the most power, ethnic minority adolescents had the developmental task of constructing meaning around the following: What does it mean to be an ethnic minority in a Euro American dominated society? This question becomes even more salient as ethnic minority adolescents experience discrimination, consider intercultural relationships, and struggle between allegiance to their home culture and the pressures to assimilate to the dominant culture.

***Cross's Model of Black Racial Identity.*** Consider, for example, Cross's (1991) model of Black racial identity. In the *preencounter stage* of racial identity, Black students accept what they have learned about Euro American dominance and value. To accept this, Black students often distance themselves from their ethnic roots and minimize the roles race and ethnicity play in their lives. The *encounter stage* is often initiated when Black students experience some overt form of discrimination and thus holding a color-blind orientation will not suffice. The third stage, *immersion–emersion*, is characterized by a pro-Black/anti-White life orientation. The characterization of the angry Black adolescent may typify this stage of identity development. The fourth stage, *internalization*, is apparent in the person who still holds on to a pro-Black orientation but is now able to forge cross-cultural relations, especially with those who seek to be allies with and demonstrate respect for Blacks. Finally, *internalization–commitment* is evident in students committed to a Black racial identity, to advancing the concerns of the Black community, and to using their Blackness as a departure point in search of more universal truths (Cross, 1991).

***White Identity Model.*** Provocative work also has been forged around White identity development, especially as White students come to understand what it means to be privileged in a society that neither wants to acknowledge, let alone question, Whiteness. Yet, to have more constructive cross-cultural relations and to work actively to create inclusive classrooms, society must ensure that students come to understand their own White ethnic identity development.

Helms's (1990) description is instructive in this instance. In the *contact* stage, the White adolescent, unaware of the privileges associated with being White, may have a curious, if not fearful, reaction to those who are not White. People who have little or no contact with ethnic racial minorities may never move beyond this stage. When situations force students to acknowledge that racism exists, they may experience *disintegration*, the second stage. They may feel guilt and shame because of the racist system and the ways in which they have been advantaged. To deal with this, many will either deny that race plays a role in their own privileges or deny the reality of racism. Alternately, the White students might become aware of how racism factors in their own lives (racist jokes made by family members, for example) and begin to talk with others about racism and question others' racist behavior. Should they meet with outright rejection, coupled with the pressure to accept the status quo, White students often experience *reintegration*, the third stage. Relationships with White peers run smoothly and the guilt felt initially often turns to anger at non-Whites for raising the issue of racism.

Again, many White students can easily end their development here, especially in the absence of non-White peers or lacking the opportunity for continual examination of racism in their society. However, given this examination, White students will move into the *pseudo-integration* stage. In this stage, White students begin to abandon beliefs of White racial superiority, actively seeking out more information, and often benefit from relationships with non-White peers who can help in this regard. However, behaviors and beliefs that still rely on, and perhaps perpetuate, our race-based social system, also characterize this stage. With Whiteness now questioned, students may begin searching for a new way to be White that seeks alliance and advocacy with people of color. Students continue in this *immersion–emersion* stage as they have the opportunity to read about and meet people who are White who have become antiracists. This is critical for developing an image of the antiracist White. Having such an image facilitates *autonomy*, the final stage. Autonomy facilitates constructing friendships across racial lines, questioning racism in contexts in which students find themselves, and working actively for social justice and equity.

## Implications for Teachers

Let's refer back to several key challenges associated with physical development that may occur during the adolescent stage of development. The eating disorders anorexia nervosa and bulimia are not uncommon. The ever-increasing possibility of sexual activity brings issues of responsible sexual behavior to the foreground with irresponsibility leading to the potential for a myriad of sexually transmitted diseases, unwanted teenage pregnancy, or both. In addition, adult-like freedom also means the opportunity to explore alcohol and drug use with the potential for abuse. Adolescents and their caregivers, including their teachers, must remain vigilant about all these social issues.

Additionally, with specific regard to identity, consider the implications for teachers in multicultural classrooms in which both White and ethnic minority students may be at different stages of identity development. While some White students may be at a stage at which they desire ethnic minority friendship (*pseudo-independent*), some ethnic minority students may be at a stage that is anti-White (*immersion–emersion*). The segregation within schools often evident on many high school campuses can be understood in terms of these varying stages of ethnic identity development (Tatum, 1999). Teachers can provide multiple opportunities for students to explore their own identity via a multicultural education; to discuss the race-based system of privilege and oppression as a higher order thinking activity; to serve via development projects in those communities most affected by social oppression; and to be informed about both ethnic minority and White people who have moved beyond the limitations of racism in America and forged positive, constructive relations across racial lines in service of seeking true social equality.

It is important to note how identity development plays out in academic disciplines. How students come to define themselves academically (such as "I'm not a reader" or "I'm very mathematical") critically affects their education. Many teachers have to work to change students' identities when these perceptions hinder progress in secondary classrooms. Importantly, ethnic identity development interacts with academic identity development. Many ethnic minority students believe that being academically successful is akin to "acting White." Alternately, consider the pressure to meet expectations imposed on many Asian American students to be nearly exclusively academic oriented. Being aware of the interaction between academic identity and ethnic identity and providing opportunities for ethnic minority students to see people of their own ethnicity as academically successful (or as more than just academic oriented) will go a long way to dispelling the notion that academic success is a Whites-only reality.

Recall that the chief developmental task of adolescents is identity attainment without getting stuck in role confusion. Students who struggle with identity attainment often have trouble adjusting to school and community contexts. Teachers would do well to inform themselves about how identity challenges factor into depression and suicide as major developmental challenges.

### *Putting It Into Practice:* Activity 2.3

Observe a teacher who deals with students from 9th through 12th grades. Try to notice the developmental differences between 9th graders and 12th graders. How do they differ across developmental domains discussed so far? How does the teacher deal with these students differently? Also notice whether any differences in students exist based on gender, ethnicity identity, English language proficiency, or intelligence preference. Why do these differences occur? Interview the teacher. Ask about developmental differences in the classroom and how the teacher thinks about and responds to them. Also ask about the differences the teacher sees across gender, ethnicity, English language proficiency lines, or intelligence preferences. Write up your observations and interview data. Work to make connections to the developmental frameworks described so far in this chapter.

## SECTION 4: SOCIAL AND ETHICAL DEVELOPMENT

"No person is an island," as the adage goes. Indeed, we are social beings. Focusing on how we think about others, both those physically close to us—peers, caregivers, teachers—and more distant others—such as people in other parts of the world—is central to social development. Any contact with adolescents leads to the conclusion that peers, in particular, become increasingly important in their lives. Part of this is due to the fact that adolescents spend more time with peers than with any other group of individuals, including family members. The central developmental task of dealing with peers prepares adolescents for their adult roles as members of a community.

### Relationships

A desire for closeness and faithfulness especially marks peer friendships in adolescence. A change occurs from having many friends to having a few close friends, which is characteristic of most adult relationships. The similarities between friends, more than the differences, also tend to mark peer friendships. Close friendships serve many important psychological and social developmental functions. Related to these close friendships is the establishment of cliques. Cliques can serve many useful functions, including providing a sense of belonging as adolescents move away from their families, helping them to experiment with new identities and social roles, and creating a place to talk through the stresses associated with adolescence.

Several other findings about adolescent social development include the following (Bigelow, Christensen, Karp, Miner, & Peterson, 1996; Brendtro et al., 2002; Selman, 1980):

- Cliques, which are more tightly structured and exclusive than in earlier years, usually develop around areas of interest.
- Cliques decrease in importance later in adolescence.
- Dating increases in adolescence and provides a healthy way to learn how to behave with members of the opposite gender across a wide range of social contexts.
- Friendship relationships are usually more intimate than dating relationships.
- Conformity to peer pressure peaks during adolescence, especially around short-term matters such as dress or music preferences, but it does not lead to blind acceptance of the dictates of the social group (in fact, parents still largely influence basic values, educational choices, and future aspirations).

***Selman's Stages of Social Development.*** Selman (1980) has been instrumental in helping identify movement from *egocentric* to *prosocial* stages of development, based on our ability to infer what others are thinking and feeling (empathy). He asserts that students begin at an *egocentric* stage of development, characterized by believing that everyone thinks and feels as they think and feel. At the *social information role* stage, students understand that others think and feel differently than they do and can even understand what others in their social sphere are thinking and feeling. In the *self-reflective role* stage, students begin to imagine that others have a perspective of them and that friendships involve reciprocal perspectives. In the *multiple role-taking* stage, beginning in early adolescence, students can empathize with others who are similar to them even if the others are not part of their immediate social group. In middle adolescence, students develop a *social and conventional system-taking role* wherein they can empathize with anyone, including those unlike them.

Selman's work around *social perspective taking* has shown that students who are able to operate at these higher levels of empathy tend to be more respectful, kind, and considerate (prosocial). Students unable to develop these higher levels of perspective taking do not feel guilt or remorse when committing aggressive acts. Activities teachers use to help students to see other worldviews and to develop an empathetic orientation to others can facilitate movement toward these more advanced stages. We recommend *Rethinking Our Classrooms* (1996) by Bigelow et al. as a resource for suggestions on activities such as social perspective taking role-playing.

The lack of social perspective taking results in delinquent behavior. It is considerably more difficult to hurt someone when you are capable of imagining what it might feel like. Coupled with the pressure to conform to groups, including those groups engaged in antisocial behavior, the increase in involvement in gang activity among adolescents becomes understandable. Viewed in light of the Circle of Courage model, this antisocial behavior stems from a need for Belonging that is not being met in a healthy way. In addition to struggling to find artificial or distorted ways to belong, adolescents may also withdraw and be reluctant to form attachments, becoming guarded, distrustful, and isolated (Brendtro et al., 2002).

## Moral Development

As students develop cognitively toward more hypothetical and abstract forms of reasoning, we might imagine accompanying changes in moral–ethical reasoning. Although Piaget (1965) hypothesized how moral development might proceed, Lawrence Kohlberg (1969) has done the most notable work. Critical to Kohlberg's notion of moral development is a focus on the reasoning individuals use to respond to moral dilemmas.

Kohlberg suggests three levels of moral development with two stages within each level. The first level is the *preconventional level*, associated with childhood, marked by students conforming to what others say is right or wrong, or what is punished or rewarded. At the *conventional level*, most typical of adolescence, moral development is characterized by a belief in and desire for the current social order and smooth social relationships. At the *postconventional level*, students are guided by principles and abstract moral values beyond what others, including the society at large, assert and reward or punish. This theory of moral development is about the movement from the moral–ethical development as embedded in others to the moral–ethical principles that one develops for oneself. For Kohlberg, this postconventional development is most characterized by an ethic of justice. Few people, including adults, move to this third level of moral–ethical development.

Carol Gilligan has criticized Kohlberg. In response to studies that showed that females lag behind males in moral development as defined by Kohlberg, Gilligan (1982) asserted that females are motivated not exclusively by a sense of justice but also by an ethic of care. In this regard, she suggests moral–ethical development proceeds from a care about self, to a care for others, to a care for both the self and others. For Gilligan, this ethic of care is a different but not a deficient ethic as compared to that of characterizing the levels of development Kohlberg proposed. Importantly, when these two ethics, justice and care, come together, the student, regardless of gender, seems to exhibit the highest degrees of ethical behavior.

Teachers can move students toward higher levels of moral–ethical development by presenting them with moral dilemmas and space to discuss with peers how to resolve them. Focus should especially be turned toward asking students why they think the way they do. An opportunity for adolescents to give something to others is another way to assist this moral–ethical development. The development of the spirit of Generosity in students assists them to become caring, supportive adults. Classroom strategies of collaborative work (shared expertise) or becoming involved in service-learning community projects can aid this aspect of an adolescent's development.

## The Humanist Perspective's Connection to Teaching

Generally, Rogers (1962) and Bolton (1986) argued that humans are, by nature, positive beings who will do the right thing given the opportunity to make healthy choices. However, unhealthy relationships and social structures that derail people from making affirming choices in their lives often taint this positive nature. For Rogers, the quality of the relationships teachers have with students is the central feature determining whether students grow and learn in productive ways. Given his interest in the qualities of a helping relationship that lead to students' functioning fully as human beings, Rogers identified three central constructs. These constructs can assist teachers as they develop strategies to help students develop fully each aspect of the Circle of Courage.

***Genuineness.*** First, Rogers discusses the importance of *genuineness*, being fully one's self, and avoiding facades and false personas. Genuineness entails being aware of your own inner emotions, thoughts, hopes, and dreams. Once you can be aware of these, you must accept that they are part of who you are. After acceptance, then you must be willing to share them with others. Rogers encourages people to show those aspects of their selves that are their vulnerabilities. In so doing, students learn how they can deal with their own human imperfections.

***Empathy.*** A second construct to healthy relationships is *empathy*, being able to understand another person's world without losing yourself in that world. It is not apathy, feeling nothing, nor sympathy, feeling sorry for someone. Rather, empathy involves listening to how others are feeling and trying to understand why they feel that way. Teachers demonstrate empathy when they listen attentively to their students, reflect back their understandings, and mirror the emotions being expressed by the other.

***Unconditional Positive Regard.*** The third construct Rogers describes is *unconditional positive regard*, of having a concern for the well-being of your students, but doing so without trying to possess them and without conditions often evident in statements that begin "I will care about you if. . . ." Rogers suggests that you may not like people's behavior but you can still demonstrate unconditional positive regard and goodwill toward them. Demonstrating unconditional positive regard involves the degree to which you can show respect and warmth toward others. It suspends judgments and evaluations and distinguishes that being critical of behavior is acceptable and being critical of the person is not acceptable.

Although some have argued that it is impossible to always be genuine, be empathetic, or offer unconditional positive regard, and it may not be appropriate to be so transparent with students that you reveal your innermost feelings, the constructs can be helpful in professional relationships. In particular, when students are experiencing a life difficulty, feel as though they need to develop a stronger relationship, or find themselves in a difficult place and do not know how to respond, consider the strength that you can gain from genuineness, empathy, and unconditional positive regard.

In addition, keep in mind the qualities that distinguish humans from nonhumans. Humans are unique, capable of thought and making choices in their lives, feeling, and acting and taking responsibilities for these actions. Whenever you share with students the things that make you unique, your thoughts and choices, your feelings, and the responsibility you take for your actions, you are acting humanly. Likewise, when you are aware of these characteristics in your students, you validate their humanity.

Rogers's three constructs of being genuine with students, demonstrating empathy, and being human by modeling positive regard and goodwill toward others correspond with the Circle of Courage, which highlights the universal need for belonging. Throughout history, the tribe, not just the nuclear family, ensured the survival of the culture. Though parents might fail, the tribe was always there to nourish and come to the aid of the next generation. All those involved with teaching need to be aware of how establishing appropriate relationships and connections with their students can develop a sense of community to which all those in the classroom can belong. Most importantly, for teachers, by modeling these qualities you feel more fully human and students tend to reflect their humanness back to you. Indeed, how can the human natural tendency toward growth be any more fully realized than in such nurturing relationships?

## Putting It Into Practice: Activity 2.4

In this activity, spend a day with an adolescent. It is best if the student is unlike you in terms of gender, economic class, and ethnicity. Make arrangements to observe the student from a distance, with permission from the student, parent, and school. Notice changes that may occur as the day progresses and across a variety of academic disciplines. When does the student seem most energetic and enthusiastic? When is the student's low point of the day? At some point during the day, interview the student about likes or dislikes about school, home, and community. Ask questions that pinpoint the student's physical, social, moral, cognitive, and personality development. For example, with respect to identity, how does the student describe his or her own ethnicity? How does the student understand issues of race or racism in America? Write up your thoughts about what you learned from your interview and observations. Your write-up should make connections to the developmental frameworks this chapter describes. Were they helpful in describing the student? Why or why not?

## SECTION 5: CHAPTER SUMMARY AND REFLECTION

The goal of this chapter was to help you understand how adolescents develop and learn so that you will be able to provide learning opportunities that support their intellectual, social, and personal development. This chapter has only begun the exploration around adolescent development. Section 1 examined the hypotheses of developmental theories, fixed stages, the hierarchical nature of development, and the speed at which growth occurs in adolescents. The section also provided an overview of the major models of learning and development.

Section 2 focused on the various perspectives of cognitive (intellectual) development. One model in this section, Gardner's multiple intelligence theory, included specific ideas teachers might use to allow more students the opportunity to connect with material being taught. This section also covered the philosophy of epistemology as it concerned how humans come to know, what they believe about knowing, and how these beliefs influence thinking. This section concluded with language development and a focus on second-language acquisition. Both stages of language acquisition and distinctions with second-language acquisition along with the challenges this understanding presents were explored.

Section 3 focused on the biological and psychological development of adolescents, including a discussion of identity development. Understanding and making appropriate use of this information can be instrumental in crafting engaging lessons for students.

The chapter concluded with an overview of issues related to the social and moral development of adolescents. As the Circle of Courage model reminds teachers, this important aspect of development cannot be overlooked in schools if students are going to have the opportunity to lead healthy fulfilling lives. The work of Carl Rogers on developing quality relationships with students illustrated how relationships connect to teaching and learning.

As you have seen in this chapter, there is a whole academic field associated with developmental psychology. The complexity of developmental theories, the controversies that many of them have engendered, and an appreciation for their specific applications can be gained by a more thorough and comprehensive study of these theories in each of the developmental areas reviewed. The understanding of development will better equip you to use effective communication techniques to foster active inquiry, collaboration, and supportive interaction in the classroom.

For now, you will be best served by looking at development, including your own, as lifelong, always moving forward. As teachers, you must recognize that your students will be moving between stages depending on the situations in which they find themselves. Finally, we hope that you consider the frameworks described here not as rigid descriptions of the complex range of human possibility but rather as flexible frameworks that offer clues to today's learners.

## References


Ausubel, D. P., Novack, J. D. & Hanesian, H. (1978). *Educational psychology: A cognitive view.* New York: Holt.

Baxter Magolda, M. B. (1992). *Knowing and reasoning in college: Gender-related patterns in students' intellectual development*. San Francisco: Jossey-Bass.

Belenky, M. F., Clinchy, B. M., Goldberger, N. R., & Tarule, J. M. (1986). *Women's ways of knowing: The development of self, voice, and mind.* New York: Basic Books.

Bigelow, B., Christensen, L., Karp, S., Miner, B., & Peterson, B. (1996). *Rethinking our classrooms*. Milwaukee, WI: Rethinking Schools, Ltd.

Bolton, R. (1986). *People skills.* New York: Simon & Schuster.

Brendtro, L. K., Brokenleg, M., & Bockern, S. V. (2002). *Reclaiming youth at risk: Our hope for the future.* Bloomington, IN: National Education Service.

Bruner, J. (1960). *The process of education*. New York: Vintage.

California Task Force (1992). *Second to none*. Sacramento, CA: Department of Education.

Chikszentmihalyi, M., & Larson, R. (1984). *Being adolescent: Conflict and growth in the teenage years.* New York: Basic Books.

Council of Chief State School Officers (1992). Model standards for beginning teacher licensing, assessment, and development: A resource for state dialogue. Washington, DC: Author. www.ccsso.org/content/pdfs/corestrd.pdf

Cross, W. E., Jr. (1991). *Shades of black: Diversity in African-American identity.* Philadelphia: Temple University Press.

Cummins, J. (1981). The role of primary language development in promoting the educational success of language minority students. In Office of Bilingual Bicultural Education, California Department of Education (Ed.), *Schooling and language minority students: A theoretical framework* (pp. 3–50). Los Angeles: Evaluation, Dissemination and Assessment Center, CSU.

Duckworth, E. (1987). *The having of wonderful ideas.* New York: Teachers College Press.

Erikson, E. (1963). *Childhood and society.* New York: W. W. Norton.

Gagne, R. M. (1977). *The conditions of learning*. New York: Holt, Rinehart and Winston.

Gardner, H. (1983). *Frames of mind*. New York: Basic Books.

Gardner, H. (2000). *Intelligence reframed: Multiple intelligences for the twenty-first century.* New York: Basic Books.

Gilligan, C. (1982). *In a different voice: Psychological theory and women's development.* Cambridge, MA: Harvard University Press.

Helms, J. E. (Ed.). (1990). *Black and White racial identity: Theory, research and practice.* Westport, CT: Greenwood Press.

Kohlberg, L. (1969). *Stages in the development of moral thought and action.* New York: Holt, Rinehart and Winston.

Krashen, S. D., & Terrell, T. D. (1983). *The natural approach: Language acquisition in the classroom.* New York: Pergamon/Alemany.

Marcia, J. E. (1980). Identity in adolescence. In J. Adelson (Ed.), *Handbook of adolescent psychology.* New York: Wiley.
National Association of Secondary School Principals (1996). Breaking ranks: Changing an American institution. Reston, VA: NASSP.
Perry, W. G. (1970). *Forms of intellectual and ethical development in the college years: A scheme.* New York: Holt, Rinehart and Winston.
Piaget, J. (1928). *Judgment and reasoning of the child.* New York: Harcourt Brace Jovanovich.
Piaget, J. (1965). *The moral judgment of the child.* New York: Free Press.
Piaget, J. (1973). *To understand is to invent.* New York: Viking Press.
Rogers, C. (1962). The interpersonal relationship: The core of guidance. *Harvard Educational Review, 32,* 416–429.
Selman, R. L. (1980). *The growth of interpersonal understanding.* New York: Academic Press.
Sternberg, R. J. (1989). *The triarchic mind: A new theory of human intelligence.* New York: Penguin Books.
Stowell, L., Rios, F., McDaniel, J., & Christopher, P. (1996). *Working with middle school students.* San Diego, CA: Teacher Created Materials.
Tatum, B. (1999). *Why are all the Black kids sitting together in the cafeteria?* New York: Basic Books.
Vygotsky, L. S. (1978). *Mind in society.* Cambridge, MA: Harvard University Press.
Vygotsky, L. S. (1986). *Thought and language.* Cambridge, MA: MIT Press. (Original work published in 1934)
Wadsworth, B. J. (1996). *Piaget's theory of cognitive and affective development.* White Plains, NY: Longman.

# Unit II

# Planning Instruction

# Chapter 3

# Assessment

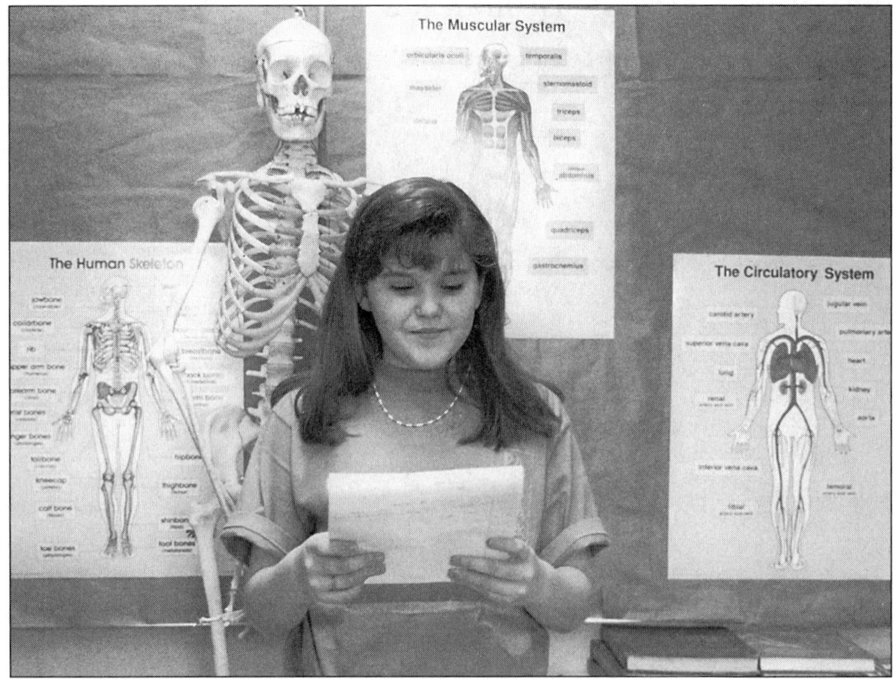

**INTASC Principle 7:** The teacher plans instruction based upon knowledge of subject matter, students, the community, and curriculum goals.

**Key Disposition**

- The teacher believes that plans must always be open to adjustment and revision based on student needs and changing circumstances.

**INTASC Principle 8:** The teacher understands and uses formal and informal assessment strategies to evaluate and ensure the continuous intellectual, social, and physical development of the learner.

**Key Dispositions**

- The teacher values ongoing assessment as essential to the instructional process and recognizes that many different assessment strategies, accurately and systematically used, are necessary for monitoring and promoting student learning.
- The teacher is committed to using assessment to identify student strengths and promote student growth rather than to deny students access to learning opportunities.

**INTASC Principle 10:** The teacher fosters relationships with school colleagues, parents, and agencies in the larger community to support students' learning and well-being.

**Key Dispositions**

- The teacher is willing to consult with other adults regarding the education and well-being of his/her students.
- The teacher respects the privacy of students and confidentiality of information.

## Introduction to the Chapter

We have placed this chapter on assessment here, ahead of the chapter on developing unit and lesson plans, in agreement with Wiggins and McTighe's philosophy that to be able to truly assess students' understanding and to inform teaching, classroom curriculum should be designed backward. In other words, teachers should use the academic standards and the broad curriculum goals appropriate to their course, and then identify the desired results. "What should students know, understand, and be able to do? What is worthy of understanding? What enduring understandings are desired?" (1998, p. 9). Once you determine the big concepts you want students to understand, skip to the end, to the assessment tools needed to determine the extent to which students know and understand the material and concepts they have been taught. Then, once you determine the assessment strategies, move on to plan learning experiences and instruction to build understanding so students can successfully complete the assessment projects and activities determined to be beneficial and meaningful. Introducing the concepts of assessment early in the text can help you develop instruction that allows for the authentic assessment practices mentioned throughout the book.

Section 1 of the chapter begins with a brief historical background of assessment as a means to better understand its evolution, including the controversy surrounding the use of standardized tests. The section then focuses on standards for assessment, addresses types of assessment, and emphasizes the importance of the validity and reliability of all assessment tools.

Section 2 focuses on designing tools to assess student understanding, beginning with a look at Bloom's taxonomy and how it relates to developing a variety of assessment strategies at all levels as part of an assessment plan. We then move on to the use of formative and summative assessment and matching them to the layers of knowledge and skills in the curriculum. The examples and suggestions provided will assist you in effectively using authentic assessment tools, including construction of rubrics. You will have the opportunity to create your own assessment plan, utilizing the models provided.

Section 3 looks at professional considerations for assessment related to teachers. Discussion centers on the importance of teacher expectations for students as well as the need for good reporting methods of student learning to parents, school, and district administrators and the community. Finally, this section provides suggestions for you as the teacher to evaluate your own instruction and curriculum using a method termed action research.

Throughout the chapter the four sections of the Circle of Courage—Belonging, Mastery, Generosity, and Independence—function as key considerations in designing and using assessment tools (Brendtro et al., 2002). Meaningful assessment demands that students experience a sense of Belonging and Independence in the assessment process. Students are the most important stakeholders in the entire process, yet often they do not understand how and for what reason they are being assessed. This chapter offers methods to help students comprehend the connections between their learning and assessment and to learn over time how to self-assess their own progress.

## SECTION 1: ASSESSMENT PRACTICES

A teacher's instructional methods, the choice of tools and materials by which to deliver instruction, knowledge of the academic content, and the quality of the assessment plan function as vital ingredients to student achievement. The key to decisions regarding assessment is balance. No one, including accomplished veteran practitioners, views assessment as a simple task. There are many factors to consider when implementing assessment strategies. We begin with a brief review of assessment practices to better understand the evolution of assessment as the school system has changed.

### Review of Assessment Practices

As you will recall from Chapter 1, secondary education until the early 1900s existed primarily for a few students almost exclusively from the upper class. Before that time, society did not expect students to complete a high school education, nor considered it necessary to become gainfully employed and be a productive citizen. Events moved more quickly in the 1920s to 1940s, when more young people started attending high school. Following World War II, the GI Bill presented veterans of all social and economic classes with the previously unimaginable opportunity of going to college. In a short period of time, unprecedented numbers of students in high schools and universities challenged the U.S. education system.

Under pressure to teach the masses and to judge their achievement, the practice of "grading" came into play. Even though educators knew then and still know how subjective grading can be, it became a necessary part of monitoring and keeping track of students and their progress. In an effort to take a subjective system and standardize it, the 1950s and 1960s saw a rapid growth in the standardized testing market. Initially, such tests were not usually made public because educators considered the achievement level of a child a private matter between parents, teacher, and student. Teachers and schools generally used standardized test scores to corroborate their own judgments and data at the end of a year, or to make learning diagnoses and curriculum decisions at the beginning of the following year.

***Changes in Schools.*** Today the debate over the use of standardized test scores continues. One of the more complex aspects of this issue involves the country's increasingly diverse population of multiple cultures, languages, and socioeconomic status (SES). Students from higher SES backgrounds often have an advantage when it comes to the kinds of experiences and information incorporated in standardized achievement tests (Popham, 2001). As teachers you need to be aware of this.

The diversity of students also profoundly affects the overall assessment decisions that teachers, school districts, and states make. In addition to the number of ethnically and linguistically diverse students entering schools, assessment of learning faces challenges from an increasing number of students with learning problems, who come from single-parent homes and have parents with little formal educational backgrounds. Gonzalez, Brusca-Vega, and Yawkey (1997) remind us how important it is to make sound judgments based on valid assessment tools.

> While a number of culturally and linguistically diverse (CLD) students may have personal characteristics that contribute to a lack of academic progress (for example, a genuine disability or an unstable home life), they may also be at-risk because characteristics of the school setting are detrimental to the learning process. In fact, our own inability (or perhaps unwillingness) as educators to distinguish between internal and external factors in the learning problems of CLD students may be the major contributor to their school failure. (p. 6)

A range of thinking exists on this topic. However, if you can continue to focus on the primary purpose of assessment, thinking about how data help inform teachers in ways to improve student learning, you will be able to make the best use of most assessment systems to improve your practice. Because everyone has a personal history with evaluation and grading, teachers need to constantly be aware of their own biases and remain open to the range of assessment strategies available.

***Changes in Assessment.*** Efforts to restructure America's schools have redefined the mission of schooling and the job of teaching. Rather than merely "offering education," schools must "ensure" all students learn and perform (INTASC, 1992; California Task Force, 1992; National Association of Secondary School Principals, 1996; National Commission on Teaching and America's Future, 1996). Assessment monitors students' progress and understanding and helps teachers determine how to ensure content achievement. Teachers must primarily focus on and spend class time on assessing students' understanding, solving problems, and adjusting teaching accordingly, so that students learn and achieve. A teacher must be able to track what students are learning through various forms of monitoring as well to track what you, the teacher, are learning about your students.

Good teachers recognize that classes of students don't learn or not learn; rather, individual students do. You want to keep a pulse on how each class understands the concepts you are teaching, but you must not lose individual students in the "average." After all, very few students are average.

### *Putting It Into Practice:* Activity 3.1

Think about a positive experience you have had with grading, as a student yourself, as well as a time when you had a negative experience with grading. How did you feel? How did the grade affect the rest of your experience with the subject? How did your feelings about the teacher develop? In both cases, what were the consequences of the grade? Share these within a small group, then with the whole class. Make a list of what you believe to be the implications of your findings in terms of your future teaching practice.

## Standards for Assessment

Most professional organizations offer standards for assessment. In addition, several authors and web sites indicate basic principles for assessment. Although the following list is not inclusive, it seeks to serve as a foundation to begin making decisions regarding assessment.

1. **When making decisions about assessment, the interests of the students are paramount.** Students must reflect upon their learning and understanding in productive ways. Do they understand how information links to what happened before and what is to happen next in the curriculum? Are they synthesizing and analyzing information?
2. **The primary purpose of assessment is to improve teaching and learning.** The teacher must be able to analyze assessment results. On a test, for example, look to see whether several students missed the same question or group of questions. If so, go back and reteach the concept they didn't understand. For example, if you find that the students have a hard time answering essay questions, help them learn to organize their thoughts around the information you teach and model for them how to answer essay questions. However, prior to taking this step, make sure when several students do have trouble with the same test items, you also consider whether the problem could be with the test item rather than the teaching or learning processes.
3. **Assessment must reflect and allow for critical inquiry into curriculum and instruction.** Inquiry is seldom effectively assessed on multiple-choice, short answer, and true/false tests. Students should write, debate, discuss, and make oral presentations about their ideas and understandings. Multiple methods of assessment should make up the overall assessment plan.
4. **Assessment must be fair and equitable.** Children who differ culturally, linguistically, and in learning styles do not do as well with traditional (paper-and-pencil and standardized tests) means of assessment. A balance of traditional and authentic assessment methods helps assure fair and equitable opportunities for all students to be judged on their achievements.
5. **The consequences of the assessment procedure are the first and most important consideration in establishing the validity of the assessment.** What

assessment improves determines its value. Any assessment procedure that does not contribute positively to teaching and learning should not be utilized. If the teacher uses tests, grades, and standardized tests that include only a limited range of skills and basic knowledge, the narrow curriculum that is emphasized rarely promotes inquiry or critical thinking.

6. **The teacher acts as the most important agent of assessment.** The teacher must have a deep knowledge of the content and take responsibility for making and sharing judgments about students' achievement with the entire educational community, including students, parents, teachers, administrators, policy makers, and the public.

The National Council of Teachers of English (1996) and McMillan (2000) recommend these and other similar standards and principles for assessment.

## Formative and Summative Assessment

As we continue in this chapter, we will ask you to make decisions about what types of assessment tools to include in your plan so that you and your students will know how they understand the concepts and material you are teaching. In any plan, you will consider two basic uses of assessment: formative and summative. Formative assessment tells you in an ongoing, daily manner how your students are acquiring knowledge and building understanding. Summative assessment, which happens at the end of the unit of study, tells you and the students how well and to what extent they understand the concepts. The list in Table 3.1 is not exhaustive but gives you some concrete examples of formative and summative assessment tools. Remember the true difference between these types of evaluation tools can be how you use and interpret them.

***Criterion-Referenced and Norm-Referenced Tests.*** It is important to clarify and make distinctions between two types of widely used tests, criterion-referenced tests (CRTs) and norm-referenced tests (NRTs). CRTs measure how well a student has learned a specific body of knowledge and skills. These would typically be the types of tests you would design for your own classroom, or you might use the textbook-designed test

**TABLE 3.1** *Examples of Formative and Summative Assessment*

| Formative Assessment | Summative Assessment |
|---|---|
| (ongoing) usually assesses factual information, concepts, and discrete skills, which are necessary to build understanding | (summary) tends to involve more analysis, synthesis, or evaluation of information in order to make judgments, form opinions, explain concepts |
| • Mastery checklists of skills acquired<br>• Quick quizzes<br>• Journal entries<br>• Homework practice<br>• Oral questions<br>• Observation (individual and group)<br>• Daily or weekly rubric for social interaction | • Research paper<br>• Projects<br>• Debate<br>• Position paper<br>• Persuasive paper<br>• Collage<br>• Oral presentation/speech<br>• Chapter or unit test (especially essay tests)<br>Many of these are referred to as authentic assessments. |

if you had taught most of the material from the textbook. CRTs usually determine whether a student has learned the material taught in a specific grade or course. An algebra CRT would include questions and problems based on what was supposed to be taught in algebra classes. It would not include geometry questions or more advanced algebra than contained in the curriculum. Most all students who took algebra could pass this test if the teacher taught them well, they had studied enough, and the test were designed appropriately.

In contrast, norm-referenced tests (NRTs) compare students to one another. That means that about half of the students have to do poorly.

> NRT standardized achievement tests should not be used to evaluate the quality of students' schooling because there are mismatches between what is tested and what is supposed to be taught, and those mismatches are often unrecognized. (Popham, 2001, p. 46)

Much controversy exists regarding the use of NRTs. You need to be knowledgeable of specific and appropriate assessment and interpretation practices. Teachers must be able to explain those practices to parents, their principal, or even politicians, who might just want items to be taught that will help raise specific NRT test scores. That pressure is real, and the stress placed upon superintendents cannot be discounted, who, in turn, pass it along to principals, who pass it along to teachers, who sometimes, inadvertently, pass it along to students. As a knowledgeable teacher who has a solid, effective, meaningful assessment plan that helps students to learn and also informs your teaching, you should be able to explain how students understand and students need to be able to do the same thing, to a certain extent. You should also be able to explain the differences in the interpretation of data for CRTs and NRTs and distinguish their purposes.

## Validity and Reliability

No matter what assessment tool teachers select to administer, they must ensure that the assessment tool can provide accurate information. Two important concepts used when discussing the quality of assessments are *validity* and *reliability*. *Validity* refers to the extent to which the assessment tool measures the curriculum objectives and content standards it is intended to assess. To be valid, you must be able to identify in the assessment where and what in the curriculum and standards are being assessed. This is known as *content validity*. In addition to content validity, you need to determine whether the task and assessment are designed such that students do well on similar tasks. This is known as *concurrent validity*. In other words, a student who does well in a town meeting simulation should also do well in a debate or mock trial. A student who does well in preparing a poster should also do well when preparing a pamphlet or other visual artifact.

It is probably harder to achieve reliability, especially considering the isolated nature of teacher grading and assessment. *Reliability* refers to how repeatable the scores are. Would the conclusions drawn about student ability be the same regardless of when in the school day the assessment were given, which form of the assessment the student received, or which rater happened to score the work? Do equal scores indicate equivalent performance across students, days, and raters? How comfortable would you feel if the same student work received vastly different scores from two different raters or from the same rater on two different days? Obviously, if an assessment is not *reliable*, it cannot be *valid* (Linn, Baller, & Dunham, 1991).

A good example of ensuring reliability is the strategy used to score science projects at a science fair. Multiple raters assess each project to ensure reliability in scoring. To help maintain reliability in your own assessments, try exchanging papers with a colleague once or twice a semester to see how someone else rates your students. Ask a colleague to come in and have a look at the posters your students have done to see how close your assessment judgments are. This offers you the opportunity to "talk" about student work and your expectations. It also helps to give you some consistency in expectations across your department, which helps students to be more successful. Additionally, ask your students to self-assess to see whether you and the students are "on the same page."

## SECTION 2: ASSESSMENT OF STUDENT UNDERSTANDING

As you read this chapter and design your own plan and assessment tools, ask yourself the question, "How will my students and I know whether they *understand* the concepts I am teaching?" *Understanding* is the most important criterion in all assessment decisions. In the Circle of Courage model, Mastery and Independence cannot be achieved without understanding. Knowledge alone cannot offer students a sense of Belonging or Generosity in a community of learners and in a democratic society at large; they must also understand how they know what they know.

### Considerations in Designing Assessments

Another important consideration about learning that will enable the teacher to design new or modify existing curriculum is asking the initial question: "What is the students' attitude toward what they know about 'this topic' before they begin studying it?" Doing this *preassessment* before the course of study can be very important in guiding overall planning (including what types of formative and summative assessments might be used) for the course as well as for individuals in the class.

#### A Closer Look

Chapter 5, Unit and Lesson Plans, contains a section called Student Focus, which addresses the need to preassess your students' entry-level attitudes and skills as well as their backgrounds and relationships. That section also provides a sample survey as a preassessment tool for your students.

#### A Closer Look

For those of you interested in probing deeper into individualized prediagnostic testing for a specific student, **Instructional Resource B** provides a sample method for literacy preassessment. Once a preassessment process is complete, the teacher can adapt and modify the existing curriculum and determine the appropriate assessment tools to use.

FIGURE 3.1 Bloom's Taxonomy

| Level of Taxonomy | Cognitive Implication |
|---|---|
| Evaluation | The student judges the value of ideas, materials, and methods by developing and applying standards and criteria. |
| Synthesis | The student puts together similar elements to form new ideas or concepts, requiring original and creative thinking. |
| Analysis | The student breaks down significant components of complex issues into constituent elements. |
| Application | The student transfers theories, methods, concepts, and principles to new situations. |
| Comprehension | The student understands the meaning of information provided. |
| Knowledge | The student recalls or recognizes the specific facts, concepts, and principles given. |

Note: From Benjamin S. Bloom et al., *Taxonomy of Educational Objectives.* Copyright © 1984, published by Allyn and Bacon, Boston, MA. Copyright © 1956 by Pearson Education. Adapted by permission of the publisher.

In their book, *Understanding by Design*, Grant Wiggins and Jay McTighe (1998) urge teachers to design curriculum and assessment to maximize student understanding. Students can learn the basic facts and information involved in the life cycle of an earthworm and answer 90% of the multiple-choice and short answer test items correctly. Yet, they may never really understand where and how the life cycle of plants and animals fits into the ecosystem, much less what their roles and responsibilities are in the preservation of the environment in which they live.

Think about Benjamin Bloom's taxonomy as it is illustrated in Figure 3.1. For the most part, multiple-choice and short answer test items generally deal with lower end knowledge and recall (though a skilled test writer can sometimes measure beyond knowledge and recall). Debate or position papers more likely ask students to move up on Bloom's taxonomy, by synthesizing, analyzing, and applying that knowledge. Importantly, the teacher needs to know what basic knowledge students have learned before asking them to think about it and apply it in other ways. A variety of assessment strategies at all levels of Bloom's taxonomy should be a part of the plan.

You have most likely studied Bloom's taxonomy in a previous course, yet you may want to refresh your memory on this concept as it will be utilized often when planning assessment, planning instruction, and selecting teaching strategies. See Box 3.1.

In addition to considering the various levels of understanding as outlined by Bloom's taxonomy, it is also important to address the assessment of all forms of learning objectives. Most often teachers focus on the assessment of understanding (cognitive objectives) but often neglect the consideration of the other types of critical

*Box 3.1*

**Bloom's Taxonomy**

In 1956 Benjamin Bloom led a team of education psychologists to develop a classification of levels of intellectual behavior important in learning. They identified six levels within the cognitive domain (Figure 3.1) from simple recall through the more complex and abstract levels of thinking. Interestingly, during the study, Bloom's team discovered that over 95% of test questions given to students required them to think at only the lowest cognitive level, recall. Bloom's taxonomy is easily understood and educators continue to widely use it today.

objectives, such as affective, psychomotor, and word, in their respective assessments. Affective objectives consider a full range of social skills such as valuing, empathy, responding, and applying one's attitudes toward a particular area of study (Krathwohl, Bloom, & Masia, 1964). This form of objective can also be situational in that it might include student attitudes toward the logistics of how the student studies (such as the use of cooperative learning or the use of a mentor or the integration of technology to the learning process). Because educators consider attitude toward learning to be one of the critical determinants of effective learning, measuring outcomes in this area is extremely important, although often neglected (Morgan, 2004). Psychomotor objectives refer to how effectively a student can master the use or manipulation of a particular tool (such as a microscope or a paintbrush) or the performance or demonstration of some physical task.

Consider the following objective: Students will work effectively in a cooperative group to complete a project. One example of how to assess this affective objective would be to have students do a quick write at the completion of a cooperative project. The teacher would pose the following questions and facilitate discussion:

1. In what ways was your group successful in working cooperatively to complete the project?
2. What did you learn that you probably would not have had you done it alone?
3. What issues or challenges occurred to you and your group as you worked together?
4. Do you see an advantage of working as a team as opposed to working individually?

Word objectives identify target language that is to be learned by the student. Understanding the word's meaning is important to grasping the overall concept being taught. An example of an assessment that combines the understanding of a word objective with a psychomotor objective would be the following:

Students will be able to use the names of 10 common household kitchen items in a conversation in Spanish I class. Students would be paired and asked to design and perform (psychomotor) a 5-minute skit incorporating the appropriate application of 10 household words (items) in Spanish (word objective).

***Curriculum Layers.*** In addition to levels of understanding and types of objectives, another consideration in determining the most appropriate assessment tools concerns the different layers of the curriculum you will be teaching and how to assess

### A Closer Look

Chapters 5 and 7 on lesson planning and designing interdisciplinary thematic units elaborate upon all of these types of learning objectives. It is important to note that use of affective objectives can also be important as criteria to consider when designing assessments.

each layer so that you build knowledge and understanding throughout the unit, semester, and year. Teachers must address three basic layers of the curriculum in their work with students (Wiggins & McTighe, 1998). The first layer contains the knowledge and skills students must know and be familiar with in order to begin to understand more complex issues; for example, content knowledge that students should be able to recall on quick quizzes or use to answer oral questions for review. Formative assessment strategies can provide a teacher with useful information about student understanding of this material.

Teachers must make the determination of what material to present at this layer; students cannot be expected to know or memorize everything in the textbook. Choices on what material to include should be guided by an understanding of what material will allow students the best opportunity to build on in order to access more complex concepts in the next curriculum layer. Students will probably retain the material presented in the first layer throughout the unit or semester but not much beyond.

The second layer of material contains the important key concepts of the discipline you are teaching. These concepts create a foundation for a deeper understanding of science, history, or mathematics, for example. Students use the material at this level to understand both material presented throughout the current course, as it builds to other complex ideas, and beyond to content in other courses. For example, material learned initially from this layer of the curriculum in a physical science class not only continues to be important throughout many successive units of this course but also contributes to the students' understanding of key concepts in a chemistry class that follows the next year. Teachers will create plans that devote more time for these deeper, more important concepts at this level and will assess understanding with both formative and summative assessment strategies.

Finally, the deepest layer of each unit or course of study contains what Wiggins and McTighe (1998) refer to as *enduring understandings*, the ideas that teachers want students to remember long after they have left their classrooms and schools. These enduring understandings enable students to transfer skills to their lives beyond formal schooling. Such understandings allow them to develop problem-solving strategies when confronted by new challenges, to be critical consumers of the torrent of information unleashed by today's technologies, and to make appropriate choices for their own careers and lives. These ideas make a difference in the types of citizens our students become, the ways they understand themselves and their part in their communities and in the world, as well as the ideas that lead to leadership, invention, and global perspective. These ideas also help each student to acquire Belonging, Mastery, Independence, and Generosity as illustrated by the Circle of Courage.

## A Closer Look

Chapter 5, Unit and Lesson Plans, in the section Determination of Course Goals, contains further description of enduring understandings as well as pertinent examples.

In your next activity we would like you just to begin exploring the concept of enduring understandings.

### *Putting It Into Practice:* Activity 3.2

In a small group, organized around your subject area, brainstorm a list of what are thought to be enduring understandings in your discipline. Additionally, provide examples of first-layer material (necessary to build to the next two layers) and middle-layer materials. Also include in the list an explanation of why you selected the items and how these enduring understandings will help students meet all sections of the Circle of Courage.

## Authentic Assessment

In devising your assessment plan for each unit, for the entire semester, and eventually for the entire year, you will need summative, formative, traditional, and authentic tools. You must appropriately apply each type and know when to use which assessment tool. For example, traditional assessments, such as multiple-choice tests, are inadequate as the sole assessment strategy in a classroom. However, when the teacher uses them to follow students' acquisition of the knowledge that provides an important part of the foundation for understanding, this type of assessment does have an important place.

Authentic assessment strategies provide a better technique of checking for deeper understanding. These strategies place a greater emphasis on individual learning styles and allow more students a wider range of opportunity to demonstrate what they know and are able to do.

In addition, student participation in assessment should be an integral part of all decisions teachers make. For example, self-assessment using a rubric can be beneficial to involve and empower students. A rubric is a printed set of guidelines that distinguishes performances or products of different quality. A rubric contains descriptors that define what to look for at each level of performance. When using a rubric to assess a written paper, a project, or social participation in cooperative learning groups, teachers should ask the students to self-assess with the rubric before handing in the project and rubric. After students have self-assessed, teachers can then use a different-colored pencil or marker on the same rubric to add their own comments and explain any place that they don't agree with the student's assessment.

### *A Closer Look*

We will discuss construction of rubrics further with examples provided in the section Construction of Rubrics.

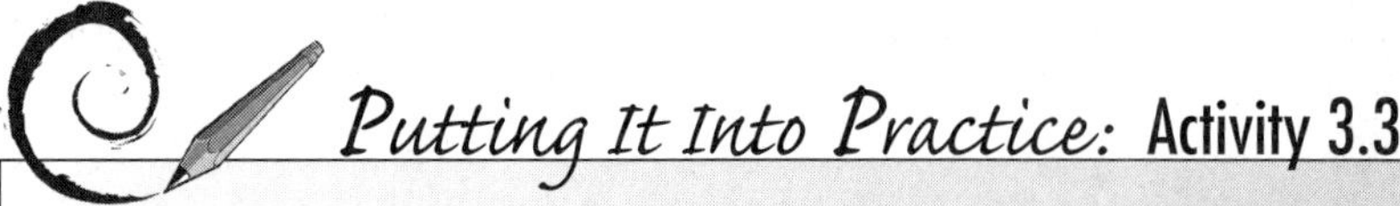


To understand authentic assessment, make a list. If you weren't going to teach tomorrow or next year, how would you use the skills and knowledge you have by virtue of your content area? Take 5 minutes to make your list.

This is one English teacher's list:

If I weren't teaching English or language arts tomorrow, how would I use the skills that I teach?

- Technical writing: instruction books, manuals, policies, and procedures
- Editing for other writers
- Writing persuasive letters as a lobbyist
- Writing articles in magazines
- Novelist
- Reading for information: newspapers, instructions, policy manuals

The assessment of daily assignments, homework, tests, quizzes, and projects must be clear to the student. Hand out rubrics at the beginning of the assignment. Post grades either on a computer grading system, to which students have access, or randomly by anonymous student number on a regular basis. Although time is precious in teaching, make sure formative individual assessment conferences take place in an ongoing manner, and summative assessment conferences are held at least two times during each grading period.

Now think about your list. Look at the "real" and "authentic" things that writers, scientists, mathematicians, historians, and others do. Perhaps this is how one should teach. How do people really use their knowledge of a particular content? As much as possible, those are the types of projects you should be designing for your students. Using your list, in groups with other preservice teachers, discuss applications for teaching.

***Authentic Assessment Decisions.*** The basis of traditional education, following a perennialist or essentialist model, as described in Chapter 1, is the transmission of knowledge model. It views teachers as possessing all of the knowledge, then imparting it to students, and finally testing to see how much of it they can recall. More recently, teachers have used the constructivist model to encourage students to learn about the world around them by thinking critically and using knowledge to construct understanding. The roots of constructivism can be identified in the progressive model described in Chapter 1. If you want students to construct personal meaning from new information and prior knowledge, then you have to employ strategies and assessments that foster analysis, synthesis, and creativity.

Elliot Eisner (1994) eloquently urged teachers always to consider "the real world" in making curriculum and assessment decisions. What does the real world allow people to do? Most importantly, it gives people choices about how to relay personal understandings of their lives and their experiences:

> After a trip to Paris, some people may write poetry, others may paint pictures, some show the photographs that they have taken and talk about their experience. It is precisely in the diversity of response to "common experience" that our cultural lives are enriched. (p. 210)

Eisner outlines eight features of authentic assessment:

1. The tasks used to assess what students know and can do need to reflect the tasks they will encounter in the world outside of schools, not merely those limited to the schools themselves.
2. The tasks used to assess students should reveal how students go about solving a problem, not only the solutions they have formulated.
3. Assessment tasks should reflect the values of the intellectual community from which the tasks are derived.
4. Assessment tasks need not be limited to solo performance. Many of the most important tasks we undertake require group efforts.
5. New assessment tasks should make possible more than one acceptable solution to a problem and more than one acceptable answer to a question.
6. Assessment tasks should have curricular relevance, but not be limited to the curriculum as taught.
7. Assessment tasks should require students to display sensitivity to configurations or wholes, not simply to discrete elements.
8. Assessment tasks should permit students to select a form of representation to use to display what they have learned.

## Authentic Assessment Tools

Generally speaking, the assessment strategies in Figure 3.2 include most of the features for authentic assessment Eisner identified. Now look at the authentic assessment suggestions in Figure 3.2 and mentally put yourself through one of them. You will have to *think critically* in order to accomplish the task. Notice that you must also employ multiple learning styles and multiple intelligences (described in Chapter 2) to complete the tasks. For example, a poster project decrying the misuse and destruction of rain forests done in pairs requires interpersonal, intrapersonal, visual–spatial, oral, and linguistic intelligences to successfully create and present the poster. Think about how appropriate these multidimensional assessment tools are for linguistically and culturally diverse students. All of these projects help to forward the students' use and development of their oral and written language skills.

Time for planning and assessing is precious. Textbook companies have provided a wealth of resources for teaching, and you can use some of the multiple-choice and short answer worksheets provided with your teacher's manual to help assess your students' knowledge. It isn't necessary to reinvent the wheel. Instead, use your time to create authentic assessment tools to assess understanding.

In order for the teacher and the students to know how they *understand* their roles and responsibilities in environmental preservation, you could give students a menu of summative, authentic assessment projects from which to choose. That menu might look something like Figure 3.3.

Mock trials, debates, and town meetings are excellent oral assessments that require deep understanding of the content principles in order to participate intelligently. In preparing these types of simulations, you must take great care

FIGURE 3.2 Types of Authentic Assessment

| Authentic Assessment | Description |
|---|---|
| Portfolios | Collection of student work to show progress over time. All work should not be included. The student and teacher should choose artifacts jointly and reflective pieces should accompany each entry. |
| Projects | Posters, science projects, models, brochures, pamphlets, PowerPoint presentations, designed to indicate the learner's understanding of particular content concepts. Can be done individually or in pairs. |
| Experiments and demos | Students complete an experiment or demonstrate how to do something. The method of demonstration can be oral, written, or both. |
| Writing samples | Students write a narrative, expository, persuasive, or research paper. Learning logs and journals are helpful for formative assessment. |
| Reading comprehension | Students give main ideas and pertinent details or answer questions from a book, orally, or in writing to demonstrate comprehension. |
| Teacher observation | Teacher observes student attention spans, interactions with other students, nonverbal behaviors. |
| Role-play and simulation | Teacher observes student performances and participation to determine understanding and identify misconceptions. |
| Constructed-response items | Students respond in writing or orally in interviews to open-ended questions. |

with the details. Identify the individual characters and their roles. Conduct whole-class brainstorming regarding the pro and con arguments the characters might use. Then have students prepare and write down their individual character's arguments in small groups, getting and giving ideas to one another. In this way, you are ensuring that the simulation more nearly mirrors the actual event of a town meeting, and you are designing opportunities for the students to *think* about the knowledge they have and *understand* its implications in a setting outside the classroom.

FIGURE 3.3 Projects for an Environmental Unit

- Create a poster, depicting the life cycle of a plant, animal, or fish. Indicate where and how the life cycle is disrupted when an industrial plant dumps waste into the river upstream.
- As a service–learning project, organize a trash cleanup day with a local elementary school. Create a pamphlet informing the children about the environmental problems in a specific area and why they need to join you in cleaning up and preserving this particular environment.
- Design a PowerPoint presentation to present to fellow students or a local civic organization describing the pros and cons of building a power plant on the edge of town.
- Choose a specific environmental issue in your community. Write a persuasive essay or letter to the editor convincing people to take action; for example, cleaning up an illegal trash dump, stopping the clear-cutting of forests, seeking alternative clean energy sources such as wind and solar-powered generators.
- Have all students participate in a simulation, whereby they become members of a community who must decide the fate of an outdated coal plant in a town meeting. The issues are clearly jobs versus environmental safety.

***Designing Authentic Assessment.*** When designing authentic assessments, you must first identify the task, which is the project, activity, or assignment. You then assess student responses to the task. Tasks can be formative—for example, short answer, discussion, or group participation—or summative—such as writing an essay, giving a speech, conducting a long-term experiment, participating in a simulation or role-play, such as a mock trial or town meeting. You need to describe the task in order to assess it. Only after you have identified and described the task can you decide upon a specified method of evaluating student performance on the task. Methods could include the assignment of points for the "correctness" of responses, checklists of response features, and rubrics requiring professional judgment (Winkling & Bond, 1995).

## Construction of Rubrics

If you determine the task would best be assessed using a rubric, you may use the following to construct a rubric:

1. Identify the judging criteria or essential elements that ensure the outcomes will be high in quality. These will become the rows in your rubric. Be sure to include the content, skills, and aspects of the task. Include criteria associated with the process of completing the task, if important.
2. Decide on the levels of achievement that you will include as column headings in the rubric.
3. In the cells of the rubric, develop clear descriptions of performance at each achievement level for each essential element of quality. Avoid undefined terms such as *significant* and *trivial* and value-laden terms such as *excellent* and *poor*.
4. Enumerate the consequences of performing at each level of quality and include descriptions of them in the commentary.
5. Decide on a rating scheme that fits in with your grading system and build it into the rubric.

As an example, refer back to the town meeting project in Figure 3.3. Determine how you would describe excellence for each criterion. Figures 3.4 and 3.5 are examples of two types of rubrics, holistic and analytical, that you could use for authentic assessment of a town meeting simulation. Consider these sample rubrics as you begin the process of developing your own.

You need to provide students with the task description and scoring rubric at the beginning of the unit. They need to know what is coming. If they know, they begin to file away information in their brains and in their notes that will help them to complete the culminating project. When you have identified the task up front, it also helps you as the teacher to focus your teaching and remind students when you are covering information that will be useful for the final project.

Just because an assessment is "authentic" and "fun" does not mean it is high quality (Winkling & Bond, 1995). It does no good to design or use fun and interesting assessment activities that do not address student learning targets or your curriculum standards and benchmarks.

> I can only hope that with responsible and articulate interpretation, authentic assessment will be understood and valued by the public-at-large. If it is, assessment will not only contribute to better schooling for children, it will also contribute to a broader, more generous conception of education itself. (Eisner, 1994, p. 210)

**FIGURE 3.4** Sample Holistic Rubric for Town Meeting Simulation

Rate yourself according to each of the criteria, and write a reflection indicating why you gave yourself the score in each area.

| Criteria | Proficient 4 | Acceptable 3 | Needs Improvement 2 | Below Expectation 1 |
|---|---|---|---|---|
| Accurate knowledge of environmental issues evidenced in oral presentation. Speaks confidently using facts from notes and readings. | | | | |
| Believable portrayal of community character. Speaking voice is clear and audible with some theatrical nuances appropriate to the character. | | | | |
| Productive and beneficial participation in group preparation. Helped other group members with information and practice, as well as completing own written argument. | | | | |
| Individual notes and written argument exhibit understanding of the issues. Written argument is legible, using conventional sentence structure and syntax. Facts are correct and arguments are logical. | | | | |

**FIGURE 3.5** Sample Analytic Rubric for Town Meeting Simulation

Rate yourself according to each of the criteria, and write a reflection indicating why you gave yourself the score in each area.

| Criteria | Proficient 4 | Acceptable 3 | Needs Improvement 2 | Below Expectation 1 |
|---|---|---|---|---|
| Content knowledge | An abundance of material clearly related to and representative of accurate knowledge of environmental issues. Points clearly made and supported by evidence. | Sufficient material related to and representative of accurate knowledge of environmental issues. Good points made but not always supported by evidence. | Material not always related directly to environmental issues. Insufficient information to suggest good understanding of the issues. | Material not clear, most not related to environmental issues. No understanding of the issues reflected in the performance. |
| Presentation | Poised, clear voice, good eye contact, and enthusiasm. Believable portrayal of assigned community character. | Clear articulation, lacked enthusiasm. Portrayal of community character was realistic most of the time. | Some mumbling, little eye contact, no expression in delivery. Portrayal of community character lacked believability. Did not always stay in character. | Inaudible or too loud, no eye contact, spoke to quickly or too slowly. Seemed uninterested in portraying the community character. |
| Creativity | Very clever and had originality in the presentation. Unique approach added to the performance. | Clever at times, thoughtful and unique in the presentation, which added somewhat to the performance. | Added few original touches to the presentation. Performance was not unique. | Little creativity used during the presentation. |
| Group participation | Enthusiastic participation with team members, shared responsibility for completing project. Performed assigned role effectively. | Participated continuously with team members, met most responsibilities for completing project. Performed assigned role well. | Uneven participation with team members, missed some deadlines and other responsibilities for completing the project. Was uneven in performance of assigned role. | Failed to participate with team members. Missed deadlines. Did not add to completing the project. |

## *Applying Technology:* Activity 3.1

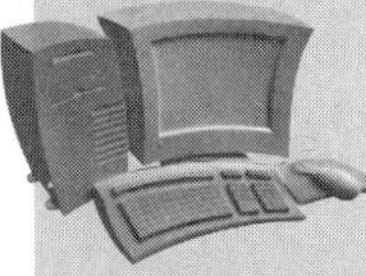

The following authentic assessment Internet sites may be helpful in completing this activity:

www.teachnology.com
www.landmark-project.com
www.lessonplansearch.com
www.schooldiscovery.com
www.teachervision.com
www.uni.edu

Determine an aspect of a unit plan that you or your cooperating teacher have been involved in teaching, and design an authentic assessment project to help you understand whether students have learned and can apply the main objectives or standards. Your project assignment should provide a clear description of the task including:

1. the outcomes that will be assessed;
2. the expectations of students, how they will produce the project;
3. time lines and due dates;
4. choices students may have in showing evidence of completing the project (e.g., presentation, written report);
5. the scoring criteria that will be assessed; and,
6. a rubric that will assess the students' final product.

List which Internet sites were the most helpful and explain what they had to offer.

# SECTION 3: PROFESSIONAL CONSIDERATIONS FOR ASSESSMENT

> To put it badly, in some school systems a student's career is somewhat determined as of the day he enters school simply on the basis of his clothing, appearance, and other factors related to the socioeconomic status of his family but not necessarily to his ability or potential. (Good & Brophy, 1994, p. 9)

## Teacher Expectations for Students

What we expect of our students is generally what we get. The messages a student receives concerning expectations, whether verbal or nonverbal, contribute in some degree to the relative success of that student's performance. In schools, the most powerful expectation signals arguably come from teachers, and the success of individual teachers' students can depend significantly upon the communication of those expectations.

In an historical overview of teacher expectations, Cooper and Good (1983) found that in 112 studies, 40% revealed significant support for the existence of teacher expectation effects. Good and Brophy (1994) suggest that teachers should send clear messages with positive expectations. In assessment, that means describing the assessment plan to students, defining excellence, and making clear that you expect them to achieve excellence.

Brophy and Good (1980) defined expectations as inferences that teachers make about the present and future academic achievement of students. Equally as important is the teacher's belief in the extent to which a student's achievement and attitude can be altered (Cooper & Good, 1983). A verbalized expectation becomes a belief (Brophy & Evertson, 1981). For example, when an algebra teacher expects all the students to master competencies before they move on, and the assessment plan includes frequent mastery checks with chances to improve scores and retake quizzes, then students are likely to pass algebra, even when other algebra classes have high failure rates. Because of the teacher's own expectations, the teacher may call on the students more often, give praise, and spend additional time helping those who are struggling.

As you develop your overall assessment plan and make assessment judgments, be aware that expectations play a significant role in your students' achievement. In his list of the six essential elements of effective schools, Edmonds (1979) rates teacher expectations as one of the determinates of the effectiveness or ineffectiveness of a school. In his observations and research he has found that teachers in ineffective schools prefer to call on the students whom they expect to answer correctly and generally do not ask those who they believe do not know the answer. Students who are not asked to participate eventually decide that the teacher does not expect them to know anything. As a result, these students are least likely to achieve Mastery. By contrast, teachers in effective schools are more likely to encourage all students to respond. Teacher expectations critically determine student success.

## Importance of Reporting Student Learning

Reporting student learning is an important aspect of the work of a teacher. Teachers are accountable for what they teach and how their students are learning. Because education is very public, teachers inevitably have a responsibility to let the public know how their students are doing. Reporting learning should not be perceived as an onerous task by which you are endangering your job. Rather, you and your students should view a report on their learning as beneficial for all those involved in public education. These stakeholders include parents, students, policy makers, and taxpayers. When you have developed a sound assessment plan, you will be able to confidently answer questions that parents, principals, or even school boards ask about what you are teaching and how your students are learning. See Figure 3.6 for an overview of what to report, for whom, and how you can report student learning.

All school districts have assessment plans for content areas that teachers can use to help guide their own assessment practices. Just as your teaching strategies and methods should be varied, so should your assessment plans. You should include assessment plans as part of course syllabi and distribute them to students and parents alike. Additionally, a letter to parents explaining the course expectations, a general overview of the topics covered, a list of typical assignments, and the assessment plan can build connections with this important group. One letter each semester will go a long way in getting cooperation and support from parents.

## Evaluation of Instruction and Curriculum

Just as it is important to find ways to assess the progress of our students, of equal importance is finding ways to evaluate the overall effectiveness of curriculum choices as well as our teaching practice as they apply to student learning. The authors believe action research is one strategy that can assist you in addressing these needs. Action research makes use of classroom assessment data as well as classroom

**FIGURE 3.6** Options for Reporting Student Learning

| What to Report | Stakeholders | How to Report |
|---|---|---|
| • Content knowledge<br>• Life/workplace skills<br>• Overall achievement<br>• Progress and mastery<br>• Effort, attitude, social skills<br>• Norm-referenced test scores<br>• Standards/criterion-referenced test scores<br>• Performance/project level of success<br>• Literacy level | • Students<br>• Parents<br>• Teachers<br>• Policy makers (legislators)<br>• Boards of education<br>• Postsecondary institutions<br>• Employers<br>• Taxpayers and general public | • Letter grades<br>• Numerical scores/percentages<br>• Skills checklists (mastery)<br>• Rating scales<br>• Teacher-written narrative reports<br>• Student-written narrative reflections<br>• Portfolios with student reflection<br>• Conferences<br>• Public performances, project displays |

## *Putting It Into Practice:* Activity 3.4

With other preservice teachers in your content area, look at the state or district content standards for the subject you teach. Prepare an assessment plan for a semester or a 9-week grading period. Refer back to Figures 3.1 and 3.2 to make sure you include a variety of assessment methods in your plan. Use the graphic organizer provided here to help you organize your ideas. (Graphic organizers will be discussed further in the next chapter.) Under content standards, your team will need the set of content standards you would expect to cover in the specified time period. Once you have determined these standards, identify a range of assessment strategies you will utilize both as formative and summative tools.

Your assessment plan should include brief explanations of decisions reached around selected standards. It should also provide a rationale for each assessment tool that includes what information your team believes this type of assessment will provide in order to help you make teaching and learning decisions.

**Assessment Plan Graphic Organizer**

**Course:** ____________ **Level/Grade:** ____________ **Grading Period:** ____________

| Content Standards | Formative Assessment Requirements | Summative Assessment Requirements |
|---|---|---|
| | | |

observations, reflection, interviews, and even small focus groups. Because so much of the data gathered comes from good teaching practice, relatively little additional work is required to provide the teacher with information valuable for improving teaching.

This section introduces the concept of action research and explains how you might apply it. Shannon (1990) has defined action research as inquiry that "applies scientific thinking to real life problems, as opposed to teachers' subjective judgments based on folklore with the purpose of increasing instructional productivity and disseminating this information to others' practice" (pp. 143–144).

Although at this stage in your professional training your use of action research may be limited, as you move into becoming a professional in education this practice will become an essential tool. Teachers use it to assess their own practice to find out in what ways and to what degree their curriculum, instructional strategies, and assessment practices benefit student learning. In this era of reform and accountability, teachers can no longer blindly adopt new curriculum or practices without assessing the innovations' effectiveness. Teachers and schools are held accountable for results and action research can help in clearly identifying them.

The use of action research has been gaining support as efforts to reform schools have increased (Hubbard & Power, 1993). Among the reasons for its increasing use include:

1. connecting educational theory to applied practice;
2. producing information that can help individual teachers make better curriculum and instructional strategy decisions;
3. obtaining valuable information from students to modify practice; and
4. using problem-solving skills in a teaching situation that can assist in overcoming a challenging teaching/learning situation.

Preservice teachers benefit from some direction in this process through course work, field experiences, or practicum. Teacher preparation programs provide an ideal situation in which to develop this training. Some innovative colleges of education have already integrated action research into their curricula in both courses and field experiences.

An action research project can be as simple as a study to assess your own teaching style with your students or may be more in depth such as assessing whether a new instructional strategy or addition to the curriculum has increased student learning. Figure 3.7 offers an example of a simple assessment questionnaire to use as a student evaluation of your teaching. The data produced by student answers can guide teachers in improving their work. The teacher analyzes the data and determines whether any patterns in the responses exist across classes. You will find ways to assess what is and is not working in order for all of your students to achieve Mastery.

Knowledge gained from a simple questionnaire such as Figure 3.7 may help you decide to develop alternative assessment for student learning and set challenging, yet realistic goals for your classroom. As noted earlier in the chapter, asking students themselves to help in assessment is an effective strategy. This technique helps build a sense of Belonging to your classroom community; students feel their opinions and observations are valued.

***Research Design Proposal.*** Sound action research will show evidence of a strong research design and proposal, use multiple data collection methods that allow for triangulation, and have a clear dissemination plan for the results. To begin an action research project, the teacher should formally outline the various elements essential to the study. Following this process helps professionalize the study and increase the

**FIGURE 3.7** Student Evaluation of Teaching

Student Evaluation of Teaching: Course __________ Period__________

The following are questions to help evaluate my teaching. You need not sign your name to this form, so please be serious, honest, and fair. Place a check mark by the response you feel is most appropriate.

1. Do I speak clearly?

__________ clearly
__________ not clearly enough
__________ too slowly
__________ too fast
__________ just right

2. Do I move around the room enough?

__________ enough
__________ too much
__________ not enough

3. Do you think I have been fair?

__________ fair
__________ too easy
__________ too harsh

4. Do I make this an interesting class?

__________ part of the time
__________ most of the time
__________ none of the time

5. Do you feel free to ask me questions?

__________ part of the time
__________ most of the time
__________ none of the time

6. Do I favor some students?

__________ part of the time
__________ most of the time
__________ none of the time

7. Do I answer questions satisfactorily?

__________ part of the time
__________ most of the time
__________ none of the time

8. Do you feel I know enough about the material we have studied to do a good job of teaching?

__________ yes
__________ no

9. Do you feel that the lessons were well planned and organized?

__________ part of the time
__________ most of the time
__________ none of the time

10. Do you understand what was expected of you on:

*Assignments?*

__________ part of the time
__________ most of the time
__________ none of the time

*Tests?*

__________ part of the time
__________ most of the time
__________ none of the time

*Behavior?*

__________ part of the time
__________ most of the time
__________ none of the time

11. Do we do a variety of activities?

__________ part of the time
__________ most of the time
__________ none of the time

12. Are you aware of your progress and grade in the class?

__________ part of the time
__________ most of the time
__________ none of the time

13. What type(s) of assessment is most effective for you? You may check more than one.

__________ true/false and multiple-choice tests
__________ fill-in-the blank and short answer tests
__________ visual presentation of projects, such as posters, PowerPoint presentations, dioramas, etc.
__________ oral participation in discussions, mock debates, etc.
__________ written papers, such as research reports, persuasive essays, opinion papers, compare and contrast essays
__________ Other __________

14. What method(s) of learning do you prefer? You may check more than one.

__________ lecture
__________ small group discussion
__________ large group discussion
__________ demonstration
__________ cooperative learning
__________ read the chapter and answer the questions
__________ individual projects
__________ group projects
__________ Other __________

likelihood of dissemination to other teachers. Teachers can also use the proposal format as an abstract when the study is completed if they wish to document the study for a presentation or journal article.

***Triangulation.*** Using multiple methods of data collecting procedures focusing on the same target is called triangulation. By using this technique, findings do not rest on only one set of findings, thus increasing the power of the study (Issac & Michael, 1987). Examples of various means to triangulate collection of data include the use of pre- and postquestionnaires, reflective journals, observations, student assessments (and other work), student records, and interviews (Hubbard & Power, 1993). In the process of selecting and developing ways to collect data, teachers should collaborate with others in order to receive feedback in both the appropriateness of the method as well as the instrument itself.

***Dissemination of Results of the Study.*** Just as the design process can be a collaborative process, so can the process of disseminating or sharing the study findings. A teacher has various options for disseminating the findings from a study including department and school-wide meetings, conferences, and teacher publications. We do want to remind you that the primary purpose of action research is for teachers to learn something about their curriculum or teaching and learning strategies to improve teaching practice and student learning. Whether or not the result includes dissemination through a presentation or journal article is secondary.

In applying action research to a particular setting, the design, implementation, and data collection can utilize individual techniques and unique qualities even when the overall goals are similar. Teachers should view the framework presented for conducting action research, including the design for research proposals, as templates.

***Action Research Projects.*** To assist you in better understanding action research, Instructional Resource C provides two project reports.

Once you have taken the time to review these action research projects, you will quickly determine the process is one that you could undertake and the learning potential about your teaching is tremendous. You may want to take the opportunity during your teacher preparation program to seek out and observe teachers who have developed and are implementing action research projects. When the time is appropriate in your classes, the templates provided here as well as your experience observing the process can help you design and implement your own study.

## A Closer Look

A veteran English teacher who took a course on action research strategies designed and implemented the first project in **Instructional Resource C**, Language Arts Tutoring. This teacher's primary interest was in understanding whether he could improve the reading comprehension of second-language learners by having them tutor younger students. Because the tutoring project was a new teaching strategy that took class time from the curriculum, it was important to determine whether the learning benefits outweighed the costs. The findings of the study showed promising results.

## A Closer Look

A life science teacher in her first year of teaching developed the second action research project provided in **Instructional Resource C**, Visiting Scientist. This teacher's teacher preparation program introduced her to action research. The primary hypothesis of the study focused on the increased academic achievement of students. The project required each student to teach lessons in an elementary school taking on the role of a visiting scientist. This example provides well-grounded and descriptive findings and includes implications and reflections based on the teacher's experience.

## SECTION 4: CHAPTER SUMMARY AND REFLECTION

The topic of assessment in education is extensive and complex. This chapter serves as an introduction to the many facets of assessment, providing a foundation to help you begin developing your understanding. As you enter into the profession, you will need to continue researching assessment practices based on your own experiences to achieve a greater depth of knowledge and skills.

The preceding sections gave you the opportunity to clarify your understanding of a range of formative and summative assessments. Section 1 addressed knowing the types of assessment tools and their differences, to help you make appropriate use of the data they provide. The differences between criterion-referenced tests and norm-referenced tests are a good example; each provides assessment data but serves a completely different purpose. Understanding these differences, as well as biases that can impact accurate assessment strategies and issues of validity and reliability, will enable you to make better use of the information you obtain.

The ultimate goal of assessment is to help you, as a teacher, determine whether students have learned and can apply the concepts and skills in your course. To that end, Section 2 highlighted considerations in designing assessment. Numerous types of assessment strategies beyond traditional paper-and-pencil tests, such as authentic assessment projects, were outlined in great detail. Authentic assessment tools were explored, including the construction of rubrics.

Section 3 examined professional considerations for assessment. These included teacher expectations for students; the importance of reporting student learning to students, parents, schools, and community; and how to go about responsible reporting. Evaluation of your own instruction and curriculum was also highlighted as an important consideration.

Additionally, keep in mind the Circle of Courage model and its four sections: Belonging, Mastery, Generosity, and Independence. The assessment process must determine levels of achievement and Mastery. Although achievement is a primary purpose of schooling, the Circle of Courage clearly makes evident that achievement alone does not make a well-rounded, caring citizen who can participate rationally in a democratic society. Generosity must also be a consideration in assessment. In this context Generosity means that a community of learners in the classroom work together as a team and are knowledgeable assessors of their own work and that of their peers. They can view their classmates' work critically, give positive feedback and meaningful suggestions for improvement, as well as celebrate the successful completion of projects. This chapter emphasizes that if you reflect back to the Circle of Courage model prior to designing and implementing assessment strategies, the focus of activity will appropriately remain on students.

## References


Anderson, L. W., & Bourke, S. J. (2000). *Assessing affective characteristics in the schools* (2nd ed.). Mahwah, NJ: Erlbaum.

Applebee, A. (1987). Musings: Teachers and the process of research. *Research in the Teaching of English, 2*, 5–7.

Bloom, B. S., et al. (1984). *Taxonomy of educational objectives.* Boston: Allyn and Bacon.

Brendtro, L. K., Brokenleg, M., & Bockern, S. V. (2002). *Reclaiming youth at risk: Our hope for the future.* Bloomington, IN: National Education Service.

Brophy, J. (1994). Trends in research on teaching. *Mid-Western Educational Researcher, 7*, 29–39.

Brophy, J. E., & Evertson, C. (1981). *Student characteristics and teaching.* New York: Longman.

Brophy, J. E., & Good, T. L. (1980). *Educational psychology: A realistic approach* (2nd ed.). New York: Holt.

Brualdi, A. (2000). Implementing performance assessment in the classroom. In *Practical assessment research and evaluation, 6*(2). ERIC Clearinghouse on Assessment and Evaluation 3(5). Retrieved September 7, 2003, from *www.ascd.org/readingroom*

California Task Force (1992). *Second to none.* Sacramento, CA: Department of Education.

Calkins, L. M. (1994). *The art of teaching writing*. Portsmouth, NH: Heinemann.

Carr, J. F., & Harris, D. E. (2001). *Succeeding with standards: Linking curriculum, assessment, and action plans.* Alexandria, VA: Association for Supervision and Curriculum Development.

Cooper, H. M., & Good, T. L. (1983). *Pygmalion grows up: Studies in the expectation communication process.* New York: Longman.

Council of Chief State School Officers (1992). Model standards for beginning teacher licensing, assessment, and development: A resource for state dialogue. Washington, DC: Author, www.ccsso.org/content/pdfs/corestrd.pdf

Edmonds, R. (1979). A discussion of the literature and issues related to effective schooling. Cambridge, MA: Harvard Center for Urban Studies.

Eisner, E. W. (1994). *The educational imagination: On the design and evaluation of school programs* (3rd ed.). Upper Saddle River, NJ: Prentice Hall.

Gill, V. (2001). *The eleven commandments of good teaching* (2nd ed.). Thousand Oaks, CA: Corwin Press.

Gonzalez, V., Brusca-Vega, R., & Yawkey, T. (1997). *Assessment and instruction of culturally and linguistically diverse students with or at-risk of learning problems: From research to practice.* Boston: Allyn and Bacon.

Good, T. L., & Brophy, J. E. (1994). *Looking in classrooms* (rev. ed.). New York: Harper and Row.

Henderson, V. L., & Dweck, C. S. (1990). Motivation and achievement. In S. S. Feldman & G. R. Elliot (Eds.), *At the threshold: The developing adolescent* (pp. 109–127). Cambridge MA: Harvard University Press.

Hubbard, R., & Power, B. (1993). *The art of classroom inquiry—A handbook for teacher-researchers.* Portsmouth, ME: Heinemann.

Isaac, S., & Michael, W. (1987). *Handbook in research and evaluation.* San Diego: Edits.

Jacobs, H. (1997). *Mapping the big picture: Integrating curriculum and assessment K–12.* Alexandria, VA: Association for Supervision and Curriculum Development.

Krathwohl, D. R., Bloom, B. S., & Masia, B. B. (1964). *Taxonomy of educational goals, Handbook 2, Affective domain.* New York: David McKay.

Linn, R., Baller, E., & Dunham, S. (1991, November). Complex portfolio-based assessment: Expectations and validation criteria. *Educational Research, 20*(8), 15–21.

McMillan, J. H. (2000). Fundamental assessment principles for teachers and school administrators. In *Practical assessment, research and evaluation.* ERIC Clearinghouse on Assessment and Evaluation. Retrieved September 7, 2003, from http://ericae.net

Morgan, S. (2004). *A curriculum redesign in response to students' anxiety to math competencies at the secondary level.* (ERIC Issue: ED482912) Institute of Education Sciences. Retrieved February 2, 2004, from www.eric.ed.gov

National Association of Secondary School Principals (1996). *Breaking ranks: changing an American institution.* VA: NASSP.

National Board for Professional Teaching Standards (1999). *What teachers should know and be able to do.* Retrieved May 11, 2003, from www.nbpts.org

National Commission on Teaching and America's Future (1996). *What matters most.* New York: NCTAF.

National Council of Teachers of English (1996). A project of the International Reading Association and the National Council of Teachers of English. Urbana, IL: NCTE.

O'Malley, J. M., & Valdez-Pierce, L. (1996). *Authentic assessment for English language learners: Practical approaches for teachers.* Reading, MA: Addison-Wesley.

Popham, J. W. (2001). *The truth about testing: An educator's call to action.* Alexandria, VA: Association for Supervision and Curriculum Development.

Rist, R. (1970). Student social class and teacher expectations: The self-fulfilling prophecy in ghetto education. *Harvard Educational Review, 40,* 411–451.

Routman, R. (2000). *Conversations: Strategies for teaching, learning, and evaluating.* Portsmouth, NH: Heinemann.

Shannon, P. (1990). Commentary: Teachers are researchers. In M. Olsen (Ed.), *Opening the door to classroom research* (pp. 141–154). Newark, DE: International Reading Association.

Stall, P., & Mullen, M. (2004). Unpublished preassessment case study project used in secondary methods courses at California State University at San Marcos.

Weinstein, R., Marshall, H., Sharp, L., & Betkin, M. (1987). Pygmalion and the student: Age and classroom differences in children's awareness of teacher expectations. *Child Development, 58,* 1079–1093.

Wiggins, G., & McTighe, J. (1998). *Understanding by design.* Alexandria, VA: Association for Supervision and Curriculum Development.

Winkling, D., & Bond L. (1995). *What your school should know about alternative assessment.* Oakbrook, IL: North Central Regional Education Laboratory.

# Chapter 4

# Instructional Strategies

**INTASC Principle 3:** The teacher understands how students differ in their approaches to learning and creates instructional opportunities that are adapted to diverse learners.

**Key Dispositions**

- The teacher believes that all children can learn at high levels and persists in helping all children achieve success.
- The teacher respects students as individuals with differing personal and family backgrounds and various skills, talents, and interests.

**INTASC Principle 4:** The teacher understands and uses a variety of instructional strategies to encourage students' development of critical thinking, problem solving, and performance skills.

**Key Dispositions**

- The teacher values the development of students' critical thinking, independent problem solving, and performance capabilities.
- The teacher values flexibility and reciprocity in the teaching process as necessary for adapting instruction to student responses, ideas, and needs.

**INTASC Principle 6:** The teacher uses knowledge of effective verbal, nonverbal, and media communication techniques to foster active inquiry, collaboration, and supportive interaction in the classroom.

**Key Disposition**

- The teacher values many ways in which people seek to communicate and encourages many modes of communication in the classroom. The teacher is a thoughtful and responsive listener.

## Introduction to the Chapter

In this chapter, you will begin to explore instructional strategies, one of the tools of the teaching profession that will help you craft engaging learning experiences for your students. It is important to remember Goodlad's philosophy (1979) that when students are involved in and excited about what they are doing (to the extent of being immune to distraction), excellent learning and accomplishment proceed.

As your understanding of the range of instructional strategies available becomes more complete, you will see how crucial the selection of the right strategy is to meeting the goals of your lesson. Every teacher needs a repertoire of effective teaching strategies, because no one best strategy meets every student's needs all the time.

Active teaching requires setting clear learning goals and selecting strategies that will offer your students the best opportunity to meet those goals. This means you will need to provide examples, conduct demonstrations, and exhibit realia if you hope to help your students acquire a deep understanding of the topics they will be studying. We accompany all the strategies outlined in this chapter, whether teacher-centered or student-centered, with suggestions on how to get students actively engaged in the learning process and how to guide them as they construct their own understanding of the topics presented. Of course, your stance as a teacher—that is, your own enthusiasm, modeling of high expectations, and ways of building connections between ideas—remains a critical factor in student learning.

Broadly speaking, the two primary categories of instructional strategies presented in this chapter are teacher-centered and student-centered. Teacher-centered strategies deliver information directly, telling in a didactic way. The teacher or textbook or both pass on knowledge and information. Student-centered strategies allow students to access the information and experiences more directly, enabling them to develop knowledge and skills. Ultimately, your skill in choosing from the continuum of instructional strategies and aligning it to both the selected assessment strategy and your lesson goals will assist you in crafting powerful learning experiences.

Section 1 of this chapter begins by introducing you to, or reacquainting you with, various teacher-centered strategies. We have included a subsection on questioning strategies at the end of Section 1 because we believe effective questioning strategies are essential regardless of whether you use a teacher-centered or student-centered approach. Questioning strategies serve as a link between the two categories of instructional strategies.

Section 2 provides information on three broad categories of student-centered instructional strategies: discussion, problem solving, and simulations. In both Sections 1 and 2, the similarities within the direct or indirect categories will become apparent; mastering a few strategies in each category will allow you to build and add to your repertoire as you gain experience. Keep in mind strategies described in both sections are intended as an introduction to instructional methods. You will explore teaching strategies much more completely in your subject area methods courses.

Section 3 may be the most critical part of this chapter. This section will add to your thinking on how to take any strategy you have selected and enhance it to ensure that all students in your classroom, including English language learners, have more opportunities to access the information.

Section 4 is devoted to technology, not to use as an add-on strategy, but rather to effectively infuse throughout your lessons. Taken together, the information in this chapter will assist you in using a variety of instructional strategies in order for your students to be successful in a rigorous curriculum and increase their desire to continue learning.

As you proceed through this chapter, note that the framework of the Circle of Courage guides the strategies presented. Mastery of knowledge, skills, and dispositions of each of your subject areas is one focus and often, from the old paradigm of teaching, the only one considered. However, in acquiring the skills of teaching, including instructional strategies, the other outcomes of the Circle of Courage require equal attention. Selecting a variety of strategies as you teach will allow you to focus on Belonging through collaborative groups and Independence by critically analyzing problems presented and problem solving through inquiry. Approaching instructional strategies from this broader perspective will equip you to plan more purposeful and effective lessons.

## SECTION 1: TEACHER-CENTERED INSTRUCTIONAL STRATEGIES

Teachers have a number of teacher-centered strategies available. The common strand among them is that each is a form of expository teaching. A teacher might select one of the teacher-centered strategies to cover a considerable amount of information in a short period of time, for example, to convey information about first-layer material. According to these methods, the authority—teacher, textbook, film, or computer—presents information with limited interaction with or among students.

## Lecture

Perhaps the most widely used method in this category of strategies is the lecture. You probably have recent experience with this strategy in your college classes. Lectures contain fast-paced, well-organized lessons intended to assist students in acquiring a specific set of limited knowledge in a short period of time. Lectures frequently introduce students to major concepts—layer two or three materials—they will be investigating in a unit. Teachers also use this strategy to add to information in a text or when they wish to heighten students' interest in a topic. Through this approach, students learn the basic facts, concepts, or rules needed in subsequent learning (Anderson & Block, 1987; Good & Grouws, 1987; Lindsley, 1991).

You would not want to select lecture as your primary instructional strategy if your goals were to provide students opportunities to synthesize, analyze, or evaluate information. If they have already learned the fundamentals of the unit, you will want them to become more engaged in problem solving and critical thinking.

The goal of the teacher conducting a lecture is to organize and convey large amounts of information in a time-efficient manner. Along with lectures, this can be accomplished through readings and providing tasks for students to integrate what has been learned. A fundamental task of teachers using this strategy is to help scaffold new information for their students during the lecture process. *Scaffolding* functions as instructional support that allows students to perform a skill or understand a new concept. In this process, the teacher breaks a complex skill or concept into subcomponent parts, adjusts the level of difficulty in questioning, provides examples, and offers prompts and cues to students (Eggen & Kauchak, 1996). We will examine scaffolding techniques more closely in Chapter 5, Unit and Lesson Plans.

***Advanced Organizer.*** One frequently used form of lecture is the *advanced organizer*. Used at the beginning of a lesson or unit, this lecture strategy organizes material in advance by previewing and structuring new content and linking it to students' existing schemata. *Schema theory* as a theoretical view of knowledge construction suggests data stored in memory consists of networks of organized and interconnected ideas, relationships, and procedures (Good & Brophy, 1994). Those interconnected ideas, relationships, and procedures are called *schemata* (Anderson, 1990).

When you have decided to use the *advanced organizer* strategy in conjunction with other strategies, three primary steps are useful in helping the learning experience be positive for students. In step one, the teacher clarifies the aims of the lesson, presents new concepts, and prompts for connections with students' previous knowledge and experience.

In step two the teacher focuses on helping students grasp the essential features of the new concept, which must be clearly identified and explained. The teacher, through a wide range of delivery modes such as lecture, discussion, film, experiment, and reading, will present the essential features, explain them, and provide examples.

In the third step, the teacher strengthens students' cognitive organization by testing information against existing ideas. Learning is anchored by reminding students of the connections to previous learning. The teacher asks students to summarize or describe the new material, provide additional examples, or examine and describe in their own words alternative ideas from various perspectives.

***Benefits and Challenges.*** As with all instructional strategies, benefits exist in the use of lectures and advanced organizers. They can be highly effective in providing background information when the teacher wants to begin a unit or create a frame of reference. Additionally, a good lecturer can bring together or summarize ideas previously covered in a lesson, creating a manageable framework of knowledge for students.

There are also definite challenges in using the lecture strategy. All too often a teacher's lecture creates a passive learning environment in which students are not actively involved in their learning. Typically they sit quietly, taking notes, and are not challenged or guided to develop skills in thinking or problem solving. The passive nature of lecture may promote student boredom, result in decreased retention of the material presented, and create discipline problems.

However, you can learn techniques to overcome the challenges of lecture, usually by blending strategies. The most successful lectures tend to be relatively short and well organized. Your role as the teacher is to clearly identify the goals and main points of the lecture. You should immediately make students aware of the goals at the beginning of the lecture and present only one main idea at a time. Your introduction should serve as a hook, intended to both stimulate and motivate students. Be certain to explain your expectations of what students will be doing during the lecture: note taking, completing an outline, or responding to your verbal prompts. Organize and present the information sequentially, with a beginning, middle, and end. Monitor students to ensure comprehension of each point before moving on to the next.

***Visual Organizers.*** Providing students with *visual organizers* when presenting more complex ideas will also help them acquire the information. You might select from numerous types of visual organizers to enhance your lecture, including *diagrams, charts, concept maps, graphs,* or even your own lecture outline. When using a visual organizer you will need to repeat difficult or complex points and should include specific examples. Figures 4.1 and 4.2 are visual organizers depicting examples of a diagram and concept map. Figure 4.1 is a Venn diagram and Figure 4.2 is a concept

FIGURE 4.1 Venn Diagram

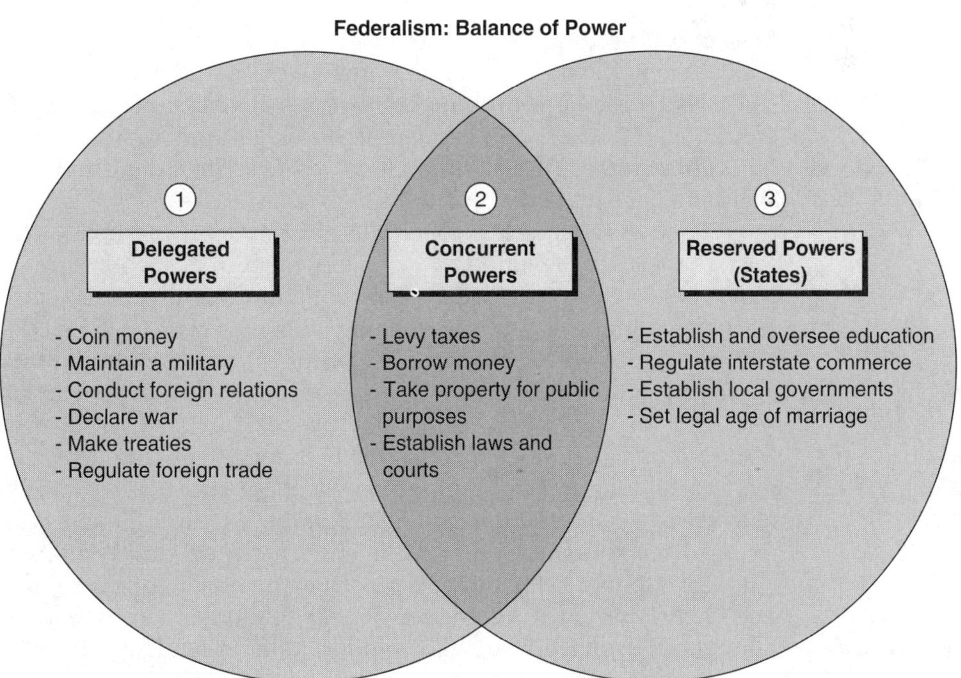

FIGURE 4.2 Concept Map (Spider Map)

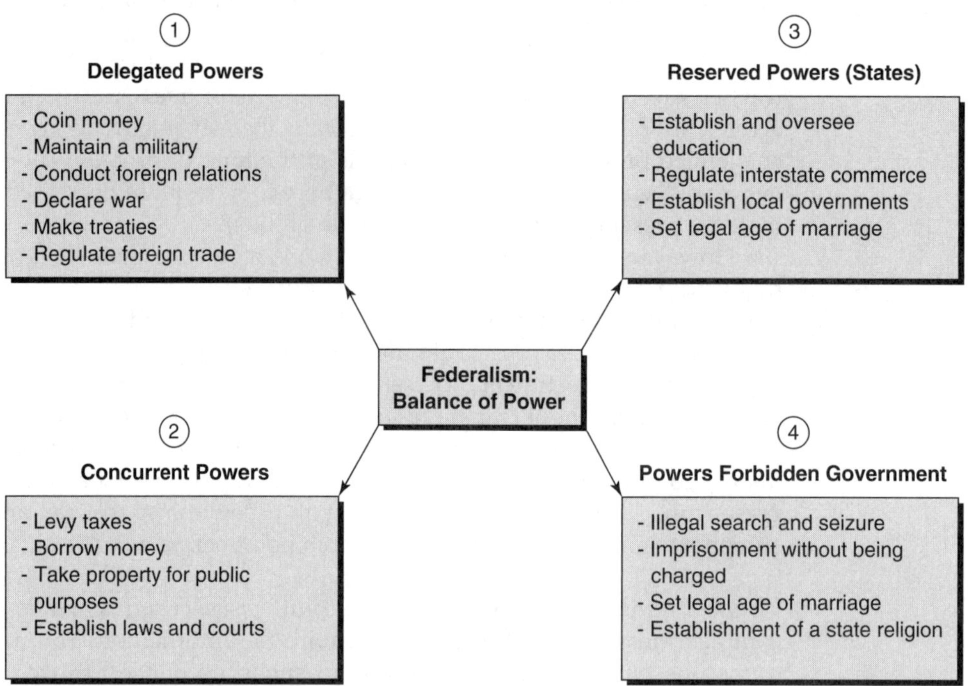


map, referred to as a spider map. Both examples focus on the same concept, balance of power between states and federal government, and illustrate how concepts can be visualized in various ways. A good resource for teachers that provides many examples of visual organizers can be found at www.graphic.org.

***Modeling.*** Lecture, when used appropriately, can be an important strategy to use with students. *Modeling,* as an important aspect of this instructional strategy, allows students to observe your thought processes. Research has shown that modeling is a critical aspect of learning because students will imitate the behaviors observed in others (Bandura, 1986, 1989). Modeling will assist students in learning the complex skills you have presented.

A good example of this concept is a history teacher who is lecturing on the Civil War. The teacher may model the development of a hypothesis and throughout the lecture use supporting evidence for validation. Students in class can observe the teacher's pattern of analysis leading to a reasoned conclusion. When asked to develop their own hypotheses on a historical question, by imitating the teacher's approach, students will offer a hypothesis followed by supporting data.

***Lecture Interaction.*** *Lecture interaction* strategies provide one type of variation on the lecture. Like lecture, the purpose of these strategies is to help students learn new bodies of information in a short period of time. Taking the strengths of the lecture (clear presentation of ideas and efficiency) and combining them with an interactive format helps students construct their own understanding of the concepts. The lecture provides the framework for students; other techniques interspersed throughout the lecture will allow you to monitor student understanding. Although there are several strategies to create interaction during the lecture, asking questions of students is one of the most commonly used techniques. Teachers pause during a lecture to check for understanding by directing questions to students.

Another interaction strategy is to stop your lecture every 10 to 15 minutes and ask your students to summarize what they have heard and identify, either verbally or in writing, aspects of the new material that they have questions about or what is confusing to them. Once you have clarified or answered their questions, you will be able to move ahead with more student comprehension of the material. Similar to the previous strategy, after students have written a quick personal reaction or summary of what they have just heard and any questions they might have, ask them to share their responses with a partner. We present a number of other specific strategies to mediate lectures in Section 3, Lecture Strategies.

A good lecturer also needs to be mindful of the pace of the talk, show enthusiasm, vary tone of voice, and move throughout the room. Avoid the temptation to stand at the front of the room the whole time. Finally, be certain to design a summary, including visual organizers, that connects the information you have presented to what you intend students to learn.

Following the lecture, design some guided practice for your students to provide them the opportunity to practice new skills or categorize other examples of a new concept. Monitor their work and assist with feedback. Finally, assign students independent practice or homework to encourage retention and transfer of skills or concepts (Eggen & Kauchak, 1996). In summary, numerous ways exist to create a more interactive lesson during a lecture. Each helps by breaking up the amount of "teacher talk" and allows the teacher to monitor and assess what students have learned.

## Demonstrations

Similar to the lecture, the teacher's goal during demonstrations is to explain a new concept or model skills. To begin, the teacher needs to think like a student, not one who has already mastered the concept, and organize the presentation in a simple way that makes sense to students. During a demonstration, the teacher can either explain the phenomenon as it is happening or ask students to hypothesize what is occurring. Demonstrations often include the use of materials or displays, but the teacher is the only person in the room actively involved in the process.

A science teacher demonstrating the appropriate steps in an experiment is a good example of this strategy in action. In front of the class, the teacher can safely model the necessary steps in the experiment. Similar to the lecture, the teacher will clarify students' expected behavior during the demonstration and will question for understanding throughout the lesson. Again, summarizing the important points closes the process. If the intended learning/experiment is complex, the teacher may want to repeat the entire demonstration. During a second demonstration, the teacher can pause periodically and prompt students to explain what steps come next, sequentially. This same strategy can be useful in a number of subject areas. In math, for example, when teaching a new formula, the teacher can ask students to explain the procedures of each step in the problem, giving the opportunity to check for understanding.

***Benefits and Challenges.*** Strengths of this method include efficient use of class time, modeling of appropriate use of equipment, clarification of detailed steps in a procedure, and main ideas made much clearer than if the students were given only oral instructions for the experiment. Challenges in using this method are similar to those of lecture, primarily making certain you constantly monitor and assess for student understanding throughout the demonstration. Make sure all students can see and participate in the demonstration. You may want, for example, to change the room configuration or use a video camera to broadcast the demonstration onto a larger screen in the classroom.

## Questioning Strategies

> The interactions that lead students to develop new insights, deeper understanding, and greater thinking skills are those in which a teacher or classmate presses the student through questioning and sharing ideas to go beyond his current thinking. (Oakes & Martin, 1999, p. 210)

Next to lecture and small group work, the most commonly used strategy in the classroom is that of asking questions. Whether you have determined a teacher-centered strategy or a student-centered approach best matches your goals for a specific lesson, questioning will play a significant role in being a successful teacher. It is very important for teachers to understand their critical part in this process and to learn how to use questions effectively. Just as Bloom's taxonomy can be helpful in planning for authentic assessment, discussed in Chapter 3, his taxonomy is also useful when using questions as a teaching tool.

Studies of teacher questions asked of students indicate that most questions are directed at the lowest level of Bloom's taxonomy (Figure 3.1). Teachers tend to ask students simply to recall newly acquired information, knowledge level. If a primary goal of instruction is to promote higher level thinking, then teachers need to be prepared in their classrooms to ask questions that lead to this important result. A first step in the questioning process is to create a classroom environment that encourages student questions and discourages the teacher from being the only questioner.

Depending on the instructional strategy being used in your class on any given day, your questioning strategies will differ. During direct teacher instruction, questions may be specific and to the point, aimed at a single right answer. If you are using a student-centered, indirect strategy, your questions should cause students to seek their own answers with minimum help from you. Both types of questions can contribute to the learning process and both can help a teacher assess student understanding.

Questioning skills also create teacher–student interactions that help promote higher order thinking. A skillful teacher will use student ideas and responses to create an understanding of the targeted concepts or skills of the lesson. This process prompts students to use examples from their own experiences to help them construct meaning from the ideas or skills being taught in your lesson. By building connections to your students' own interests, concerns, and problems, you will be providing a way for them to connect new information to what they already know.

***Convergent Questions.*** Part of the art and skill of questioning is the ability to formulate questions at the appropriate level and then be able to follow up one question with other probing questions. Questions can follow either a convergent or divergent pattern. *Convergent questions* focus on narrower objectives and on central themes. Often they ask for responses that are at the lower level of Bloom's taxonomy: knowledge recall or comprehension. For example, in a world language course, the teacher might use convergent questions to help students develop their oral or vocabulary skills by asking them to recall single right answers.

***Divergent Questions.*** *Divergent questions* elicit a wide range of responses from your students. Unlike convergent questions, divergent questions usually do not have one right answer and are often used to create student-led discussions. When employing divergent questions, the teacher must model a high degree of acceptance of the wide range of responses your students will offer. You desire creative responses as a good way to get students connected to your lessons.

***Using Questions Skillfully.*** In preparing to use questions for any type of lesson, it is important to write, in advance, specific questions you may want to ask. Your questions should help students clarify and understand information being presented. In preparing questions, be aware that your students may lack experience being asked divergent questions. If that is the situation, you will need to model expected behavior and show patience as students learn a new process of acquiring information. Be prepared for them to ask, "Why don't you just tell us the answer?" Let students know you expect multiple answers, not just a single answer. Over time, your students will learn not only to respond to your questions but also to build on other classmates' answers, either by asking clarifying questions, offering a different perspective, or adding new information.

You may also want to use probing as a questioning strategy as a means to follow up your questions. You can use this approach when you believe a student response lacks depth or is incorrect. Probing questions are usually aimed at correcting, improving, or expanding on a student's initial response. Use of good probing questions allows you to help students increase their level of learning and understanding.

You need to avoid a few common mistakes when using questions. One that occurs all too frequently involves the failure of teachers to allow for a period of silence when posing questions to their class. This period of time, known as wait time, has been divided into two specific pauses: wait time I, the period of teacher silence that follows the initial question to the class, and wait time II, the pause that follows a student's initial response. Both of these important strategies improve the quality of student responses (Tobin, 1980). Many teachers, for example, fail to allow any wait time after asking a question. They ask a question of one student and immediately move on to another student or answer the question themselves. As a result, students can feel a sense of failure and become less comfortable answering questions in the future. According to research studies, the average wait time of a teacher after asking a question is 1 second. When wait time is increased from 3 to 5 seconds, researchers discovered several positive results. First, the length of student responses increased as they had more time to bring their thoughts together. Next, more students were able to offer answers, even those not asked the question. Finally, and importantly, the level of student confidence increased (Rowe, 1974a, 1974b, 1978). Wait time is important; using appropriate wait time and learning how to prompt students will increase their engagement.

***Questioning Tips.*** As you develop your own questioning skills, there are several tips to bear in mind.

- Frame clear and understandable questions.
- Prepare questions in advance while developing your lesson plan.
- Keep in mind the importance of wait time.
- Avoid the tendency of many teachers to call repeatedly on those students they believe will know the answer.
- Direct your questions evenly around the room.
- Ask only one question at a time.
- Do not ask too many questions in any single lesson.
- Plan questions so that they range from easy to difficult.
- Listen closely to your students' responses.
- Allow time for other students to comment or react.

One final tip: Teachers who respond to student answers in a nonevaluative way tend to increase student participation. A response such as "interesting," or "can anyone add to this thought?" will open up the discussion. A teacher response of "good" or "right" will probably end the dialogue at that point.

Effective questioning strategies either can be a part of the teacher-centered approaches or may be infused into the student-centered strategies. Becoming an artful questioner in your classroom will help you increase your students' critical thinking and understanding.

The following boxes may be helpful in illustrating the use of questioning strategies in high school class discussions. Box 4.1 lists 12 keys to questioning strategies. Box 4.2 shows an actual class discussion in the first column. The second column identifies the questioning strategies the teacher used from Box 4.1, illustrating convergent questioning strategies to help students in a biological science activity on classification systems. Box 4.3 depicts divergent questioning strategies. During this activity students brainstorm the variety of different variables in physical science to consider in designing a potentially successful mousetrap-propelled "Mousemobile." The use of a common subject area helps readers see that both types of questioning strategies have value, depending on the situation.

Box 4.1

**Key to Questioning Strategies**

1. Use of Bloom's taxonomy to *vary the complexity of the types of questions* from simple identifying responses to more complex justifying (analysis), higher-level responses.
2. *Positive and nonjudgmental teacher response* (using words that denote they have the "correct" or "incorrect" answer). This encourages all students to respond and feel comfortable as well as sends the message that even if a response may be technically "correct," you want to hear from all other respondents.
3. *Wait time* demonstrates, by modeling, the importance of processing an answer and then following it up.
4. Ask for *clarifying or elaborating* on a response. This will assist other students to understand the response as well as get their added input.
5. Teacher suggests the *reason why* the student response is very appropriate. This is in addition to the positive/nonjudgmental teacher responses.
6. *Varying respondents* so that all students have an opportunity to participate (and everyone learns that expectation) even if it means calling on those who do not have their hand up.
7. Use of a *visual prompt* or realia as a valuable context to the questioning prompt, which provides a reference point that all can see, use, and understand.
8. Soliciting *multiple perspectives* or potential hypotheses for the same question.
9. *Student-centered* focus allows students to suggest and use choices while at the same time they are able to justify and defend those choices.
10. *Use of student drawings* or graphic organizers to clarify understanding of responses.
11. *Limiting response time* for one individual to prevent dominance by anyone.
12. Frequent *summarizing* by both teacher and student on the information or ideas they have suggested.

As a preservice teacher, these examples may help you understand how and when to use convergent and divergent questions and provide a potential template to prompt you to anticipate, prior to a lesson, what questions might be asked. The numbered notes in the second column of Boxes 4.2 and 4.3, next to the dialog, identify which strategy the teacher used and why. These notes are keyed to Box 4.1, which summarizes each type of questioning strategy. The final questions ask you to consider what might have been added (or deleted) to enhance the discussion.

***Convergent Questioning Example.*** Background: In this activity a science teacher is introducing the concept of classification that would lead to using biological classification keys, which means a specific organism will be placed in one and only one category or class of organisms (convergence). In addition, in the broader sense it will assist students in the understanding of concepts in evolution. The teacher gave each student group the same ten common objects (visual prompting). They were asked first to place the objects into four groups in which each object shared some common trait and to name that trait. They were then asked to put the object in two more comprehensive groups with a common trait, name it, and finally place all the objects in a larger single group and give the group a common name.

The teacher asked one group questions (while the others watched) to observe student understandings. Each successive group explained its groupings/names/traits with the teacher as well as other students outside the group involved in the discussion. As a follow-up assessment activity the teacher could ask these students to develop a simple dichotomous key to use to identify any one object from their classification system and give it to another group to see whether they are able to use and identify the student team keys.

### Box 4.2
### Convergent Questioning Strategies

| | |
|---|---|
| **Teacher:** What are the names of each of the four groups (with their objects) and why did you give that name to the group? (1) (7) | 1. **Vary complexity**<br>7. **Visual prompts** |
| *Student A:* Metallica, because each object in the group is made from some metal parts. | |
| **Teacher:** OK, that seems to makes sense. (waits a few seconds then . . .) Hmmm. How do you know it is a metal? (2) (3) | 2. **Positive and nonjudgmental response**<br>3. **Wait time** |
| *Student B:* I know what brass and steel look like. I have seen them before. | |
| **Teacher:** Good response, from your past experiences, I take it. Anyone else have a suggestion why these are all metals and belong together? (8) | 8. **Multiple perspectives** |
| *Student C:* I looked at the keys and they are shiny and hard and the coins are also. That's one of the characteristics of metals I remember. | |
| **Teacher:** OK, from your firsthand observation, that is how we formally get information in science. (5) Good job, team, defining that group. Now let's repeat the process with the other three different groups you have classified. What are each of the other groups' names? (4) | 5. **Prompt for further response**<br>4. **Clarify/elaborate** |

### Box 4.2
### Convergent Questioning Strategies *(continued)*

By repeating the process with this team's selection of groups' names and later with the other teams, the teacher is reinforcing/training the students to be able to defend their responses. (Teacher continues using the same line of questions illustrated here.) After discussing the names given to four groups, followed by division into two groups, the teacher discusses the name they have assigned for the whole group: all 10 objects (convergence).

| | |
|---|---|
| **Teacher:** What name did you select for the whole group? (See whether they can converge the objects into one group.) (1) | 1. **Vary complexity** |
| *Student D:* (Teacher calls on D because he has not spoken much yet.) We decided on calling the group "artificial" because people make them all and they are nonliving. (6) | 6. **Vary respondents** |
| **Teacher:** Sounds like a reasonable choice. How did your team decide they were nonliving? (1) (4) | 1. **Vary complexity**<br>4. **Clarify/elaborate** |
| *Student A:* They are all made out of either plastic or metal or paper or combinations of each, which are nonliving things. So, we called them artificial. | |
| **Teacher:** OK. (wait time) (3) Just a thought. Were any of these materials ever living? Would anyone else like to clarify? (4) (6) (8) | 4. **Clarify/elaborate**<br>6. **Vary respondents**<br>8. **Multiple perspectives** |
| *Student B:* (Teacher asks B to answer even though A has hand up.) That's what I told them, that paper is made from wood, which was once living, but they still went with nonliving. (6) | 6. **Vary respondents** |
| **Teacher:** Good job. That is a good strategy to solve problems, the fact that you question all ideas. That is how science works. (5) Is there any way that your team could adapt the name assigned this group that incorporates this idea that some of the objects may have been made from living things? (1) (4) | 5. **Validate response**<br>1. **Vary complexity**<br>4. **Clarify/elaborate** |
| *Student B:* What about "not living now"? | |
| **Teacher:** Good, any other possibilities? (6) (8) | 6. **Vary respondents**<br>8. **Multiple perspectives** |
| *Student C:* Abiotic? I heard that word earlier in the year. | |
| **Teacher:** That is an important scientific word. Could you clarify what it means? (4) | 4. **Clarify/elaborate** |
| *Student C:* Nonliving but maybe it would not include paper because it was made from something that was once living. | |
| **Teacher:** Hmmm, that is a great point. I am not sure either. Perhaps you could look that up and let us all know. (9) I think you are on the right track and with this final clarification have made some good decisions. At any rate, I think your group did a great job of modeling for all of us how you justified your groupings. (2) (5) That will help all the rest of the class as we go through their responses. Thanks again. (2) | 9. **Student-centered focus**<br>2. **Positive and nonjudgmental response**<br>5. **Validate responses** |

***Divergent Questioning Strategies.*** As part of the physical science curriculum, the teacher facilitates students in a team project involving the construction of a "Mousemobile," a mousetrap propelled only by a single rubber band. The students are challenged to induce (derive) or deduce (validate) some of the principles of physics they have studied such as Newton's laws of motion, gravity, friction, momentum, acceleration, engineering design, and energy. After the student groups finish the construction of their vehicles they have to test the efficiency of the vehicles over a specific course under different conditions including (1) over a flat surface through a given distance, (2) over a set of "hills," and (3) through a maze of balloons that they have to pop with the vehicle.

In this initial questioning process of brainstorming with the whole class, the teacher is leading a discussion by questioning students on the potentially different (divergent) ways to construct their vehicles and how these tasks might be accomplished. The class is later divided into smaller cooperative groups to complete the tasks.

Box 4.3

**Divergent Questioning Strategies**

| | |
|---|---|
| **Teacher:** (Teacher clarifies the task of building a mousetrap-propelled "Mousemobile" and the different tasks and conditions under which it has to function. In addition, individual class members have a mousetrap in front of them.) (7) Let's start with a key question to brainstorm ideas: What are the design considerations in making the Mousemobile? Let's make a list on the board of the ideas you have to assist you. (7) | 7. **Visual prompts** |
| *Student A:* How do you transfer the energy from the trap to the Mousemobile itself? | |
| **Teacher:** Good start. What are some ways you might do this? (1) (8) (9) | 1. **Vary complexity**<br>8. **Multiple perspectives**<br>9. **Student-centered focus** |
| *Student A:* What about a string attached somehow between the trap lever arm and front wheels? | |
| **Teacher:** OK, hmmm. (2) (3) I'll write this idea down on board and you can each sketch it next to the words. (Teacher also asks for appropriate labels and clarification as the student sketches his or her ideas.) (3) (7) (10) So let's continue to focus on this question related to transferring energy from the trap to the vehicle. (8) | 2. **Positive and nonjudgmental response**<br>3. **Wait time**<br>7. **Visual prompt**<br>10. **Student drawings**<br>8. **Multiple perspectives** |
| *Student B:* The string is a good idea but how about using something that can overcome friction like a rubber band that would not slip as much on the front axle. | |
| **Teacher:** Good suggestion. . . . and two questions: What do you mean by "friction" and why might your idea work better than the string? (2) (3) (4) | 2. **Positive and nonjudgmental response**<br>3. **Wait time**<br>4. **Clarify/elaborate** |

Box 4.3

**Divergent Questioning Strategies** *(continued)*

| | |
|---|---|
| (Teacher continues to affirm student responses and then probes for the reasons/justification for their ideas. Teacher also elicits responses from other students to encourage greater participation. Teacher continues to have them sketch their ideas next to the summary of their words. Teacher allows enough time until everyone who wants to gets a chance to respond, getting more than 75% of the students involved in this first questioning prompt). (5) (6) (8) (9) (10) (11) (12) | 5. **Prompt for further response**<br>6. **Vary respondents**<br>8. **Multiple perspectives**<br>9. **Student-centered focus**<br>10. **Student drawings**<br>11. **Limiting response time**<br>12. **Summarizing** |
| **Teacher:** Now that we have some ideas on how we can make the vehicle move, let's brainstorm one of the challenges it will have to overcome as it is moving. (The teacher explains the three tasks as outlined in the background above and asks students to decide which one they think they should address first.) (9) (12) | 9. **Student-centered focus**<br>12. **Summarizing** |
| *Student C:* Well, I think the second task is a bit more daunting than the other two because the Mousemobile has to go up and over two successive ramps with a 10% and 15% grade and it is also timed whereas on the other two tasks it goes over a flat surface. (Teacher motions the student with his hand and asks the rest of the class whether there is a general consensus to brainstorm this problem first.) Student C continues: I think we ought to use large wheels on the back and have rubber bands around them and also use a very light body and . . . . | |
| **Teacher:** Wow, those are all very good possibilities, but let's slow down a bit and clarify some of your ideas (and have you draw them) while I give the rest of the class a chance to share their different ideas. (1) (2) (3) (4) (6) (11) Thanks for your ideas ! | 1. **Vary complexity**<br>2. **Positive and nonjudgmental response**<br>3. **Wait time**<br>4. **Clarify/elaborate**<br>6. **Vary respondents**<br>11. **Limiting response time** |
| **Teacher:** OK, class. Now what are the potential benefits or issues with using large wheels on the back and small ones in front? (The teacher then lists the student-generated pros and cons of this design consideration again using student drawings when appropriate that explain each of their ideas. (12) (When this is done, he summarizes the manner of brainstorming/questioning they have used and repeats this line of questioning for the other design ideas: brainstorm, clarify, draw, and list pros and cons.) (12) | 12. **Summarizing** |
| **Teacher:** You have all done a wonderful job of proposing very different (divergent) ideas on designing your vehicle and completing some of the required tasks. I like the fact that you have also been able to justify these ideas. | 1. **Vary complexity**<br>5. **Prompts for "why"** |

*Box 4.3*

**Divergent Questioning Strategies** *(continued)*

| | |
|---|---|
| When you actually make and test your vehicle under the three task conditions, you will find out how well it works. (1) (5) Now you can use this same approach on your individual teams as you work your way from brainstorming to construction to testing and the final competition. I will now place you on teams to work on brainstorming some of the additional tasks you will have to address (which were listed on board and are outlined on the worksheet). | |
| **Teacher:** (The teacher opens it up to the students to see what general questions they might have in completing the tasks in this problem). What general questions do you have related to "solving" this problem? (9) | 9. **Student-centered focus** |
| A variety of students (10 out of 25) ask questions. Several follow below: (1) (4) (8) (9) (12) | 1. **Vary complexity**<br>4. **Clarify/elaborate**<br>8. **Multiple perspectives**<br>9. **Student-centered focus**<br>12. **Summarizing** |
| *Student D:* Can we modify the mousetrap itself? | |
| **Teacher:** You can, of course, make the car out of any material you want but the original mousetrap and its parts can be modified without adding any other additional parts. (10) | 10. **Clarify/elaborate** |
| *Student E:* How much time do we have to actually build it? | |
| **Teacher:** Time limits and my intermediate checks are on the worksheet. (10) | 10. **Clarify/elaborate** |
| *Student F:* Will our grades be decided on how well our Mousemobile achieves the tasks? | |
| **Teacher:** There will be certain minimums to accomplish as outlined in the worksheet/task sheet, but generally your grade depends on the process of building and testing the vehicle, your active participation, understanding of the physics involved, and ability to work effectively on your team. (5) (10) | 5. **Reasons why**<br>10. **Clarify/elaborate** |
| **Teacher:** These are all important questions . . . continue to ask each other and me these types of concerns as you proceed through the process. Good luck to all of your teams. (2) | 2. **Positive and nonjudgmental response** |

## *Putting It Into Practice:* Activity 4.1

Observe one or two teacher-centered lessons at your assigned site. Record your thoughts and observations on the effectiveness of the strategy, and identify "keys" that helped the lesson be successful or issues that prevented the lesson from reaching the desired outcome. Pay particular attention to what students are doing during the lesson and the teacher's strategies to keep them engaged in the lecture.

## SECTION 2: STUDENT-CENTERED INSTRUCTIONAL STRATEGIES

Active engagement of students in their own learning has been a goal of educators for at least the past century. As a means to reach this goal, teachers have been crafting lessons designed and sequenced to connect student learning with the students' own experiences. In this way, students can construct understandings that make sense to them, rather than receive information organized and delivered by their teachers. Strategies that allow this form of learning are known as *indirect or student-centered.* This section explains several examples of student-centered strategies. As noted earlier, knowing how to implement a strategy is important; knowing why and when to use it to match with your assessment tools will make the lesson purposeful.

A primary goal of student-centered strategies is to provide students in your classroom the opportunity to learn and practice skills of higher order and critical thinking. Many, if not all, student-centered strategies are grounded in a *constructivist* view of learning. As you recall from Chapter 2, constructivists believe learners develop their own understanding of the way the world operates as compared to information being delivered to them through the teacher. From this viewpoint, students are an active part of the process and will, when guided appropriately, construct meaning that makes sense to them.

A teacher usually selects a student-centered strategy when the goal is to teach content at a deeper level, information and skills described in Chapter 3 as the middle and third layers. These strategies will help students acquire the enduring understandings. Even though student-centered strategies may require more time than teacher-centered strategies because there is less control over the pace of the lesson, they can be more effective in meeting the goal of a particular lesson. The trade-off for using student-centered strategies is that a smaller quantity of information will be covered, but the depth of learning will be enhanced as it becomes an active process and provides students with opportunities to practice critical and higher order thinking, allowing them to acquire enduring understanding. The role of the teacher differs when using student-centered approaches. Teachers act more as a guide, or facilitator, and creator of participatory experiences. The following three broad categories represent the range of student-centered strategies to consider in any lesson: discussion, problem solving, and simulations.

### Discussion

Think of a time in your secondary school experience when powerful conversations occurred among students. The energy in the class came alive; students were focused on the topic at hand and were actively following the thoughts of other students on issues important to them. You were being asked to think critically and draw on your previous knowledge. These powerful learning experiences were student-centered discussions.

Discussion, one of the most commonly used student-centered strategies, is not a lecture plus a few questions along the way; rather, in true student-centered instruction, students dominate the conversation. These are not open, freewheeling talk fests; instead, educators purposefully design discussions to allow for focused student exchange of ideas and direct them toward specific learning goals.

The teacher's role is no less important than when using teacher-centered strategies; it is just a different role—one of facilitation. Through appropriate questioning, the teacher facilitates the discussion to keep its focus so that more students become engaged in the conversation. As a caution, sometimes the teacher whose predominate style is lecture, can also dominate a class discussion. The teacher should be involved by keeping the discussion moving and on track by posing effective questions. In this role the teacher works to keep any student or small group of students from controlling or dominating the discussion. A teacher skilled in this strategy encourages many student voices and occasionally offers an alternative viewpoint to keep the discussion going.

Students must be appropriately prepared prior to a discussion. They need to have read or reviewed pertinent information and they must work to follow class norms, be active listeners, and show respect for differing opinions. Keeping all students engaged is evidence of a powerful discussion and a strong learning experience for students.

***Opening Questions.*** Initiating a discussion session can be done by the use of two types of questions. The first type, *divergent questions*, discussed earlier, is effective because there is not a simple answer. For example: What are the underlying causes of poverty? What issues would be created if medical science found a way to significantly retard the aging process? Divergent questions are open to interpretation and allow students to demonstrate their deeper understanding of issues, concepts, or ideas.

The other primary type of opening question focuses on controversial issues. For example: Will racism always be a part of a multicultural society? Can democracy find success in all cultures? Is security more important than civil liberties since 9/11? These types of questions can be explored to allow students to examine and reevaluate their attitudes, values, and behaviors on important adolescent and societal issues such as drug abuse or sexually transmitted diseases.

You can also use the discussion strategy to introduce a new topic. Questioning allows you to obtain an idea of what your students currently know about the idea or concept. Additionally, you may use discussion to explore a previous topic more deeply, looking at other resources or data. The discussion may also open up another avenue for collaborative group work. We will discuss collaboration more completely in Chapter 6, Cooperative Learning. Again, keep in mind that students will need to learn the skills of discussion and will improve by repeated opportunities to practice these skills.

***Facilitating Successful Discussions.*** Several strategies enhance the chances for successful discussion. Structuring discussions using the following tips will provide your students with the opportunity to be actively engaged in the process. To enhance the possibility of a class discussion being effective, a safe and interactive learning environment is essential. Remind your students of the basic ground rules of discussion: Use active listening; do not interrupt other students; respect differing viewpoints; and keep the discussion focused on the issue versus letting it become personal (that is, no questioning the person rather than the idea).

In designing a discussion, teachers need to select a question or topic that will hook students into conversation. The teacher will also want to limit the time allowed for discussion. As you begin to use this strategy, start with 20 to 30 minutes as a time frame before moving to full class periods. The way the room is arranged will also be important. An arrangement that clusters students in a circle or semicircle provides a better venue for students to talk with each other. You might also begin with minigroups of 6 to 8 students clustered for discussion before moving to whole-class discussions. Remember to assign specific roles to group members. Although it is always important to assign roles in cooperative groups, in informal small groups work roles might not be needed and could, in fact, hinder the natural course of a discussion or activity. In some cases students need to negotiate their own roles if we want them to learn to be more independent.

## Problem Solving

Problem solving is an important skill for all students to develop and practice, and as such, teachers need to use this instructional approach regularly in their classrooms. Like other student-centered strategies, problem solving involves students in their own learning, requiring them to solve problems through direct experiences the teacher provides.

This strategy encourages students to be active rather than passive learners. Also, due to the fact that students at this stage of adolescence are characteristically curious, they are motivated to actively seek out answers to problems. As a result, students tend to retain more information and skills learned because they were applied rather than just memorized.

Of course, certain limitations to this type of strategy exist. Students receive less direct feedback from the teacher as they independently explore alternative answers to problems. Another issue to consider with the problem-solving strategy is that it takes a great deal of time; it targets quality rather than quantity of content coverage as the goal. Students focus primarily on the process of solving problems, knowing what questions to ask and which data are valid. Use this strategy to apply information and skills and typically focus on the enduring understandings identified in the unit.

***Inquiry.*** *Inquiry* is a form of problem solving often used in classrooms. It differs from other forms of problem solving (for example, discovery) in that its emphasis is on the process of investigating a problem, not necessarily finding one correct solution. Additionally, whereas discovery provides a defined process for students to follow, inquiry encourages students to explore various approaches to solving problems. A primary goal of this strategy is for students to develop a sense of independence.

Inquiry's focus on developing critical thinking as well as the skills required for conducting research through the process of realistic classroom research makes it a valuable strategy. Students generate the problem or the question for the inquiry from their inquisitiveness about the content being studied. The classroom teacher needs to model and facilitate the research skills required for the inquiry of students. All inquiries can be related to district, state, or national content standards. Review the standards in your content area as well as the textbooks and other materials you use in your classes. Decide on themes that lend themselves to integration of content areas so students can transfer knowledge from other classes to the inquiry process. This enables students to understand that what is learned in one class is actually transferable to another class.

Rather than just assigning a topic for students to research, students need to learn how to ask questions about a specific area of a broad topic they are studying in class. For example, in a class studying about systems, you might decide to conduct an inquiry about the system of student life on students' high school campus. They may ask questions about how the groups that exist on campus came to be. Where did they get their names? How are "territories" on campus defined? Where are the territories? Who defined them? How is knowledge of these territories transmitted to other students? To newly arrived freshmen? Do the teachers and administrators on campus know about these territories? Do they try to do something about the issues or do they care?

Students can and should be trained to read, interview, write, or create sketches, grids, and graphs to answer questions they have generated, rather than plagiarize by simply downloading information from the Internet or copying out of books. You may find Figure 4.3 to be useful in teaching students to (1) state their goals, that is, define what they really want to know; (2) brainstorm as many ideas as possible about all aspects of the topic in which they are interested; and (3) carefully choose the best idea from all of the ideas they have generated.

Tishman, Perkins, and Jay (1995) suggest that the skills necessary to find a good inquiry project must be explicitly taught along with each of the subskills or building blocks required to complete the process. Figure 4.3, adapted from their work, outlines thinking challenges students encounter while searching for topics for inquiry as well as the strategies or building blocks teachers need to explicitly teach and model.

The purposes of teaching students the strategies outlined in Figure 4.3 are to provide them support in the development of the topic and questions for their

**FIGURE 4.3** Searching for Inquiry Topics

| Thinking Challenges | Strategies or Building Blocks |
|---|---|
| When I need to be clear about what I am doing and how I am going to get there | State the problem or question.<br>State what I want to accomplish (my goals).<br>State the context of my problem, such as where it is and what is there.<br>Include facts that help the reader understand what the problem or question really is. |
| When I need to think about (to "see") the entire picture of what I am trying to do | Search for as many ideas about this problem as I can.<br>Search for as many possibilities I can think of or can find.<br>Ask how else I might think about it. Ask some "what if . . . ?" questions about this problem.<br>Think about the causes.<br>Think about the effects.<br>Think about who might not agree with me or question what I have to say.<br>Identify other questions I have.<br>Think about what I will do with my information. What does it mean? So what?<br>Who will I have to convince that the solutions I suggest are do-able? |
| When I need to assess, rate, or decide something | Think critically (evaluate) about my questions, plans, facts I found, and my goals. |
| When I need to think or rethink the details of the plan I am suggesting | Find more information from other sources.<br>Add more explanations (elaborate).<br>Do I want to start all over again or should I just change a few things in my plan? |

Note: From S. Tishman et al., 1995, *The Thinking Classroom: Learning and Teaching in a Culture of Thinking* (p. 102). Published by Allyn and Bacon, Boston, MA. Copyright © 1956 by Pearson Education. Adapted by permission of the publisher.

inquiry project and to help them develop a plan that will guide their research as well get them to think critically about what they have decided to do. Students will need support if and when they decide that the plan they develop has flaws; however, the process of self-generated topics around which to build an inquiry, and the interest and enthusiasm that it generates, results in extremely positive academic returns for students because of the motivation involved in working on the inquiry.

Teachers will need to help facilitate the thinking of those students who are having trouble generating questions for their inquiry. You might start by giving resistant students an interest inventory in the areas your class covers. For example, you might ask students whether they would like to work on a science investigation in the classroom or outside the classroom, whether they like to interview people or read about what people have done.

Figure 4.4 offers an example of an interest inventory that you can use as a beginning. You can adapt it for use in any content area. You may also want to add questions that you feel are more appropriate.

The purpose of the inventory is to find a place for students to start to ascertain whether they will be interested in a hands-on project, one in which they will be able to sketch and label parts of their inquiry, or whether they prefer to conduct their inquiry through reading. Once you determine the preferred mode of investigation, you can look for possible project questions that fit the ways students want to learn about something. You can also stimulate interest by having students look at a variety of realia (such as costumes, medical instruments, musical instruments), books, newspaper articles, or listen to a story read, or view a portion of a video. Your next step is to teach students how to generate questions that can be researched in the inquiry process based on those areas that seem to have piqued their interest.

You need to conduct an assessment of inquiry projects in order to give students feedback and to let you know how each is progressing. A simple checklist, like the example in Figure 4.5, can help you assess students while they are working on their inquiries.

**FIGURE 4.4** Sample Interest Inventory

| Questions | Always | Sometimes | Never |
|---|---|---|---|
| I like to learn about ________ by actually doing it (activities, diagrams, sketches, etc.). | | | |
| I like to learn about ________ by reading about it. | | | |
| I am interested in knowing about the people who have accomplished a lot in ________. | | | |
| I enjoy working with others to learn ________. | | | |
| I enjoy learning ________ by myself. | | | |
| I enjoy ________ because ________. | | | |
| I do not enjoy ________ because ________. | | | |

FIGURE 4.5 Teacher Checklist for Assessment of Student Inquiry Projects in Progress

STUDENT INQUIRY PROGRESS CHART

STUDENT NAME: ______________________________

| Criterion | Date | Date | Date | Comments |
|---|---|---|---|---|
| Has a question that can be researched | | | | |
| Has developed a do-able plan | | | | |
| Knows the materials needed | | | | |
| Uses sketches to support thinking and planning | | | | |
| Can relate what is observed to the plan | | | | |
| Questions the quality of the plan | | | | |
| Notes causes and effects and understands them based on the analysis | | | | |
| Understands that the plan is meant to convince an audience to support a specific viewpoint | | | | |

Decide on the dates you will check on students' progress. List the criteria you are looking for, that is, what you can determine to be progress based on the elements you have taught and modeled for students. Write brief yet concise comments that you will be able to use to plan instruction.

Remember, the teacher's primary role in the inquiry approach is to allow students the opportunity to create their own process for solving problems. Teachers help students become more conscious of learning to analyze their own thinking. The Circle of Courage emphasizes "guidance without influence" (Brendtro et al., 2002). Student empowerment is required to foster the belief that students are in control of their own learning process. This promotes the development of Independence within the context of the Circle of Courage model.

## Simulations

The last major grouping of student-centered strategies overviewed in this chapter falls under the heading of *simulations*. Activities such as role-playing or enacting minidramas to recreate significant events or problem situations needing solutions are included in simulations.

***Drama.*** Role-playing as a form of creative drama seems to come naturally to many students. Role-playing often helps teachers gain insight into how students feel about a particular issue as well as find out what is important to them. In order to assess students' attitudes about specific issues, teachers should encourage students to choose what they will role-play in a specific content area as well as how they will role-play an issue. Participation in role-playing should be voluntary, and at no time should anyone ridicule or embarrass a student.

During role-playing, students take on a persona such as that of landowners during the Civil War. You can combine the underlying philosophy of drama as education with role-playing to add richness to the process. In drama as education, students do not pretend to be someone. They read about a specific situation, the people, the context (historical or social), and then become the people in the drama, assuming the perspectives of those they have been studying. The teacher is also a part of the drama, leaving the drama or stopping the drama when students need more information on people, objects, places, social or historical contexts, and culture, in order to process an issue they have been studying.

***Group Interviews.*** Role-playing can naturally take place in secondary classrooms in the context of a group interview, with the teacher serving as the interviewer. For example, if the class has been reading about underwater devices, the inventors, and the users of the devices, the teacher may spontaneously place students in roles as the inventors and users of the various underwater devices. Through the process of questioning, the teacher leads students to discuss the inventions, their uses, and the advantages or disadvantages of underwater breathing devices.

***Tableaus.*** Role-playing can also include tableaus or freeze pose, whereby a group of students demonstrate a given scenario or a vocabulary word. They discuss, research the scenario or word, and decide how they will best represent the idea or concept in a tableau or freeze pose. The teacher then uses the group freeze pose to guide the class in unpacking the meaning of a concept or word as portrayed in the tableau.

***Students Exploring New Situations.*** Simulations allow students to practice their communication skills as well as test their analytical skills. Encourage them to focus on aspects of the situation that seem important to them. You may even give students the opportunity to play themselves in an unfamiliar situation. After identifying the various issues involved, students can examine alternative solutions through critical thinking. As they explore these solutions, students learn to analyze and evaluate the consequences of various outcomes. Keep in mind strategies such as these offer students with different learning styles an alternative means to demonstrate their understanding.

***Using Simulation Strategies.*** A teacher using simulation strategies takes the following into consideration: A well-managed classroom is important; even actively involved students need clear boundaries. To create simulation activities, teachers are bound only by imagination and their students' opportunities to investigate various issues. Teachers can also use simulation activities prepared by a publisher such as Teachers' Curriculum Institute (www.historyalive.com). In any case, purposefully designed simulations with well-articulated learning goals are essential to the success of this student-centered instructional strategy.

Student-centered strategies offer teachers and students a variety of means to enable the subject matter to stir the imagination and challenge thinking to find new and innovative solutions. As you have read, student-centered strategies form their own continuum of student involvement. Only by experimenting and using various techniques will you discover your own comfort zone in incorporating them into your classroom. Keep in mind if you are just learning to implement these student-centered strategies without much prior experience, you will need to practice and refine your own skills in implementing them. Some teachers give up too quickly because they are uncomfortable with their own role. Practice and experience will allow you to move beyond this point and increase your range of strategies to actively engage students in learning.

### *Putting It Into Practice:* Activity 4.2

Observe one or two student-centered lessons at your assigned site. Record your thoughts and observations on the effectiveness of the strategy, and identify "keys" that helped the lesson be successful or issues that prevented the lesson from reaching the desired outcome. Pay particular attention to what students are doing during the lesson and the teacher's strategies to keep them engaged in the student-centered activity.

### *Putting It Into Practice:* Activity 4.3

Develop a list of benefits and challenges that apply to both teacher-centered and student-centered lessons. Share these lists with your colleagues and attempt to identify strategies to mitigate the challenges involved with using either teacher-centered or student-centered strategies.

## SECTION 3: STRATEGIES FOR MULTILINGUAL/MULTICULTURAL CLASSROOMS

Secondary classrooms today reflect the very pluralistic society educators serve. Teachers must be prepared to mediate (modify) any of the strategies presented in the previous two sections. Though teachers modify the approach to teaching the content or skills of the lesson, they do not lower their expectations of meeting the standards and objectives of the unit. All teachers face this difficult challenge. In this section, you will explore a variety of ways to meet this challenge. Although this discussion particularly emphasizes mediating for English language learners (ELL), each of the techniques described can help all students in your class be more fully engaged and learn.

### Lecture Strategies

When teachers decide to use lecture to meet the goals of the lesson, much of the time they are uncertain whether students really comprehended the ideas presented. Typically teachers rely solely on student note taking as a demonstration that students understood the lecture. When they begin to check for understanding more closely, teachers often discover that students have only a vague notion of the critical concepts of the lecture. For example, some English language learners, although having been tested and identified as being "advanced" in English language development, may still struggle to process information in large chunks, especially when it is delivered orally. Teachers need to find ways of mediating comprehension of material delivered in a lecture format. The following strategies might help you mediate understanding of the content of your lecture for students.

***Ten/Two.*** Think about the time a teacher spends talking during a lecture. As noted earlier in this chapter, length is a critical factor; a teacher should not lecture for too long a period at any one time. Students will find it difficult to keep up with the content when too many points are covered during a specific time frame. When a student is processing complex, abstract, academic information for a long period of time, receptively (listening or reading), the words seem to fall over each other, often reduced to a kind of incomprehensible babble over time. To address this challenge you should lecture for no more than 10 minutes at a time, especially when teaching English language learners. Pause after 10 minutes and facilitate students to process the information shared in the lecture for 2 minutes. They can share in a small group of three or four. During the 2-minute sharing, instruct students to identify and agree on the main points discussed in the lecture and compare notes with one another. One person in each group should write down the main points during each 2-minute pause and then share them within their group after the entire lecture is over. Continue this pattern until you have concluded the lecture.

***Quick Write.*** Another strategy to help students access the important ideas in a lecture is to pause after covering no more than three important points related to a major concept and have students do a quick write for 2 minutes. They should individually identify the important points of the lecture up to the time you stopped. Next have students quickly share their own notes with the class. As successive students present, have them share only new ideas. That is, if someone who speaks ahead of you shares the main point you were going to present, you should share a new point or "pass." It is important to consider that English language learners may be able to process only a few points during the pause. For these students, lectures have very little context to support comprehension and present a cognitive challenge because of the content.

***Think-Pair-Share.*** A variation of the quick write is the think-pair-share strategy. Again, pause periodically during your lecture and ask students to list quickly the main points you have covered. Next, have them share their ideas with a partner and finally with the entire class. When you listen to what students share, you will be able to assess quickly which students comprehend the content of the lecture and which do not. That information will help you target your reteaching for the students who need the additional support.

***Visual Supports.*** As mentioned previously, using visuals such as diagrams that are large and clearly labeled to support student comprehension of the material about which you are lecturing allows access to the information in a different way. Whenever possible, illustrate a concept (refer to Figures 4.1 and 4.2). You may also want to stop the lecture and ask students to visually represent the content about which you have been lecturing. If the students are English language learners, you may want to ask them to share their visuals and explain how the visuals demonstrate the content. This also serves as an assessment to guide any reteaching that may be necessary.

When you use support mechanisms to mediate understanding of the content of a lecture, you will find that comprehension of content increases because students have had the time to share and process information. Though you may not be able to cover all of the material as quickly as you would like, if your goal is to help all students understand and master the content, then the time must be made to mediate comprehension.

## Student-Centered Strategies

Student-centered instructional strategies focus on what students already know, are presented through experiences that actively involve them in the learning, and provide the necessary scaffolds or supports to ensure that students learn and master the content. Student-centered instructional strategies evolve from careful planning. Students, who they are, what they already know, their cultures and their interests, should be the first considerations in planning. First, focus on students to ensure that you meet the diverse needs of the classroom during teaching (Villa & Thousand, 1992). Next, carefully analyze the tasks and the skills or competencies required of students in order for them to perform the tasks in which they will be engaged during the lessons.

Finally, determine appropriate scaffolds necessary to ensure that students will learn the content we teach as well as actively engage in the learning. Several types of scaffolds support student learning, such as modeling, metacognition, bridging or activating background knowledge, building background knowledge, and representing text in comprehensible ways. Section 3 of Chapter 5 on differentiated instruction fully describes scaffolding techniques for struggling students as well as for those requiring additional challenges.

You will need to utilize bridging or activating background knowledge up front as one of the scaffolds for English language learners in your class. Look at district assessment records and speak to their other teachers to help determine students' strengths and areas of need in language and content area literacy. You should also prepare a list of strengths and needs determined from authentic classroom experiences. Figure 4.6 shows a sample graphic organizer utilizing this scaffold. Student considerations listed give you an idea of the information you will need to assemble regarding the English language learners in your class.

***Dyad/Triad Groupings.*** Dyad or triad groupings provide a context for all students to talk. Instead of the teacher having to call on individual students, groups of students process information, answer questions, generate questions, summarize information, and solve problems. You must carefully structure the dyads or triads for them to function productively. The structure includes (1) a way for students to take turns so that each group member actively participates, and (2) a way for the students themselves as well as the teacher to evaluate the process.

You can structure turn taking in a dyad in a variety of creative ways. For example, two students can share one book so that one is reading while the other listens. When they complete the reading, the listener asks the reader at least three questions about what was read. You must teach students the types of questions to ask to ensure that their questions are not all recall or literal questions.

When performing an experiment, one student can record the information while the other student reads thermometers, for example. The way this exchange is structured depends on the content being taught. The important thing to remember in dyads, as in other groups, is that you are certain that every student is participating in

FIGURE 4.6 Graphic Organizer

| MEDIATING STUDENT-CENTERED STRATEGIES FOR ENGLISH LANGUAGE LEARNERS | | | | |
|---|---|---|---|---|
| **Student Name** | **What I Know** | **Tasks** | **Skills Required** | **Required Scaffolds** |
| Ramón | Spanish is L1.* Syntax is difficult in writing. Vowel sounds in Spanish are substituted for vowel sounds in English. Getting the "gist" of a selection and determining main idea is difficult. How to elaborate on ideas in writing needs support. | | | |
| Chou | Vietnamese is L1. Syntax is difficult in writing. Needs additional help to elaborate and support main ideas in writing. | | | |
| Luz | Tagalog is L1. Has adapted well to the English curriculum. Needs support in elaboration of ideas in writing. | | | |
| Aída | Spanish is L1. Comprehension of main ideas is difficult. Elaboration of main ideas in writing needs support. | | | |

* L1 refers to the student's primary language or the language the student speaks the most often.

an interesting, compelling activity that requires at least two people to complete, and that they understand what they have to do as active participants.

Another structure that supports a dyad is the *think-pair-share* strategy (Kagan & Kagan, 1992), described previously in this section. This structure, after the teacher models it, provides opportunities for students to think about what they know individually, then pair with a partner to clarify thoughts and assumptions, and finally to share ideas the pairs have discussed. In the *think part* of this structure, give students 2 to 3 minutes to think individually and then jot down their thoughts about answering the question, or solutions to a problem or conflict. In the *pair part* of the structure, two students discuss thoughts each has had in response to the prompt. Give students 2 to 4 minutes to do this.

Next, in the *share part* of the structure, each pair shares the ideas they have discussed with the entire class. As suggested earlier, each sharing of ideas should be new or novel to avoid repetition of ideas. The teacher should use prompting questions to encourage pairs of students to clarify or extend their ideas when necessary. Record all student responses on chart paper for future reference as well as to preserve the thoughts of the group. This structure can occur anywhere in the lesson.

You can structure a triad in a kind of *round robin* talking structure (Kagan & Kagan, 1992) whereby students take turns speaking, must actively listen, and need to be able to paraphrase what others have said as well as extend the discussion. This type of triad can start with a question or prompt that is related to the content being taught. You can give each triad a different question or a different problem to solve. The first student suggests an answer to the question or the problem. The second student paraphrases what the first student suggested and either agrees or disagrees but must explain his or her response. The third student paraphrases what both students have suggested as solutions to the problem and adds a response. Once again, you have to model the process so the participants understand what they have to do in order to participate and answer the question or suggest a solution to a problem. After all three students have shared their viewpoints, the group prioritizes solutions or responses and shares with the entire class. Each group member has a responsibility in the group process. One student must facilitate the group process, one student records responses, and the third student shares the group's responses with the class. If you give more than one question or problem prompt to the same group during the same class period, rotate roles (facilitator, recorder, reporter), including who shares first in the round robin.

Triads can also include writing. In a *write around*, one student begins a response to a question or problem solution. The second adds to or extends the response. The third takes the ideas put forth by the first two students and concludes the argument or answer. The group then discusses the response they have written, works together to clarify their ideas, and then shares with the class. Sharing can be done in a carousel fashion. Each group tapes on the wall its response recorded on the large chart paper. Triads then circulate the room to read all of the group responses. Triads may respond to the postings; however, responses must include positive comments as well as suggestions for clarity of ideas. At the next level, if appropriate, the class can discuss responses. When appropriate, and especially if the class is linguistically diverse, precede the writing with the K part of a KWL session whereby students share what they know or think they know about the issue or concept about which they will be writing (Ogle, 1998, in Tierney & Readance, 1999). Figure 4.7 shows a sample KWL chart.

**FIGURE 4.7** Sample KWL Chart

| What I Know or Think I Know | What I Want to Know or Wonder About | What I Have Learned |
|---|---|---|
| | | |

***Increasing English Language Learners' Participation.*** You can give English language learners (ELLs) the opportunity to hear academic language in authentic contexts while engaged in either dyads or triads. The more often they participate, the more adept they become at understanding not only the group structure but also the kinds of language used when involved in a group structure. However, for ELLs who are unsure about the language required for active participation in the grouping structures and the content the course requires of them, you will need to create a group for them and directly facilitate their language. Teach them the language structures: (1) how to say they agree or disagree; (2) how to begin to express their own opinions; (3) how to look for and use support from text or other sources; and (4) how to question text, authors, concepts, ideas, and sources. Specifically teach your ELLs the functions of classroom language such as agreeing or disagreeing, problem solving, evaluating, questioning, and describing (Gibbons, 1993). Develop a list of all the phrases they can use when involved in group structures, and post the phrases and sentences visibly to make them readily accessible for students to reference while working in dyads, triads, or small groups. Using strategies such as these, in which task expectations are clear, develops an inclusive atmosphere in which each student can feel like an important member. This approach will foster a sense of Belonging and draw students into your lessons (Brendtro et al., 2002).

**FIGURE 4.8** Sample Chart for Standards of Behavior

| WAYS TO SHOW THAT PARTICIPATION IN YOUR GROUP IS ACTIVE AND PRODUCTIVE | |
|---|---|
| **What You and I Will Hear** | **What You and I Will See** |
| Encouragement such as "That was a great answer . . . ," or "I like that idea. . . ."<br>"I agree with . . . because. . . ."<br>"I disagree with . . . because. . . ."<br>"What would happen if we . . .?" | Group members looking at each other<br>Group members having their heads together to listen to others in the group<br>Heads nodding in agreement or shaking in disagreement |

***Assessment of Group Performance.*** The assessment component makes dyads, triads, projects, group research papers, or any other grouping structure successful. Students should assess their own performance and the performance of the other members of the group. The teacher also needs to assess group performance. The following can be helpful in the assessment process.

After having modeled the behavior expected in the group, tell students that you need their help to describe the norms for active participation. As students share what they think the norms should be, categorize student responses into either the things you will hear or the things you will see as you monitor group process and participation. Write student responses on chart paper and post them visibly for all students. Figure 4.8 offers a format for written responses.

This list becomes the standard for behavior and you should frequently refer to it to keep students focused on the expectations for group participation. The same list becomes the criteria both the teacher and students use to evaluate the performance of the group and its members. Student cooperation in assessment can foster a spirit of Generosity, as described in the Circle of Courage. Learning to help others greatly increases self-esteem and self-worth. There is a responsibility to consider the welfare of everyone in the group (Brendtro et al., 2002).

Figure 4.9 illustrates another way to encourage self-reflection on the part of students with regard to participation and contributions to the group process. Either the teacher may use this type of open-ended assessment of expected behaviors for productive group participation to evaluate the group, or individual students may assess the quality of their own participation in a group. If the teacher and students use the same evaluation instrument, discussions about group performance can be more constructive because both will be talking about the same standards for participation. If students have helped develop the assessment standards, once again discussions about performance will have more meaning for them.

**FIGURE 4.9** Sample Student Self-Assessment Chart

| **Group Evaluation** | |
|---|---|
| Name of the Group: ______<br>Date: ______<br>Task: ______<br>Evaluator: ______ | |
| Things we did well as a group and why: | Things we could do better as a group and why: |

## Participation of English Language Learners in Inquiry

If you know the level of language acquisition of students in English, you will be able to provide appropriate scaffolds to support their choices, thinking, and learning in the inquiry process. ELLs will need support in how to generate topics. At first, the teacher guides student thinking as well as the topics they select. Using information from the interest inventory (Figure 4.4 in Section 2 of this chapter), you can begin the brainstorming by suggesting some questions you developed based on inventory data.

Provide ELLs with opportunities to sketch what they are investigating and then writing to describe what they are investigating in detail. Figures 4.10 and 4.11 provide examples of support mechanisms you may want to use to assist English language learners in identifying and then planning their inquiry projects.

Using these strategies to assist students to develop competence will help you provide your students with multiple ways to access what is being taught. These

**FIGURE 4.10** Sample Support Mechanism for Defining an Inquiry Project

| **Sketching What I See** |
|---|
| Name: ______ Date: ______<br>What the weather was like (outside) ______ |
| Use the space below to sketch what you see. Label your sketch. Under your sketch, list how the object of your sketch is connected to your question. |

FIGURE 4.11 Sample Support Mechanism for Planning an Inquiry Project

**Planning Sheet for My Inquiry**

Name: ______________________________ Date: ______________

My Question(s):

What I need to do first: ______________________________

______________________________

______________________________

Things I will need: ______________________________

______________________________

______________________________

Draw what happened: ______________________________

______________________________

______________________________

List what you observed and why you think it is important: ______________________________

______________________________

______________________________

strategies will support a teacher's efforts to help each student reach Mastery. All students can learn if given opportunities for success in ways that work for them. In this view of Mastery, success becomes a possession of the many, not of the privileged few (Brendtro et al., 2002).

## SECTION 4: TECHNOLOGY AS AN INSTRUCTIONAL TOOL

In the world today, technology plays an important role as a tool for school, work, and in our personal lives. Teachers need to prepare students for using and applying technology in effective ways for accessing current and relevant information,

organizing and interpreting data, communicating with people globally, and publishing or presenting their ideas in a professional way. As a teacher, you must be prepared to support students in their use of technology by providing the tools, resources, and opportunities for effective use of these tools in your classroom.

## ISTE Student Foundation Technology Standards

The International Society for Technology in Education (ISTE) published standards (2000) for the use of technology for students, teachers, and administrators (www.iste.org). The following section will discuss integrating the National Educational Technology Standards (NETS) for Students into the secondary classroom. The ISTE groups student foundation technology standards in the following broad categories:

1. Basic operations and concepts
2. Social, ethical, and human issues
3. Technology productivity tools
4. Technology communications tools
5. Technology research tools
6. Technology problem-solving and decision-making tools

The ISTE has developed profiles of expected student performance for grades 9 through 12. It would be helpful to you as a preservice teacher to refer to the NETS student standards on the ISTE web site when planning lessons for the classroom. Technology should not be an isolated topic but integrated into lessons, activities, and units that you plan for student learning experiences. In order to be prepared for the integration of technology in teaching and learning activities, teachers will need to be proficient in the following areas:

1. Technology operations and concepts
2. Planning and designing learning environments and experiences
3. Teaching, learning, and the curriculum
4. Assessment and evaluation
5. Productivity and professional practice
6. Social, ethical, legal, and human issues

Educators have found the use of technology in teaching and learning matches well with models using project-based learning and student-centered activities. The active involvement of students in problem solving and higher-level thinking processes can lead to desirable skills for their future careers. The management of these environments requires the use of instructional strategies and planning that lead to effective uses and desirable outcomes.

***Social and Ethical Use.*** ISTE NETS for Students and for Teachers both include a standard focusing on the social, ethical, and legal use of equipment, software, and materials. Be sure to review fair use guidelines and be aware of the school and district acceptable use policies (AUP). These contain specific information regarding copyright infringement, harassment, privacy, and software piracy. Stanford University Library offers a comprehensive list of resources on copyright and fair use (http://fairuse.stanford.edu/internet). Teachers should require a reference list or bibliography including listing sources of information, graphics, and photographs on all student projects. You can find the American Psychological Association and the MLA guidelines on the Internet (www.columbia.edu/cu/cup/cgos/idx_basic.htm). It is a good idea to provide an example sheet of the format you would like your students to use.

*Netiquette* is a term used to describe expectations for behavior in online environments. Ask students to review some resources and facilitate class discussions on social behavior related to technology use. At this time, have students help develop a list of rules and consequences for inappropriate use of technology and online tools to be posted in the classroom for quick reference. If the rules and expectations are clear, you will have fewer problems with behavior. If they are not clear, the students will be more likely to challenge and test the system.

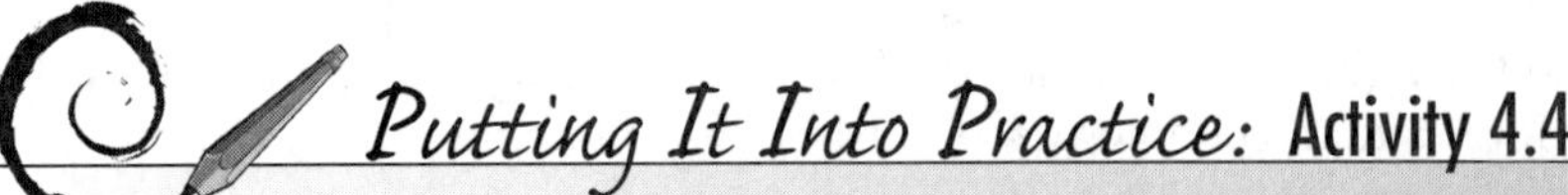

### Putting It Into Practice: Activity 4.4

Select a local school in a district in which you will be placed for fieldwork and investigate that district's fair use guidelines and acceptable use policies for technology. Prepare a short executive summary on the selected school's policies. Be certain to include information on copyright infringement, harassment, privacy, and software piracy. Conclude your report with thoughts on how you will explain them to students and build these policies into your own classroom rules.

## Technology Management Strategies

Many schools have computers in the classroom and often provide computer labs that teachers can reserve for additional use with their classes. Both options offer effective environments for using technology, but the management strategies differ. Investigate the resources and environments available to you at your school and plan accordingly.

***Computer Labs.*** A lab offers the opportunity for students to learn a new software program as a group, introduce a project, or complete activities that are on a short time frame. There are usually rules posted and log-in procedures required, so you should check ahead of time to be prepared for efficient use of lab time. Be sure to enforce the lab rules and leave the lab in good order when you are finished. It is a good idea to review directions and activities with students beforehand in order to save time and avoid confusion when you enter the lab. Give students a task sheet and specific directions and plan for what they will do if they have wait time in accessing resources.

Teachers often use a web page to post links and information about an assignment. Projection devices are usually available in the computer lab for demonstrations. Practice the use of these tools ahead of time so you are confident about their use when you present to the class. Allow adequate time for saving, logging off, and cleanup. Consider the following list of questions in preparing your lesson in the computer lab:

- Will students be working in teams?
- Will they need materials such as disks, texts, notes, and charts to supplement the use of computers?
- What should they do if they need assistance or have computer problems in the lab?

***Classroom Computers.*** In contrast to a computer lab, classroom computers offer easy access and flexibility in the use of computers for activities. Your planning and organization should take into consideration the ratio of students per computer, resources available on each computer, and access provided to networks.

If using cooperative groups, make sure you have clearly assigned roles and responsibilities before the groups begin working. Designating which students are going to be on the computer and for what purpose or period of time helps keep them on task.

You can plan a signup sheet, time schedule, or rotation to accommodate all students or groups accessing the technology they need for activities. You can also use these organizational tools for checking out technology devices such as cameras, portable keyboards, probes, and scanners. Give students an assignment sheet with directions for how and when they access the technology, the task, and a time line for completion of activities. Consider the following list of questions in preparing your lesson in the classroom setting:

- Will you be teaching groups of students when others are on the computers or be available to students during computer time?
- What will students do if they have a question or problem at the computer?
- How will you control noise and monitor use of equipment, completion of tasks, cleanup, computer breakdown, and materials such as printing supplies?
- What will you do if the network is down or student files are lost?

## Software Applications

Many types of software can be used to support secondary curriculum. Some software applications are general tools that students can use across all curriculum areas. For example, a *basic library of software* for a classroom or school computer network usually includes word processing, database, spreadsheet, email, Internet browser, desktop publishing, graphics, and multimedia programs. *Specialized software* for content curriculum areas can be identified for a grade level or department to supplement curriculum areas and is specific to the needs of students. Examples of types of software packages include simulation, drill and practice, tools for analysis, and tutorials. Libraries or media centers usually make *reference software* available for students to use in searching for resources on specific topics. In addition, the school network often provides *teacher productivity software* for attendance and grading.

Technology can support evaluation and assessment for students. Grade-management programs assist teachers in managing grades and reporting. Some online programs and resident software programs offer the ability to post grades online with password protection. Be cautious of laws and policies that may determine how to handle this. *Digital portfolios* are also becoming a popular form of student assessment; however, criteria and evaluation rubrics need to be developed. You also need to consider storage and access privileges for student work when using this type of assessment.

***Multimedia.*** Video technology is expected to dominate the twenty-first century. Digital cameras and editing software are becoming a common resource in schools and labs. Students can create digital reports, documentaries, and portfolios of their work.

Multimedia, by definition, involves the use of computers to present a combination of text, graphics, color, video, animation, and sound in an integrated way. "Multimedia provides students with a powerful medium of communication and offers students new insights into organizing, synthesizing, and evaluating information" (Ivers & Barron, 1998, p. 2). The use of multimedia dramatically changes the way students can explore information and investigate topics. Publishing multimedia products over the Internet provides the added dimension of allowing a distant audience to view students' work.

Many software programs exist for creating multimedia presentations. Students can incorporate topics and threads as bullets enhanced by graphics, photos, movies, text, and sound. They can publish their products on the Internet or on a video or CD-ROM for distribution and presentation. These products are becoming powerful tools to support learning and incorporate real-world experiences into secondary as well as college classrooms.

Laser technology has evolved over the past decade. Teachers have used laser discs and players as supplementary materials for enhancing the curriculum by incorporating a combination of video and still images. Some laser discs come with a controlling software program that integrates the use of the computer with the resources stored on the laser disc. Other laser discs are a compendium of resources in much the same way as a set of encyclopedias. Compact discs, or CDs, became a valuable resource for storage and sharing information. Though not having the capacity of laser discs, CDs can easily hold projects created by students and can be "burned" at a very low cost. Digital video device (DVD), high-quality video, music, and other resources can be intermixed and accessed at high speed. The resources are searchable and you can use clips in multimedia.

## The Internet

The Internet offers resources to supplement classroom materials and provides access to real-world connections, primary source documents, and virtual environments. Many textbook publishers maintain web sites with discussions, drills, and templates for use with curriculum materials. Online collections of lesson plans can be found on most topics and grade levels. One of many excellent resources is the Blue Web'n site, sponsored by Pacific Bell Knowledge Network (www.kn.pacbell.com/wired/bluewebn/index.html). This page provides a searchable database of lessons and hot lists of resources.

Students researching the Internet for information need to develop the important skill of evaluating web sites. As mentioned previously, ISTE provides a rubric on its web site, and other rubrics can be found on Kathy Schrock's Guide for Educators (http://school.discovery.com/schrockguide/assess.html). These may be good resources for you as a preservice teacher. You may want to design a lesson for your own students, asking them to pick a site that demonstrates effective use or reliable sources for them. Ask your students to justify their decisions. Practice in evaluating sites will lead to good judgment in selecting resources for their projects.

***Webquests, Filamentality, Web Page Design.*** A *WebQuest* (www.webquest.sdsu.edu) is a model of an Internet-based inquiry lesson that utilizes online resources. The model, developed by Bernie Dodge and Tom March at San Diego State University, has spread all over the world and examples can be found for any curriculum topic

### Putting It Into Practice: Activity 4.5

Visit a district or regional educational software preview center or Internet site that provides reviews of software titles. Make a list of the software available at your site and the resources available to support your content area. Identify publishers of textbooks and check their web sites and materials for additional supplementary technology resources. Evaluate the software using a rubric such as the form ISTE provides on its web site.

area. *Filamentality* is an online tool for easily creating WebQuests and other formats of Internet-based lessons.

You may want to look into *web page design* for the future. The Global Schoolnet Foundation and the ThinkQuest organization have sponsored web page competitions to inspire teachers and students to publish their projects on the Internet. Cyberfair projects are based on community collaborations in curriculum areas. ThinkQuest offers students and teachers opportunities to collaborate on curriculum topics and develop Internet resources to share with the global community.

Some schools and districts require class or teacher web pages. If you plan to develop a class web page, take time to review other school and class web pages and evaluate the desirable outcomes. It is important to consider how much time it will take to keep the page up to date and have information available in an easy-to-find format.

***Distance Learning.*** Tools on the Internet are available to support a variety of learning experiences for your students. Email, list servs, chat rooms, and threaded discussions are a few you may want to utilize. Each of these tools requires the teacher to set and organize guidelines. If your students are using email, identify how it will best support the projects you have planned. Require students to copy you on emails related to projects or prewrite and submit important communication information. This will help them develop effective skills and lead to success in the responses they request. Closely examine any online tools ahead of time to make sure they are appropriate for the grade or subject you are teaching. Also check to make sure students are invited to participate in the online environment you have identified. Some require permission for student participation in a listserv, chat room, or other environment.

The most important consideration when selecting technology for your classroom is what tools will best support teaching and learning. How will the use of technology address student learning styles, instructional goals, and contribute to student understanding? By using effective technology integration strategies and careful, thoughtful organization and planning, technology can motivate and empower students to think more critically and engage in more meaningful learning. Teachers should plan for periodic professional development in technology on a regular basis to stay current with advancements and new developments in software.

## SECTION 5: CHAPTER SUMMARY AND REFLECTION

In this chapter you have had the opportunity to explore a range of instructional strategies along the teacher-centered, student-centered continuum. One goal of this chapter has been to reinforce the notion that the continuum of teacher-centered to student-centered methodologies is just that, a continuum. The skilled teacher can use the most appropriate strategy along this continuum to meet the needs of students and assist them in obtaining stated goals.

This chapter has also offered guided activities that require you to observe identified strategies in practice and analyze their effectiveness in reaching learning objectives. This chapter has started your process of reflecting on the value of all strategies as measured by their effectiveness in student learning, and understanding that matching the right instructional strategy with your lesson objectives is critical to student learning.

Section 3 introduced techniques for modifying the instructional strategies presented in the previous sections, to help meet the needs of all students in your

## A Closer Look

Take a look at the INTASC Principles 3, 4, and 6 and their key dispositions in **Instructional Resource A.** Each of these will assist you in developing a strong repertoire of techniques that will serve you well in your career.

class. You need to develop a broad understanding of the diverse needs of the learners, including English language learners, in your classroom and provide them with opportunities to access your course material. As school demographics continue to change, these skills become increasingly critical to your success as a teacher.

Finally, Section 4 presented an overview of technology as a tool to help your students reach their learning goals. As you proceed through this text, you will be asked to build or reinforce your skills in applying technology to the work you do in your own classrooms.

As you move into the next chapter on developing unit and lesson plans, keep in mind that instructional strategies and assessment must match as you craft effective lesson plans. Experience with the tools of our profession will help you develop the skills you need in your own teaching.

## References


Anderson, J. (1990). *Cognitive psychology and its implications* (3rd ed.). New York: W. H. Freeman.

Anderson, L., & Block, R. (1987). Mastery learning models. In M. J. Dunkin (Ed.), *International encyclopedia of teaching and teacher education* (pp. 58–67). New York: Pergamon.

Ausubel, D. P. (1968). *Educational psychology: A cognitive view.* New York: Holt, Rinehart and Winston.

Bandura, A. (1986). *Social foundations of thoughts and action: A social cognitive theory.* Englewood Cliffs, NJ: Prentice Hall.

Bandura, A. (1989). Social cognitive theory. In R. Vasta (Ed.), *Annals of child development* (Vol. 6, pp. 1–60). Greenwich, CT: JAI Press.

Beyer, B. K. (1987). *Practical strategies for the thinking of thinking.* Boston: Allyn and Bacon.

Beyer, B. K. (1997). *Improving student thinking: A comprehensive approach.* Boston: Allyn and Bacon.

Bloom, B. S., et al. (1984). *Taxonomy of educational objectives.* Boston: Allyn and Bacon.

Borich, G. D. (2000). *Effective teaching methods* (4th ed.). Upper Saddle River, NJ: Merrill.

Brendtro, L. K., Brokenleg, M., & Bockern, S. V. (2002). *Reclaiming youth at risk: Our hope for the future.* Bloomington, IN: National Education Service.

Corkill, A. (1992). Advanced organizers: Facilitators of recall. *Educational Psychology Review, 4,* 33–67.

Costa, A. L. (Ed.). (1985). *Developing minds: A resource for teacher thinking.* Alexandria, VA: Association for Supervision and Curriculum Development.

Council of Chief State School Officers (1992). Model standards for beginning teacher licensing, assessment, and development: A resource for state dialogue. Washington, DC: Author. www.ccsso.org/content/pdfs/corestrd.pdf

Eggen, P. D., & Kauchak, D. P. (1996). *Strategies for teachers: Teaching content and thinking skills* (3rd ed.) Boston: Allyn and Bacon.

Gibbons, P. (1993). *Learning to learn in a second language.* Portsmouth, NH: Heinemann.

Good, T., & Brophy, J. (1994). *Looking in classrooms* (6th ed.). New York: HarperCollins.

Good, T., & Grouws, D. (1987). Increasing teachers' understanding of mathematical ideas through in-service training. *Phi Delta Kappan, 68,* 778–783.

Goodlad, J. I. (1979). *What schools are for* (2nd ed.). Bloomington, IN: Phi Delta Kappa Educational Foundation.

Graphic Organizer Home Page (2003). Retrieved August 19, 2003, from www.graphic.org

Halcomb, E. L. (1999). *Getting excited about data: How to combine people, passion and proof.* Thousand Oaks, CA: Corwin Press.

Hensen, K. T. (1996). *Methods and strategies for teaching secondary and middle schools.* White Plains, NY: Longman.

Hoetker, K., & Ahlbrand, W. (1964). The persistence of the recitation. *Educational Research Journal, 6,* 145–167.

International Society for Technology in Education (ISTE) (2000). *National educational technology standards for students: Connecting curriculum & technology.* Eugene, OR: ISTE.

International Society for Technology in Education (ISTE) (2002). *National educational technology standards for teachers: Preparing teachers to use technology.* Eugene, OR: ISTE.

Ivers, K. S., & Barron, A. E. (1998). *Multimedia projects in education: Designing, producing, and assessing.* Englewood, CO: Libraries Unlimited.

Joyce, B., Weil, M., & Calhoun, E. (2003). *Models of teaching* (7th ed.). Boston: Pearson Allyn and Bacon.

Kagan, S., & Kagan, L. (1992). *Cooperative learning structures.* Malibu, CA: Kagan Cooperative.

Lindsley, O. R. (1991). Precision teaching's unique legacy from B. F. Skinner. *Journal of Behavioral Education Analysis, 25*(1), 21–26.

Moore, K. D. (1999). *Middle and secondary school instructional methods.* Boston and New York: McGraw-Hill College.

Oakes, J., & Lipton, M. (1999). *Teaching to change the world.* Boston: McGraw-Hill College.

Ogle, D. (1998). In R. Tierney & J. Readance (Eds.). (1999). *Reading strategies: A compendium.* Boston: Allyn and Bacon.

Orlich, D. C., Harder, R. J., Callahan, R. C., & Gibson, H. W. (2001). *Teaching strategies: A guide to better instruction* (6th ed.). Boston and New York: Houghton Mifflin.

Rowe, M. B. (1974a). Relation of wait time and rewards to the development of language, logic, and fact control: Part two, rewards. *Journal of Research in Science Teaching, 11*(4), 291–308.

Rowe, M. B. (1974b). Wait time and rewards as instructional variables, their influence on language, logic, and fate control: Part one, wait time. *Journal of Research in Science Teaching, 11*(2), 81–94.

Rowe, M. B. (1978). Wait, wait, wait. *School science and mathematics, 78,* 207–216.

Sirotnik, K. (1983). What you see is what you get: Consistency, persistence, and mediocrity in classrooms. *Harvard Educational Review, 53*(1), 16–31.

Steffe, L., & Gale, J. (Eds.). (1995). *Constructivism in education.* Hillsdale, NJ: Erlbaum.

Tishman, S., Perkins, D. N., & Jay, E. (1995). *The thinking classroom: Learning and teaching in a culture of thinking.* Boston: Allyn and Bacon.

Tobin, K. (1980). The effect of an extended wait-time on science achievement. *Journal of Research in Science Teaching, 17,* 469–475.

Villa, R., & Thousand, J. (1992). *Creating an inclusive school.* Alexandria, VA: Association for Supervision and Curriculum Development.

Vygotsky, L. (1978). *Mind in society.* Cambridge, MA: Harvard University Press.

Wolfe, P. (2001). *Brain matters: Translating research into classroom practice.* Alexandria, VA: Association for Supervision and Curriculum Development.

Wulf, K. M., & Shane, B. (1984). *Curriculum design.* Glenview, IL: Scott, Foresman.

# Chapter 5

# Unit and Lesson Plans

INTASC Principle 1: The teacher understands the central concepts, tools of inquiry, and structures of the discipline(s) he or she teaches and can create learning experiences that make these aspects of subject matter meaningful for students.

**Key Disposition**

- The teacher realizes that subject matter knowledge is not a fixed body of facts but is complex and ever-changing. She/he seeks to keep abreast of new ideas and understandings in the field.

INTASC Principle 7: The teacher plans instruction based upon knowledge of subject matter, students, the community, and curriculum goals.

**Key Dispositions**

- The teacher values both long term and short term planning.
- The teacher believes that plans must always be open to adjustment and revision based on student needs and changing circumstances.
- The teacher values planning as a collegial activity.

## INTRODUCTION TO THE CHAPTER

This chapter will help you put into practice the strategies for assessment and instruction we have explored in previous chapters. On the surface, the process of planning unit and lesson plans may appear to be simple, and in the past many have perceived it that way. This chapter, however, approaches planning as a complex task and as one of the most important elements in helping students achieve Mastery in a content area. In order to help you look at planning from this perspective, this chapter addresses the following issues. Section 1's focus on planning for instruction begins with considering your students' backgrounds to help prepare for their instructional needs. It includes suggestions for assessing your students' skills and their attitudes regarding both the subject matter and school in general. These will help you engage students in your lessons. Next, this section examines the different levels of planning and the need to align all goals and objectives with district and state content standards. Finally, we address how to make decisions on course goals and critical concepts your students must know in order to be skilled users of the content.

Section 2 describes the process to plan for instruction. It explores course, unit, and lesson plan goals. We discuss lesson objectives in terms of cognitive, psychomotor, word, and affective outcomes including how to determine the assessment task to evaluate student work. The section also identifies the importance of supporting students throughout the lesson. Section 2 concludes with descriptions of unit and lesson plans and activities that will help you gain experience in these essential teaching skills.

Section 3 examines the importance of differentiating instruction within the lesson. We include it with this planning chapter because it is an essential aspect of crafting as well as implementing lesson plans. You will be able to apply your previous learning about assessment and instructional strategies to the knowledge and skills you learn in this chapter. They are at the heart of being able to create powerful learning experiences that will enable your students to acquire the skills and knowledge to be effective learners.

## SECTION 1: OVERVIEW OF INSTRUCTIONAL PLANNING

Experienced teachers understand that planning is a process focused on addressing the learning needs of students. When a teacher looks at planning simply as a way to lay out what will be done the next day in class to keep students busy, it oversimplifies a complex process and hence lessons rarely add in a meaningful way to a student's growth. Planning involves research, data gathering, and thinking about students and learning. On a broader scale, it may also involve observing, communicating, and collaborating with other teachers, a process called lesson study, proven to be a valuable model in the support and evaluation of lesson plan development and implementation (Byrum, Jarrell, & Munoz, 2003). In this process, keep in mind the Circle of Courage (Brendtro et al., 2002); it will help you frame your approach with students and develop learning activities in the best way to potentially meet all of a student's needs. Promoting a sense of Belonging by thinking about students first and getting to know their individual and creative talents is an important aspect of planning.

### Student Focus

Daily lesson plans usually start with cognitive objectives. In addition, as discussed in Chapter 3 on assessment, you need to consider incorporating affective, psychomotor, and word objectives. In this way you do not limit instruction and assessment to a focus on the learning of only content knowledge but rather broaden them to include the students' attitudes toward the topic (affective), their demonstrating/performing understanding of knowledge (psychomotor), as well as the appropriate integration of vocabulary (word). If you start with an understanding of who your students are, the experiences they have and have not had, as well as how they feel about the content you are teaching, you will be able to target cognitive objectives designed to teach students new content rather than content they already know (Open Society Institute and the International Reading Association, 2004). You will want to do some background work to obtain the following information to help you understand who you have in your classes:

- What cultures are represented in each of your classes?
- What languages do your students speak?
- Are there materials in your content area you can use that are representative of the cultures in your classes?
- Have any students received special services such as former English language development (ELD) or special education placements?
- Do any students have an individualized education plan (IEP) or an accommodation plan? If so, what are their unique objectives and accommodations?
- What prior experiences have students had with the subject matter you are teaching (course prerequisites or life experiences)?

Finding out who your students are helps you plan for challenges you may encounter during instruction. Plan for individual needs ahead of time rather than waiting to see whether something out of the ordinary occurs during instruction.

***Gauging Students' Entry-Level Attitudes and Skills.*** You need to obtain a sense of how your students learn and relate to the content area you are teaching. Once you understand these factors, you can be proactive in the planning process, determining ways to engage students and balance appropriate instructional strategies. Designing a brief student survey will give you information on a range of topics including:

- experiences your students have had in school;
- things they like to learn about in your content area;
- successes or failures they have experienced in learning the material you are teaching;
- learning style preferences, groups or individual learning; and
- types of homework assignments that help them learn more effectively.

Results of an informal survey can help you better understand your students to assist you in planning. You will have a clearer idea of how to design effective lessons focused on what you want students to learn and how you want them to learn it. Figure 5.1 contains a survey for a science class that could be adapted for other content areas.

The design of Figure 5.1 as an open-ended survey allows you to understand how your students process questions and respond to them in writing. You may also want to give a content area preassessment to ascertain the level of content knowledge and skill your students already have. For example, you might give students a short list of significant terms that will be used regularly in the course and find out what students think they know about the concepts these terms represent. You could also give students sample problems to solve that require them to use fundamental, underlying knowledge and skills needed to engage in your course work. Each of these examples helps assess your students' prior attitudes and skills as they begin your class. This information will assist you in developing or modifying plans to support student learning.

## Levels of Planning

As you begin the process of determining what content and skills you will be teaching your students, you need to consider various levels of planning. The first level is *course-long planning,* by which you will establish long-term course goals for student

**FIGURE 5.1** Sample Survey to Gauge Students' Entry-Level Attitudes and Skills

**Science Survey**

1. Is science important? Why? Why not?
2. How do you try to figure out what difficult words or terms mean when you are reading a science book?
3. Do you think science is important for everyone to learn? Why or why not?
4. How do we use science in our daily lives?
5. Why is it important to learn to think like a scientist?
6. Why is it important to combine reading and writing with labs or experiments in science?
7. Do you enjoy hands-on experiments?
8. Do you prefer to work in a small group or individually? Why?
9. Is the writing follow-up to experiments (the lab report) easy or hard for you? If easy, why? If difficult, why?
10. What do you feel you need in order to be a better learner in science?
11. What is easy for you in science?
12. What is hard for you in science?
13. Does homework help you learn science? Why? Why not?
14. What about school do you enjoy? Why?
15. What about school frustrates you? Why?

learning and identify *enduring understandings* that students should acquire by the end of a course of study. Teachers must consider what concepts, skills, and attitudes they want students to master by the end of the course.

The next level is *unit planning*, which breaks down the course goals into chunks of study that can last anywhere from 2 weeks to 2 months. Each unit will identify clear goals that you expect students to meet at its conclusion. When students meet the unit goals, they will move closer to meeting the established course goals.

Finally, there is *lesson planning*, which breaks down each unit into short lesson plans. For example, a 3-week unit would include approximately 15 daily lesson plans (some lesson plans may cover more than one day). Each lesson plan will be based on explicit objectives (cognitive, affective, psychomotor, and word) that identify what students will master and be able to do by the end of the lesson. When students can demonstrate mastery of the lesson plan objectives, they will have moved closer to meeting the established unit goals and course goals.

Design daily lesson plans to build on previous lesson plans just as each unit builds on previous units. Teachers provide students a better opportunity to achieve course goals if they have carefully prioritized, sequenced, and planned lessons. This does not mean that a plan is inflexible; rather, it means that a teacher maintains a long-term perspective on which directions students should be going in their learning and makes careful plans to meet those outcomes. A thoughtful teacher reflects carefully at the end of every lesson and unit to determine the necessary changes or adaptations for the next lesson or unit. Plans should be flexible to meet the needs of students and to accommodate new information teachers learn about their students during the teaching process. Always make these changes with the long-term goals in mind. Figure 5.2 provides a visual overview of the process.

## Determination of Course Goals

Deciding on the critical knowledge and skills your students must know in order to be proficient consumers and users of the content is the next step after getting to know your students. As a secondary teacher with subject area expertise, you will make decisions on goals, critical concepts, and skills students should learn in your classes. As you make these determinations, the following considerations should guide you in part.

1. **State and district content standards.** What do they list as critical concepts or skills for the subject matter or course you will be teaching?
2. **School or department goals.** Do any documents exist that identify course goals or critical concepts related to your content area?
3. **Textbook and other resources.** What concepts do these materials suggest as appropriate for the content area you are teaching?
4. **Your expertise and experience.** What do you consider important for students to learn in your content area? Think about the *enduring understandings*. What concepts lay a strong foundation to enable transfer of learning in your content area?

For example, if you teach social studies and you have decided, after reviewing all the suggested documents listed previously, that learning about the concept of power is a critical enduring understanding in order for students to be able to understand and reflect on history, then you may plan a unit that addresses the concept of power. We know that the concept of power may be studied over time in many ways because it permeates all aspects of life. However, you could focus on the manifestation and effects of power in the historical period(s) covered at your grade level. An example of a critical concept is "Power is the basis of all humankind's interactions with each

FIGURE 5.2 Unit and Lesson Planning

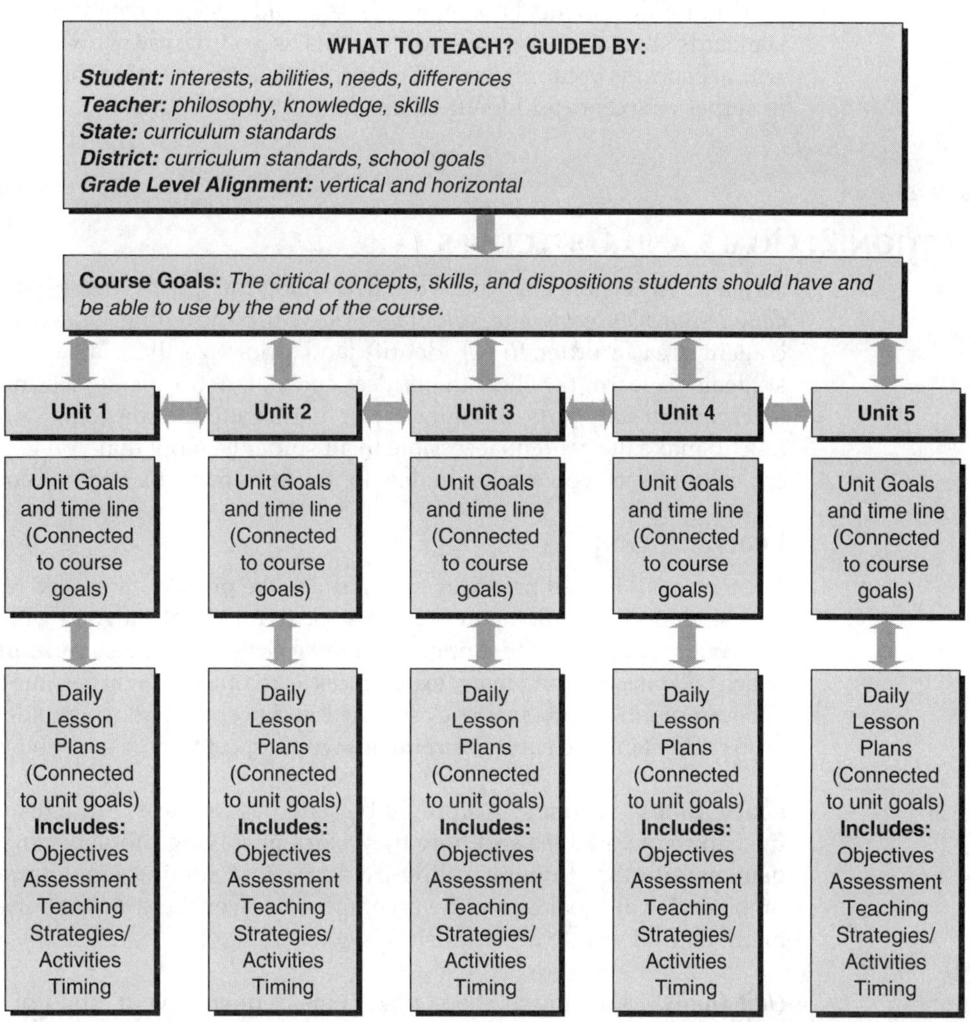


other." You could narrow the focus of the concept by concentrating on the forms power has taken in terms of structures and interactions within groups of people in society, again within the context of the era students are studying.

***Alignment with Content Standards.*** The planning process begins by thinking broadly about your subject area, examining the concepts identified in state or national content standards; district, school site, and department goals; and textbook and other materials. Then, you will need to decide which are the most important or critical and focus on those.

Keep in mind that a district working with its teachers and school community might have already developed alignment agreements that stipulate which critical concepts will be taught and where they will be taught in the curriculum. These agreements can include both horizontal and vertical alignment. Horizontal alignment is the sequencing of instruction across a common course or grade level, such as alignment across all U.S. history classes. Vertical alignment is the sequencing of instruction between grade levels. Examples may include alignment of curriculum through grades 9 through 12, all

English classes, or a discipline-based sequence: algebra, geometry, and algebra II. These curriculum documents have most likely already been aligned with the state content standards. You must use these documents as you narrow down and prioritize your critical concepts because you will be responsible for ensuring that your students meet or surpass the concepts identified in your part of the sequence.

## SECTION 2: GOALS AND OBJECTIVES

As stated in Section 1, as you work to develop the *specific course goals, unit goals,* and *daily lesson plan goals* and *objectives* you will be teaching, you must analyze your content area in order to (1) identify and prioritize the critical concepts for your students to learn; (2) align the critical concepts with the subject matter and grade level content standards for your state or district and the site goals; and (3) think about how to make the content accessible to all students. Now that you have identified the critical concepts, you can begin developing specific goals and objectives.

### Learning Goals

The term *goals* is used primarily to determine the purpose, aim, and rationale for what your students will be doing in your class. Goals are closely aligned with state standards. The concepts you have identified as *learning goals,* those most enduring and complex, which will take time and many experiences to accomplish, will become the course goals. For example, in a mathematics class, a critical concept or enduring understanding might be to understand the nature of variables with respect to problem solving.

***Course Goals.*** A *course goal* might be stated as follows: "Students will understand the nature of variables and how they work in solving problems and will be able to demonstrate that understanding by accurately solving single and multivariable problems." This goal cannot be accomplished over the course of one unit. In fact, it might take all year to accomplish this goal.

***Unit Goals.*** Looking at the course goals, sequence your units of instruction and establish *unit goals.* A first unit in an algebra course, for example, might be a review of basic math functions and how they relate to algebra. A second unit might focus on solving single-variable equations. You will determine the number of units in a course by how you conceptualize the units: thematically, chronologically, or by texts, and how many chunks you need in order to break down the more complex course goals. As you establish your *specific unit goals,* you will focus on the course goals. For example, a unit goal for the single-variable equations unit might be stated as follows: "Students will know and be able to demonstrate how to solve a single-variable equation." This unit goal directly links to the course goal of understanding the nature of variables in problem solving.

***Lesson Plan Goals and Objectives.*** The task for the teacher is, at this point, to develop *daily lesson plan goals* and *objectives* that when accomplished will lead to students mastering the unit goals. *Objectives,* drawn from the unit plan, focus on what students will do to acquire the necessary knowledge and skills. Objectives describe exactly what students will be able to do during a specific lesson, under certain conditions, and how they will demonstrate they understood and learned the objective. For example, the first lesson of the single-variable unit might include an introduction to variables and how they represent a quantity. A specific lesson plan objective might be stated as follows: "Students will be able to identify figures, from a group of figures, are the variables in a given set of equations"; or "Students will be able to solve a set of simple equations by substituting given numbers for the variables." These *lesson plan objectives* are specific to the day's lesson and are also aligned to unit and course goals. Notice that the wording of the goals and objectives identifies what students will be able to know, do, or be like.

> **A Closer Look**
>
> Chapter 3 reviewed Bloom's taxonomy in the section Considerations in Designing Assessment.

***Cognitive Goals and Objectives.*** Bloom's taxonomy can be useful in developing the language of goals and objectives and in determining the level of learning you are seeking.

For example, do you want recall level understanding or evaluation level? It is also helpful to start with the words "Students will be able to . . ." or "Students will . . ." as you write goals and objectives. This keeps the focus on what students' learning will actually look like, and it helps to clarify the specific skill, attitude, and knowledge you are seeking from your students.

When you have established your curricular priorities, you will know your cognitive goals and objectives for your students. Those goals and objectives are specific to the content area knowledge and skills, including the language needed to process the content material.

***Psychomotor Goals and Objectives.*** A teacher must also consider goals and objectives that are psychomotor, affective, and word. Psychomotor goals and objectives have to do with how students physically work or create in an environment. For example, in a biology class the teacher might design a unit goal that focuses on students' abilities to manipulate a microscope accurately. A math teacher might design a unit or course goal related to how a student manipulates a graphing calculator. An English teacher might implement a course goal that has to do with students creating a portfolio.

***Affective Goals and Objectives.*** Affective goals and objectives concern attitudes, beliefs, experiences, and working with others. For example, a course goal in math might be for students to develop a greater sense of confidence about working with abstract concepts. A Spanish lesson plan objective might be for students to work productively in small teams to develop a skit.

***Word Goals and Objectives.*** Word goals and objectives have to do with understanding and appropriate use and application of key vocabulary. For example, in a social studies class on democracy, a word objective might be to have students use these words in their writings, oral communication, and informal conversations in groups. Obviously the students need to know this is the teacher's objective and when and how the teacher will assess this knowledge (Roberts & Kellough, 2000).

***Using Goals and Objectives.*** In stating all four types of goals and objectives—cognitive, affective, psychomotor, and word—the teacher more likely will teach the skills related to each of the goals and objectives and will assess students' progress toward meeting these. If the teacher's objective is that students will work productively in teams in a Spanish class to develop a skit, then the teacher must also teach them what it means to be productive: how to deal with conflict and how to establish roles. It also means observing or using other forms of assessment to gauge students' success in meeting goals. Psychomotor, affective, and word goals and objectives become very important in helping to uncover skills that students need but are often taken for granted in our classes.

The Circle of Courage supports the holistic view of learning that includes psychomotor and social skills (Brendtro et al., 2002). Students will be better able to achieve Mastery if the teacher can identify the lack of skills that could potentially lead to frustration. By taking into consideration skills needing to be developed in all students, the teacher is more likely to be able to build self-esteem in all students, which in turn will better prepare them to meet the objectives.

***Content Standards.*** Once you have analyzed the skills you want your students to learn and the concepts you want them to master, you can more easily align the learning goals and objectives with the state or district content standards at the appropriate grade level. The idea is not to teach standards in isolation or as a "checkoff" approach, but rather to teach them as an integral part of the content. If the standards require that students know and be able to use the scientific method in investigations, writing, and problem solving, then ensure that the teaching of the scientific method is part of the lesson as a means to learning the cognitive objective rather than planning to teach a lesson on the scientific method. Standards are attainable if you make them an integral part of the teaching and learning process.

The web sites of various teacher organizations provide excellent information on content standards. Here is a list of five that you can use in planning your lesson and unit plans.

International Society for Technology in Education (ISTE)
www.iste.org

National Council for the Social Studies (NCSS)
www.ncss.org

National Council of Teachers of English (NCTE)
www.ncte.org

National Council of Teachers of Mathematics (NCTM)
www.nctm.org

National Science Teachers Association (NSTA)
www.nsta.org

## *Putting It Into Practice:* Activity 5.1

Use the sample activity chart in Figure 5.3 to gather planning information from your cooperating teacher. Find out the course goals and how they sequence the units of instruction.

**FIGURE 5.3** Sample Activity Chart Course and Unit Goals Information

Ask your cooperating teacher for the COURSE GOALS for students. Get samples of cognitive and affective goals that deal with the acquisition of knowledge and skills (these should be critical concepts).

| Cognitive and Language Goals | Affective Goals | Psychomotor Goals |
|---|---|---|
| | | |

Ask your cooperating teacher what units are planned for the school year. Get the names and length of units. If this is not available for the whole year, just gather as much information as you can. Star the unit(s) you will be involved in teaching during your student teaching experience.

Name of Unit
Unit length

Unit 1:

Unit 2:

Unit 3:

Unit 4:

Unit 5:

Unit 6:

Unit 7:

Unit 8:

Unit 9:

Unit 10:

Unit 11:

Unit 12:

Unit 13:

Ask your cooperating teacher about the *current* unit being taught. Find out the name, length, resources (materials), and goals of this current unit. If there are differentiated goals for different students (English language learners, for example), note the differences.

Current Unit

Name:

Length:

Resources:

Unit goals (cognitive and affective):

## Elements of Planning Instruction

Once you develop goals and objectives, plan backward to ensure that you are taking into consideration the necessary support mechanisms for student learning. Recall discussions in Chapter 3 on planning backward. Table 5.1 illustrates one way to conceptualize this.

Having identified the cognitive, psychomotor, word, and affective goals and objectives students should learn, you will need to identify the assessment task(s) used to measure student achievement of the critical concepts. If, for example, a critical concept is knowing how to use the writing process to develop a polished piece of writing, then an assessment tool might be assigning students a final essay to include all the work from each step of the writing process (prewriting, drafting, reader response, revision, editing, metacognition). This allows the teacher to evaluate a student's ability to use each step of the writing process as well as the finished

**TABLE 5.1** *Sample Chart for Support Mechanisms in Planning*

| Goal/Objectives (Critical Concept) | Assessments | Knowledge/Skills | Support Mechanisms (Scaffolds) Required |
|---|---|---|---|
| Students will be able to demonstrate the use of the writing process in a completed essay. | Final essay | How to:<br>1. use each step of the writing process<br>2. work in groups for feedback<br>3. plan and organize an essay | (examples)<br>• Pair with a partner to review steps.<br>• Review rules/procedures for working in groups.<br>• Demonstrate the steps in writing an effective essay. |
| | | OR | |
| Students will be able to identify and describe the immigration patterns in the United States from 1700 until the present. | Presentation | How to:<br>1. read primary source material<br>2. describe cause and effect<br>3. synthesize and organize data<br>4. demonstrate visual and oral communication skills<br>5. work effectively in groups | (examples)<br>• Teacher-led demonstration on how to approach primary materials.<br>• Review examples of cause and effect studied previously.<br>• Provide a practice exercise in breaking down data using graphs and charts.<br>• Model and list the skills in effective presentation.<br>• Review rules/procedures for working in groups. |

product (the essay). If a critical concept is understanding patterns of immigration to the United States from the 1700s to the present, then an assessment tool might be a group presentation in which students identify and explain these patterns.

***Necessary Skills.*** Following identification of critical concepts (goals) and assessment tasks, determine the necessary skills students must attain in order to learn the concepts and meet the demands of the assessment task. Given the concept of the writing process and the assessment task, students would need to learn the following knowledge and skills: (1) how to use each step of the writing process to develop and improve a piece of writing, (2) how to work effectively with other people, and (3) how to plan and organize an essay. Given the immigration example, students would need to acquire the following knowledge and skills: (1) how to read the primary source documents that relay demographic information about the U.S. population; (2) various immigration patterns and the causes and effects of those patterns; (3) how to develop a presentation by synthesizing and summarizing information; (4) how to use both visual and oral methods of communicating their information; and (5) how to determine the roles each member of the group will play.

It is often useful to think about yourself as a learner in your own content area. What do you have to do in order to be an efficient learner and teacher of English or social science? What kind of reading is necessary and what skills would you need in order to read that material? What kind of thinking? writing? oral language or discussion skills? observation skills? group dynamics skills? attitudes?

***Support Mechanisms.*** Now that you have identified the necessary skills, anticipate the scaffolds or learning support mechanisms necessary to meet the needs of your students, based on what you already know about them. For example, if you have students who are English language learners in your science class, model the strategy you want students to learn in order to write a coherent lab report. You will have to model the process of transferring what one sees into writing. That may mean that for a specific group of students, you demonstrate how to write a group lab report based on an actual experiment, walking students through the process step by step. Next, you may want to pair students so they can produce a lab report, teaching them how to work in pairs so both partners evenly assume the workload. You may also want to develop a rubric ahead of time that clearly describes the features expected of a quality lab report. Distribute the rubric to students before they write their lab reports to support the thinking and writing process.

When students are clear about the expectations, you can hold them accountable for their own performance through the appropriate assessment, such as the rubric. This sense of autonomy is an intrinsic motivator fostering Independence as described in the Circle of Courage (Brendtro et al., 2002). Importantly, in diverse classrooms do not expect less from some students than you expect from other students. Use your teaching skills to make the objectives achievable by all students.

Suppose, for example, you have a group of students that needs refinement of observation skills; that is, these students need to be able to be clear and specific about what they actually see in an experiment and then be able to display the data. Support this process by modeling how to look at what is actually happening and explicitly teaching ways to display data that can later be used in writing a lab report. There are several types of scaffolds to consider. Some students will require a variety of support mechanisms, whereas others will not need as much support or as many scaffolds to meet the expectations you have set for the class.

You may have students who are ready to exceed your expectations for a particular lesson. These students require a different kind of scaffolding; they need help in moving to a more challenging level of work. Examples of trying to meet this need may include asking those students to start the work without as much modeling or additional practice; complete the lab report as a multimedia report; or go further with the lab, analyzing or researching other features of the experiment that the rest of the class might not do. These kinds of scaffolds are not about giving *more* work to the students who need a challenge; rather, it is about providing them a *different* kind of work, *differentiating instruction*, that allows them to build on the skills and knowledge they already have achieved.

Once you have made these determinations, it is incumbent upon the teacher to provide the scaffolds or temporary supports for all students, which model through authentic activities what the expectations and tasks look and sound like. If you have gathered data on who your students are and what they already know, you can be much more efficient in meeting students where they are in terms of knowledge, skill, and confidence. Your instruction can build on these prior experiences and propel them toward content mastery in your subject area.

***Effective Lessons.*** Students will more easily master content if careful planning takes place (that is, when the use of a variety of learning scaffolds supports student learning; the teacher monitors the learning process while it is occurring; and the teacher provides students with corrective feedback). Students must develop content mastery in order to use the acquired knowledge to learn more challenging content in the next sequence. Good teachers ensure that their students acquire the language and the critical concepts necessary to master the content they are studying. This then positions students to master additional concepts in any content area (Cummins, 1980).

As noted in Chapter 3, content area mastery can be assessed in a variety of ways, including:

- authentic assessments in which teachers give students a problem to solve, and, in the problem-solving process, students demonstrate the understanding of the critical concepts taught;
- teacher-developed tests in which students apply critical concepts; and
- student presentations and demonstrations whereby they plan a project based on understandings of critical concepts and demonstrate mastery of learning.

Wiggins (1998) notes in his work on assessment that when students plan and present or demonstrate content in situations in which they are the experts, they master content at a much higher level. The work of Chamot and O'Malley (1994) validates that concept and adds that students can become experts when teachers facilitate the learning process; when students are researching and working in areas of extreme interest and application of academic knowledge; and when teachers provide them with corrective feedback during the learning process.

### A Closer Look

Section 2, Assessment of Student Understanding, of Chapter 3, contains several subsections that include more examples of authentic assessments.

## Unit Plan Development

Now that we have explored developing course, unit, and lesson goals and objectives, we will move on to a process to create actual unit plans. The following unit plan design method includes a suggestion for self-assessment and reflection for the teacher as part of the process:

1. State the grade level(s), content area/class, and unit topic and length (for example, the unit will last 13 classes; each class will be 60 minutes).
2. Consider the key facts about your students that you are incorporating as you plan. What are your students' learning needs, styles, and dispositions?
3. Consider your rationale for this topic/unit. In other words, what is important about it? Why does it matter? How does it fit into the overall scheme of this course and your course goals for the students?
4. Determine the specific goals and objectives for the unit you are working on (cognitive, affective, psychomotor, word). How do they align with state and district curriculum standards? What are the critical concepts? What will you be working to accomplish with just this unit (what do you expect the students to know, do, and be like long after this unit is over)? You should connect these with the course goals you identified, because they represent the stepping-stones to achieving those goals.
5. Determine assessment strategies you and the students will use to demonstrate achievement of each unit goal. What evidence will you have that students have met each unit goal? How will they have demonstrated it? Will the students value these assessments for relevance and authenticity? You should include a range of assessment types that are both summative and formative, including self-assessment by the student.
6. Consider the knowledge, skills, and scaffolds your students need in order to meet the expectations you have set. What teaching and learning experiences will equip students to demonstrate the targeted understandings? Organize these by thinking about what teaching and learning experiences you'll set up to get your students:
   a. *INTO the unit.* What will you do to hook your students, to draw on previous experience, and to build foundational knowledge or skills?
   b. *THROUGH the unit.* What will you do to scaffold students' learning as they develop the skills and acquire the knowledge associated with the unit goals and assessments? How will your instructional activities/experiences build on one another and create momentum? Are your approach and sequencing coherent?
   c. *BEYOND the unit.* How will you create closure for this unit and transition to the next? It is also about helping students to make the "global" connection to those things beyond the classroom. Think of culminating, synthesizing experiences.

   (*Note:* It is often helpful to set this up as a calendar so you can see the flow of the unit as you write specific information in each calendar block.)
7. Identify materials, resources, books, films, speakers, realia, field trips, and anything else you and the students will use over the course of the unit.
8. Carefully develop the individual lesson plans of your unit (focusing in on each calendar block). Each lesson plan should include information about objectives (cognitive, affective, psychomotor, and word), assessment (formative and summative), instructional strategies/steps, timing for each step, and, materials needed.
9. As you complete your unit plan, step back and assess your work. The following questions can help guide that self-assessment and reflection:

a. In what ways have you differentiated instruction and goals to meet the varying needs of your students (including your high achievers, English language learners, and struggling students)?
b. To what degree have you set up experiences for students that include reading, writing, oral language skills, and technology in your unit?
c. What strengths and possible limitations do you see in your plan?
d. What unanswered questions do you have about your plan, and whom can you work with to get your questions answered?

## A Closer Look

**Instructional Resource D** provides two completed unit plans, one in chemistry and a second in English language arts, to assist you as you begin learning how to design unit plans.

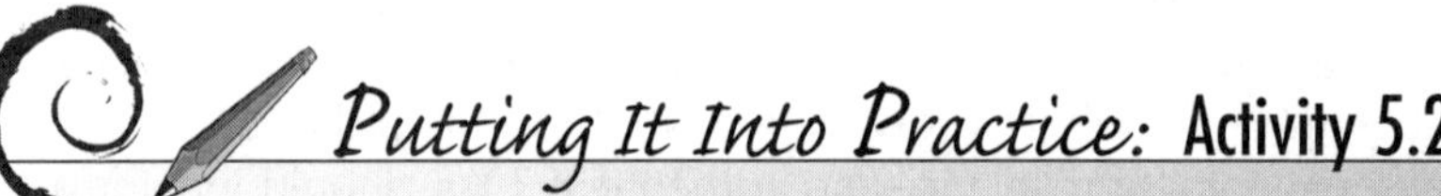

## Putting It Into Practice: Activity 5.2

Outline your own unit plan using the template provided in Figure 5.4. As mentioned previously, Instructional Resource D includes two completed sample unit plans for your review.

FIGURE 5.4 Sample Unit Plan Template

Step 1: State the grade level(s), content area/class, and unit topic and length.

Step 2: Decide what key facts about your students you need to take into consideration as you plan.

Step 3: Explain your rationale for this topic/unit.

Step 4: Identify both the specific goals and objectives for the unit (cognitive, affective, psychomotor, word) and how they align with state and district curriculum standards. Explain the critical concepts.

Step 5: List assessments (evidence) used to demonstrate success of unit goals and attainment of benchmarks.

Step 6: Describe teaching and learning experiences; the knowledge, skills, and scaffolds students need to meet the expectations you have set.

- INTO
- THROUGH
- BEYOND

Step 7: List materials and resources.

Step 8: Design lesson plans.

Step 9: Write your self-assessment and reflection.

***A Preservice Teacher Reflects on Planning.*** The following is a preservice teacher's reflection after working through the unit planning process the first time. Her reflections are often typical of a teacher's initial attempts with this process.

> When I first thought of unit planning, I imagined it to be something like planning a vacation—deciding where and when to go, how long to stay, what activities best suit everyone's wishes and when to do them, what modes of transportation to use, how much money is available to spend, how much food to bring, and so on. I can see there are definite connections between vacation and unit planning. Consider the "backward" approach to planning. I have learned that in unit planning, figuring out the modes of assessment prior to activities is crucial if I am to effectively meet the unit goals. Likewise, in planning a vacation, you first need to determine what modes of transportation are available before choosing activities. For example, exploring a distant island would be impossible without a plane or a boat, and imagine downhill skiing without those essential skis.
>
> There are, however, a number of differences between vacation planning and unit planning. I have realized that vacation planning, as much of a headache as it can be, seems much easier to do than unit planning! I do not remember the last time I have thought so intensely and invested so much passion and mental effort into anything; this unit plan was truly a challenge for me. I squeezed every ounce of my brain so hard that my gray matter turned white and went numb for a while. I spent a great deal of time and energy brainstorming and reading, analyzing, and researching my topic. I vaguely recall the long hours I worked on an interdisciplinary thesis in college, but this unit plan wins the prize hands down, and I am so much more proud of my efforts here than I ever was of any of my efforts in college.
>
> I have also learned that most students probably do not have a clue how much effort goes into teaching. I think I had a fair idea of the amount of work involved when I began the credential program, but in both high school and college, it was difficult for me to assess how much work the teachers actually put into teaching their unit coursework. For example, if a teacher is ineffective, I think a student naturally assumes little planning went into the lesson, and the more ineffective, the less planning involved; on the other hand, if a teacher is moderately to highly effective, lessons sometimes appear to be so fluid and flawless, I think a student could easily be fooled into believing far less effort and planning went into the lesson than in actuality. All in all, I know this first go-round in unit planning for me seemed slow, but hopefully planning will be easier for me as I move through my teaching career.

## Lesson Plan Development

After working through course goals, unit plan outlines, and sequencing, this section begins to address individual lesson plans. Though there are a variety of lesson plan designs, and your program may require a specific model, most include a set of common elements. Lesson plans reflect previous work a teacher has completed: identification of critical concepts, enduring understandings, course goals, unit goals, and the continuing alignment of each to district and state standards. Elements common to most lesson plans include goals and objectives, resources needed, an anticipatory set, procedures to follow, assessment strategies, adaptations to accommodate students, follow-up activities, and teacher reflection.

Section 2 has explored the identification of goals but only briefly described objectives to this point. Lesson plan objectives set the target for a lesson and provide the basis of decisions about other elements in the plan. Well-written objectives—the terms *behavioral, learning,* and *performance* describe them—identify observable student behaviors or actions, and teachers use them to make judgments about learning. Learning to write objectives, an important skill needed in the teaching profession, requires practice and experience to become accomplished in this aspect of the work. A well-written objective communicates clearly what the intended learning is in the lesson.

***Lesson Objectives.*** Lesson objectives describe what students do to form the basis for making a determination about their learning. Teachers develop objectives from unit plan goals and set a specific time in which they are to be achieved. They describe what students will be able to do during, or at the end of, a lesson that can be observed under certain conditions (e.g., given a diagram of the brain . . .) and to what degree (e.g., identify the five main . . .). In short, students will need to demonstrate their learning.

Consider these two example objectives:

1. The student will be able to understand the terms *neuron, axon, dendrites, neurotransmitter,* and *synapse.*
2. The student will identify and define the terms *neuron, axon, dendrites, neurotransmitter,* and *synapse.*

In the second example, the teacher could assess the learning of students by checking on what terms they identified and how they defined those terms. However, in the first example, it would be difficult for a teacher to assess understanding. Teachers learn what students know by specific tasks they perform to a set level. *Understanding,* as the assessable term, would not be possible for a teacher.

Verbs to consider using in writing cognitive objectives may include those in Table 5.2. Of course, you can use many other verbs to construct objectives. Your list will grow as you gain experience. The similarity of the verbs listed is that the teacher can assess each to find out whether the student achieved the intended learning of the lesson.

***Materials.*** Though seemingly a simple part of the lesson, more than one teacher has begun a lesson only to find the necessary equipment or materials not available or working properly. By creating a list of resource needs, you can do a quick check of your classroom to make certain everything is ready.

**TABLE 5.2** ***Verb Prompts for Writing Objectives***

| Cognitive | Affective | Psychomotor | Word |
|---|---|---|---|
| Apply (a rule) | Empathize | Perform | Incorporate |
| Demonstrate (use of) | Value | Demonstrate | Integrate |
| Describe | Communicate effectively | Illustrate | Use appropriately |
| Diagram | | | |
| Classify | | | |
| Construct | | | |
| Identify | | | |
| Locate | | | |
| Label | | | |
| Order | | | |
| Predict | | | |
| Solve | | | |

***Anticipatory Set.*** The next step in designing the lesson plan, to create an anticipatory set, will be based on several factors, including your knowledge of your students. What will "hook" them in? What connections to previous lessons should you consider? The anticipatory set is a short activity that helps students focus on the lesson about to be introduced. It could be a question such as "What is the strangest animal you have ever seen?" It could be a handout for students to review on evolution or prompts to be answered on the board. The anticipatory set assists in engaging learning from the beginning of the lesson.

***Procedures.*** Procedures describe what your role will be in teaching the lesson: how you will introduce the lesson, what types of instructional strategies you will use, and how you will bring closure to the session. As discussed in Chapter 4, Instructional Strategies, it is important to vary your teaching strategies as well as to make certain each is a good match for your identified student objectives. Additionally, procedures include specific information about what students will be doing during the lesson (group work, individual work, or other activities). Consider how to draw ideas together for students at the end of a lesson. In what ways will you provide feedback to students to correct their misunderstandings and reinforce their learning?

Some teachers will break down the various procedures and assign an estimated time to complete each part. A teacher needs to remain flexible in following these time estimates. Expect to make adjustments throughout a lesson, because the lesson plan is only a detailed outline of your expectations.

***Assessment Strategies.*** Because an entire chapter of this book has been devoted to assessment, the most important consideration in selecting your strategy is that the assessments are aligned to and match the objectives. You would not want to use a performance-based assessment to assess student learning of a finite list of terms and definitions. A short answer or matching quiz might be more appropriate. The goals of assessment should be to gauge whether students have met the objective and to inform them of what they have and have not learned. In addition, as discussed in Chapter 3, assessment should consist of both ongoing, more informal checks for understanding, referred to as formative assessment, as well as culminating assessments and activities, called summative assessment.

***Adaptations.*** As a part of the plan, you must identify what additional steps might be needed to adjust or scaffold information in order to enable all students access to the content and skills. We have discussed these strategies throughout the text and, in an effort to assist in your planning, devote Section 3 to this topic.

***Follow-Up.*** In each lesson you design you will need to provide students with the opportunity to practice what they have learned as well as knowledge and skills to be

### A Closer Look

The two sample lesson plans in **Instructional Resource E** include examples of both formative and summative assessment strategies.

assessed. At this time, do not introduce new material but instead offer reinforcement material that students can use to practice, enrich, or remediate the content or skills you have been teaching.

***Reflection.*** At the end of every lesson be sure to take time to review what happened. Identify those aspects of the lesson that went well and those that need to be adjusted to make the lesson more effective. Taking the time right after the lesson, or as close to the experience as possible, will prevent your repeating similar mistakes in the future. Reflective practice is one of the keys to becoming a successful teacher. Reflecting on

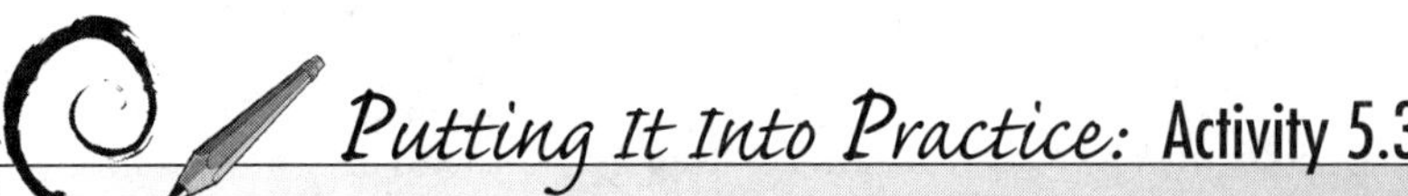

## *Putting It Into Practice:* Activity 5.3

Using the unit plan you designed in Putting It Into Practice Activity 5.2, select one of the goals you think would create a strong focus for a lesson. Next, follow the lesson plan template in Figure 5.5 to create a lesson plan. Don't forget to try to include all four types of objectives and appropriate formative and summative assessments for each goal. You should identify and describe what you would do in each component. If possible, design the lesson to be taught in your own class during your field experience.

FIGURE 5.5 Sample Lesson Plan Template

Title ____________ Subject Area ____________

Grade Level _______

| | Notes on Each Area |
|---|---|
| Lesson Goals: | |
| Objectives: | |
| Materials Needed: | |
| Anticipatory Set: | |
| Procedures: | |
| Assessment Strategies: | |
| Follow-Up: | |
| Reflections: | |

your lesson, as written and enacted, helps in becoming a reflective practioner. Now that you have read through the various steps in designing a lesson plan, it is time to attempt one yourself.

> **A Closer Look**
>
> **Instructional Resource E** provides example lesson plans based on the template provided. To judge the clarity of your plan, trade lessons with a colleague and see whether he or she would be able to implement it without clarifying any aspects with you.

## SECTION 3: DIFFERENTIATED INSTRUCTION

We have included a specific section on differentiated instruction in this chapter because it is a critical aspect of planning. A well-crafted lesson plan reflects considerable thought and includes strategies on engaging all students in the learning process. Knowing how to differentiate instruction to meet the needs of English language learners, struggling students, those with special needs, and students who require additional challenges does not mean that we water down the curriculum, add extra busy work, or ask students to engage in tasks that are do-able but do not teach content. The standards and expectations in a lesson remain the same for all students, including those with different needs. This section addresses specific ways to scaffold student learning and differentiate the instruction as well as practice to ensure student success. Although this section presents scaffolding in the context of its use for students who are English language learners, the same strategies work for all students who are struggling with content mastery.

### Scaffolding Techniques

Educators have categorized several types of scaffolds in terms of what teachers actually do to support student learning. This section covers each of the following types of scaffolds: (1) modeling, (2) contextualization, (3) metacognition, (4) bridging or activating background knowledge, (5) building background knowledge, and (6) representing text in comprehensible ways.

***Modeling.*** *Modeling* is central to teaching. When using modeling as a scaffold, you will need to consider where your students are in the learning process. You will probably first model the task for the entire class. Students who feel they are ready to begin the assigned task, should proceed. You will need to pull together the English language learners or others who either let you know they are not ready to perform the task or whom you have observed struggling, and model again for this group. If, when you check for comprehension, you see that some are ready to proceed, have them leave the group to begin the task. Supply additional instruction in each aspect of the task to those who are still not ready. You should model each step of the task or use another example, perhaps one that is closer to their lives. Continue the support until students feel confident and are ready to perform the task. Perhaps some complete the task as partners first and then individually the next time.

***Contextualization.*** *Contextualization* as a scaffold encourages students to understand that words, phrases, or concepts take on different meanings based on the words, phrases, and paragraphs that surround them. With English language learners, use context as a means of supporting understanding of the entire "picture." English language learners need to be able to see concepts in their entirety, whether you use pictures, labels, flowcharts, maps, or graphic organizers. Sometimes, the teacher supports contextualization through the use of a read aloud by reading a small section of text to students. Through questions and thinking about the concepts in the section, as well as engaging in summarization, the teacher can model for students how context affects meaning. These aids help students see relationships among the parts of the whole, and this context gives them a *gestalt* for learning.

***Metacognition.*** *Metacognition* is the practice of thinking about a mental process while it is occurring. That is, a person thinks about thinking while thinking. One thinks about the process of reading while reading and thinks about writing while writing. The purpose of this scaffold is to encourage students to focus on the mental processes in which they engage, to arrive at answers or solutions. Teachers model this process of metacognition by thinking out loud about their own thinking. Teachers should also model the process with a student while other students observe. Next, students try the process in pairs while the teacher monitors and provides feedback on the scaffold, always letting students know how this helps with comprehension and content mastery.

***Bridging.*** *Bridging* as a scaffold helps students activate their background knowledge for content they will be learning. It provides opportunities for students to use comparative and contrastive situations from their personal experiences to connect with new information. For example, students might note that the effect of air pressure compares to how they feel when they walk uphill and their ears feel plugged up. Eventually they "pop" and that's how a change in air pressure has personally affected them.

Teachers may use a variety of strategies to bridge old (background) knowledge with new knowledge. For example, you can utilize KWL charts, as described in Chapter 4, to ask students what they know or think they know about a topic as well as questions they might have about the topic. As the lesson emerges, ask students daily to list what they have learned about the topic on the chart. The process includes validating students' background knowledge by revisiting the K part of the chart, answering the questions students had in the W part of the chart, and making connections between new knowledge (the L part of the chart) with old knowledge.

Figure 5.6 provides an example of an anticipation chart, another method of helping students make connections between what they think they will learn and what they actually do learn. Ask students to make predictions about what they will learn about a specific topic such as an animal. They predict whether they think the animal is a predator, how the animal interacts with people, what the animal eats, and so forth. They read to gather information from texts or other media. Once they have gathered information, they compare their predictions with what they learned. This provides students opportunities to express their curiosity as well as to validate their predictions with the content they read.

***Building Background Knowledge.*** When students do not have the experiences to connect to what they are learning, *building background knowledge* is critical,

**FIGURE 5.6** Example Anticipation Chart

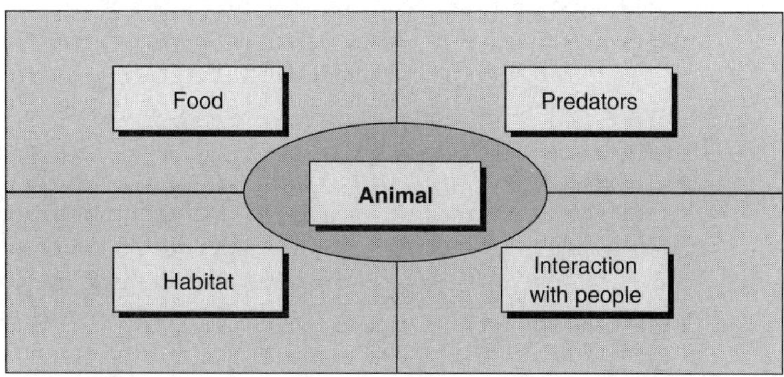


especially for English language learners. Building background knowledge means that teachers must first expose students to concrete objects to support the use of sensory learning. If objects are not available, teachers may want to use mime and drama, if applicable. Next they use pictures to provide a visual image of what students will be learning. Another strategy to use is a graphic organizer; however, a graphic organizer can be abstract, which may make it difficult for students to perceive the connections. It is important to use pictures and realia to create that first experience. Once students have had experience and built background knowledge, they begin to make the mental comparisons and contrasts, which enable them to activate what they know about something that is similar to what they are learning.

***Text Representation.*** The teacher uses the process of *text representation* to make difficult content comprehensible. This does not mean that the teacher waters down the content. Instead the teacher may use a graphic organizer, already partially filled in, to depict the concept to be learned. An explanation of the graphic organizer would precede the reading of the text or engaging in an activity. Students would then use the organizer as a map to guide them through the text or the activity. As they encounter the remaining content that would be filled in to complete the graphic organizer, they would do so. A graphic organizer could contain diagrams or pictures with labels. A graphic organizer could be a partially filled in flowchart or a partial map of a text showing its structure and relationships between the parts of the text.

Students can also use text representation to show what they know about content and may accompany it with an oral presentation. They may use a graphic organizer, a picture, a creative diagram, or any other visual device that demonstrates understanding.

## Needs of Struggling Students

Whereas English language learners might "struggle" in the content area as they are acquiring a sufficient level of cognitive academic language proficiency (CALP), other students might struggle for a variety of other reasons: poor reading or writing skills, a lack of confidence, poor foundational math skills, or many other problems. The scaffolds discussed will help both the English language learners as well as others who are struggling, though you might find that some students still need additional supports. You may consider using supplemental texts to augment your core textbook. These texts would present the same content material as the textbook but at a reading level more accessible to your students.

Deliver your content material using multiple modes: presentation, audio, video, demonstrations, reading, and interactive methods. You might consider using small group instruction led by a peer who has attained mastery in the material (and who has had direction in how to lead the group). You might need to offer specific small group instruction to a select number of students to give them more of your guidance and modeling. This can happen in class if you plan your lesson in a way that the whole class gets started on a task or activity that they can do with minimal guidance from you while you meet with the small group of students needing further instruction. Focusing on the specific needs of your struggling students is often challenging, and it requires you to check in frequently with individual students to evaluate what strategies are really working for each student. This conscientious attention will pay off with more engaged students and increased learning.

## Students Requiring Additional Challenges

Paying attention to students' special needs also means identifying those students in your class who are ready for increased challenges. These students might be ready to be challenged for a variety of reasons: They have strong background knowledge or experience in the content material; they learn material very quickly and can move at a much quicker pace; they are highly motivated and want more than the "required" experiences; or they have strong reading, writing, or technology skills.

You might challenge these students by augmenting your core textbook with supplemental readings that move into the subject matter more deeply or take a different angle on the subject matter being studied. You might offer these students opportunities to conduct research in a topic area that they could later present to the rest of the class or turn in to you. These students might teach a section of the content material to the class with your guidance. Additionally, these students might act as peer tutors or small group leaders to assist other students in class. Keep a variety of strategies in mind to challenge these students and do not rely simply on the peer tutoring model. Many students become resentful when they perceive that they are not allowed to build on their skill and knowledge but are doing the "teacher's work." As much as we value peer mentoring and tutoring and know the power behind teaching others as a way to cement our own understandings, it is difficult for students to appreciate this when it's the only way in which their instruction is ever differentiated. Variety is important.

Again, remember not to give these students *more* work or increased homework; rather, provide them with a *different* kind of work, a way to move deeper and further into a topic. It is also critical to keep in mind that a student's skill level might not be the same for all of the topics studied in your content area. While students might be masterful at animal classification, for example, they might not have the same skill and confidence with genetics. Teachers need to assess students' prior knowledge and experiences with each new unit of study to determine who might struggle and who might need more challenge.

Reiterated often in this text is that once you have taken the time to find out who your students are, you will be better able to plan a variety of different activities that will support all learners and enable each student to meet or exceed the same standards and expectations. You will need to group within your classroom. Differentiated planning and instruction means looking at teaching in a different way that challenges the effectiveness of always delivering content in the context of the entire class or whole group. Using flexible grouping models to give additional support to students, having students tutor one another, or giving them different

directions than the rest of the class can be crucial to the success of all students (Tomlinson, 1999). Again, the Circle of Courage comes into play when Generosity is fostered through cooperative interpersonal relationships, communication skill building, and the feeling of pride that comes from helping others (Brendtro et al., 2002).

## SECTION 4: CHAPTER SUMMARY AND REFLECTION

One of the most complex tasks all teachers must tackle is that of planning instruction. Your thoughtful preparation of both unit and lesson plans critically determines whether students will be engaged in your course and learn the necessary knowledge, skills, and dispositions of your discipline. This chapter has provided a detailed means for you to become skilled in creating purposeful and meaningful learning experiences for your students.

Sections 1 and 2 prompted you to think before putting pencil to paper or hands to a keyboard, and consider a range of elements that influence the final lesson: student background and skills, course goals and objectives aligned to standards, and various strategies to differentiate instruction to diverse learners. By considering student characteristics, teachers are better able to understand how to develop and modify appropriate strategies within a lesson. The alignment of goals and objectives to standards allows for clear targets of instruction and guides thinking about appropriate assessment strategies.

Section 2 presented a backward planning approach as a means to building a well-designed lesson based on the ideas noted in the previous section. Once you have decided on the goals and objectives to be targeted in a lesson and have identified appropriate assessment tasks, then you can identify the skills students will need to be successful, as well as necessary scaffolding strategies. Backward planning will assist you in creating a lesson inclusive of all the necessary elements that afford students a better opportunity to learn.

Section 3 described strategies that can assist you in helping all students to learn necessary content and skills. It also explored techniques to assist students in acquiring the language and critical concepts needed to master content. It focused on the ever-present need to differentiate instruction by scaffolding instruction to help students succeed and presented a number of scaffolding strategies. Additionally, this section considered ideas on meeting the needs of those students who continue to have difficulty in accessing the knowledge and skills necessary to be successful learners, as well as those who require additional challenges.

This chapter highlighted two sections of the Circle of Courage: Belonging and Mastery. Very few students who sit in a classroom and day after day feel like a failure because they have been unable to connect with the learning will feel a sense of connection or belonging. Instead they withdraw, if not physically, by being frequently absent from your class, then intellectually, to protect themselves. Every teacher should strive to create lessons that engage learners by using strategies that allow all students access to the information. Success builds on success and once successful, students will gain a sense of Belonging. Through powerful lessons, teachers can help their students reach Mastery and open up endless opportunities for them. Lesson and unit plans are more than ideas to fill a class period; through them teachers apply their own knowledge and skills as well as their art to create the foundation for all the learning that occurs in a classroom.

# References

Anderson, J. (1990). *Cognitive psychology and its implications* (3rd ed.). New York: W. H. Freeman.

Bandura, A. (1986). *Social foundations of thoughts and action: A social cognitive theory.* Englewood Cliffs, NJ: Prentice Hall.

Bandura, A. (1989). Social cognitive theory. In R. Vasta (Ed.), *Annals of Child Development* (Vol. 6, pp. 1–60). Greenwich, CT: JAI Press.

Beyer, B. K. (1997). *Improving student thinking: A comprehensive approach.* Boston: Allyn and Bacon.

Bloom, B. S., et al. (1984). *Taxonomy of educational objectives.* Boston: Allyn and Bacon.

Borich, G. D. (2000). *Effective teaching methods* (4th ed.). Upper Saddle River, NJ: Merrill.

Brendtro, L. K., Brokenleg, M., & Bockern, S. V. (2002). *Reclaiming youth at risk: Our hope for the future.* Bloomington, IN: National Education Service.

Brophy, J. E., & Evertson, C. (1981). *Student characteristics and teaching.* New York: Longman.

Byrum, J. L., Jarrell, R., & Munoz, M. (2003). *The perceptions of teachers and administrators on the impact of the lesson study initiative.* (ERIC Issue: ED467761) Institute of Education Sciences. Retrieved September 2, 2003, from www.eric.ed.gov

Chamot, A. U., & O'Malley, M. (1994). *Calla handbook: Implementing the cognitive academic language learning approach.* Reading, MA: Addison-Wesley.

Corkill, A. (1992). Advanced organizers: Facilitators of recall. *Educational Psychology Review, 4,* 33–67.

Costa, A. L. (Ed.). (1985). *Developing minds: A resource for teacher thinking.* Alexandria, VA: Association for Supervision and Curriculum.

Council of Chief State School Officers (1992). Model standards for beginning teacher licensing, assessment, and development: A resource for state dialogue. Washington, DC: Author. www.ccsso.org/content/pdfs/corestrd.pdf

Cummins, J. (1994). In C. Leyba (Ed.), *Schooling and language minority students: A theoretical framework* (2nd ed., pp. 3–46). Los Angeles: California State University, Los Angeles.

Eggen, P. D., & Kauchak, D. P. (1996). *Strategies for teachers: Teaching content and thinking skills* (3rd ed.) Boston: Allyn and Bacon.

Gibbons, P. (1993). *Learning to learn in a second language.* Portsmouth, NH: Heinemann.

Gonzalez, V., Brusca-Vega, R., & Yawkey, T. (1997). *Assessment and instruction of culturally and linguistically diverse students with or at-risk of learning problems: From research to practice.* Boston: Allyn and Bacon.

Hensen, K. T. (1996). *Methods and strategies for teaching secondary and middle schools.* White Plains, NY: Longman.

Moore, K. D. (1999). *Middle and secondary school instructional methods.* Boston and New York: McGraw-Hill College.

National Council of Teachers of English (1996). A project of the International Reading Association and the National Council of Teachers of English. Urbana, IL: NCTE.

Oakes, J., & Lipton, M. (1999). *Teaching to change the world.* Boston: McGraw-Hill College.

O'Malley, J. M., & Valdez-Pierce, L. (1996). *Authentic assessment or English language learners: Practical approaches for teachers.* Reading, MA: Addison-Wesley.

Open Society Institute and the International Reading Association (2004). *The reading and writing for critical thinking project.* (ERIC Issue: ED480266.) Institute of Education Sciences, Retrieved November 8, 2004, from www.eric.ed.gov

Orlich, D. C., Harder, R. J., Callahan, R. C., & Gibson, H. W. (2001). *Teaching strategies: A guide to better instruction* (6th ed.). Boston and New York: Houghton Mifflin.

Roberts, P., & Kellough, R. (2000). *A guide for developing interdisciplinary thematic units.* Upper Saddle River, NJ: Merrill/Prentice Hall.

Tishman, S., Perkins, D. N., & Jay, E. (1995). *The thinking classroom: Learning and teaching in a culture of thinking.* Boston: Allyn and Bacon.

Tomlinson, C. A. (1999). *The differentiated classroom: Responding to the needs of all learners.* Alexandria, VA: Association for Supervision and Curriculum Development.

Wiggins, G. (1998). *Educative assessment: Designing assessments to inform and improve student performance.* San Francisco: Jossey-Bass.

Wiggins, G., & McTighe, J. (1998). *Understanding by design.* Alexandria, VA: Association for Supervision and Curriculum Development.

Wolfe, P. (2001). *Brain matters: Translating research into classroom practice.* Alexandria, VA: Association for Supervision and Curriculum Development.

Wulf, K. M., & Shane, B. (1984). *Curriculum design.* Glenview, IL: Scott, Foresman.

# Unit III

# Approaches for Engaging Learners

# Chapter 6

# Cooperative Learning

**INTASC Principle 5:** The teacher uses an understanding of individual and group motivation and behavior to create a learning environment that encourages positive social interaction, active engagement in learning, and self-motivation.

**Key Disposition**

- The teacher values the role of students in promoting each other's learning and recognizes the importance of peer relationships in establishing a climate of learning.

## INTRODUCTION TO THE CHAPTER

Johnson, Johnson, and Holubec (1994b) defined cooperative learning as an instructional strategy whereby students work together to accomplish shared goals. Others have described it as a strategy whereby students want to succeed as a team, encouraging and helping others succeed as preparation for the complex problems in life, and as a means to not only reduce prejudice but also increase common humanity in the social process of cooperation (Allport, 1954; Dewey, 1970; Slavin, 1995). Researchers such as Piaget (1928) and Vygotsky (1978) also understood cooperative groups as important to learning. They noted that collaborative activity promotes growth through the modeling of behaviors that often take place and that social arbitrary knowledge such as language, values, rules, morality, and symbol systems can be learned only in interaction with others.

Chapter 6 introduces you to this important and effective instructional strategy. Section 1 provides an overview of cooperative learning beginning with a brief comparison of three predominant learning approaches: competitive, individual, and cooperative. Additionally this section identifies implications for student performance, characteristics of effective groups, organizational guidelines, and individual student accountability.

Section 2 describes the critical skills needed by students and important considerations in preparing them to participate effectively in cooperative learning projects. It provides several activities to use with students to facilitate development of these skills.

Section 3 introduces cooperative learning models, describes their characteristics, and provides specific examples of cooperative learning activities to be used in classrooms. Exercises such as Putting It Into Practice and Applying Technology will provide a platform for you to apply and assess these techniques in an actual field study situation. The cooperative learning methods discussed and applied in this chapter are excellent matches for the common theme of this text, the Circle of Courage (Brendtro et al., 2002). Students gain Mastery of knowledge through collaborative interaction and teacher facilitation. They develop Independence working independently, in addition to developing social interdependence and a sense of Belonging through the processes of group work. This collaboration extends beyond their group to the other members of the class and in some cases involves the larger community outside the classroom, thus providing opportunities to demonstrate Generosity.

## SECTION 1: OVERVIEW OF COOPERATIVE LEARNING

There are three predominate learning patterns as defined by particular teachers' strategies: competitive, individual, and cooperative. In the *competitive model* students basically work against each other to achieve a teacher-derived goal and are graded on a norm-referenced basis. A common assessment outcome of this structure is the application of a grading curve. One result of the competitive model is the formation of a negative interdependence among students creating a classroom of "haves" and "have-nots." Inevitably some will succeed and others will fail. Some students will work hard to do better than their peers, while others will give up because they have begun to believe they can never succeed.

Students come to perceive themselves as locked in fierce competition with each other in schools that espouse the competitive type of teaching and learning. The sole use of this model may cause high levels of anxiety in students and increased levels of selfishness, self-doubt, aggression, and poor communications (Johnson, Johnson, & Holubec, 1994a; Kohn, 1986). The model may be effective in situations in which well-learned materials need a review before an exam. For example, you could use game-show trivia-type competitions for competition related to knowledge of the learned material.

Students taught primarily using the *individual model*, work by themselves in relative isolation. They usually learn at their own pace and may in fact work on learning goals unrelated to others in the class. They are expected to focus on their own efforts and success and view others' success or failure as irrelevant (Johnson & Johnson, 1994). There is very little interaction with others socially or academically, and as a result, sharing of outcomes rarely happens. Although the model does allow for individualized progress in learning, the lack of interaction and sharing with other students is a crucial drawback.

The third model, *cooperative learning*, utilizes activities in which individuals seek outcomes that are beneficial to themselves as well as to other group members. Positive interdependence exists in cooperative situations, as students perceive that they can reach their learning goals if others reach theirs.

## Implications for Performance

A meta-analysis of over 375 experimental studies on achievement findings indicated that cooperative learning resulted in significantly higher achievement and retention of subject matter (at a variety of grade levels) than in competitive or individual models (Johnson & Johnson, 1989). In addition to achievement, researchers noted significant differences in other outcomes compared to competitive and individualistic learning: more high-level reasoning, frequent creation of new ideas and solutions, and greater transfer of learning from one situation to another. Furthermore, these gains occurred in cooperative strategies that were not pure manifestations of cooperative learning (that is, they had incorporated individualistic or competitive elements).

In addition, the findings suggest that the use of cooperative learning influenced other related affective and social factors. These included increases in interpersonal attraction (the quality of relationships and social support in groups) and psychological health (self-esteem).

Research also suggests that all of the factors are interdependent: Caring and committed friendships come from mutual accomplishment and bonding from joint efforts. The more people care about each other, the more likely they are to produce quality work. Self-esteem increases with the success of the group. Likewise, psychologically healthy individuals maintain and strengthen these social characteristics and continue to grow academically because of them (Johnson & Johnson, 1994).

When applied effectively, cooperative learning can assist teachers in meeting a number of important goals simultaneously. This is accomplished when the strategy helps raise achievement of all students, including those who are gifted and those who are academically challenged. Second, it helps build positive relationships among students, which is at the heart of creating a learning community that values diversity and establishes a spirit of Belonging. Third, it gives students experience vital to healthy social, psychological, and cognitive development (Johnson, Johnson, & Holubec, 1994a). Many countries that academically have outperformed the United States have emphasized the use of cooperative learning with evidence suggesting that this strategy may be one of the prime reasons for heightened performance (Rosenbaum, 2003).

## Characteristics of Effective Groups

Johnson et al. (1994b) also suggest that high-performance groups exhibit characteristics students need when working cooperatively. These include trust, respect, caring, encouragement, skills of effective communication and building and maintaining trust, as well as providing leadership. The ability to communicate feelings as well as ideas to all members of the group is essential to a successful cooperative learning situation. Specifics that contribute to success include the ability to use and interpret both verbal and nonverbal communication, asking for feedback on ideas, using paraphrasing to clarify meanings and feelings, avoidance of personal attacks or criticism, and a fair critique of ideas.

Building and maintaining trust among group members is a critical element. Group success requires each group member's efforts and unique contribution to the group's effort because of individual resources, roles, and task responsibilities. In properly formed cooperative groups, the success of one means the success of all, sometimes referred to as *positive interdependence*. Positive interdependence can be developed by an open exchange of ideas, sharing of materials and resources, rejection of nonsupportive behaviors, and periodic group monitoring and self-monitoring through formal or informal evaluation procedures.

All members of a learning group will typically improve leadership skills by their involvement in a cooperative activity. They may do this by assuming individual situation-specific leadership in a group; for instance, each member may assume leadership for particular tasks or, in a larger role, oversee the work of the entire group. Teachers need to help students develop leadership skills that will allow them to organize, motivate, set goals, and resolve conflicts so that they can better manage group activities.

## Organizational Guidelines for Cooperative Groups

In well-organized cooperative learning activities, more students can achieve a degree of success, often to a greater extent than seen in the competitive or individual model. However, without proper planning this strategy can dissolve into a chaotic classroom situation. Cooperative learning requires specific organizational and social guidelines essential to successful implementation. Teachers must be certain the students are taught and understand the guidelines. Guidelines include clear time constraints, responsibilities within the group, specific methods to plan the topic of study, descriptions of how to make use of resources, and definitive evaluation plans as well as techniques for students and their peers to interact effectively with each other (Sharan & Sharan, 1992).

Simply placing students in the same room together in such configurations as study groups, lab groups, project groups, or homerooms and calling them cooperative does not ensure that this will in fact take place (Johnson et al., 1994b). A teacher who wants to utilize cooperative learning should consider the following broad questions while planning to implement this strategy as part of the curriculum:

1. What are the most important personal skills students need when working cooperatively?
2. What organizational and curricular components increase the level of cooperation and consequently learning success within a classroom?

The first question regarding personal skills has been addressed in previous paragraphs. Answering the second question on the organizational and curricular components involved with cooperative groups requires developing clear expectations, composition, and size appropriate to the task. Clearly stated expectations are important, and teachers should provide them in both written and oral formats. Discussion of expectations prior to moving into cooperative groups is essential to ensure students understand the guidelines to the activity. Students should be able to grasp the overall purpose of the cooperative project, as well as the individual tasks expected of them.

Written task sheets formulated by student groups assist them in appropriate task and time management. In considering group composition and size appropriate for the task, teacher experience in using a particular assignment, as well as knowledge of individual students' strengths and weaknesses, can be helpful in the process of team formation.

The teacher's goal in appropriately applying cooperative learning will be to seek Mastery of the curriculum objectives from each member of the group. Consequently, this encourages a degree of Independence, while at the same time group members provide collaboration in the form of support and assistance to each of the other members of the group (Generosity and Belonging), in line with the Circle of Courage.

## Accountability in Cooperative Groups

Teacher assessment techniques that define individual and group accountability within a group project ensure the maximizing of both the individual tasks and the overall goals of the project. A common criticism of cooperative learning is that a few members do all the work while the remaining members of the group get full credit (in spite of their lack of work). Besides individual and group assessments, incorporating formative assessments in addition to the summative assessments can overcome this potential issue. The teacher should frequently give feedback to and receive it from both individuals and the whole group. These checks can provide motivation (in the form of a grade, for example) as well as inform students regarding the quality of their progress.

Teachers should also have mechanisms in place prior to summative assessments that allow each group member to synthesize the information incorporated by other members of the group. Opportunities to share concepts are crucial to making this process truly collaborative. Summative assessments, at the end of the project, will more likely indicate better learning results if you provide specific time to allow the group the opportunity to synthesize their ideas. This virtually ensures the success of the group's project on the summative assessment. Evidence suggests that all of these strategies can potentially increase individual achievement levels (Munoz & Clavijo, 2002) as well as the social behavior of the participating students (Brandt & Christensen, 2003; Goldberg, Foster, Maki, Emde, & O'Kelly, 2002).

***Use of Relevant Interpersonal and Small Group Skills.*** The students' skills in the areas identified previously, such as communication skills, conflict management, and leadership, should be apparent, and the teacher should be able to note them either directly or indirectly. Both teachers and students must constantly review, reinforce, and evaluate these skills. A very important, yet often neglected, small group skill is scheduling time for teams to meet and present to each other their "works in progress" in order to receive feedback and assistance in their various tasks. Including this time avoids a common situation in cooperative learning whereby team members work in isolation of each other and none of them has a complete understanding of the process or content of the final product.

***Evaluation of Cooperative Learning Skills.*** Evaluate cooperative learning skills using postproject whole-group discussions and individual written self-evaluations. These strategies will stress the importance of cooperative learning skills in the overall learning process and provide both you and the students with important feedback regarding progress in this area.

***Involvement and Participation of the Audience During Final Group Presentations.*** In addition to the learning that takes place within a team, consider how to ensure that accountability for learning takes place with those individual students in the audience when team presentations are made. This might take on the form of a quiz (designed by the presenting team), some questions formatted by the audience to the team, a quick write that outlines what was learned (or not learned), or a formal test on selected elements of the presentations. This aspect of cooperative learning keeps the audience involved and models essential elements of cooperative learning on a larger scale (whole class).

## SECTION 2: STRATEGIES TO IMPROVE COOPERATIVE SKILLS

In preparing students for cooperative learning activities, pretraining sessions and continuous teacher feedback improve the experience. This section describes how to use three interactive simulation games to develop and reinforce a variety of cooperative personal learning skills. These games provide a good match to the interpersonal and small group skills Johnson and Johnson (1994) described as essential to effective group learning. These skills include communication, trust building, leadership, and conflict management skills. The games introduce and reinforce each of these skills as they are presented sequentially. The simulation games are *Five Stage Rocket*, *Verbal/Nonverbal Communication*, and *Leader of the Pack*.

Although teams earn points for "successful" achievement in each game and can get team awards, teachers should emphasize the skills being learned as the primary motive for doing them. In order for the games to be an effective learning strategy, teachers must incorporate reflection throughout the games. Students need to understand the importance of the skills being learned, which should be reinforced throughout the school year. You can accomplish this by:

1. posting the essential skills for effective cooperative learning on visible charts and lists around the room;
2. reviewing the skills before each group project;
3. providing formal and informal feedback on these skills to each group and to individuals during and after completion of a group process; and
4. providing group process self-evaluation forms as part of the group process.

### Communication and Trust Building

The *Five Stage Rocket* simulation game, developed by Elizabeth Cohen (1986), facilitates students' practice of two of Johnson and Johnson's (1994) essentials of effective

**FIGURE 6.1** Spaceship Problem

The object of this game is to select seven people to go on a spaceship for a voyage to another planet. You have just been alerted that a giant meteor is on a collision course with the planet Earth, and because of its size and impact area, this is expected to be catastrophic for all life on Earth. In fact, this will very likely mark the end of human civilization as we know it on Earth. This will, therefore, be an effort to continue our life form on another planet (Mars). The spaceship has the capacity to set up life on Mars. The twelve people below were originally chosen to go on the ship; however, a maximum weight (mass) error was made, and now it turns out that there, is room for only seven. Your group must decide which seven people will go to start life on the new planet.

Remember: Only seven people can fit in the new configuration of the ship. Your team must have an agreement and a rationale for the seven members you choose.

1. A 30-year-old male symphony orchestra violin player
2. A 67-year-old male minister
3. A 23-year-old engineer and his 21-year-old wife (they refuse to be separated)
4. A 40-year-old police-officer who refuses to be separated from his gun
5. A young male college student
6. A 35-year-old male high school dropout, recently arrested for armed robbery
7. A 32-year-old female 6th-grade teacher
8. A 40-year-old female medical doctor
9. A 50-year-old female artist and sculptor
10. A 25-year-old male poet
11. A 1-year-old female child (unrelated to any of the others)

cooperative learning: communication skills, and building and maintaining trust in each other. The five stages of the simulation emphasize (1) conciseness, (2) active listening (not interrupting each other), (3) wait time to allow information to be processed, (4) incorporating previous responses in replies, and (5) inclusion of all members in discussions. After each stage, scores are tallied and all members of each group, including the observer, share with the class the value of the skill addressed in that stage.

The following describes the Five Stage Rocket simulation game:

**Step 1:** Introduction to the activity

- Teacher discusses the purpose of cooperative groups and a specific problem that will be used in the simulation game. Figure 6.1 spells out the spaceship problem.
- Groups discuss the problem for 3 to 5 minutes without any specific directions on group processes to use.
- Based on this exercise, the teacher and students brainstorm both the strengths and the impediments they observed in their group efforts to resolve the problem.

**Step 2:** The stages

Prior to beginning each stage, assign three students in each group these roles: observer, timer, and recorder. The observer enforces rules by assigning penalties, the timer keeps the group on task, and the recorder records details of the group process. Rotate roles at the end of each stage so that all group participants play at least one role in the activity. At each stage students discuss the same problem presented in Figure 6.1.

- *Stage One rules.* Tell participants to value *conciseness* in their responses (15-second maximum response time). Long responses tend to be repetitive and limit time for other members to contribute. The observer/timer assesses violators one penalty point per violation. Have the group discuss the same problem for 3 minutes.

- *Stage Two rules.* Note—continue to enforce all rules from the previous stage. Be sure participants do not *interrupt* another participant while talking, so that all members have the opportunity to complete their responses. Assess violators one penalty point. Discussion time is 3 minutes.
- *Stage Three rules.* Tell participants to allow for *wait time* (3 seconds) between responses, so that all group members can process information. Assess violators one penalty point. Discussion time is 3 minutes.
- *Stage Four rules.* Tell participants they must *clarify, restate,* or *elaborate* the previous respondent's ideas before replying. This rule encourages active listening and value of others' responses. Failure to do so results in a penalty of one point. Discuss the same problem for 3 minutes.
- *Stage Five rules.* Give all participants an opportunity to reply to any statements made. Each person must speak or pass before a person who has spoken once can speak again. This will encourage everyone to voice ideas and play a role in the outcome, ultimately resulting in the strength of group solutions. Failure to do so results in a penalty of one point. Discuss the same problem for 3 minutes.

**Step 3:** Closing the activity
At the end of stage five, give each group a brief opportunity to share scores and any general observations about their success (or lack of) regarding the application of these communication skills.

- The new observer assesses only positive points (one each) every time the group has applied all rules from each step successfully. No penalties are assessed.
- The group discusses the problem for 3 minutes. It formulates the solution and rationale for a presentation.
- The group presents the final solution to the class. The total score (points and deductions) is tallied.
- The teacher facilitates a debriefing closure on the challenges and value of each skill practiced, and continues to reinforce these skills throughout the school year using strategies mentioned earlier (e.g., posting charts with skills listed).

## Reinforcement of Interpersonal Communication

We developed the *Verbal/Nonverbal Communication* simulation as an interactive, hands-on game to highlight the importance of all forms of interpersonal communication and to illustrate the wide range of differences in the understanding of words (both written and spoken) and body language individuals use. The activity also reinforces building and maintaining trust.

**Step 1:** Introduction to the activity
Group students into teams of three and assign each one of three roles: architect, builder, or observer. The architect initially creates a drawing of a structure incorporating the materials provided in the group's design. The builder must recreate the design without being able to see it. The observer keeps track of the interactions, both positive and negative. Rotate these roles throughout the game as teams proceed to different levels of problems so that each team member is provided an experience to help the team understand communication from different perspectives.

The four levels of problems are ordered in increasing difficulty.

- *Level One:* Information is conveyed and questions are asked orally.
- *Level Two:* Information is conveyed orally; however, no questions may be asked.
- *Level Three:* Information can be conveyed only in writing. Written statements and questions may be used.
- *Level Four:* Only nonverbal communication can be used. The team must develop and implement a system to communicate information.

At each successive level of difficulty, award teams higher points for success, thus providing opportunities for even late starting groups to be successful. After each problem level, the teacher leads a reflective discussion with groups based on the observations of successes and challenges experienced at that level of the game. Conduct a broad debriefing at the end of the game regarding implications and lessons learned from it. You can award rewards (points) in a variety of ways: to successful teams at each level; cumulatively for all levels; or for creative solution approaches to the problems.

**Step 2:** The activity

- Group students into teams of three.
- Give each group (team) four objects: pencil, rubber band, paper clip, and toothpick.
- *Roles.* The *architect* designs a structure from the materials provided and then must communicate how to construct it to the *builder* without actually showing the structure. The *observer* will watch both the architect and the builder but will not have any interaction with either. The observer's role is to write down everything observed during this exercise.
- *Time Limits.* Specific time limits are allotted for each step of the game. The recommended allotment is 3 minutes for problem 1; 6 minutes for problem 2 (3 minutes to write and 3 minutes to solve); 6 minutes for problem 3 (3 minutes to write and 3 minutes to solve); and 8 minutes for problem 4 (5 minutes to develop a nonverbal system prior to starting and 3 minutes to solve).
- *Reflection/Discussion.* A brief conversation follows each problem level and includes all members of the team. Input from the observer at this point is quite helpful. A more extensive reflection, discussion, or quick write is included in step 3.

***Problem 1:*** The architect can use only verbal communication. The builder is allowed to solve the problem only by asking questions. Additionally, these two students will face away from each other so that the builder cannot see the drawing and the architect cannot see the structure being built. Team scores are based on how accurately the structure resembles the drawing.

***Problem 2:*** The architect and the builder can communicate only in writing and only in the form of questions to solve the challenge. No symbols may be used, and again students will face away from each other. Team scores are based on how accurately the structure resembles the drawing.

***Problem 3:*** In this phase, only the architect can communicate in writing to the builder. No symbols may be used, and again students will face away from each other. Team scores are based on how accurately the structure resembles the drawing.

***Problem 4:*** The two team members can use only nonverbal communication strategies. No sounds or written words are allowed. Students can face each other to communicate but cannot point at or direct movement in the building of the structure.

**Scoring**
Base points earned during the exercise on a correct structure being assembled, one that closely resembles the architect's drawing. Each problem level added a degree of difficulty so points increase appropriately:

| | | |
|---|---|---|
| Problem 1 | = | 1 point |
| Problem 2 | = | 2 points |
| Problem 3 | = | 3 points |
| Problem 4 | = | 4 points |

**Step 3:** Closing the activity
Facilitate students' exploring of the following questions related to both verbal and nonverbal communication. This may be accomplished in a group discussion or individual quick writes, later shared with the team and class as a whole.

- What techniques did your group's communication system use (both verbal and nonverbal)?
- What problems did you observe in your group's efforts to try to communicate together at each step of this game?
- What suggestions do you have for improving your group's communication skills (either verbal or nonverbal)?
- What did you learn about language and/or communication in general?
- How might this apply to working cooperatively together in future group projects?

## Leadership and Conflict Management

The primary purpose of the simulation game *Leader of the Pack* is to assist students in defining, identifying, and practicing the strengths of good leaders. It also facilitates practicing conflict management skills. Additionally, the importance of interpersonal communication skills, and building and maintaining trust, as practiced in the first two simulation games, continues to be reinforced. With this in mind, you may use the Leader of the Pack simulation most effectively after the other simulation games, because it incorporates all of Johnson and Johnson's (1994) essential interpersonal skills for cooperative work, making it a good culminating activity before beginning actual group assignments.

**Step 1:** Introduction to the activity
For all three subsets of Leader of the Pack, arrange students in teams of four to six (with one observer taking a rotational role). Also, like the two previous games described, place emphasis not on the teams' performances but rather on reflecting on what was learned and how students can use these ideas in group work.

**Step 2:** Opening the activity
The teacher facilitates students to brainstorm those skills considered important for leadership in a group process. Some likely examples will include:

- good organization skills
- contributing member of the group
- conflict management skills

- group motivator and goal setter
- able to help others move toward closure on tasks
- charisma

### Round One

1. **Model.** Use one team to model the simulation for the rest of the class. Appoint one person as the leader of this team and pose a specific problem for the team to use as the context for discussion. For example, you might ask the team to decide the consequences for a group of students who arrive repeatedly late to your class.
2. **Audience participation.** While the class observes this group simulation, have them (a) list leadership behaviors (or lack of) from the previous brainstorming session demonstrated by the designated leader, (b) rate the leadership skills from 1 to 5, and (c) include a justification for their evaluations.
3. **Analysis of findings.** Following the simulation, discuss the findings of the class regarding the strengths and weaknesses of the leader's individual skills.

### Round Two

1. **Divide the class into teams.** Appoint a group leader and observer for each group. Give each team leader a problem to resolve and a specific amount of time to accomplish the task. Observers in each group will take notes on the interplay between the leader and the group, assigning a rating of 1 to 5 points for the leadership displayed in that round, then orally report the outcomes to the class during the discussion.
2. **Reinforce.** You may repeat the activity with two or three different individuals acting in roles as leaders and/or observers.
3. **Reflect/discuss.** At the end of each game, debrief the process with the whole class by first discussing each group's solutions for all problems. Then have observers report on the strengths and weaknesses of various leaders. Total accumulated scores may be tallied for each team. An overview/list of characteristics of effective leadership as derived from the games might be appropriate to use as a reinforcing strategy throughout the year.

### Round Three

1. **Organizing skills.** Assign a problem and allow the leader 5 minutes to get a consensus of what roles are needed, who will do what, and in what time frame (see the task sheet template for round 1 in Figure 6.2). Class observers rate leadership performance on a 1 to 5 point scale and list strengths and challenges as observed. Average points for each team's leaders will reflect that team's overall score.
2. **Conflict management.** Have one or two members role-play a conflict, which the leader has 3 to 5 minutes to resolve. Examples of possible conflicts could be refusing to do assigned tasks, refusing to work with one or more team members, interrupting tasks, or doing subpar-level work. Class observers rate leadership performance on a 1 to 5 point scale and list strengths and challenges as observed using the task sheet template for round 3 in Figure 6.2. Average points for each team's leaders will reflect that team's overall score.
3. **Group motivation/goal setting.** Have each leader give a motivational presentation in which a series of group goals are stated in 1 to 2 minutes. The teacher could assign typical leadership scenarios such as a leader of a science

FIGURE 6.2 Task Sheet Templates

| Round 1: ORGANIZING SKILLS | | |
|---|---|---|
| **Tasks** | **Who Will Do It** | **When** |
| | | |

| **Strengths Observed** | **Challenges Observed** |
|---|---|
| | |

| Round 2: CONFLICT MANAGEMENT | |
|---|---|
| **Strengths Observed** | **Challenges Observed** |
| | |

| Round 3: MOTIVATIONAL OR GOAL-SETTING SKILLS | |
|---|---|
| **Strengths Observed** | **Challenges to Leadership Observed** |
| | |

group school project on inventions, captain of a women's soccer team, or supervisor of a work crew. Class observers rate leadership performance on a 1 to 5 point scale and list strengths and challenges as observed using the task sheet template for round 1 in Figure 6.2. Average the points for each leader from class scores.

The second sample problem for use with Leader of the Pack (see Figure 6.3) is a more complex scenario called Envy-Free Cake Division. Again, the context of the problem teaches the key leadership skills of organization, conflict management, and goal motivation. This sample problem is from "Formulas for Fairness: Applying the Math of Cake Cutting to Conflict Resolution" (Peterson, 1999). All parties in a conflict receive at least some of what they really want, resulting in a final resolution whereby the mediator feels that all the parties have been equitably treated in the process.

FIGURE 6.3 Envy-Free Cake Division Problem

Arrange students in teams of five: one mediator, two conflicting parties (husband and wife getting a divorce, business partners dissolving business, family members in an inheritance battle etc.), and two lawyers to represent each of the two conflicting parties. The processes of leadership including organization (1–2), conflict management (1–3) and goal/motivating (1–3) are embedded throughout the simulation game and will be discovered and explored in the process and the follow-up discussion.

**Procedures**

1. The team will establish a list of all the "assets" that have to be divided. For example, in the divorce situation each team might consider a different socioeconomic situation such as low-, middle-, or upper-income family for variety and a range of assets. These are combined to make one master list. (20 minutes)
2. Each party privately (without the other present) and in collaboration with the lawyer must now place a point value on each asset in the master list with a total of 100 points total available for distribution. They can assign a point value of from 0 to 100 for any individual asset depending on how importantly they value that asset. (20 minutes)
3. The teams meet with the mediator, who develops an equitable procedure to go through each item awarding the asset to the party who has assigned the highest point value to it. The mediator and the teams can derive additional agreed-upon compromising procedures to divide those assets that are close in point value or for which large points are assigned to an asset but are "lost" to a higher value of the other party. All three of these procedures involve simulations of important learning strategies; that is, how well the teams organize, mediate, and motivate each other enhances one's ability to "accept" a position or argument. (20 minutes)
4. After the "resolution" has been reached by each team (or least almost completed), each team should take 5 minutes to explain the processes of achieving the resolution of its assets to the whole class. Each member of the team (two conflicting parties and the mediator) should explain how they feel about the details of resolution; their strategies for organizing the assignment of assets, their strategies for mediation of conflicts as coordinated by parties and mediator, and how the parties and mediator motivated and or set goals for this to be accomplished. The teacher facilitator should keep a listing of the comments by category on the board.
5. The class should provide feedback to each team by asking questions and offering comments related to the perceived strengths or weaknesses noted in each area of leadership: organizing skills, mediation, and goal setting/motivation.
6. After this discussion with each team, the members of the class use a Likert scale-scoring sheet (0–5 with justification for scores) provided by the teacher to rank the other teams in each of the three areas of leadership. A total score for "Leader of the Pack" for each team is obtained by adding the three subscores and then using this to get an average from the whole class. The teams with the highest average scores would be awarded first, second, and third place and receive extra credit or an award for their exemplary efforts. Alternatively, teams might also be given an award for high scores in some subset of the game.
7. The teachers should facilitate closure for this activity on leadership by keeping a tally on the board of each team's overall strategies and holding a discussion on which ones might be most important when working in teams. Those highlighted as most important could be listed and should be reinforced by the teacher in future cooperative activities by way of informal or formal teacher feedback and/or by self-evaluation by members of the teams.

### Putting It Into Practice: Activity 6.1

This activity applies cooperative learning simulation games to a classroom setting. As part of a structured lesson plan, apply at least one of the cooperative learning interactive simulations with your classes such as the Five Stage Rocket, Verbal/Nonverbal Communication, or Leader of the Pack. Write a reflective journal entry that includes the context of the lesson plan and the effectiveness and challenges of your implementation as perceived by you and your students. Share these findings as part of a whole-group discussion.

## SECTION 3: COOPERATIVE LEARNING MODELS

This section provides an overview of the essential methods used in most cooperative learning models as well the results of studies conducted to support their use. Additionally, Section 3 introduces several widely used models and approaches for implementing the cooperative learning strategy and details three examples of cooperative learning approaches.

### Essential Characteristics

Robert Slavin studied and reported the most widely used models of cooperative learning. He categorizes all of the methods by the inclusion or exclusion of six characteristics and compares them to traditional group work, which typically includes none of these characteristics (Slavin, 1995).

The six characteristics of cooperative learning used by Slavin to compare the various methods encompass the following:

1. **Group goals.** These might include achievement goals on formative and summative assessments and recognition for meeting predetermined criteria.
2. **Individual accountability.** This may involve individually assigned tasks and perhaps a final grade, based on individual quizzes or accomplishments. In some cases, the final group grade may be the sum of the individual grades.
3. **Equal opportunity for success.** All students can improve and have the opportunity to improve. Mechanisms are in place to change, adapt, or redo any elements of work that the instructor deems less than appropriate.
4. **Team competition.** Competition between teams may be used as motivation if done appropriately.

### A Closer Look

You may also want to refer to **Instructional Resources D** and **E** (discussed in Chapter 5) in which unit and lesson plans also integrate some of these models of cooperative learning.

5. **Task specialization.** Each team member is responsible for specific tasks to help accomplish the team goals.
6. **Adaptation to individual needs.** Accommodation and allowances are made for individual student needs, such as writing and reading.

## Student Team Models

These methods share the common element that all cooperative learning methods incorporate: Students work together to learn and are responsible for their teammates' learning as well as their own. In this broad model the students' tasks are not to do something as a team but rather to learn something as a team. The following models all have the characteristics of team awards, individual accountability, and equal opportunities for success (Slavin, 1995).

***Student Teams–Achievement Division (STAD).*** In the STAD model, students' placement in heterogeneous groups of four or five is by achievement level, gender, and ethnicity. In this model of student team learning, the teacher initially presents a lesson. Students work together in teams to make sure all members have mastered the lesson. Students then take individual quizzes on the material, which are compared to past averages, and points are awarded based on the degree of improvement for each member of the team. The cumulative effect of each team's total points would be a basis for a team award or certificate. Teachers primarily use this model to assess concepts, computations, and language skills.

***Teams–Games–Tournaments (TGT).*** David DeVries and Keith Edwards (1973) developed another model of student team learning, the TGT. It uses the same concept of a teacher presentation as the STAD method, but with an added element. Instead of assessing students with quizzes, teachers use academic games as an assessment tool. To prepare for the games, students assist each other with worksheets and by explaining problems to each other. Once the games begin, an equal opportunity for success is provided, because the top scorer at each table receives 60 points. Students might compete in mathematics against students with similar past records. Through this method, any team may receive a team award. Equal opportunities for success and individual accountability and team awards characteristize this method.

***Cooperative Integrated Reading and Composition (CIRC).*** The CIRC model, a program for teaching reading and writing that is effective in middle school and high school, works especially well with second-language learners (Madden, Slavin, & Stevens, 1986). Teachers place students in appropriate ability groups, then pair up students of different abilities within the groups to complete tasks such as reading to each other, summarizing stories, making predictions, practicing spelling, decoding, and learning vocabulary.

Students also work in their whole teams to master main ideas and comprehension. They engage in process skills such as writer's workshops, whereby they might publish long-term projects such as group or class books. All of these student activities follow carefully designed teacher instructions. The model measures student contributions to their team by individual quizzes, composition, or their role in the writing projects, thus ensuring individual accountability. Like the other models in this group, it ensures individual accountability by the fact that student contributions to their teams are task-specific.

## Additional Cooperative Learning Methods

Using the student team learning methods, students work together in various cooperative arrangements to gain a better understanding of some concepts and the teacher assesses them both individually and as a team. In the models that follow, the academic outcomes are often more than learning particular concepts and may include a variety of products, both group and otherwise. As with the previous methods, they all include critical elements of defined group goals, individual accountability, and task specificity.

***Group Investigation.*** Yael and Shlomo Sharan (1992) developed group investigation in which students use cooperative inquiry, group discussion, and cooperative planning to produce a project within a teacher's unit plan and defined rubrics in the form of a final report or presentation. Students work on individual tasks (task specificity) toward the ultimate goal, and the teacher holds them accountable within the project to inform other group members about the information they have gathered. The group synthesizes the information and prepares a final report or presentation for the class. The teacher holds the whole class accountable for the information presented by each group investigation through tests or other forms of evaluation. As part of the project, the presenting group might in fact develop the assessment to be given to the whole class. The teacher's role is critical, acting as a facilitator throughout the process in preparing an initial overview of the project (with clear rubrics), providing formative assessment (intermediate) to each team member, and group and summative assessment (final) to the individuals and teams.

***Learning Together.*** David and Roger Johnson (1994) developed the learning together model of cooperative learning that places equal emphasis on both achievement and social development as outcomes of cooperative processes. This method emphasizes four elements: (1) positive interdependence whereby students work together for common goals; (2) individual accountability whereby each must demonstrate mastery of material; (3) face-to-face interaction (in four- to five-member groups); and (4) interpersonal and small group skills as students are taught effective mechanisms to work together and are assessed on their progress in this area.

### A Closer Look

Example 1, Group Investigation: Solving an Energy Crisis, in **Instructional Resource F** provides a good description of the application of this model in secondary schools. 11th- and 12th-grade students used this teacher-developed project in an environmental science class. In this cooperative group investigation, students collaborated to determine the feasibility of using alternative forms of energy to solve a state's energy crisis. The example details the six implementation stages of group investigation projects, as outlined by Sharan and Sharan (1992). It also includes a sample assessment rubric in Table F.1.

### A Closer Look

An example of a project incorporating the learning together strategy can be found in **Instructional Resource F**, Example 2, Learning Together: Film Class. This project was developed to teach the basic artistic and technical elements of creating video to students who normally would not have had access to the skills and tools of contemporary media. Objectives of the project included improving language arts skills, developing higher order thinking skills, increasing cooperative organizational skills, and increasing parent–teacher–student interaction. The project is representative of creatively applying the learning together model to address multiple needs of a targeted population.

***Complex Instruction.*** Elizabeth Cohen (1986) developed the complex instruction method of cooperative learning, which emphasizes discovery-oriented projects, particularly in science, math, and social sciences. This method, widely used in bilingual and heterogeneous classes, places a high value on the individual strengths of the student when working on a team. For example, a student who has strengths in artistic areas would be assigned a role on a team to do a blueprint of a building to illustrate a team design. An additional goal is to give English language learners a higher level of context to apply oral and written applications to the English language. They would also be accountable, as in previous methods, to understand the overall project. Each team member's collaboration comes from an area of strength.

***Structured Dyadic Methods.*** Unlike other cooperative methods, which typically use four to six team members, the dyad method pairs students to work together in situations in which each student alternately takes on the role of teacher and student, or tutor and tutoree (one student directing teaching of another). The teacher's role may be as an informal facilitator or a more active guide (providing scripted prompts for the pairs). A variety of research evidence has shown that both scripted pair learning (Dansereau, 1988) as well as class-wide peer tutoring (CWPT) produce favorable achievement outcomes compared to control groups (Greenwood, Delquadri, & Hall, 1989).

### A Closer Look

Similar to the previous two models described, Example 3, Complex Instruction: Mousetrap Mobile Races, in **Instructional Resource F**, presents an example of the implementation of the complex instruction method. This example not only describes the strategy as it was implemented but also includes a description of the innovative project used in the cooperative learning experience. Ninth-grade students from a Navajo reservation who had previously failed the course learned how to (1) identify and apply the principles of motion and energy, (2) creatively present their findings demonstrating their language skills, and (3) improve their cooperative learning skills.

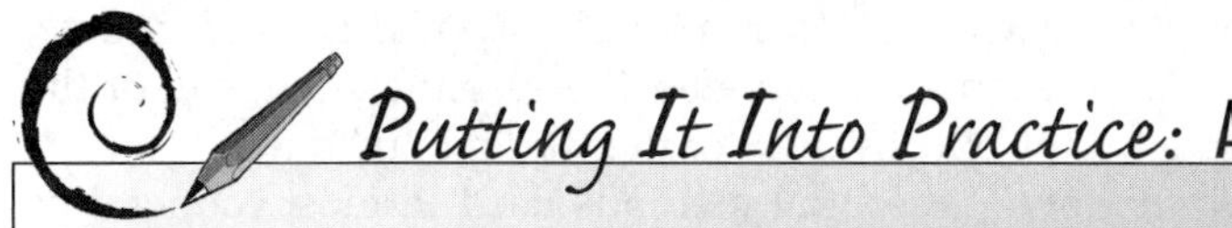

## Putting It Into Practice: Activity 6.2

Using one of the cooperative learning methods described in this chapter, design a lesson plan within your discipline that incorporates this model. Implement it in the classroom and provide a reflective journal entry that discusses the effectiveness of the implementation related to the learning of content material and cooperative group processes. The journal entry should include data and perceptions from both you and your students. Present the findings as part of a whole-group discussion.

## Applying Technology: Activity 6.1

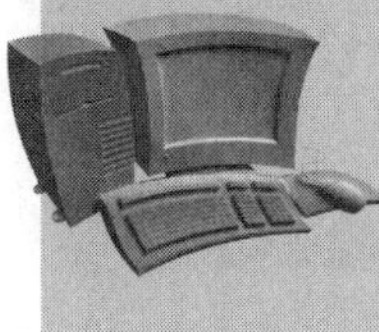

In this activity you will use digital cameras and computer editing equipment, if available, to document implementation of cooperative learning simulation games and cooperative learning methods. Select either Putting It Into Practice Activity 6.1 or 6.2 and document the implementation of the selected exercise. Your final edited products should be no longer than 5 to 10 minutes and should capture for the audience the essence of the implementation process with that particular model.

## SECTION 4: CHAPTER SUMMARY AND REFLECTION

In this chapter, an overview of the research findings on cooperative learning in Section 1 suggests its use as a teaching method can improve achievement and social skills and is highly effective compared to competitive and individual methods. This assumes the incorporation of certain essential elements for the students and the teacher into the process. This section addressed characteristics of elements for effective groups. The elements for students include clear goals and rubrics introduced from the beginning; critical skills necessary for small group cooperative and communication skills; individual and group accountability; group processing time; and evaluation of academic and social processes. The elements for teachers include explaining academic tasks and rubrics (including formative and summative assessments); structuring positive interdependence through training; deciding group composition; establishing roles within the group; arranging for materials and resources; arranging the room; and facilitating overall academic and social achievement.

Section 2 provided strategies to improve cooperative skills by suggesting cooperative learning simulation games as an important element to train students prior to engaging in cooperative learning. These games help students learn small group interpersonal social skills of conflict management, leadership, communication skills, and building and maintaining trust. The Five Stage Rocket, Verbal/Nonverbal Communication, and Leader of the Pack simulation games explained and modeled these skills. Putting It Into Practice Activity 6.1 provided practice in implementing and evaluating the effectiveness of these simulation games.

Instructional Resource F provides extensive examples/models of actual classroom implementation of three of the major methods of using cooperative learning. These examples included (1) group investigation, an environmental studies course, "Solving an Energy Crisis"; (2) learning together, a language arts course,

"Film Class"; and (3) complex instruction, a remedial physical science course, "Mousetrap Mobile Races." Each example integrated the essential elements of the cooperative method and reported the effectiveness of the student outcomes.

Section 3 provided an overview of essential methods used in most cooperative learning models as well as studies conducted to support their use. Several widely used models and approaches for implementation were detailed, including specific student team models as well as additional cooperative learning methods such as group investigation, learning together, complex instruction, and structured dyadic methods. Putting It Into Practice Activity 6.2 provided an opportunity to design and implement your own lesson plan to incorporate cooperative learning methods.

Cooperative learning matches up well with the Circle of Courage, as mentioned in the chapter introduction. At this point, it should be clear that all four parts of the circle (Belonging, Mastery, Generosity, Independence) can be developed through the various applications of cooperative learning strategies explored in this chapter.

## References


Allport, G. W. (1954). *The nature of prejudice*. Reading, MA: Addison-Wesley.

Brandt, M., & Christensen, R. (2003). *Improving student social skills through the use of cooperative learning, problem solving, and direct instruction*. (ERIC Issue: ED465929). Institute of Education Sciences. Retrieved March 7, 2003, from www.eric.ed.gov

Brendtro, L. K., Brokenleg, M., & Bockern, S. V. (2002). *Reclaiming youth at risk: Our hope for the future*. Bloomington, IN: National Education Service.

Cohen, E. (1986). *Designing group work: Strategies for heterogeneous classroom*. New York: Teachers College Press.

Council of Chief State School Officers (1992). Model standards for beginning teacher licensing, assessment, and development: A resource for state dialogue. Washington, DC: Author. www.ccsso.org/content/pdfs/corestrd.pdf

Dansereau, D. F. (1988). Cooperative learning strategies. In C. E. Weinstein, E. T. Goetz, & P. A. Alexander (Eds.), *Learning and strategies: Issues in assessment, instruction, and evaluation* (pp. 103–120). Orlando, FL: Academic Press.

DeVries, D., & Edwards, K. J. (1973). Learning games and student teams: Their effects on classroom. *American Educational Research Journal, 10*, 307–318.

Dewey, J. (1970). *Characters and events; popular essays in social and political philosophy* (J. Ratner, Ed.). New York: Octagon Books.

Dodge, B., & March, T. (1995). *WebQuest overview site*. Retrieved April 13, 2003, from http://webquest.sdsu.edu/overview.htm

Embry, (2000). *Alternative energy sources in WebQuest examples matrix*. Retrieved April 4, 2003, from http://webquest.sdsu.edu/matrix/9–12–Sci.htm

Goldberg, K., Foster, K., Maki, B., Emde, J., & O'Kelly, M. (2002). *Improving student motivation through cooperative learning and other strategies*. (ERIC Issue: ED455464.) Institute of Education Sciences. Retrieved April 4, 2003, from www.eric.ed.gov

Greenwood, C. R., Delquadri, J. C., & Hall, R. V. (1989). Longitudinal effects of class-wide peer tutoring. *Journal of Educational Psychology, 81*, 371–383.

Johnson, D., & Johnson, R. T. (1989). *Cooperation and competition: Theory and research*. Edina, MN: Interactive Book Company.

Johnson, D., & Johnson, R. T. (1994). *Learning together and alone*. Boston: Allyn and Bacon.

Johnson, D. W., Johnson, R. T., & Holubec, E. J. (1994a). *The new circles of learning*. Alexandria, VA: Association for Supervision and Curriculum Development.

Johnson, D. W., Johnson, R. T., & Holubec, E. J. (1994b). *The nuts and bolts of cooperative learning*. Edina, MN: Interactive Book Company.

Kohn, A. (1986). *No contest: The case against competition*. Boston: Houghton-Mifflin.

Madden, N., Slavin, R. E., & Stevens, R. J. (1986). Cooperative integrated reading and comparison. *Teacher's manual*. Baltimore: John Hopkins University, Center for Research in Elementary and Middle Schools.

Munoz, M. A., & Clavijo, C. (2002). *Educational opportunities for minority students: Lessons learned from a summer high school math and science program*. (ERIC Issue: ED463149.) Institute of Education Sciences. Retrieved April 3, 2003, from www.eric.ed.gov

Peterson, I. (1999). Formulas for fairness: Applying the math of cake cutting to conflict resolution. *Science News, 149*, 284.

Piaget, J. (1928). *Judgment and reasoning of the child*. New York: Harcourt Brace Jovanovich.

Rosenbaum, J. E. (2003). *High schools' role in college and workforce preparation: Do college-for-all policies make high school irrelevant? Spotlight on student success*. (ERIC Issue: ED474216.) Institute of Education Sciences. Retrieved April 3, 2003, from www.eric.ed.gov

Sharan, Y., & Sharan, S. (1992). *Expanding cooperative learning through group investigation*. New York: Teachers College Press.

Slavin, R. (1995). *Cooperative learning*. Boston: Allyn and Bacon.

Vygotsky, L. S. (1978). *Mind in society*. Cambridge, MA: Harvard University Press.

# Chapter 7

# Interdisciplinary Thematic Units (ITUs)

**INTASC Principle 1:** The teacher understands the central concepts, tools of inquiry, and structures of the discipline(s) he or she teaches and can create learning experiences that make these aspects of subject matter meaningful for students.

**Key Disposition**

- The teacher appreciates multiple perspectives and conveys to learners how knowledge is developed from the vantage point of the knower.

**INTASC Principle 7:** The teacher plans instruction based upon knowledge of subject matter, students, the community, and curriculum goals.

**Key Disposition**

- The teacher values planning as a collegial activity.

## Introduction to the Chapter

The focus on planning so far has been on the individual teaching strategies and planning curriculum within your own subject matter disciplines. This has included the basics for designing individual lesson plans as well as the broader concept of the unit plan. The next logical step in this process is a discussion of strategies to integrate curriculum from one content area with that of other disciplines in a meaningful, seamless, thematic manner. We will refer to this as using interdisciplinary thematic units (ITUs).

Section 1 describes the use of ITUs including their purpose and value from the perspective of different curriculum models. It also covers research studies related to the effectiveness of using ITUs in schools.

Section 2 takes you through the process of developing an ITU as a team and provides activities to prepare you to implement this strategy in your field experience. Though you are not expected to design a complete ITU at this stage of your training, the activities and guidance provided in this section will enable you to undertake such a project should it fit into your field or course work needs. You can also examine an example of an ITU developed by a team of preservice teachers.

Section 3 explores the various challenges teachers might encounter when attempting to implement an ITU in their own schools. Though none is insurmountable, it is always better to be aware of the various issues that must be dealt with prior to beginning rather than encountering them along the implementation path.

A primary goal in using the ITU curriculum approach is to enable your students to gain Mastery over the concepts and skills that bridge several discipline areas. Once students have obtained these skills, they will be better able to apply the knowledge, skills, and dispositions they learn anywhere to a variety of situations and contexts. This is true Mastery of the learning process, which will help students long after they complete secondary education.

## Section 1: Introduction to ITUs

The education field has also referred to interdisciplinary learning by a number of other interchangeable terms, including *multidisciplinary learning, integrated learning, holistic education, integrated curriculum*, and *thematic learning*. As noted by Roberts and Kellough (2000).

> All refer to a way of teaching and a way of planning and organizing the instruction program so that discrete disciplines of subject matter are interrelated in a design that matches developmental needs of students and helps connect students' learning that is meaningful to their current and past experiences. (p. 4)

This often runs counter to what is typically seen in most schools today, where curriculum tends to be teacher-centered, text-driven, and uses standard, traditional assessment as the sole indicator of evaluation. Contrary to this type of teaching, interdisciplinary instruction, or *interdisciplinary thematic units (ITUs)*, as it is referred to here, typically maintains these unique characteristics:

1. focus on a central theme;
2. exploration of a theme by applying skills and techniques derived from a variety of disciplines, with an emphasis on applying both content and process (Wood, 1997); and
3. performance of multilevel tasks by a group of students.

## The Purpose of ITUs

A group of teachers using ITUs have a number of goals to keep in mind, which are to:

1. promote the major concept (to students) that learning is interrelated and cuts across disciplines;
2. promote individual interests of students through individualized and personal instruction;
3. promote student motivation and independent problem solving through learning what they need to know, rather than dictating what the teacher wants them to know; and
4. provide a context for, and facilitation of, cooperative learning.

***Reform, Philosophic, and Research Support.*** A number of education groups and researchers have advanced strong justification and support for this teaching approach. Philosophically, national reform documents related to secondary education, including those referred to previously—such as *Second to None* (California Task Force, 1992), *Breaking Ranks* (National Association of Secondary School Principals, 1996), and *What Matters Most* (National Commission on Teaching and America's Future, 1996)—each discuss the merits of interdisciplinary instruction. Additionally, a number of key researchers in learning theory—including Piaget (1928), Dewey (1938), Vygotsky (1978), Bruner (1986), and Gardner (2000)—suggest valuable outcomes resulting from teaching students in a more holistic, interdisciplinary manner.

In addition to support from major educational reform groups and prominent learning theorists, there has also been an accumulation of recent empirical support evidenced by the number of research studies focused on the potential effectiveness of using ITUs with secondary school students. This chapter presents a sample of that research, representative of the findings and inclusive of a variety of subject areas and range of student abilities.

One study involved Navajo students in an interdisciplinary course entitled Senior Honors Seminar (Keating & Stall, 1990). These students represented a population that typically performs poorly in traditional classroom settings. The teacher-researchers used a series of six interdisciplinary units in a year-long course to evaluate the effectiveness of the ITU versus traditional course work (separated into distinct subject areas by teacher). This study used some of the instructional elements common in all ITUs; for example, student-centered/hands-on activity-based experiences; cooperative learning; cultural connections; field and community-based activities; linkage to state standards in English, science, and social science; and both traditional and authentic assessments. Findings from this small study indicated gains (as compared to control groups) in these variables (from pre- and postsurveys and tests of achievement): (1) attitudes toward school, (2) language arts skills (oral and written language), and (3) cooperative/social skills. This study successfully produced gains in critical areas when compared to students in a control group enrolled in traditional course work. A major implication of this study was the value of including cultural connections and community resources in ITUs representative of students' cultural background.

A special 10-week enrichment summer program utilized the integration of math and writing in inner-city Los Angeles schools. This study involved a large number of students who had finished 9th grade and had performed poorly in traditional school environments prior to the study. Researchers found an increase in both problem solving and writing ability compared to control groups (Bell & Bell, 1985). The findings suggested the value of integrating writing to improve both higher level understanding of math and the quality of writing.

The integration of science with technology, language arts, and societal issues was used in a 2-year study of an integrated Science 1 and Science 2 course conducted in a higher socioeconomic California high school. Researchers compared the outcomes to students in more traditional science courses over this same 2-year period (Keating, 1996). Findings suggested student differences in levels of problem solving, social skills, attitudes toward science, and achievement in science as compared to the same variables in control groups. These differences were noted regardless of student socioeconomic status, again implying the value of using interdisciplinary teaching and learning with all students.

Robert Yager (1992) conducted four studies involving the effectiveness of the interdisciplinary science/technology/society (STS) approach as compared to a more traditional approach to the teaching of science. This curriculum model emphasizes the development of student interest through the integration of societal issues, science, and technology. By focusing on meaningful community issues, students take on leadership in studying and becoming active participants in solutions to problems. Results from the four studies indicated no statistically significant differences found in achievement related to concept development; however, significant differences were reported in the application domain for grades 8 and 9, as well as for low-ability students in the attitude domain. STS research also indicated a strong positive effect on the attitudes of females toward science. Finally, implications of these results in the areas of curriculum reform, assessment, and the professional development of teachers concluded that the four studies provide "hard" empirical evidence in favor of the STS interdisciplinary approach for students as well as for teachers.

Although most of these studies focused on student outcomes, a study by Yvonne Meichtry (1990) concentrated on a variety of effects on teachers' involvement as influenced by their participation in the development of interdisciplinary curriculum. Using a variety of sources of data, her findings suggest that middle school teachers involved in this process were observed to model positive changes in their own individual classroom practices in the areas of curriculum planning, delivery of instruction, evaluation of student performance, and behavior management. These findings further suggest that the experience process of collaboration with other teachers exerts profound influence on teacher practice. Although the Meichtry study focused on middle school teachers, Paul Spies (1995) suggests a corollary to this study is that high schools can learn much about interdisciplinary teaching from the middle school reform movement in which middle school teaching has been focused and centered around team teaching and ITUs. He points out that many of the positive outcomes (such as more coherent and relevant curriculum, improved attendance, reduced failure rate, improved social skills, and improved relationships with community members) seen in middle school education would be transferable to the high schools.

Another study focused on the importance for teachers to understand the nature of interdisciplinary teaching and learning and the elements critical to its success. This meta-analysis study analyzed a number of studies that were conducted on teachers claiming to be participating in interdisciplinary teaching (Cotton, 1982, 1999). The findings produced mixed results in that students in controlled classes (traditional curriculum) produced greater gains in academic areas compared to experimental classes (those supposedly using ITUs). Further analysis suggests that these differences may actually be attributed, at least in part, to teacher misconceptions related to interdisciplinary teaching. These would include both the types of strategies incorporated in ITUs as well as lack of a clear understanding of how to facilitate the process with students. These findings suggest the importance of teachers utilizing some common "best practices" in designing and implementing ITUs, especially in terms of what strategies they use with students and how they facilitate this process.

Much support for incorporating interdisciplinary teaching and learning in high schools exists in national reform documents (and task forces), learning theorists, and empirical studies. How then does this translate to the practitioner who appears to be more and more restricted by demands of state and national standards?

Contrary to this apparent dilemma (restriction to subject matter content standards) is the fact that state and national committees that produce national educational standards have recommended the incorporation of interdisciplinary teaching as a desired methodology in secondary schools. *Many states have also followed that lead in their own subject matter standards by encouraging integration of other disciplines.* A sample of how interdisciplinary curriculum is encouraged can be found in *Goals 2000: The National Education Goals* (refer to web page www.negp.gov).

Figure 7.1 provides a visual of an interdisciplinary concept model to give you an idea of how the pieces may fit together in an integration of disciplines to form an ITU.

***A Continuum for ITUs.*** ITU planning is not an all-or-nothing curricular adaptation. When you decide to initiate an ITU, keep in mind it may not always be logistically or academically appropriate to integrate all discipline topics smoothly. In fact, a continuum of possibilities exists for interdisciplinary teaching, ranging from a nonintegrated model—with individual teachers working in their own classes who teach only within their disciplines, without any active attempt to

**FIGURE 7.1** Interdisciplinary Thematic Units Concept Model

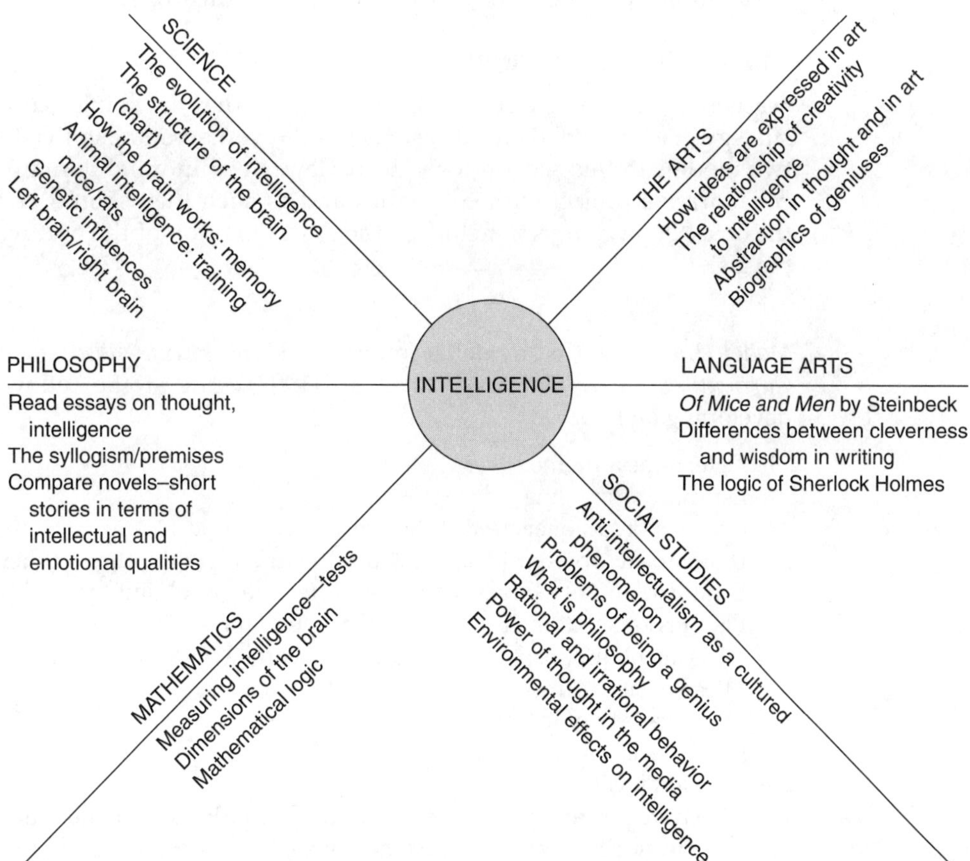


Note: From *Interdisciplinary Curriculum: Design and Implementation* (Figure 5.3, p. 58), edited by Heidi Hayes Jacobs, 1989. Alexandria, VA: Association for Supervision and Curriculum Development. Copyright 1989. ASCD. Reprinted by permission. All rights reserved.

integrate other disciplines or teachers, but still work around a theme—to a complete integration of teacher discipline teams. At this end of the continuum the teacher team will team teach thematically across the whole curriculum with little or no subject matter boundaries. In between, on the continuum, teachers from two different disciplines might actively coordinate or parallel what is taught in each other's classes, but never physically combine the two groups. In this model, they may or may not incorporate common themes. Using this third model teachers and students may collaborate intensely around a central theme within two or more disciplines.

Using some level of an ITU can create situations in which learning in your classroom is more closely connected to students' reality, their lives, and other subjects that interest them. The use of ITUs provides students an opportunity to see the connections in a way that makes sense from their own experiences. From the perspective of the Circle of Courage, utilizing interdisciplinary teaching serves the spirit of Mastery well. Mastery can be accomplished more easily as concepts are assimilated in a context that will be long lasting for students.

## Models for ITU Design

Teachers have a variety of models to examine if they are going to use this curricular strategy. Each model delineates steps to follow to accomplish this task. We present two models in this section for your review. Keep in mind you are undertaking a collaborative project with colleagues and as such they should be involved from the onset of any project, including the determination of the best way to approach the task.

*Model One.* The first model is from a book entitled *Interdisciplinary Approaches to Curriculum*. In it, Thomas Post et al. (1997) suggest the following outline in developing an ITU:

1. Determine a theme.
2. Estimate a time line.
3. Create a broad overview of the topic.
4. Brainstorm topics or ideas related to the theme with other teachers.
5. Establish unit objectives (cognitive, affective, psychomotor, and word).
6. Plan lessons that include an appropriate sequence incorporating many of the assessment and instructional strategies you have examined in previous chapters. These desired curricular areas include:
   a. a variety of learning styles;
   b. questioning strategies encompassing various knowledge and comprehension levels;
   c. strategies for inclusion of all students (multicultural, gender-fair, and physically or emotionally challenged);
   d. assessment tools (both informal and formal); and
   e. evaluation of the effectiveness of the ITU.

Evaluating the ITU is an important aspect of this model. Teachers must assess the value of ITUs. They can use action research (Chapter 3) as a useful evaluation method. Based on findings from assessing the practice, this model allows for continuous revision of the ITU. Another important aspect of this model is that the design highlights the issue of inclusion of all students.

*Model Two.* A second model, developed by Wood (1997), suggests the following eight-step approach to designing ITUs:

1. Consider students' developmental backgrounds including cognitive strengths and limitations as well as learning styles.
2. Brainstorm activities and procedures that might address developmental background.
3. Prepare a complete lesson plan for the introductory lesson.
4. Include a brief description of other lessons.
5. State the general objectives of the unit.
6. Determine tentative evaluation methods and techniques.
7. List essential materials.
8. Select a unit theme involving students in this process.

Remember that, as you read in Chapter 5, all steps for models such as these appear to be sequential in nature. However, actual planning never follows a strictly linear path. Ideas will be sparked at various stages in planning and teams must be flexible enough during the development stages (and even in the delivery phase) to revise ideas continuously, always with the goal of developing the best ITU possible.

## ITU Teams

Patricia Roberts and Richard Kellough in their text, *A Guide for Developing Interdisciplinary Thematic Units* (2000), place an emphasis on the initial importance of how to work together as an interdisciplinary team. Their ideas are very similar to the models of cooperative learning for students discussed in Chapter 6. They emphasize the importance of the essential skills of communicating and group processing skills used in cooperative learning. In addition, other initial tasks include selecting a team that includes teachers from different disciplines, designating roles (such as team leader and other appropriate roles), scheduling regular meeting times, and having an organized action plan for the completion of the ITU.

Content considerations for the team are also very important and include familiarity with local, state, and national standards; student textbooks; primary sources; resources from Internet and other sources (people and places); as well as professional literature related to the ITU. It would be helpful to develop a working title for the theme at this time to help focus discussion of the ITU.

Figure 7.2 provides a visual of a sample brainstorming activity as an example of how to begin planning an ITU by using a webbing diagram.

**FIGURE 7.2** Sample Brainstorming Activity to Plan an ITU by Using a Webbing Design

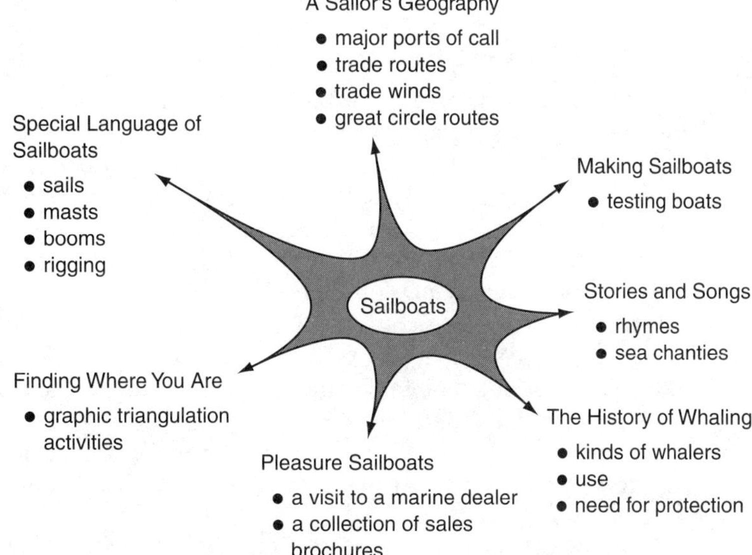


Note: From *Interdisciplinary Approaches to Curriculum: Themes for Teaching* (p. 27) by Post, Humphreys, Ellis, and Buggey, © 1997. Reprinted by permission of Pearson Education Inc., Upper Saddle River, NJ.

## Putting It Into Practice: Activity 7.1

This activity will help you initiate the process of developing an interdisciplinary thematic unit using a collaborative process. You will need to form a small team with members representing three or four different subject areas. The tasks of the team are to select a theme for study and prepare a presentation to the rest of the class on how your team made decisions throughout the process.

1. Your team must decide which sources you will consult prior to selecting an appropriate theme. Use this checklist to guide your discussion.
   a. National curriculum standards for a particular subject
   b. State curriculum frameworks
   c. Local curriculum guides and documents
   d. Student textbooks and teacher's guide for adopted textbooks
   e. Student interests and questions
   f. Resources on the Internet
   g. Professional literature
2. Next, working individually, brainstorm as many word and phrase associations about the theme from your own discipline as possible, and construct a visual web. Then share your ideas with others in your group. One member of the group should record the ideas and develop a visual web for the team to use as a resource as you continue to develop your ITU ideas.
3. Share and discuss both the product and process your team used as you developed the initial pieces of the ITU.

# SECTION 2: THE ITU DEVELOPMENT PROCESS

In any model selected, certain key elements will help your design and implementation efforts to be successful. Teachers must know the standards they are responsible for teaching. You should identify enduring concepts that will cause students to think critically, solve problems, and look at the world in different ways. This focus on concepts while designing ITUs helps students understand important concepts rather than just learn facts to recall. Concepts used in this strategy should be broad ideas such as *change* or *conflict*.

You could use the concept of change, for example, to study ecosystems and evolution in science in a way that offers students a chance to understand how cause and effect produce change. Further, they could begin exploring how change in their own lives has cause and effect. Students can discuss moral issues such as the failure to compromise or change in scientific terms, in a social, historical context, and through literature and writing.

## Essential Questions

Following the identification of a concept, essential questions then guide the critical thinking and understanding of the unit. Jacobs (1997) believes that essential questions are at the heart of the curriculum. "It is the essence of what you believe students should examine and know in the short time they have with you" (p. 26). She identifies eight criteria for writing essential questions:

1. Each student should be able to understand the question.
2. The language of the questions should be written in broad, organizational terms.
3. The question should reflect the teacher's conceptual priorities.
4. Each question should be distinct and substantial.
5. Questions should not be repetitious.
6. Questions should be realistic given the amount of time allocated for the unit or course.
7. There should be a logical sequence to a set of essential questions.
8. Questions should be posted in the classroom.

In the example using change as the theme, questions posed might be something like the following:

1. What is the nature of change?
2. How has change affected the environment?
3. How has change affected society through history?
4. How has change affected you and your community?

## *Putting It Into Practice:* Activity 7.2

For this activity, you will need to regather your interdisciplinary team formed for Putting It Into Practice: Activity 7.1. The next step in this process is to develop your skills in identifying essential questions and in selecting specific resources related to your emerging ITU. For this activity, use the ideas and themes you developed in step 2 of Activity 7.1, and begin to write essential questions that cover the range of your theme and could help guide the development of the ITU. The previous example of the change theme offers ideas on how questions might be framed.

Each team should determine a specific theme and develop at least five essential questions that could be used in designing student learning experiences throughout the ITU.

## Scope and Sequence

Once you have developed the essential questions that frame your ITU, the next step is to focus more directly on specific concepts to be learned in each subject area. Clarifying the theme and essential questions makes this task easier. Similarly, by using the theme, essential questions, and specific target concepts, your ITU team will be able to examine textbooks, curriculum guides, standards, and other resources to determine whether these resources will be useful in implementing the ITU.

At this point your team must begin to sketch out the scope and sequence of the project: To what depth will ideas and concepts be specifically covered and over what time period? During this phase, your team will sequence the order of content to be taught and identify instructional and assessment strategies to be used at various points in the unit. Additionally, your group will consider the various roles and expectations of both students and teachers at different stages of the process.

## Assessment Strategies

Following the development of essential questions and planning the scope and sequence, focus on what assessments you will use with students that will tell you what they understand. If you use the backward planning model discussed in previous chapters, these steps will help in determining assessment strategies:

1. Identify desired results.
2. Determine assessment strategies.
3. Plan learning experiences and instruction.

You need to link the desired results to the school district or state content standards. Students should be able to provide evidence of understanding in a variety of ways through writing, performance assessment, and oral presentations. Once you have determined how to assess students, then and only then can you make decisions about the lessons and the instruction you will need to provide to build their schema and knowledge base in order to successfully demonstrate their knowledge and understanding at the end of the unit.

***Sample Assessment Plan.*** Continuing with the example of change as the theme, the following will illustrate this process for you.

**Concept:** Change

**Standards:** These should be identified by content area based on the state or district curriculum standards.

**Essential questions:** These should be general enough to be used across the curriculum.

**Assessment:** This final project or menu of projects will allow students to demonstrate their understanding of the concept and essential questions. You can best assess these projects using rubrics. For example, the final projects can be content-specific or conducted jointly between disciplines and might include the following:

1. Students simulate a town meeting to discuss whether or not to adopt a science textbook with evolution, one with evolution and creationism, one with neither.
2. Students write a position paper taking a stand on evolution or creationism, analyzing, synthesizing, and evaluating information learned to draw their own opinion.
3. Students prepare a PowerPoint (or other visual) presentation depicting major industrial changes throughout American history and the effect those changes have had on society.
4. Students participate in a small group Socratic Seminar, teacher-led, discussing past effects of change, predicting future changes, and determining personal responsibility to the global and local community.

**Instructional experiences:** This is background knowledge, examples, and experiences students will need in order to successfully demonstrate their understanding in the final projects (examples are listed).

1. **Science:** resource books, text chapters, guest speakers, and experiments on change.
2. **English:** opinion and persuasive writing, reading and literary analysis, discussion analysis essays, and Socratic Seminars.
3. **Social Studies:** research using primary and secondary sources to gain knowledge of key events and change throughout American History, preparation of PowerPoint presentations depicting key issues and drawing conclusions, and Socratic Seminars.

Within the same interdisciplinary teams you have been working with, use the ideas generated by the last two Putting It Into Practice activities to develop a general scope and sequence plan for teaching your sample ITU. Your team should develop a plan that covers at least 2 to 3 weeks of instruction using the template provided in Figure 7.3. Include ideas of how you might use assessment in your plan.

**FIGURE 7.3** Scope and Sequence

| Week: _____<br>Concepts/<br>Essential Questions to Focus On: | Science | Social Science | English |
|---|---|---|---|
| 1.<br>2.<br>3.<br>4.<br>5. | | | |
| Materials to Be Used (e.g., text pages/chapters): | | | |
| Teacher's Role: | | | |
| Student's Role: | | | |

## A Closer Look

**Instructional Resource G** contains an example developed by a team of preservice teachers representing English, social science, and science disciplines. This successfully implemented ITU shows that ITUs can be utilized in secondary schools even if only by a small dedicated team that wants to bring this experience to students. The sample daily lesson plans included in **Instructional Resource G** detail what each teacher will do to participate in the implementation of the interdisciplinary thematic unit. This plan represents how a team used the model to help design its unit in a way that allowed team members to be able to implement it as well as the action research strategy used to assess its effectiveness.

Figure 7.4 is a shell outline for an overall ITU. You can use it to guide your interdisciplinary team in the completion of an ITU should you wish to do so in the future.

FIGURE 7.4 ITU Shell Document

| Team Member Names | Discipline Areas | Grade Levels |
|---|---|---|

1.
2.
3.
4.

**Working Theme of the Unit and Essential Questions**

**Rationale**

Provide a justification based on:

1. appropriateness for students and school site;
2. frameworks and standards from each discipline; and
3. personal and team curriculum philosophy.

**Unit Overview**

1. Goals
2. Standards addressed in each subject area
3. Major questions to address
4. Major objectives (cognitive, psychomotor, and affective)
5. Major summative and formative assessments methods matched to these objectives
6. Scope and sequence

**Instructional Strategies**

A list of (a) activities (discipline or interdisciplinary specific); (b) major teaching strategies; (c) organizational patterns; and (d) specific resources (people, places, and things), including what technology applications will be used.

**Organizational Patterns and Resources**

Include people, places, and things as well as consideration of how specific technology applications will be used.

**Strategies for Inclusion**

Detail specifically how all students will participate and succeed, including specifically designed academic instruction in English (SDAIE).

**Individual Lesson Plans in the Context of the ITU**

Individual lesson plans from each member of the group with a brief description of how each connects to the ITU theme.

**Action Research Design and Evaluation Plan**

Draft a brief action research design that would evaluate the success of the ITU.

## SECTION 3: ESSENTIALS FOR ITU IMPLEMENTATION

If teachers in secondary schools plan to utilize the ITU strategy, they must overcome various challenges. Some challenges arise because interdisciplinary curriculum is not yet a common practice in secondary schools, one reason being that most ITU curriculum is somewhat more customized and not typically available in the marketplace in the form of texts and other supplemental resources. As a result, teachers at school sites need time to develop the curriculum and select (or create) appropriate resources. Ideally, this means not only initial planning time to write the curriculum but also common time during implementation in order to meet to organize, evaluate, and adapt the curriculum and strategies as needed (common preparation hours, for example).

## Support of School Administrators

School administrators must understand interdisciplinary connections to be an effective learning strategy and support the logistics that can maximize the development and implementation of ITUs. Optimally, in addition to the planning time and common prep periods, support would also include any additional required curriculum materials. All of these may involve increased financial commitment from schools.

Implementation of interdisciplinary curriculum may very well involve longer periods of time for students to complete than more traditional curriculum. One reason for this is that students are making choices on what and how they learn. The learning process may not always be linear, because students design and redesign what they want to do. Although this is one of the cognitive strengths of the process, some parents, students, teachers, and administrators outside the process may view it negatively as a lack of time on-task.

The potential for this perception makes it even more critical for administrators as well as teachers to be well informed on the theory and research that justifies interdisciplinary curriculum, resulting in the incorporation of appropriate strategies that maximize the potential for success. Empowered by this expertise, they can inform and involve parents and students in the ITU process and make them aware of the value of integrating the curriculum (and of the possible need for more time to accomplish the goals).

## Teacher Buy-in and Expertise

Teachers involved with ITUs must buy in to the process and be willing to be flexible as part of a consensus-building team that decides what to include and exclude in the ITU. As subject matter specialists, teachers are accustomed to having individual control over what content they include. They should also be willing to involve students' suggestions and input as a crucial element in shaping their interdisciplinary plans.

Additionally, students experience freedom and flexibility when involved in interdisciplinary curriculum, which means teachers will have to trust them to work independently and with their teams. This is all part of the cooperative learning process, discussed in Chapter 6. Teams on-task may involve a greater noise level in a class and less structure than normal (students in and out of their seats and the room) as they attend to their various tasks. Some teachers may be uncomfortable in relinquishing traditional controls over students and may not have the personal communication skills to facilitate well in this work environment. Therefore, teacher knowledge or training in appropriate classroom management skills and the effective use of cooperative learning are essential corollaries to the implementation of the ITU process.

## Commitment to Innovation

Assessments in interdisciplinary learning tend to be more performance based and less traditional. Use of paper-and-pencil type assessments such as multiple-choice, true/false, and matching exams is replaced by more authentic forms of assessment, such as the use of portfolios, group projects, and performance. Using these forms of assessment involves a paradigm shift in how evaluation is done and in some cases may mean the participating teacher's training in or relearning of the process of evaluating student work.

Any team of teachers that decides on an ITU approach will need to take all of these issues into consideration. Practically speaking, if educators consider ITUs a fairly innovative practice on a school site, it would be most appropriate to start with less ambitious attempts identified earlier in the ITU continuum. Two teachers can combine efforts to initiate an ITU project, sharing the process and results with colleagues as they proceed.

It is only in schools committed to the ITU strategy that teams of teachers are likely to have the support needed to be successful at the upper ends of the continuum. If, however, a teacher's focus is always on student learning, some form of the ITU strategy will be part of the curriculum during a semester. Application of one of the ITU models gives students experiences that will allow them to develop in all aspects of the Circle of Courage.

## SECTION 4: CHAPTER SUMMARY AND REFLECTION

Chapter 7 introduced you to interdisciplinary thematic units, one of the more advanced and complex ways to present your curriculum to students. When implemented appropriately and in collaboration with involved teaching colleagues, the results can be powerful for students because learning becomes more meaningful. Curriculum that connects across disciplines provides students with a more integrated means of understanding the relationships among the content areas they are studying.

Section 1 of this chapter provided an overview of models for designing interdisciplinary units and offered strategies for working together effectively as a team with your colleagues in this process. Teachers may have creative and useful ideas on building interdisciplinary connections across the disciplines, but unless the group can build and teach the unit together, they will remain only ideas.

Section 2 described the practical steps of developing an ITU and offered a template to follow as well as several exercises to provide you with some experience in crafting such a unit. Section 3 examined the various needs that facilitate the development process, not only while creating the ITU but also in thinking through issues of resources and gaining colleague support to undertake such work. Keep in mind the various levels of ITUs and approach your initial efforts in a practical way. Start from less complex designs until you acquire the skills and experiences to begin using more elaborate ITUs with others.

The efforts of finding the resources and time to work with colleagues on ITUs are rewarded with student understanding not only of the specific curriculum objectives but also in learning to connect ideas across various disciplines. In this way, you will assist students in reaching the Mastery section of the Circle of Courage at a level that will allow them to transfer knowledge and skills from one area to another.

## References


Bell, E., & Bell, R. (1985). Writing and math in problem solving: An argument in favor of synthesis. *School Science and Math, 85*(3), 210–221.

Brendtro, L. K., Brokenleg, M., & Bockern, S. V. (2002). *Reclaiming youth at risk: Our hope for the future.* Bloomington, IN: National Education Service.

Bruner, J. (1986). *Actual minds, possible worlds.* New York: Cambridge University Press.

California Task Force (1992). *Second to none.* Sacramento, CA: Department of Education.

Cotton, K. (1982). *Effects of interdisciplinary team teaching: Research synthesis* (ERIC Issue: ED230533). Institute of Education Sciences. Retrieved March 18, 2003, from www.eric.ed.gov

Cotton, K. (1999). *Research you can use to improve results*. Portland, OR: Northwest Regional Educational Lab.

Council of Chief State School Officers. (1992). Model standards for beginning teacher licensing, assessment, and development: A resource for state dialogue. Washington, DC: Author. www.ccsso.org/content/pdfs/corestrd.pdf

Dewey, J. (1938). *Experience and education*. Bloomington, IN: Kappa Delta Pi.

Gardner, H. (2000). *Intelligence reframed: Multiple intelligences for the twenty-first century*. New York: Basic Books.

Hough, D., & St. Clair, B. (1995). The effects of integrated curricula on young adolescent problem-solving. *Middle Level Education Quarterly, 19*(1), 1–25.

Jacobs, H. (Ed.). (1989). *Interdisciplinary curriculum: Design and implementation*. Alexandria, VA: Association for Supervision and Curriculum Development.

Jacobs, H. (1997). *Mapping the big picture: Integrating curriculum and assessment K–12*. Alexandria, VA: Association for Supervision and Curriculum Development.

Keating, J. (1996, December). *Preliminary results, implications and applications from a study comparing a traditional and an integrated high school science program*. Paper presented at the Annual Global Summit on Science and Science Education, San Francisco, CA.

Keating, J., & Stall, P. (1990). Evolution—A topic for interdisciplinary study. *New Mexico English Journal, 5*(2), 19–21.

Meichtry, Y. (1990). *Teacher collaboration: The effects of interdisciplinary teaching on teacher interaction and classroom practice*. Paper presented at the Annual Meeting of Mid-Western Research Association, Chicago.

National Association of Secondary School Principals (1996). *Breaking ranks: Changing an American institution*. Reston, VA: NASSP.

National Commission on Teaching and America's Future (1996). *What matters most*. New York: NCTAF.

National Education Goals Panel (2000). *Goals 2000: National Education Goals*. Retrieved December 9, 2002, from www.negp.gov

Piaget, J. (1928). *Judgment and reasoning of the child*. New York: Harcourt Brace Jovanovich.

Post, T., Humphreys, et al. (1997). *Interdisciplinary approaches to curriculum*. Upper Saddle River, NJ: Prentice Hall.

Roberts, P., & Kellough, R. (2000). *A guide for developing interdisciplinary thematic units*. Upper Saddle River, NJ: Merrill/Prentice Hall.

Spies, P. (1995). *Turning the tables: The growing need for high schools to follow the lead of middle level reform through interdisciplinary teaming*. Paper presented at the Annual National Middle School Association Conference, New Orleans, LA.

Vygotsky, L. S. (1978). *Mind in society*. Cambridge, MA: Harvard University Press.

Wiggins, G., & McTighe, J. (1998). *Understanding by design*. Alexandria, VA: Association for Supervision and Curriculum Development.

Wood, K. (1997). *Interdisciplinary instruction*. Upper Saddle River, NJ: Prentice Hall.

Yager, R. (1992). The STS approach: Reasons, intentions, accomplishments and outcomes (ERIC Issue: ED356945). Institute of Education Sciences. Retrieved March 18, 2002, from www.eric.ed.gov

# *Unit* IV

# Creating Supportive Environments for Learning

# Chapter 8

# *Diverse Inclusive Classrooms*

**INTASC Principle 5:** The teacher uses an understanding of individual and group motivation and behavior to create a learning environment that encourages positive social interaction, active engagement in learning, and self-motivation.

**Key Dispositions**

- The teacher takes responsibility for establishing a positive climate in the classroom and participates in maintaining such a climate in the school as a whole.
- The teacher understands how participation supports commitment, and is committed to the expression and use of democratic values in the classroom.

## Introduction to the Chapter

This chapter describes the classroom environments intended to support the primary outcomes of the Circle of Courage (Brendtro et al., 2002). All students must experience a sense of Belonging to the learning community a teacher establishes and be connected to others in the class. While learning to be responsible for considering the welfare of everyone in their learning community, they also develop a sense of Generosity. As members of a classroom, students learn to be productive in pluralistic settings, valuing diversity for the strength it represents. Ultimately, inclusive classrooms encourage Independence as students become decision makers who are also responsible for decisions made. Mastery can be achieved when attention is given to classroom environment as one of the critical foundational aspects of learning.

Hoover and Kindsvatter (1997) have suggested that "Classroom climate is a pervasive but intangible factor composed of the sum of the perceptions and impressions about the classroom that exist in the minds of students and teachers" (p. 130). Teachers who have thought through the many elements involved in diverse inclusive classrooms are able to design environments in which students feel welcome and included in the events of the classroom. This is no small accomplishment in a secondary classroom in which you will often meet with 150 students a day, each needing a safe learning environment, each individual coming to the class with different needs. However, putting some common ideas into action can help us develop classrooms that provide the optimal chance of creating a positive place for students to engage in learning.

These central elements form the basis of this chapter. Section 1 briefly introduces the concept of democratic classrooms and why many educators believe creating such environments is central to our teaching. One such educator, John Goodlad, believes that if teachers are to fulfill the educational mission of schools, they will need to help prepare citizens for a democratic society. He further argues that society primarily depends on the ability of teachers to cultivate a democratic setting and create learning opportunities that embrace all students (Goodlad, 1996).

In Section 2, the focus turns inward. We will ask each of you to begin to examine and understand your own filters of perception, those that influence the manner in which you interact with others who are different from you. Through this self-examination, we encourage you to undertake a process of becoming more culturally competent. Without an understanding of personal biases, teachers will likely make judgments and decisions about students that may perpetuate and reinforce existing cultural relations and conditions. These unexamined judgments can lead to actions that often have a negative impact on students. Becoming culturally competent is important in the process of becoming a teacher because it provides a real source of power to manage a classroom and help resolve student conflicts. Like many teaching skills, reaching this level of competence does not happen quickly but requires experience and maturity. Therefore, begin such development as early as possible in your efforts to become a powerful teacher, so that you gain the self-knowledge, confidence, and skills to be able to establish safe classrooms.

Section 3 explores the ideas of designing and setting up inclusive classrooms. The discussion examines various practices that enhance the prospect of being able to create and maintain safe and inclusive classroom environments, as well as the underlying principles that enable these classrooms to exist. As a preservice teacher learning how to develop these environments, you need to look beyond the traditional classroom structures you have likely seen during your observations and experiences in schools (those in which the teacher is the dominant and authoritarian figure). You will be challenged to create classrooms that may seem to contrast with these traditional management models and practices and instead promote democratic ideals of participation, fairness, equality, and justice. In brief, your challenge is to create classrooms that reflect and perpetuate the ideas of inclusive democracy and provide students with an experience that serves to teach and reproduce those ideals.

## SECTION 1: OVERVIEW OF DEMOCRATIC SCHOOLS

Establishing democratic schools and classrooms is not a new idea. In the early part of the twentieth century, the call to public schools to help train a citizenry for a more democratic society was reemerging. Noted education philosopher John Dewey—a strong voice in these efforts—believed in the necessity of a commitment from all Americans to help build communities that make their efforts and resources available to all members of the society to provide them the opportunity to reach their potential (Westbrook, 1996). Dewey's directive to schools was more specific: If people are to secure and maintain a democratic way of life, they must have opportunities to learn what that way of life means and how it might be led (Dewey, 1916). He believed schools were the responsible agent for providing these opportunities to learn about democracy.

Much more recently, other education scholars, such as Ted Sizer, have elaborated Dewey's beliefs for secondary schools. As Sizer noted, "High schools are one of America's most ubiquitous intentional communities. They exist to prepare youth for the adult world" (Sizer & Sizer, 1999, p. 9). What does this mean to the next wave of secondary teachers? It means that each of you will need to create an environment that provides all students the opportunity to acquire the knowledge, skills, and dispositions to help them build successful lives and careers.

If we accept the notion that classrooms in secondary schools should reflect and perpetuate democracy, then we must consider whether our own classrooms, classroom management strategies, and discipline actions actually teach, as well as model, those ideals. This is a challenge because many often perceive the school system as the least democratic institution, even though one of the roles society expects the system to fill is that of transmitter of the practice of democracy.

### Participatory Decision Making

Altering this perception means that teachers will need to work explicitly on creating inclusive democratic classrooms. To do this we must address perhaps the most important condition of democracy: respect. As Randy Hoover and Richard

Kindsvatter have noted in their book, *Democratic Discipline* (1997), without an environment of respect in the classroom, those in power establish the agendas and those lacking power become alienated and marginalized. This may be particularly true in schools and classrooms in which the teacher has little or no respect for students. Democracy implies participation; for schools and classrooms this means students need to be involved in decisions (Apple & Beane, 1995; Hoover & Kindsvatter, 1997). As one of the most important transmitters of this core American value, it is not hard to understand why many educators believe schools should be democratic places. Adults in the schools must model such ideas in the many roles they play. In classrooms, this implies that students and teachers should engage in collaborative planning to reach decisions that respond to the concerns, curiosities, goals, and interests of both. There is also a genuine attempt to allow all individuals in the classroom the right to participate in making decisions that affect their lives.

***Student Participation.*** In inclusive democratic classrooms, all individuals are valued and the rules of classroom participation and membership are clear. Ample opportunities exist for students to become active participants. All the while, assignments challenge them to meet outcomes that result in accomplishments as defined by students, as well as those expected by society. The work in the classroom becomes the students' work, rather than solely exercises assigned by someone else: teacher, test maker, or curriculum planner.

Many educators believe that these types of democratic classrooms must be youth-driven and sensitive to students' everyday realities. Teachers in these classrooms need to be flexible in their approaches to learning and students buy in to the goals of the lessons. The work in the classroom is also intense, not marked by casual participation, and teachers serve primarily as mentors and coaches, rather than dispensers of information (Sizer & Sizer, 1999).

## An Equitable Learning Community

To be involved in democratic schools, teachers must see themselves as participants in a learning community. Because classrooms are diverse communities, teachers must demonstrate the importance of each member of the classroom community having a shared purpose to ensure equal access to the information being provided to the class. Teachers must be aware that the same sources of inequality in society can be, and often are, replicated in our schools (Apple & Beane, 1995). One goal, therefore, must be the elimination of these societal inequalities. As University of California, Los Angeles (UCLA), educational scholar, Jeannie Oakes, noted, "In a diverse democracy, classrooms must be equitable learning communities and students must experience democracy in order to believe it" (Oakes & Lipton, 1999, p. 239).

Teachers working toward democratic ideals have a choice: Either maintain the status quo, or work to transform the environment of classrooms and schools to ensure that inequality does not continue to exist in secondary school practices. In doing the latter, teachers can create learning environments in which students grow accustomed to being treated as competent and able individuals. Each teacher needs to seek and create a balance between the intertwined rights of the teacher and the students so that students can participate in ways comfortable to them (Bartolome, 1994).

***Sense of Belonging.*** Schools and classrooms that work at becoming small democracies are noted for the conversations they hold. On the one hand, all members of the community are important and must feel as though each of their voices is heard. On the other hand, you must achieve a balance in this process. There is not a completely shared power base, because teachers will still hold the balance of power so that they are able to do their job. Ultimately, your challenge is to create a place in your classroom and school where all students feel they belong. After all, they have a right to belong, which is necessary in the full development of all students.

### Positive Relationships

A democratic classroom seeks to develop positive relationships in which there is an ongoing search for information and skill development. Students are trying to identify what they know and how they know it. The teacher's search also focuses on what students know and how they know it. The relationships between teacher and students, as well as among students, shape academic learning, intrapersonal learning, learning about institutions, and learning about culture (Oakes & Lipton, 1999).

The consequences of rigidly structured and rule-bound classrooms impact these relationships and, as a result, student learning and development. Teachers dispense information to quiet students and respond to misbehaviors by putting disciplinary consequences into effect automatically, with little or no interaction between student and teacher. Calm, orderly, and productive classrooms are consequences of a caring, inclusive, democratic environment. When the teacher is credible, that is, when words and actions are consistent, students are less likely to test the teacher with misbehavior. As Vygotsky and others have shown, people learn in relationships (Oakes & Lipton, 1999). This means that cognitive development is inseparable from social development, and therefore, the classroom environment is critical to learning.

***Modeling.*** As you have or will come to observe, all schools teach by what they model to their students. School and classroom routines demonstrate lessons of substance and value. Whether done implicitly or explicitly, both students and teachers internalize these values. It is important to clearly model the intended messages. Modeling can either promote optimism or cynicism, hard work or shortcuts. Our students count on our consistency, so we need to carefully model what we intend to teach.

In looking again to Dewey concerning issues of democratic classrooms, he stressed the importance of classrooms as a part of life, not merely preparation for it. To help society maintain and enhance democracy, students must participate in the classrooms, which in reality are microcosms of democratic society. Teachers must give students a chance to learn how their actions affect the success or failure of the group (Dewey, 1916).

Now that you know a bit more about democratic classrooms, the next two sections will explore what teachers can do to prepare themselves to teach in such places. Also examined will be how to create the routines and environments that allow for the modeling of democratic practices.

## SECTION 2: THE ROLE OF THE TEACHER

Have you ever wondered how you have developed your attitudes and perspectives on issues, people, or events? If you have pondered this question, undoubtedly you realized the importance of your parents and family in the process. From a very early age, close family members help shape individuals' personal filters of the way each one views the world. Theorists have suggested that by age 3 or 4 humans have the beginnings of perceptual filters and through these lenses begin screening the input the world provides. Interestingly, the information that matches the filters passes through and serves to reinforce early beliefs. Information that provides different or conflicting viewpoints is often deflected as untrue and does not become part of one's perceptual framework.

## Perceptual Filters

Each person has built a worldview that helps in dealing with the torrent of information faced daily. In that way, these filters are necessary. On the other hand, if people never take it upon themselves to examine their filters consciously, they may react to situations in a manner that was determined by the beliefs of those who raised them, which may not necessarily match the reality of the current world.

This failure to check personal filters often results in prejudices and discriminatory views. When confronted with a new situation or individuals unlike them, people may tend to respond with old patterns of behavior. Have you ever heard yourself repeating phrases you heard over and over again from members of your family who were adults when you were a child? Behaviors and actions may also stem from a similar pattern of learning; old tapes play in the subconscious. The filters and beliefs created in your childhood are not bad, in and of themselves. In fact, they have helped you make choices and survive your adolescence into adulthood. However, because of your influence as a teacher, many of your old tapes can, and often do, negatively impact the students in your classroom.

***Biased Practice.*** The following example of how biases can be transmitted may help illustrate this point. Examine the treatment of males and females in the classroom. As a male or female in this society, you have been taught gender roles, that is, what is expected of you as a young man or woman. Gender bias has been an issue in schools for years, both instructionally by teachers whose instruction perpetuates the bias as well as informally in the curriculum. Textbooks and reading materials historically have underrepresented girls and stereotyped gender roles in terms of character traits and career options. They have often portrayed males as brave, risk takers, achievers, and problem solvers, and females as passive, dependent, incompetent, fearful, and concerned about physical appearance (Sadker, Sadker, & Klein, 1991).

In a male-dominated society, this can lead to inaccurate judgments screened by personal filters. As a result, teachers in the past have communicated different expectations of males than females, often giving male students more attention and providing them more opportunities in class (Campbell, 1996). For example, though it is changing slowly in our secondary schools, there has been a belief that young women could not and should not achieve the same expected academic performance in math and science classes as their male counterparts. As a result, many teachers, raised with the screening filters described, continued to reinforce this biased practice. Only when teachers begin to more consciously examine their filters and behaviors, do they start to understand that they may unconsciously be perpetuating social myths that never did, and certainly no longer do, have a place in classrooms and schools.

It is not difficult to move beyond this example to understand how other issues, such as race, ethnicity, disability, religion, or socioeconomic status, can impact the classroom and school environment in even deeper ways, with great consequences. These filters and old tapes can work against creating and maintaining the types of inclusive democratic classrooms teachers want. It also is not hard to understand the significant impact these biased actions have on students. They can and do begin to develop a warped view of themselves, their place in classrooms and schools, and their own potential. Do teachers really want young women in their schools to believe that they are not as capable in certain academic areas as young men are? Do they want this for any student of color or economic class or religion? Certainly not in an inclusive democratic classroom.

***White Privilege.*** Peggy McIntosh clearly described the importance of understanding one's own filters in her article "White Privilege: Unpacking the Invisible Knapsack." McIntosh set out to write about "men's unwillingness to grant that they are over privileged, even though they may grant women are disadvantaged" (1989, p. 10). Such denials, according to McIntosh, constitute taboos that surround male advantage gained from female disadvantage. However, McIntosh realized that if this male bias were true, then it was equally possible, because hierarchies in society are interlocking, that most likely a phenomenon of white privilege exists that was similarly denied and protected. McIntosh notes, "As a white person, I realized I had been taught about racism as something which puts others at a disadvantage, but had been taught not to see one of its corollary aspects, white privilege, which puts me at an advantage" (1989, p. 10). Realizing this, the rest of McIntosh's article depicts her efforts to identify and understand some of the daily effects of her privilege. She was choosing to examine her own perceptual filters and attempting to begin to change the way she approached the world around her. After this careful examination, McIntosh concluded her powerful article by suggesting the following:

> One factor seems clear about all of the interlocking oppressions. They take both active forms which we can see and embedded forms which as a member of the dominant groups one is taught not to see. In my class and place, I do not see myself as a racist because I was taught to recognize racism only in individual acts of meanness by members of my group, never in invisible systems conferring unsought racial dominance on my group from birth.
>
> Disapproving of the systems won't be enough to change them. I was taught to think that racism could end if white individuals changed their attitudes. (But) a "white" skin in the United States opens many doors for whites whether or not we approve of the way dominance has been conferred on us. Individual acts can palliate, but cannot end these problems.
>
> To redesign social systems we need first to acknowledge their colossal unseen dimensions. The silences and denials surrounding privilege are the key political tool here. They keep the thinking about equality or equity incomplete, protecting unearned advantage and conferred dominance by making these taboo subjects. Most talk by whites about equal opportunity seems to me now to be about equal opportunity to try to get into a position of dominance while denying that systems of dominance exist.
>
> It seems to me that obliviousness about white advantage, like obliviousness about male advantage, is kept strongly inculturated in the United States so as to maintain the myth of meritocracy, the myth that democratic choice is equally available to all. Keeping most people unaware that freedom of confident action is there for just a small number of people props up those in power, and serves to keep power in the hands of the same groups that have most of it already. (McIntosh, 1989, p. 12)

McIntosh states that, unless people carefully examine their own behaviors and dispositions, they may be doing very little to help resolve the problems of discrimination. All people need to check their own filters, act differently on the old tapes as they play, and in general, raise their awareness concerning personal views on issues of difference. Teachers need to understand that these types of inequalities do not stop at the classroom door. If educators are committed to creating classroom environments in

## *Putting It Into Practice:* Activity 8.1

In a short paper:

1. Describe what you believe were the powerful experiences in your life that shaped your views of gender roles, race, culture, disabilities, economic class, and so on. Such experiences could be conversations with parents or respected elders you knew as a child, your own experiences as a student, encounters with those with backgrounds different than yours, foreign travel, or any other events. Try to capture not only the events but also how you believe they influenced your perception of others and the world around you.
2. Reflect on experiences in terms of your own cultural background. For example, what has it meant to grow up female or male in a specific culture? What roles did you feel expected to play? How have those experiences shaped your filters?
3. Identify how these experiences have influenced you as a learner, teacher, and member of a cultural group. Finally, explore how your experiences and perceptions have helped shape your assumptions about schooling and education.

which students can grow in all aspects of their lives, including Belonging, Mastery, Generosity, and Independence, then it is important for individual teachers to understand themselves, their filters, and their tapes. Completing Activity 8.1 can be helpful as an initial step in this process.

## Cultural Competence

Once teachers have a better understanding of their own filters, they will be in a better position to serve students. Additionally, individual teachers must continue developing their own cultural competence, their own understanding of how they perceive and interact with the world, and, most importantly, their own actions in the classroom. This raised awareness around issues of difference will help you as a teacher to build stronger connections with all students. These relationships will help make it possible to find connections between what is being taught and your students' own lives, thus creating opportunities for more active student engagement and thus greater opportunities for learning.

Though this text is not the place to delve extensively into these extremely important concepts and issues, one other example may help challenge your own thinking and inspire each of you to explore this topic further. The term *cultural competence* has been used in the preceding pages. Next, you will find a description of various stages of cultural competence. As you read through each stage, you can begin to identify, on the scale provided, the level of competence you believe yourself to currently be working from. Hopefully, this will provoke further thought and reflection. The piece that follows came from a workshop provided by Educators for Social Responsibility (ESR). This organization reminds us that we are continuous learners in the area of creating democratic classrooms and addresses issues of diversity in a pluralistic society.

In the ESR model, four levels of cultural competence exist. These include unconscious incompetence, conscious incompetence, conscious competence, and unconscious competence.

### *Unconscious Incompetence*

> Unconscious incompetence refers to a lack of awareness of how issues of diversity affect our lives. Although we may recognize that people have differences, we downplay their importance. At this stage we might say, "I don't know how many kids of color are in my classroom. Kids are kids. I'm color blind."

### *Conscious Incompetence*

> The next stage one may move into is conscious incompetence. In this stage, we begin to relate to ourselves as cultural beings and experience differences in others as well. We realize at this stage that we have a lot to learn about dealing with multicultural issues.
>
> Things don't seem simple anymore. We begin to take in the reality that we don't all share the same values, beliefs or behaviors; we move from an ethnocentric view of the world—"Only my culture, perspectives and values are appropriate"—to a multicultural perspective. We start to have respect for cultural differences and for points of view other than our own.

### *Conscious Competence*

> The next stage, that of conscious competence, actively engages us in a give-and-take dialogue around issues of diversity. We are willing and feel comfortable in giving and receiving coaching to better understand and appreciate differences. In this stage, we can easily ask others about themselves and their experiences. We also feel comfortable responding to inquiries about our differences. In this stage, we are often engaged in dialogues about our cultural competence. We are pretty comfortable asking a blind person whether they would like a hand crossing the street, getting instructions from someone in a wheel chair on how to help them get up an incline, or asking an African-American person about the meaning of Kwanza.

### *Unconscious Competence*

> The final level of cultural competence is unconscious competence. At this stage, we are meeting each other on the same level, engaging in an equal, democratic interaction. We are more and more comfortable with conflicts that arise during intergroup interactions. We feel more and more at home adjusting the way we perceive and experience our world and shifting to other ways. At this stage, we are not likely to go into an intergroup interaction with the naive thought that "all people are alike." We are able to bridge naturally and easily from one cultural pattern to another as we interact with people from different backgrounds. At this stage, we truly value inclusion and feel our lives are richer when people with a variety of perspectives enter our schools, lives, and neighborhoods. We believe and feel we need everyone's perspective to enjoy all of life's possibilities. (Dieringer, Kreidler, & Lantieri, 1996, sec. 8, pp. 7–8)

These descriptions of each level of cultural competence can help teachers more readily understand their own development in working with diverse groups of students. No matter which level you would identify yourself with, the work of understanding how you perceive the world should be thought of as a continuous effort. Personal filters and old tapes are deeply embedded. Unless teachers are mindful of them, they can easily influence their actions and behaviors in the classroom.

## Standards for Responsibility

Having laid the foundation for understanding oneself, one's filters, and one's own resulting biases and actions, let's refocus on the strategies that can be used in the classroom. As the focus shifts, remember that it is important to stay open and work

## *Putting It Into Practice:* Activity 8.2

Once you have completed reading about the four levels of cultural competence provided by ESR, individually answer the following:

- Where do you see yourself in the ESR model of cultural competence? Explain why.
- What important events in your life moved you from one stage to another?
- With what groups do you have less or more cultural competence? For example, some of us may have a lot of interactions with people with disabilities and are more comfortable in how we relate with this group of people than we are with other groups.
- Outline a personal action plan that will help you challenge yourself to move from one level of cultural competence to another. What kinds of experiences would this plan include?

After completing your individual assessment, join with two other classmates and share your responses.

to broaden the perspectives that shape your actions. Each person has been socialized to believe many myths and stereotypes. Be honest with yourself.

An important step in creating safe, democratic schools is to challenge discriminatory attitudes and behaviors as they arise within your classroom. Ignoring these issues will not make them go away. A teacher's inaction will send the wrong message—that the teacher is in agreement with such attitudes and behaviors. Make it clear that you will not tolerate words or actions that demean an individual or group. Your role in providing accurate information to challenge stereotypes and biases is crucial. Take responsibility for educating yourself about your own culture and the cultures of others. By doing this, you can establish standards for responsibility and behavior to hold yourself and others accountable.

As we have mentioned previously in this book, we believe that all teachers are role models. Teachers' actions become part of what their students are learning. Because one important goal in democratic classrooms is to assist students in being active members of their communities, then continued work on personal self-awareness is essential. Randy Hoover and Richard Kindsvatter have pointed out in their book, *Democratic Discipline* (1997), that as teachers begin to understand their roles in helping shape citizens for a democratic society, they need to come to know the ways they serve to reproduce and reinforce cultural relations and conditions. By using this understanding, teachers may realize what is needed on their parts to create positive change in those conditions.

## SECTION 3: EFFECTIVE CLASSROOM ENVIRONMENTS

The two preceding sections covered the history behind democratic school practices and reasons for establishing them in the classroom. They also explored the critical nature of raising personal awareness and understanding individual perspectives concerning the issues of diversity and inclusion, which underlie such endeavors. This section focuses on exploring various strategies that can assist you in developing your own inclusive classroom environments. One goal of this section is to help you manage your students' behavior in class, reducing disruptions and increasing cooperative, responsible behavior.

While we will focus more closely on class management issues and strategies in the next chapter, in this current section, we cover the tone you set in your class, which is critical to developing democratic classrooms. Many management issues can be eliminated or significantly reduced by the way teachers approach their classes. Establishing safe classroom environments will ensure each student the opportunity to be engaged in learning.

## Management

It is not unusual for new teachers, early in their first year, to experience the frustration of failure in the arena of class management. Unfortunately, this can lead to a breakdown of their self-confidence. Frequently, this problem can be traced to a clash between the teacher assuming a more traditional authoritarian role and the students wanting to be able to control some aspect of their role in the classroom. The resulting power struggle creates an unproductive learning environment. These types of tense environments result in the persistent failure of both teacher and students and serve to reinforce the stereotypes, hostility, and culture clashes seen all too often in our schools today. The teacher does not need to become authoritarian in order to challenge students intellectually. Your students can learn in cooperative, democratic classroom cultures (Bartolome, 1994).

Teachers have a choice to view their roles differently from past paradigms. Teachers can elect to engage students in learning by helping to create supportive relationships in positive learning environments. As a teacher, you will need to decide on the type of class management procedures you want to establish. You must reflect on your own values as they apply to your teaching situation and select appropriate strategies if you want to promote democratic behavior and responsibility. A primary goal for the democratic teacher is to help build learning environments in which appropriate student behaviors grow from engaging lessons, reflections about ethical actions, and caring and respectful relationships (Oakes & Lipton, 1999).

***Respect.*** How you interact with the students in your classroom sends a clear message about the respect you have for them. Few students stay in a positive learning mode when placed on the defensive. Democratic teachers provide instructions or correct student misbehavior without using an aggressive, authoritarian style. These teachers focus on the behavior of students that might be inappropriate, rather than criticizing the individual. Teacher criticism will serve only to close down connections with students.

It may seem to be a subtle difference, but you will see the powerful impact. While you might be thinking about a student who is out of his seat again, "John, you are always so disruptive to my classroom work," you would be better served to say, "John, I'm concerned that being out of your seat will not help you finish this assignment. You need to return to your seat and refocus on your work." Here you have focused on the inappropriate behavior and made clear your expectations of John without attacking him personally.

Be careful about labeling and categorizing students personally; instead, keep your focus on the disruptive behaviors that need to be addressed. The same case can be made for the teacher's use of sarcasm. Like criticism, sarcasm is rarely helpful and seldom contributes to behavioral change.

Fred Jones, who has spent considerable time researching and writing about positive classroom environments, asserts that the most frequent, and hence the most important, types of class management problems are the very small disruptions. Jones found, when conducting research in both urban and suburban schools, that the vast majority of class management issues, roughly 80%, consists of students talking to neighbors, while the second largest category, 15%, consists of students being out of their seats. Most other management issues are smaller ones: pencil tapping, note passing, or playing with objects (Jones, 1987). How teachers approach these issues can make a difference.

## Connections with Students

In developing democratic classrooms, your connections with your students are important, because these relationships form a part of the search for competence. Students are looking to discover what they know and how, and the teacher, whose search is very similar, is trying to discover what students know and how they know it. In meeting this challenge, the teacher plays a significant role by crafting learning experiences in which students are able to take control over their own learning.

The teacher must access students' prior knowledge to link it with new information. In this process, the teacher allows students to present and discuss what they already know and experiences they have had using their knowledge and skills. As we detailed earlier, teachers can then use this information as a valuable resource in helping them develop lessons that connect with the students' background, languages, and cultural experiences.

> The actual strength of methods depends, first and foremost, on the degree to which they [teachers] embrace a humanizing pedagogy that values students' background knowledge, culture, and life experiences, and creates learning contexts where power is shared by students and teachers. (Bartolome, 1994, p. 190)

In developing a positive democratic environment, you will need to choose instructional strategies to help students build confidence. They need positive feedback and a safe environment to take risks in their learning. The teacher must incorporate activities and classroom routines that help guide students in developing positive interpersonal behavior and appropriate school behavior.

Your behavior will either contribute to or detract from building a democratic environment. Remember, modeling the behavior you want from your students is an important teaching tool. Teachers who are successful in creating strong learning environments learn to describe positive behavior. If you consistently repeat positive directions, you will be able to guide most students to respond without becoming defensive. Quite often in classes today, teachers make comments to students such as "You haven't started yet?" and "Why aren't you working?" Another more positive approach to these typical classroom situations would be to ask, "How did you answer the first question?" or "Is there anything I can do to assist you with that problem?" Such subtle changes in the way teachers talk to and interact with students can produce significant results, because these comments do not put the students in a defensive or reactive stance and have helped refocus and perhaps assist them in getting started.

***Clear Instruction.*** Another strategy in creating positive learning environments consists of the teacher being deliberate in providing clear assignments and directions. In the large classrooms of secondary schools, you can expect that some of your students will almost always need clarification of assignments or instructions you have provided. For example, when you see that a couple of students have not begun to work on the assigned task, it is more effective to repeat the directions, "Begin reading today's handout on page four," than it is to start meting out discipline. Be certain to provide instructions both verbally and visually. Also, rather than asking, "Are there any questions?" which often leads to complete silence, ask, "What questions do you have for me?" By using this phrase you suggest you expect questions and are open to answering them. Just as students learn at different paces, they also process information differently. Some students will require more detail before they feel comfortable beginning a task.

***Classroom Climate.*** A classroom climate does not really exist prior to the arrival of the students. Though some elements might be present, for example, the physical condition of the class or your reputation as a teacher, the students and their presence help establish the environment. Students begin forming their impressions of your class climate on day one. Teachers should not leave this first impression to chance. As we have said repeatedly, all acts of teaching are purposeful. This includes developing the class climate, which requires your full attention.

When developing strategies to enhance your classroom environments, consider the needs of your students, including allowing them to maintain their individual identities, ensuring their personal safety, creating activities that will stimulate their thinking and provide opportunities to build connections with their peers (Hoover & Kindsvatter, 1997). These issues cannot be left to chance or you will have to bear the consequences for the entire year.

All students in an inclusive democratic classroom have the right to expect to feel as though they belong in the class. Because a significant problem of the larger secondary school is that of anonymity, it is imperative that teachers work to correct the problem. Teachers must develop and use strategies to promote relationship building. Relationships are easily one of the most effective and efficient forms of class management. When teachers have created connections with their students, students have a greater willingness to cooperate (Jones, 1987).

As Jones has pointed out, "The basic fabric of social cohesion, caring and mutual respect, begins to deteriorate as soon as people become anonymous in a group" (1987, p. 66). Though building a community of learners may be more difficult to accomplish in a secondary setting, rather than an elementary setting, it is no less important. The most immediate step each teacher can take in this regard is to get to know the name of each and every student. Many other activities will assist you in this effort, and though we will not examine them in detail in this chapter, some resources for you to explore follow.

***Team-Building Resources.*** We have used the following resources in classroom team-building activities. You can also search the Web for other resources, because they are too numerous to list. New resources are also frequently added to the Web; we encourage new teachers to make use of the Internet for resources to aid and update teaching their practice.

Educators for Social Responsibility
www.esrnational.org

John Dewey Project on Progressive Education University of Vermont
www.uvm.edu

Jones, F. H. (1987). *Positive classroom discipline*. New York: McGraw-Hill. (chap. 4)

Pfeiffer, W. J. (1989). *Encyclopedia of group activities*. San Diego, CA: Pfeiffer & Company.

Pfeiffer, W. J. (1989). *Encyclopedia of icebreakers*. San Diego, CA: Pfeiffer & Company.

Secondary School Educators
http://7-12educators.about.com

## Rules and Routines

Another way you can help students connect with you and their classmates is to enlist their help on the first days of school to establish class rules. How many times in your own school experience have you walked into a classroom on the first day and been handed the definitive list of classroom rules? How many of these rules focused on the behaviors you were expected *not* to do? This list may possibly have included the consequences for any rules violation. We would never suggest that in any community of people, including in a classroom, there should be an absence of agreed-upon norms of behavior, and commonly accepted and expected routines. It simply seems that as schools have grown larger and focused primarily on the management of student behavior, they have drifted away from the important aspect of allowing students to learn and experience inclusive democratic practices, including the responsibilities. By shifting the emphasis from misbehavior and consequences to appropriate behaviors and the reasons behind them, schools create a much more positive and inclusive environment.

You will want to identify a strategy to help you develop the class rules. No matter which strategy you select, avoid problems by being aware of some of the basic misconceptions secondary teachers have about student behavior in the classroom. In his book, Fred Jones has detailed a number of the most common misconceptions and myths of class management issues. See Figure 8.1.

***General versus Specific Rules.*** Jones's work also guides our thinking to consider two types of rules: general rules and specific rules. We believe the general rules, or class norms, form the broader ideas on expected student behavior and should be generated with significant student input. By contrast, specific rules relate to the procedures and routines needed to carry out particular everyday tasks and teachers may develop them on their own in advance. Specific rules make smooth transitions between activities possible and include procedures for maintaining a safe environment. An example of specific rules in a science class is the set of procedures students must follow in gathering lab equipment, setting up and breaking down experiments, and taking care of various scientific instruments. These reliable routines are particularly important for addressing disruptions to a safe and productive classroom climate.

***Class Norms.*** General rules, or class norms, detail more of the students' expected behavior in class, as well as ideas on how students can be involved in helping shape the curriculum. In a democratic classroom, the teacher might begin on day one or two of the new year by engaging students in a process to develop the class norms. The ability to enforce classroom rules depends upon a clear understanding of what is expected of students and a knowledge that they are all of our rules, not just the teacher's (Jones, 1987). Remember that you, as the teacher, are a member of the class and will also contribute ideas, as well as abide by the rules. Of course, certain parameters must be made clear. Class rules, for example, cannot supercede school-wide rules, which were ideally developed in a collaborative way with all school community members engaged in the process.

FIGURE 8.1 Myths of Class Management Issues

| Misconception/Myth | Current Thinking |
|---|---|
| *The students should know better by this time.* | Students know from elementary school how to behave; the key for them is what they have to do (or can get away with) in your class. |
| *I can't take too much time to go over rules because I have so much material to cover.* | Teacher effectiveness research indicates that teachers with the greatest time on task and fewest discipline problems spend most of the first two weeks of the school year teaching rules, routines, standards, and expectations. |
| *Rules are general guidelines.* | General rules must ultimately be expressed as highly specific procedures, routines, and standards that spell out the proper way of doing everything the teacher wants done each day. |
| *Rules are announced.* | Rules are taught. |
| *If I do a good job teaching the rules at the beginning of the school year, I will not have to deal with them repeatedly throughout the year.* | Rules are retaught and must be consistently reinforced. |
| *Teaching rules is a matter of being strict.* | Teaching rules properly lays the groundwork for cooperation based on mutual caring. |
| *Students dislike and resent classroom rules.* | Students appreciate and respect a teacher who makes expectations clear. |

Note: From *Positive Classroom Discipline* by Fredric Jones, 1987, New York: McGraw-Hill. Copyright by Fredric H. Jones & Associates. Adapted by permission.

In starting the process of developing class rules, set the tone by asking students to reflect on classes they have had that they wanted to be in, found academically engaging, and in which they felt safe. Then ask them to jot down some ideas on the following questions: What makes a good class a good class? What do your best teachers do in their classes? What is the role of the student in a good class? What behaviors should be expected from everyone in the class, including the teacher?

***Student Involvement.*** Once students have written some responses, have them share while you write responses on the board. Allow them ample time to contribute to the list. You might be surprised with the thoughtful suggestions. Our experiences with this process in our own high school classrooms led to ideas of respect, active listening, the importance of welcoming and valuing all questions, engagement in the lesson, passion and enthusiasm for the topic being studied, not using putdowns, and many others. You should expect testing comments such as "no reading in class" or "no homework." Discuss with students the consequences of such ideas: No reading does not respect those who learn best with this learning style, and explore the idea that "no homework" really means "no busy work." Too many students have had the experience of being assigned homework that is not purposefully selected. For example, "Read Chapter Thirteen, Sections One and Two, and do the questions at the end of each section." This way of assigning homework occurs over and over again. Instead, you can include "no busy work" as a norm that will help remind you always to attempt to have the curriculum focused and assignments selected to reinforce the skill or knowledge important for a particular lesson. Not all material is of equal value, so it should not be treated as if it were.

Once you have written the ideas on the board and all students have had the opportunity to contribute, attempt to categorize and narrow down the number of class norms. You want to have a list that is reasonable in size that you can post in the classroom and refer to as necessary. The list of class norms created together accomplishes a number of things. First, you have a set of classroom rules that your students helped create and in which they share ownership. Second, you have modeled your expectation of student involvement in all aspects of the class. Third, you have begun to establish a tone of respect for your students and their ideas. These strong first impressions for your students will help you throughout the year with classroom management (Kohn, 1996; Putnam, 1997; Sizer & Sizer, 1999; Wong & Wong, 2001).

The work of noted psychiatrist William Glasser (1985, 1990) supports these ideas of involving students in the process of managing the classroom and in helping to solve actual problems. His work identified some of the important needs of students that must be met in order to improve and maintain behavior. These include the need to feel a sense of Belonging, as discussed throughout this book with reference to the Circle of Courage, to feel a sense of importance or power by being listened to by adults, and to experience the opportunity of being able to make choices in some aspect of the curriculum (Independence). As Glasser determined, "For workers, including students, to do quality work they must be managed in a way that convinces them that the work they are asked to do satisfies their needs. The more it does, the harder they work" (1990, p. 22). The more ownership students feel for the class environment, the harder they will work to support it.

***Maintenance of Class Environment.*** Once you and the students have established and posted the rules, do not make the common mistake, noted earlier, that nothing more needs to be done to maintain the classroom environment throughout the year. Teachers must frequently remind students of the routines and expected behaviors. It is also important to talk with students about what is working and what the challenges are in maintaining the rules. In the constant monitoring of the class environment, you should never ignore violations of the class rules. This sends the wrong message. Instead, you have several options to correct behavior. It may be as simple as standing next to a pair of talkative students during a group presentation, or it might be a significant enough breakdown that you will stop class and ask your students (perhaps while pointing to their posted rules) whether this broken rule is no longer in effect. These simple steps usually suffice to get a class back on track, and they also send the clear message that you will maintain the environment of the classroom.

If continuous problems with the class climate exist, the teacher should consider holding a class meeting and discussing the range of problems or concerns in an atmosphere of respect. You may want to use class meetings for more significant issues, often a breakdown of student-to-student cooperation or respectful behavior. Class meetings remind students that they are significant players in maintaining the

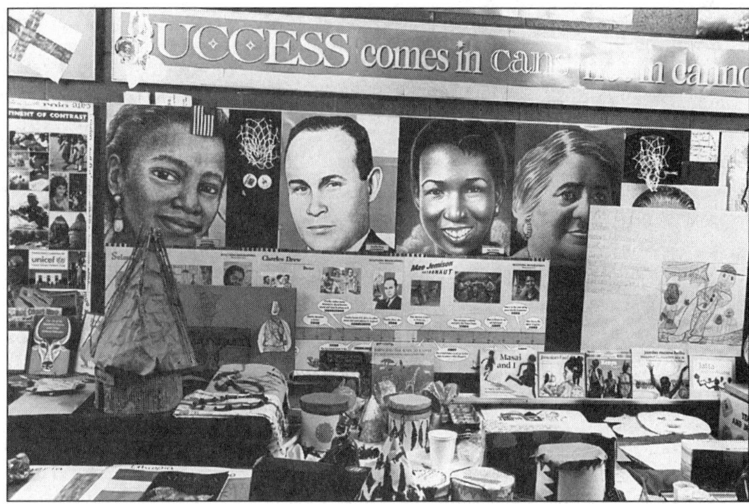


democratic environment. Using a class meeting might follow steps of bringing students together, sharing your issues of concern and allowing students to share theirs, discussing reasons behind the problem(s), talking through possible solutions, and choosing one (Campbell, 1996; Kohn, 1996; Putnam, 1997). Class meetings also offer an important way to model problem solving. The teacher provides the leadership and structure to assist students in taking responsibility for resolving class problems. Taking the time to resolve the issues as they begin to emerge will save you much more time over the course of the year, rather than repeatedly dealing with symptoms of the problems.

## Physical Climate

The last element of creating positive classroom climate discussed in this section is the physical environment. The design of your classroom, the way it is arranged, where furniture is placed, and how the walls and bulletin boards are decorated may have as much to do with reaching your instructional and behavioral goals as the rules and routines you have established. If you would like to see the impact of a thoughtful classroom design, visit a local elementary school classroom. These colorful, well-decorated spaces are inviting and engaging learning environments. The secondary classroom is often in stark contrast with bare walls and rows of desks. Psychologists often use the term *behavioral setting*, which aptly describes a classroom. Choices in the setting are important as they will encourage and discourage student behaviors. Because your goals will be different throughout the year, your classroom design will need to be flexible.

Of the many elements involved in the physical aspects of the class, two of the most important are the room arrangement and the seating arrangement. A direct relationship exists between the proximity and mobility of a teacher in the class and classroom disruptions (Jones, 1987). The best designs put the least amount of distance and fewest barriers between the teacher and any student in the classroom. Being able to wander, monitor, and assess, moving freely from one student to another, are all important.

In designing the physical layout of your inclusive classroom, avoid placing your desk between you and your students or between your students and the white board. Research by Fred Jones indicates these factors matter more than how closely you place your students together, as increased student proximity did not, in Jones's research, reveal increased disruptions (1987).

A traditional classroom design depicted in Figure 8.2 violates this rule. The arrangement sets the tone of a teacher-centered classroom, wherein the interactions are primarily between the student and the teacher. The design does not stimulate much interaction between students. Figure 8.3, by contrast, creates a different tone. The design of this room facilitates more cooperative learning and the development of relationships among the students. Of course, endless sets of variations of

**FIGURE 8.2** Traditional Arrangement: Teacher-Centered Classroom

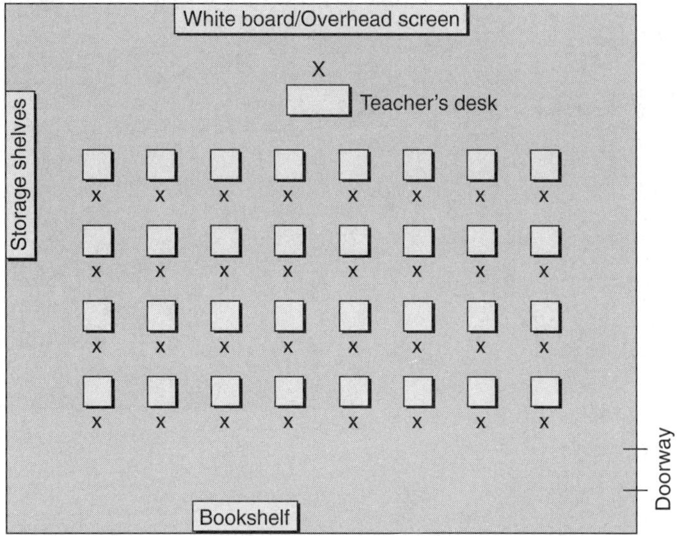


**FIGURE 8.3** Cooperative Learning Design: Interactive Student-Centered Classroom

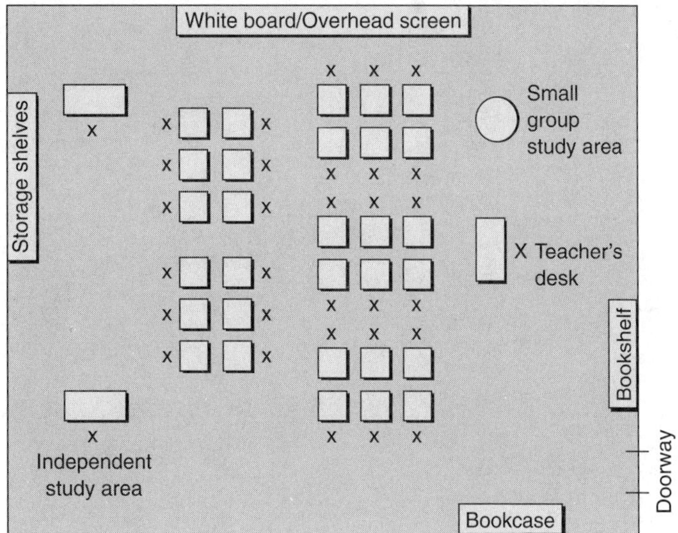

arrangements exist. Figures 8.4 to 8.7 illustrate further examples. Remember, as we have repeatedly discussed throughout this text, all actions of the teacher should be purposeful. This includes designing a physical layout to match your goals of designing an inclusive democratic classroom.

**FIGURE 8.4** Whole-Group Discussion Design: Presentations

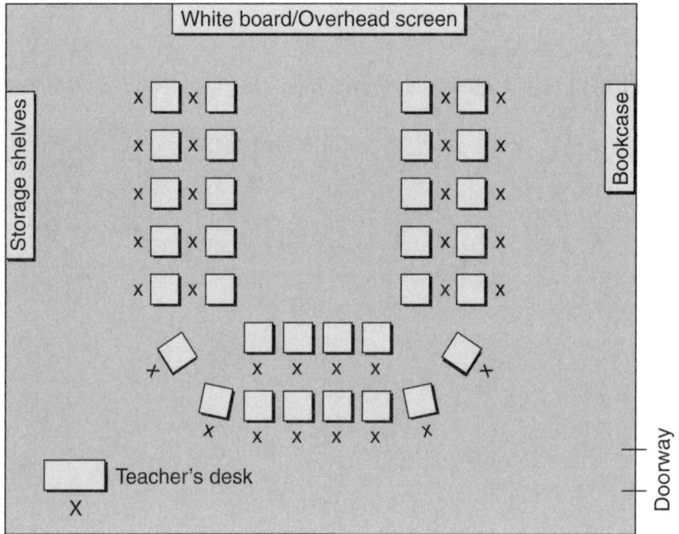


**FIGURE 8.5** Small Group Cooperative Design: U Shape

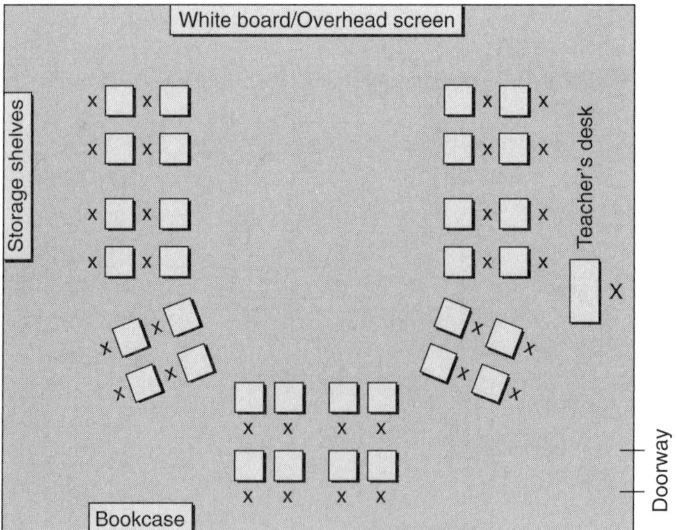

**FIGURE 8.6** Chevron Design: Presentations, Student Discussions

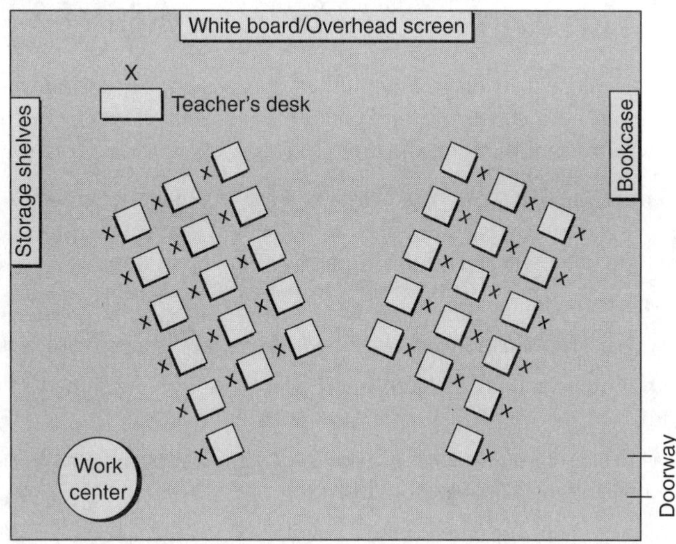


**FIGURE 8.7** Student Learning Teams: Cooperative Learning

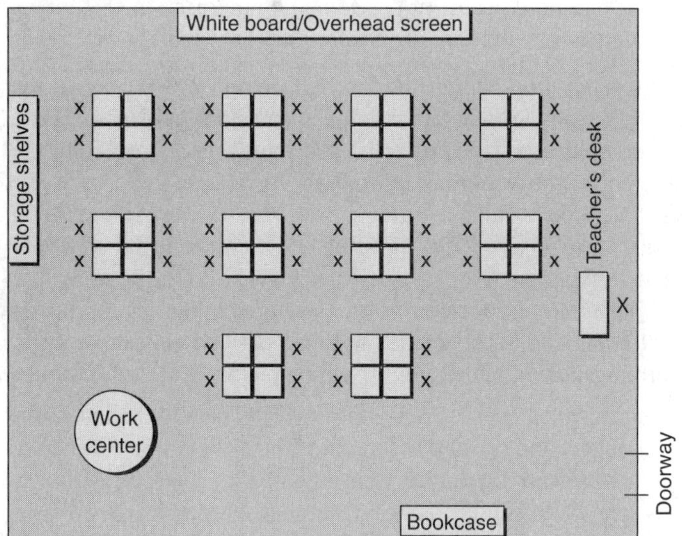

## *Putting It Into Practice:* Activity 8.3

Each of you will create a class environment plan. This assignment includes an introductory letter to parents, a map design of your classroom, and your initial ideas on class management strategies. Keep in mind these are only your current thoughts; be open to changing or adding ideas as you gain more experience.

1. *The parent/caretaker or student letter.* You will create this letter to send home to parents and caretakers, or to give to your students during the first week of the school year. The letter should be no more than one page and contain the following components:
   a. who you are;
   b. your basic philosophy of teaching (in layperson's terms, abbreviated, concise);
   c. your expectations of students and your modes of assessment (aligned with your cooperating teacher);
   d. curricular highlights such as what parents can expect their son or daughter to be learning (or what students can expect to learn);
   e. opportunities for parent involvement;
   f. how you will communicate throughout the year with parents; and
   g. how students might be involved in the communication.

Your letter should be easily readable and accessible, personable and inviting. Remember, this letter will help set a foundation and a tone for parents or students as to how they view you. With that in mind, this letter should have no mechanical/writing errors.

Another very important aspect of providing communication is planning how you will address *other-language speaking* parents and caretakers who might not read English. Think about this for discussion.

2. *The classroom map.* Design a map that demonstrates how you would physically arrange your classroom. Imagine the general shape, dimensions, and features of your classroom hypothetically (or you could use your preservice teaching classroom). Think about a specific grade level or course and what would be appropriate for students at that level or in that course. Show how tables and desks would be arranged, where workspaces would be set up, how you envision using the wall space, shelf space, and other areas. Present this in a map or diagram with everything labeled.

   Write a rationale for why you've arranged things as you have (about a paragraph in length). Include what kind of movement and learning you are preparing for with this arrangement, how this arrangement supports your teaching philosophy, and in what ways it benefits students.
3. *The "management" part.* Discuss how you'll create a positive classroom environment, fostering mutual respect and supportive learning. This writing will provide you with an opportunity to think through your learning during your time in a teacher preparation program, as well as your own values, goals, and comfort zones. Your plan should include both general and specific rules. Additionally, you should address the following components:
   a. what you'll do in the beginning of the year to help students get to know you and each other;
   b. what you'll do to create a positive learning atmosphere that fosters risk taking, respect, and creativity;
   c. what procedures you'll have in place to ensure that things move efficiently and are organized for learning such as how you want students to turn in homework, handle supplies, materials, or technology;

d. what "rules" you'll find necessary for learning to take place (could overlap with your procedures) and how these rules will contribute to a positive learning climate;
e. how you'll establish and introduce these rules to the students and how you will know whether all students perceive the rules as being fair;
f. how you'll deal with students who don't follow the rules and how you will ensure that your consequences are effective, relevant, and fair;
g. what school-wide management "rules" you are expected to adhere to (no eating in classrooms, tardy policy) and how you will work these in with your classroom expectations, using your current site's rules as a model;
h. how you will "see," reinforce, remind, and redirect students in their behaviors; and
i. anything else you deem important to your plan.

This section should be no more than two pages.

## SECTION 4: CHAPTER SUMMARY AND REFLECTION

This chapter on diverse inclusive classrooms has offered an overview of democratic practices in schools, how you can prepare yourself to teach in them, and some strategies for creating this type of environment. As with all the ideas and techniques presented in this text, you can view those included in this chapter as a starting point from which to build your practice.

Most importantly, teachers must constantly remind themselves of the need to understand their roles as molders of citizens. Section 1 addressed participatory decision making, an equitable learning community, and developing positive relationships. Your own actions can serve to reproduce and reinforce existing social and cultural conditions or, conversely, can influence positive changes in those conditions. In modeling the belief in inclusive democratic, participatory classrooms, each teacher increases the opportunity for students to learn how to be productive and active members of their own communities.

Section 2 examined the role of the teacher, beginning with the importance of exploring your own perceptual filters and how to build cultural competence in teaching today's multicultural population of students. This section also established standards for teacher responsibility in diverse classrooms. Providing accurate information to challenge stereotypes and biases is crucial to hold yourself and others accountable to appropriate behavior.

Section 3 focused on components of an effective classroom environment. A discussion of classroom management showed its powerful influence on class environment. This section addressed at length appropriate strategies for connecting with students. The discussion provided ways to establish rules and routines as well as to develop a positive physical climate for diverse inclusive classrooms, and offered opportunities to put these strategies into practice. A teacher who is able to put these into practice will be able to establish a safe and engaging learning environment for all students.

# References

Apple, M. W., & Beane, J. A. (1995). *Democratic schools*. Alexandria, VA: Association for Supervision and Curriculum Development.

Bartolome, L. I. (1994). Beyond the methods fetish: Toward a humanizing pedagogy. *Harvard Educational Review, 64*(2), 173–191.

Brendtro, L. K., Brokenleg, M., & Bockern, S. V. (2002). *Reclaiming youth at risk: Our hope for the future*. Bloomington, IN: National Education Service.

Campbell, D. E. (1996). *Choosing democracy: A practical guide to multicultural education*. Upper Saddle River, New Jersey: Prentice Hall.

Council of Chief State School Officers (1992). Model standards for beginning teacher licensing, assessment, and development: A resource for state dialogue. Washington, DC: Author. www.ccsso.org/content/pdfs/corestrd.pdf

Dewey, J. (1916). *Democracy in education*. New York: Macmillan.

Dewey, J. (1938). *Experience and education*. Bloomington, IN: Kappa Delta Pi.

Dieringer, L., Kreidler, W. J., & Lantieri, L. (1996). *Resolving conflicts in schools and classrooms: Training manual*. Cambridge, MA: Educators for Social Responsibility.

Glasser, W. (1985). *Control theory in the classroom*. New York: Harper and Row.

Glasser, W. (1990). *The quality school: Managing students without coercion*. New York: Harper and Row.

Goodlad, J. I. (1996). Democracy, education, and community. In R. Soder (Ed.), *Democracy, education, and the schools* (pp. 87–124). San Francisco: Jossey-Bass.

Hoover, R. L., & Kindsvatter, R. (1997). *Democratic discipline: Foundation and practice*. Upper Saddle River, NJ: Prentice Hall.

Jones, F. H. (1987). *Positive classroom discipline*. New York: McGraw-Hill.

Kohn, A. (1996). *Beyond discipline: From compliance to community*. Alexandria, VA: Association for Supervision and Curriculum Development.

McIntosh, P. (1989). White privilege: Unpacking the invisible knapsack. *Peace and Freedom, 49*(4), 10–12.

Oakes, J., & Lipton, M. (1999). *Teaching to change the world*. Boston: McGraw-Hill College.

Putnam, J. (1997). *Cooperative learning in diverse classrooms*. Upper Saddle River, NJ: Prentice Hall.

Sadker, M., Sadker, D., & Klein, S. (1991). The issue of gender in elementary and secondary education. In G. Grant (Ed.), *Review of research in education* (pp. 272–273). Washington, DC: American Educational Research Association.

Sizer, T. R., & Sizer, N. F. (1999). *The students are watching*. Boston: Beacon Press

Soder, R. (Ed.). (1996). *Democracy, education, and the schools*. San Francisco: Jossey-Bass.

Vygotsky, L. S. (1978). *Mind in society*. Cambridge, MA: Harvard University Press.

Westbrook, R. B. (1996). Public schooling and American democracy. In R. Soder (Ed.), *Democracy, education, and the schools* (pp. 125–150). San Francisco: Jossey-Bass.

Wong, H. K., & Wong, R. T. (2001). *The first days of school*. Sunnyvale, CA: Harry K. Wong.

# Chapter 9

# Classroom Management

**INTASC Principle 5:** The teacher uses an understanding of individual and group motivation and behavior to create a learning environment that encourages positive social interaction, active engagement in learning, and self-motivation.

**Key Dispositions**

- The teacher takes responsibility for establishing a positive climate in the classroom and participates in maintaining such a climate in the school as a whole.
- The teacher values the role of students in promoting each other's learning and recognizes the importance of peer relationships in establishing a climate of learning.

## INTRODUCTION TO THE CHAPTER

This chapter provides an overview of the major philosophical and theoretical categories of classroom management and the considerations for incorporating these techniques into the classroom. You will explore the implementation effectiveness of different approaches to classroom management. Section 1 reviews various models of class management while emphasizing that engaging students in meaningful curriculum is significant in dealing with behavior management. It also presents a summary of current classroom management research. Section 2 addresses specific applications of classroom management, ranging from the most common behavioral disruptions in secondary schools to serious discipline problems as well as an introduction to bullying.

Section 3 places a particular emphasis on bullying and its various ramifications. Bullying is a serious and critical issue that schools, teachers, and parents must address. This section introduces various school-wide responses to managing bullies as well as a list of resources that address this problem. Putting It Into Practice activities focus on exercises at field sites that include administrative interviews, classroom observations, and the creation of lesson plans that demonstrate methods for implementing appropriate classroom management procedures. Applying Technology activities suggest the utilization of tools such as digital video, digital still photography, and PowerPoint, as much as is available because technology can help document what happens in actual classroom management situations.

This chapter also reinforces the overall theme of the Circle of Courage (Brendtro et al., 2002) in that the student is always the focus in the educational process with the primary objectives of fostering Belonging to a learning community, Mastery of knowledge, Generosity toward others, and development of Independence. It will be clear that these components represent critical elements as the teacher and students collaborate to create a classroom environment that maximizes learning for all.

## SECTION 1: INTEGRATION OF MANAGEMENT IN THE CLASSROOM

Classroom management issues are frequently one of the major challenges beginning teachers face, as well as one of the main causes of teachers leaving the profession (Glasser, 1992). Some define classroom management as all the elements, in the classroom environment, both intrinsic and extrinsic, that encourage effective learning and interaction between individuals. Many suggest that classroom management primarily concerns instruction and creating a positive environment for learning (Brainard, 2001; Martin, 1997). Recommendations that have evolved from this perspective include strategies in which teachers relate to students in a positive manner in order to foster more effective learning. These techniques include (1) using a sense of humor and praising student work; (2) preventing student misbehavior by communicating in private (versus in public) about individual discipline issues; (3) adjusting learning activities when the teacher perceives ineffective learning; (4) handling student discipline situations promptly and consistently; and (5) providing and encouraging models of classroom leadership. Teachers should weave each of these into the context of teaching and learning.

Another perspective identifies classroom management as the distinct actions and strategies a teacher takes to be able to maintain order in a classroom, focusing on discipline as a separate issue, rather than as one that is integrated into the teaching and learning (Burden, 2000). This perspective defines classroom management as the required action toward a student by teachers or school officials when behavior disrupts the ongoing educational activity or breaks preestablished rules (Wolfgang, 1995). Although both of these constructs have their advocates, the overwhelming evidence finds that classroom management and its natural subset, classroom discipline, are most effective if seamlessly included as a natural aspect of the teaching and learning process.

Our perspective is that classroom management and teaching and learning are inseparable. The teacher must develop skills as a diagnostic problem solver addressing the integration of both teaching and social interaction within the class. The Circle of Courage model supports this view, emphasizing the teacher's focus on the student. The way a teacher collaborates with students on curriculum and social expectations in the learning environment is critical, influencing the effectiveness of students personally adopting the four learning components of the Circle of Courage.

There have been a number of different attempts to categorize classroom management styles used in schools. We will review two models, one by Wolfgang (1995) and the other by Froyen (1993), with the expectation that familiarity with them will help you as you determine your own classroom management strategy. Keep in mind, as with all strategies, you may need to implement approaches from across the continuum as the need arises.

## Power Relationship Model

Wolfgang uses the degree of the *power relationship* of teacher to student to classify many of today's broad management styles. This model's primary emphasis on the power relationship can be depicted as a continuum in the context of different *faces* or behavioral responses to the students. Different responses are based on the situational context the teacher has identified.

***Relationship-Listening Face.*** On one end of the continuum is the *relationship-listening face,* which uses concepts developed by Carl Rogers, who believes that "Given empathetic understanding, warmth and openness, one will choose what is best for oneself and will become a fully functioning person, constructive and trustworthy" (Wolfgang, 1995, p. 15). This face focuses priority on direct relationship between the teacher and the individual student. The outcomes of these personal social interactions between teacher and student will determine the specific actions that both will follow.

***Confronting-Contracting Face.*** Next, the *confronting-contracting face* uses the concepts developed by Rudolf Dreikurs (Adlerian theory), which focus primarily on the importance of social discipline and social development of students rather than on the interaction between an individual student and teacher. This face requires that the teacher (1) determines the level of social development of a student in order to enhance it; (2) emphasizes that responses are targeting students' actions but are not a criticism of students themselves; and (3) places students in collaborative situations in which they are expected to assist each other rather than compete (Wolfgang, 1995). The active involvement of parents, students, teachers, and administrators contributes to the success of this approach.

***Rules and Consequences Face.*** The third approach on the continuum, the *rules and consequences face,* heavily emphasizes the teacher establishing determined sets of rules, consequences, and rewards. Exceptions are not allowed; teachers expect all students to follow the rules and accept the consequences equally. This face places much less emphasis on individual student differences or the use of social collaborations as a context for establishing an effective management style. The rules, once established, typically apply in all situations for all individuals. Gathercoal's *judicious discipline model* (Wolfgang, 1995) falls under this approach. He suggests that even with clearly defined classroom rules, the wide range of teaching styles, from authoritarian to democratic, causes implementation of the management process to differ greatly by teacher. The degree of flexibility that individual teachers are comfortable with will determine how they enforce rules in their own classrooms.

***Coercive-Legalistic.*** The last approach, *coercive-legalistic,* represents the maximum teacher power control on the continuum of approaches teachers might assume. It consists of preestablished sets of procedures to deal with the most serious problems, such as assaults and other forms of violence. Many of these may involve the law or mandatory school-wide policies. In such cases, teachers may not have any discretion in what they can or cannot do. Examples might include student expulsion or legal action toward students or parents as a result of a drug, alcohol, or weapons infraction (Wolfgang, 1995).

The four categories discussed represent a teacher-to-student power continuum ranging from minimum to maximum control, summarized in Table 9.1.

## Teacher Management Model

In contrast to the power continuum categories developed by Wolfgang, Froyen (1993) uses three *teacher management functions* to describe his model of classroom management. These functions are responses to tasks the teacher must address during everyday instruction to deal with the following three areas: (1) content management (including setting functions and instructional functions), (2) conduct management (student behavior), and (3) covenant management (teacher–student agreements). This model makes extensive use of teacher discretion by utilizing teacher reflection and problem solving to establish specific actions the teacher will take within the context of the teaching task. Froyen justifies his model by taking the position that the critical element of group psychosocial dynamics shapes group behavior and that this factor varies tremendously from group to group and among individuals.

***Content Management.*** Examples of the range of issues teachers respond to while involved in a specific classroom task may include (1) addressing procedures involved in the delivery of *subject matter content functions;* (2) setting up routines for taking

**TABLE 9.1** *Continuum of Classroom Management Categories*

| | TEACHER'S POWER | | | |
|---|---|---|---|---|
| | Minimum Power | | | Maximum Power |
| *Category* | Relationship-Listening Face | Confronting-Contracting Face | Rules and Consequences Face | Coercive-Legalistic |
| *Process* | Therapeutic | Educational and counseling | Controlling, rewards, and punishment | Restraining, exclusionary, and legal |
| *Models* | Gordon's *T.E.T: Teacher Effectiveness Training, Teaching Children Self-Discipline*<br>Harris's *I'm OK–You're OK* | Dreikurs's *Discipline Without Tears*<br>Albert's *Cooperative Discipline*<br>Glasser's *Control Theory in the Classroom, Schools Without Failure, The Quality School*<br>Gathercoal's *Judicious Discipline* | Madsen/Madsen's *Teaching/Discipline: A Positive Approach for Educational Development*<br>Alberto/Troutman's *Applied Behavior Analysis for Teachers*<br>Dobson's *Dare to Discipline*<br>Canter's *Assertive Discipline, Succeeding With Difficult Students*<br>Alberti's *Your Perfect Right, Stand Up, Speak Out,Talk Back*<br>Jones's *Positive Discipline* | Nonviolent crisis management and arbitrary preestablished administrative procedures leading to physical restraint, exclusion, and legal actions toward the student or family.<br>CPI (Crisis Prevention Institute) |

Note: From *Solving Discipline Problems, Third Edition* by C. Wolfgang, 1995, New York: John Wiley & Sons. Copyright © 1995 John Wiley & Sons. This material is used by permission of John Wiley & Sons, Inc.

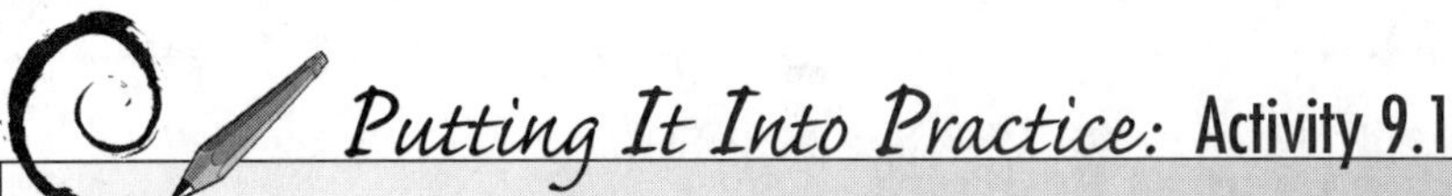

## Putting It Into Practice: Activity 9.1

Form a small team (four to six members) to investigate a specific class management program or model representative of those described in the continuum in Table 9.1. The team may decide to select a model in use in local schools or one that interests members as a possible approach to use in their own classrooms.

Each team will prepare a brief oral presentation for the entire class that includes a one- to two-page summary on the important aspects of the selected program. The presentation and written summary should include (1) an overall description of the specific program; (2) research regarding its effectiveness; (3) a representative case study illustrating its application (a local school having implemented it); and (4) the team's overall reflection and analysis of the model, including whether the model is one the team members would implement in their own classrooms.

attendance; (3) clarifying expectations for behavior during transition times; (4) determining the most appropriate physical placement of tables and chairs (those supportive of that particular instructional strategy); and (5) specifying expectations for written assignments.

***Conduct Management.*** To address tasks related to *student conduct functions*, teachers may (1) post rules and expectations, (2) apply consequences consistently, (3) periodically inform parents of both positive and negative aspects of student behavior, and (4) include colleagues in the management plan for consistency.

***Covenant Management.*** Examples of addressing tasks related to *teacher–student agreement functions* would include (1) involvement of class members in short- and long-term goal-setting processes; (2) devoting more time to establishing agreements to help develop a sense of group interdependence; (3) fostering a sense of trust and faith in each other, as well as the avoidance of ridicule and sarcasm; and (4) delegating responsibility in a way that all students succeed in becoming fully functioning members of the class.

Activity 9.2 will utilize this management model as a context for application.

### *Putting It Into Practice:* Activity 9.2

Refer to the text discussion of Froyen's three teacher management functions (content management, conduct management, and covenant management). In mixed subject area teams of three to five persons, use the management functions as a focus to observe classroom teachers. This should include some discussion with the teacher prior to and after the observed lesson. Record the different ways that the observed teacher integrates each of the functions and the type of student responses observed within the teacher's instructional period.

Meet in your teams to synthesize, analyze, and summarize the findings. This discussion should address, at the minimum, commonalities and differences of management responses, differences between disciplines, and the group's perception of the overall strengths and weaknesses of the observed teacher responses. Each discipline team should present a 5- to 10-minute overview to the class that is a representative summary of its findings. Include some form of visual technology such as overhead projectors, PowerPoint software, digital still photography, or movies to assist in illustrating the concepts related to Froyen's management functions.

## Classroom Management Research

In recent research studies related to effective classroom management, some common elements or *best practices* associated with teaching and the classroom have emerged. One of these studies, by Haberman (1995), includes best practices commonly observed in what he terms "successful" teachers. You will note that we have elaborated upon the best practices in this section throughout the textbook because they have been integrated across many areas of your teaching practice. We reiterate and summarize them in this chapter because we believe good instructional practice is integral to effective classroom management. The most common best practices include the following:

1. Discipline and management are not separate from instructional practices; instead they are linked throughout the teaching and learning process.
2. Classroom ideas are best learned if put into practice by using practical and relevant applications for students.
3. Homework is meaningfully connected to activities in which the students are involved during class time that are not dull and repetitive.

4. The teacher uses available background information about students and parents in a positive way to help students learn more.
5. The teacher demonstrates enthusiasm.
6. The teacher increases use of assessment formats that are authentic in nature and more reflective of individual student learning styles, including portfolios, cooperative group projects, and performance-based assessments.
7. The teacher demonstrates increased emphasis on the use of student-centered, versus teacher-centered, strategies and activities.
8. Student and teacher mistakes are acceptable and are used to create teachable moments.
9. The physical presence of the teacher creates an awareness of what is occurring in the classroom that is maximized by applying specific managerial skills (such as physically moving around class and picking up visual and auditory cues).
10. Students are encouraged to collaborate with each other as well as the teacher to master difficult material.
11. The classroom is established as a safe environment in which students have freedom from fear as a result of nontolerance of verbal or physical abuse.
12. Teachers frequently reflect on their practice, with the purpose of making appropriate changes and modifications for improvement when needed.

Brophy and Good (1986) also focused their research on teacher behaviors that led to successful practice. Many of their findings are similar to those from the Haberman study. These include the following:

1. Teachers demonstrate expectations for both learning and behavior for all students, regardless of native abilities. They use multiple approaches to find what is most effective with an individual student.
2. Teachers maximize the amount of time devoted to academic time on task.
3. Teachers provide appropriate pacing of a variety of different activities within the day's curriculum so that students do not get bored.
4. Teachers recognize within the curriculum that students should be the active learners with the teacher as the facilitator, as opposed to using teacher-centered curriculum.
5. Teachers emphasize mastery of knowledge through both practice and applications of the principles.
6. Evidence exists of positive teacher personalities that are caring and supportive, in a friendly environment.

In summary, current research findings include evidence that effective classroom management involves a classroom environment in which students feel safe; rules that are fairly and consistently enforced; teachers with high expectations; well-planned, student-centered curriculum; and teachers who are positive and enthusiastic role models.

## SECTION 2: APPLICATIONS OF CLASSROOM MANAGEMENT

Section 1 discussed the elements of effective practice. If implemented, many of these will promote effective learning and teaching. We have summarized some strategies by level of behavioral difficulty.

**Level 1**

- Work with students to "collaboratively" establish a set of classroom norms for teacher and student expectations for behavior and academic achievement.
- Write up a contract outlining these norms, and have it signed by the teacher, student, and parent.
- Consistently provide positive and constructive feedback regarding student behavior using many indirect, nonthreatening techniques such as standing by or calling on an off-task student or, conversely, providing a series of extrinsic rewards for positive behavior.
- Redirect the off-task student by periodically reexplaining the expectation or task, or assuming teacher responsibility for the lack of understanding of the expectation and then reclarifying.

**Level 2** (if level 1 strategies are not working with individual students)

- Hold an individual conference or interview outside the classroom setting with the off-task student that establishes (1) using praise, showing you do care for him or her and (2) concern with the ongoing misbehavior.
- If deemed necessary, create an individual "social contract" that establishes (1) an outline of goals with positive and negative consequences for that individual student both academically and behaviorally, and (2) a means for the student to achieve the goals.
- Communicate clearly with the parent/guardian what behavioral issues are involved.

**Level 3** (if levels 1 and 2 strategies are not working with individual students)

- Refer the student to the administrator, counselor, or other person responsible for addressing student misbehavior by using appropriate school district policy and guidelines.

**Level 4** (if levels 1–3 strategies are not working with individual students use the compassionate discipline model as illustrated later in Figure 9.1)

- Establish a meeting with all stakeholders: parents, counselor, teacher(s), administrators.
- Clarify medical or psychological needs of the student.
- Establish appropriate training and buy-in by all key individuals.
- Reestablish the social contract with the student that outlines expectations and goals for academic achievement and behavior at school and at home.
- Inform other students how to interact appropriately both positively and constructively with this student.
- Offer positive praise (and/or rewards) for appropriate behavior as well as consistent enforcement of social contract expectations by all stakeholders.
- Consider possible alternatives such as relocation to a different classroom setting or school site if the student fails to make progress.

## Most Common Disruptions

In spite of these practices, most teachers today still face a number of common disruptions as well as serious management issues. We consider the following scenarios representative of some of the most common forms of disruptions and sources of frustration challenging secondary teachers (Curwin & Mendler, 1988).

**Scenario 1:** Bill enters your class 3 minutes late, takes his seat, and starts talking to a friend, disrupting the beginning activity in your class.

**Scenario 2:** Linda is writing and passing notes in class when she is supposed to be completing an assignment in a textbook. She claims you never told her that there was a rule against writing notes.

**Scenario 3:** When a couple of students ask what you are having them do in class that day, and you respond, "Reviewing for a test," they tell you verbally and nonverbally that's boring.

**Scenario 4:** When you tell a student she must stay after class to talk to you about not completing her in-class assignment, she tells you (perhaps using inappropriate language), "I am not staying after and you can't make me."

**Scenario 5:** A high percentage of students are not handing in the written homework assignments you are assigning, resulting in a low grade for this quarter.

**Scenario 6:** You find that some students in the class have plagiarized a research paper.

**Scenario 7:** Three different students refuse to work in the cooperative teams to which you have assigned them. Another two are constantly disrupting the team's efforts to work.

**Scenario 8:** A student accuses Jake (who is physically large) of "bullying" him. According to the student, this includes both physical and verbal abuse. You have never observed this happening in person.

**Scenario 9:** Jose, Mary, and Aaron refuse to do a research assignment on Teddy Roosevelt and his role in the war in Cuba. They say it is counter to what they think is an important perspective and not relevant to their own cultural backgrounds.

**Scenario 10:** You are constantly being disrupted in class by having to tell students to stop talking, pay attention, or get started on written assignments.

**Scenario 11:** Some students show little or no interest in topics that you consider interesting and enjoyable.

**Scenario 12:** Many students in your class are deficient in the basic skills of writing, reading, and oral language, preventing them from getting passing grades on many of the assignments and tests that you use to grade them. They are getting discouraged and misbehave as a result.

**Scenario 13:** You have little contact with parents due to a very low turnout of parents for open houses. You would like to talk to parents about the progress of their sons and daughters, but see few of them at school functions.

**Scenario 14:** Some of your better students have after-school jobs and are not doing any studying or homework outside the class. Although they are doing well in regular class work, failure to hand in outside assignments has resulted in relatively low grades.

**Scenario 15:** Many cliques exist in your classes. Students do not interact socially, nor are they tolerant of students not in their own cliques.

**Scenario 16:** You have noticed some socially isolated students who seem to have no apparent friends. They appear sad, talk little, and other students do not encourage them during group work.

**Scenario 17:** You have a wide range of abilities and motivation in your class and find it very difficult to both motivate and assist students on either end of the learning spectrum (very bright to learning disabled). This has resulted in a variety of behavioral issues from both of these groups.

### *Putting It Into Practice:* Activity 9.3

In small teams of three or four, divide the most common disruption scenarios among each team in order to discuss implications and proposed actions. Present a simulated role-play, acting out each scenario for the class. The classroom management research discussed previously may help you in your discussions and your team's response to the scenarios. When you have presented your team's simulation, gather feedback from other class members and then continue your discussion as a team. The purpose is to determine the effectiveness and appropriateness of responses as well as to give you practice addressing some common class management issues.

## Serious Management Issues

Some of the most common (and important) but less serious behavioral management scenarios that teachers face in the classroom have just been examined. Now we will address the fact that most schools have a small (5% to 15%) number of students who are unresponsive to normal teacher-management strategies. These may result in serious disruptions for the teacher and other students, as well as for the general social climate of the classroom. Schools, teachers, and students must have strategies in place to effectively interact with these types of students and their seriously disruptive behaviors. If not dealt with immediately and effectively, such students and their resulting behaviors can cause serious, long-term ramifications for the school.

***Case Study.*** The following case study provides an overview of how a team of teachers, administrators, and students dealt with an example of a more serious, ongoing type of management issue. The basis of this case study is interview data collected from a consultant who has trained a number of teachers, administrators, and parents in the use of a model of classroom management called the compassionate discipline model, illustrated in Figure 9.1 (Keating, 2001). You will notice that the compassionate discipline model incorporates and integrates a number of concepts suggested by other models discussed earlier.

In this case study, John is a male high school student with severe behavioral problems, in a mainstream classroom. He is a 9th-grade student who lives with an adopted family. He has been diagnosed with fetal alcohol effects (FAE) for which he has been under the regular care of a psychiatrist and treated with medications. He was mainstreamed into a self-contained regular classroom in a public school. The teachers include both a regular classroom teacher and a special education teacher. Other special-needs students are included in this classroom of approximately 20 students (15 regular education and 5 special education).

John has recently been causing severe disruptions to the classroom and its students. These have included biting, hitting, screaming profanities, running away, and throwing objects. Both teachers and administrators have been unsuccessful in addressing these disruptions through the traditional school discipline policies. Safety and order for all students have become key issues.

As a result, the administration, principal and the teachers are recommending John be placed in a special school (located some miles away) that can better cope with his behavior. John's mother has requested that some alternative plan be made that would keep him in his regular school. She is concerned that he remain close to home and in this case in a school with which he has become familiar. The principal requested a special-services behavioral consultant (psychologist from the state) to assist the school in ways to address John's behavior and retain John at the school.

The psychologist explained the compassionate discipline model he has used successfully with other students who severely disrupted classrooms. The general principles of compassionate discipline are outlined throughout the case history.

The first step in the process involves all parties related to the situation. This would include John, his adoptive parents, the teachers, and the principal. The compassionate discipline model in Figure 9.1 incorporates elements of Total Quality Management (TQM) in order to achieve collaboration on issues and arrive at a consensus with all members of the team.

First, the psychologist interviewed John individually and then met with the team to discuss their perspectives. The team agreed to the following:

1. John would have a follow-up appointment with his psychiatrist to address use and dosage levels of all medications.
2. John's targeted misbehaviors and personal needs and issues would be identified.
3. All members would participate in a brief training in the compassionate discipline model.
4. The team would reach an agreement as to how to be consistent at home and at school for a 30-day trial implementation period.

### A Closer Look

**Instructional Resource H** summarizes the compassionate discipline principles.

The training sessions were completed over a total of 2 to 3 hours and included the following components:

1. Self-determine the parental management styles of each member of the team in order to assist all of them in understanding their own feelings when dealing with John (Smalley, 1992).
2. Understand the stages of motivation that adolescents go through in order to assist in determining from what stage of motivation John's actions and needs are derived. This assists in determining an action plan and resultant social contract to resolve the behavioral issues (Arroyo & Selleck, 1989).
3. Use this information to implement the action plan for the compassionate discipline model that incorporates the three components illustrated by junction points of a triangle.

**FIGURE 9.1** Compassionate Discipline Model

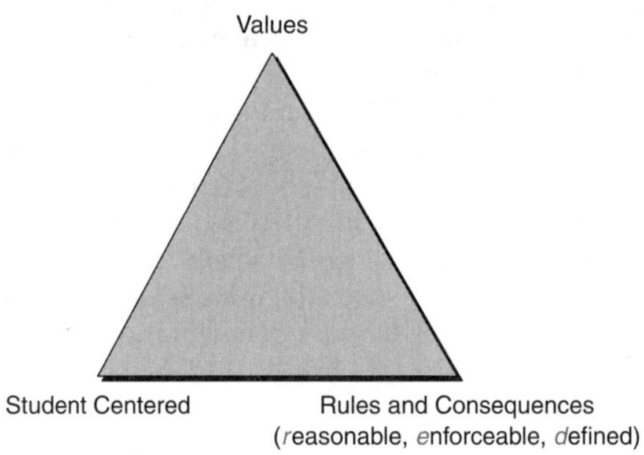


Note: From *The Compassionate Discipline Model* (unpublished) by James Keating, 2001.

The three components illustrated by the triangle in Figure 9.1 are values, student centering, and rules and consequences: essential elements for team members who interact with John. These include working with John on *values* (at the top) such as honesty, caring, and respect for others as well as establishing a work ethic.

The *student centered* aspect, the second point of the triangle, includes a list of people, places, and things that would help assist John in learning more and in becoming more comfortable in the home and classroom environments. These specific preferences could be withdrawn when inappropriate behavior warranted discipline. This component of the plan also assists all members in developing a more sincere, trusting, and caring relationship with John. Specifically, in John's case, it meant preferences such as where he would sit in the class, incorporation of more tactile material into instruction, more time spent with him individually, being able to bring books to class he had selected to read, and increased time during school for physical exercise. His mother developed a corresponding list for use at home. This list of positive actions from those around him also included the positive behaviors expected of him (to counter the negative actions he had exhibited).

The third point of the triangle indicates *rules and consequences*. The characteristic elements in this component, which became part of a social contract, were *r*easonable, *e*nforceable, and *d*efined (RED). By signing the social contract, all parties (in this case John, his teachers, parents, and principal) agreed to consistently clarify and reinforce the goals of the contract. This process included "catching" John exhibiting appropriate, positive behavior and using verbal or nonverbal praise. Just as importantly, when observing negative behavior, this included reiterating goals and expectations, using appropriate reprimands, and assigning consequences as agreed by contract. *The One Minute Teacher* (Johnson & Johnson, 1986) outlines this type of teacher–student interaction (praising, clarifying goals and expectations, and reprimands) very effectively.

Within the 30-day trial period, John initially challenged the new system and suffered some setbacks that included specific consequences for his negative actions (including time out, withdrawal of privileges and social interactions with others). After he realized that all members of the team (including his mother at home) sincerely had his interests at heart and were serious in implementing this new approach that would assist him in managing his behavior, he gradually exhibited fewer and fewer negative behaviors and engaged in many more positive interactions.

In addition, examples of positive socialization from and with the other students in the class increased as they started to accept John's increasingly positive attitude toward them. The involved parties met periodically to review progress and, when appropriate, modified the original social contract. Although John occasionally experienced some minor setbacks, the overall results were positive (both at school and at home), resulting in his becoming a more socially acceptable individual who gained acceptance from his peers and instructors. The goals to keep John at his school were achieved. He also became an active, contributing learner with social skills acceptable to his classmates.

Teachers continued to maintain the model used with John and effectively integrated it into their other classes as well. Although this case used a consultant, teachers could easily implement the basic premise of the model in a variety of settings. In fact, after observing the success with John, the principal requested that the consultant train the rest of his faculty and staff using the compassionate discipline model.

A Closer Look

**Instructional Resource H** contains details on the compassionate discipline model and the training session.

## Introduction to Bullying

Most of the classroom management problems and teaching strategies discussed previously involved basic teacher–student social interaction. In terms of degrees of complexity and seriousness, probably one of the most serious issues of classroom management that teachers face is *bullying*. Recent violent incidents in schools suggest that bullying behavior can provoke victims to retaliate against long-term victimization with even more dramatic forms of violence against the school and the bullies. The serious problem of bullying can dramatically affect students' abilities to progress academically and socially. Bullying results in direct and indirect short-term and long-term effects on the bully, the victims, and the student observers.

Bullying consists of both direct and indirect behaviors. Direct behaviors include teasing, taunting, threatening, hitting, and stealing initiated by one or more students against a victim. Indirect bullying behaviors can cause a student to be socially isolated through intentional exclusion (Banks, 1997). Researchers have identified three core elements of bullying: (1) repeated aggressive behavior, (2) negative intent directed from one person to another, and (3) power difference between the bully and victim (Marano, 1995).

Various studies have found some common profiles and causal factors of bullying. These include some evidence extracted from environmental and biological differences. In terms of their home environments, bullies often come from homes in which physical punishment is used, children are taught to strike back physically as a way to handle problems, and parental involvement and warmth are frequently lacking (Marano, 1995).

***Brain and Hormonal Research.*** Recent brain and hormonal research on teenagers suggests that a number of biological and genetic roles may come into play, resulting in bullying behavior commonly found in teenage years (LaFee, 2001). These include the following:

1. The prefrontal cortex does not fully develop until the late teenage years. This part of the brain assists in higher order thinking skills, including modulating behavior by aiding the limbic areas to think more like an adult. For example, when adults and teenagers were asked to identify facial expressions of people in fear, most of the adults could correctly identify the emotion, while most of the teenagers were not able to do so. Individuals considered "impulsive-aggressive" appear to have difficulty arousing the prefrontal cortex and thus have less ability to modify aggressive behavior.
2. The corpus callosum, which links the right and left halves of the brain (intelligence and consciousness), may not fully develop until the twenties, preventing full interaction with the limbic system. Intense neuron growth occurs in 9- to 18-year-olds in this area, as well as in the prefrontal cortex.
3. Levels of the moderating neurotransmitter called serotonin decline in the brain during teenage years. This may exacerbate feelings of emotional pain, making it easier to act impulsively.
4. Reduced levels of the hormone cortisol (released by the adrenal gland) occur in males that manifest aggression. One hypothesis is that low levels of cortisol may produce indifference to one's own actions, thus making it easier to engage in socially unacceptable behavior.
5. In the amygdala, the part of the brain believed to trigger fear and anger, heightened levels of hormones occur during puberty, possibly accounting for increased aggressiveness and irritability in both sexes.
6. The nerve coating called the myelin is not completely laid down until the post-teenage years. Myelin acts as a nerve insulator to help impulses and nerve functions be more efficient. This may be a contributing factor to increased irritability during the teenage years.

Knowing that both biology (nature) and the environment (nurture) may play a role in triggering bullying behavior, educators may be able to identify and reduce risk factors. From the biological perspective, the medical community can be of assistance. Doctors have recently used some drugs to successfully treat impulsive-aggressive individuals, reducing anxiety, depression, and anger and giving patients more time to think before they act. The use of other drugs to keep serotonin levels high helps the brain modulate its response to external stimuli. From the environmental perspective, educators should seek out parents of disruptive students and assist them through a variety of programs to become part of the ongoing solution in working with their children.

***Gender Differences.*** Both males and females are involved as bullies although gender differences exist in both the manifestations of bullying behavior and the frequency of incidents. Studies report bullying as more prevalent among males than females (Nansel, 2001). Males more commonly exhibit the physical forms whereas females manifest more verbal forms of bullying (Ahmad & Smith, 1994).

Male bullies' overt aggressive tendencies start at an early age and continue throughout their lives, interfering with work, learning, friendships, relationships, income, and mental health. They tend to become antisocial adults, who have more illnesses, shorter lives, higher rates of court convictions, more driving offenses, and they more often batter their spouses and abuse their children. This, of course, will increase the potential for producing another generation of bullies (Marano, 1995).

Bullies perceive provocation where it does not exist, in order to justify their aggressive behavior. They process social information inaccurately, believing aggression is the best solution to conflicts. They derive satisfaction from injuring others. Because they tend to lack prosocial behavior, they do not understand the feelings of others, come to deny others' suffering, and often see themselves quite positively. They tend to have few friends (two or three), who also tend to be aggressive. As bullies progress from middle school to high school, earlier peer admiration of their physical strength starts to wane (Olweus, 1993).

Female bullies tend to be less physical and more emotional than males in their aggressive behavior, sometimes called relational aggression. They also tend to exhibit many of the long-term problems of males. Some of the manipulation of relationships seen more commonly with females includes spreading vicious rumors to "get even" with someone, telling others to stop liking someone, using social exclusion to dominate a person, and using the "silent treatment" (Marano, 1995).

Both male and female bullies tend to focus their aggressive behavior against individuals in an attempt to undermine factors valued by their gender. In males it is physical strength and in females it is relationship power.

***Victims of Bullying.*** The individual victims of bullying are typically nonassertive, anxious, insecure, cautious, and suffer from low self-esteem, rarely defending themselves or retaliating when confronted. When faced with any form of conflict they are gripped with a fear sometimes called an "anxious vulnerability" (Olweus, 1993). They also may lack social skills and friends and often find themselves isolated. In general, in interactions with peers, they tend to make no attempts to verbally persuade, demand, request, or suggest. Studies of victims' home environments suggest that parents of victims tend to be overprotective and close to them. This results in an environment that offers them little or no practice in conflict resolution, a basic skill in social life and important in order to avoid becoming a victim.

Physically, victims tend to be smaller and weaker than their peers (Batsche & Knoff, 1994; Olweus, 1993). Their peers also perceive them as "weak," "nerds," and "afraid to fight back." Victims also tend to be socially introverted and like spending time in passive play (such as computer games), instead of engaging in activities directly involved with others. This isolation, social difficulty, and submissive behavior provide a mechanism for bullies to identify potential victims. Researchers have described the bully–victim relationship as a type of macabre dyad that results in mutually responsive negative interaction. In this relationship the bully gets satisfaction from dominance and the victim "feeds" the bully with compliance and sometimes physical rewards (food, objects). Without intervention, this "relationship" continues, causing physical and emotional abuse.

***Peer Spectators.*** Various studies have estimated that over 85% of bullying incidents involve peers as spectators or bystanders, and because of these experiences, this role impacts them in some capacity. Antonious Cillessen, a psychologist at the University of Connecticut, calls group dynamics the hidden purpose of bullying. Observing bullying behavior sometimes results in negative behavior or attitudes of other peers toward the victims. Evidence shows that many peers accept bullying behavior as "theater" and are aroused by it or moderately or severely upset by it (Lampert, 1998). Interviews with bystanders of bullying incidents report that less than 50% attempt to intervene. Researchers believe this to be due in part to the negative perception of victims (Charach, Pepler, & Ziegler, 1995). This evidence furnishes further proof that school-wide programs should address bullying.

## SECTION 3: SCHOOL-WIDE RESPONSE TO BULLIES

Recent school shootings and other overt forms of violent behavior, in many cases initiated by victims of bullies or by bullies themselves, have placed this issue at the forefront in many schools. Individual teachers have expressed helplessness against such systemic violence. Studies suggest that actions to deter bullying are the responsibility of the entire school community: parents, students, teachers, and administrators. Many programs and suggestions evolving from this approach have had a positive impact on identifying bullying problems and posing action plans to alleviate them (Marano, 1995).

Some interventions include general recommendations for students and parents to assist in preventing bullying and becoming a victim of bullying. Figure 9.2 lists a number of general suggestions for students and Figure 9.3 offers suggestions for parents. If you suspect issues of bullying, you might initiate a response by helping both groups deal with the problem.

Figures 9.2 and 9.3 make general recommendations for students and parents, but as noted earlier, because bullying is such a systemic problem in schools, addressing it requires a school-wide program involving the whole community. Schools can utilize a variety of tested, successful programs and handbooks to train students, parents, faculty, and staff. We now discuss a representative sample of these.

### School Programs

***Bully Busting.*** A psycho educational program for helping bullies and their victims (Newman, 1999) focuses on training teachers. It aims at the goals of changing teachers' knowledge of bullying intervention skills, teachers' use of these skills, and teachers' self-efficacy, resulting in a change in students' classroom bullying behaviors.

A research study used this model in an in-service setting for middle school teachers and compared the results to a group of equivalent middle school teachers who were not part of the in-service. Researchers found that the achievement level of all of the goals listed here significantly differed from the control group (Newman, 1999). Most importantly, the amount of bullying in each of the participant teachers' classrooms significantly decreased after the in-service training.

***Intervention Model.*** A program emphasizing a whole-school approach (Olweus, 1993), includes:

1. administering a school-wide questionnaire for students and parents to identify bullying-related problems and justify institution of the program;
2. discussing findings through parent organizations and parent conferences;
3. training teachers how to apply simulations and role-playing activities to teach students appropriate assertive behavior in order to provide strategies to assist victims, counteract bullies, and create an overall climate that does not tolerate bullying;
4. implementing school-wide interventions including individualized counseling sessions with bullies and victims;
5. increasing the use of cooperative learning activities into the curriculum to help prevent student isolation; and
6. increasing adult supervision, particularly at critical times, such as lunch and breaks. Research findings related to this program revealed a 50% reduction of bullying behaviors (Olweus, 1993).

FIGURE 9.2 Suggestions for Students on How to Handle Bullying

| What Students Can Do |
|---|
| • A wise line of defense is avoidance. Know when to walk away. It is thoroughly adaptive behavior to avoid a bully. Being picked on is not character building. |
| • Use humor to defuse a bully who may be about to attack. Make a joke, "Look, Johnny, lay off. I don't want you to be late for school." |
| • Tell the bully assertively, "Get a life. Leave me alone." Then walk away. This may be the best defense for girls. |
| • Recruit a friend. Observers find that having a friend nearby is one of the most powerful protections, especially for boys. |
| • In general, seek out the friendly children and build friendships with them. |

FIGURE 9.3 Suggestions for Parents on How to Handle Bullying

| What Parents Can Do |
|---|
| • See that your child is grounded in assertive behavior. The real first line of defense against a bully is self-confidence. |
| • Spread the word that bullying is bad for bullies. |
| • Ask your children how peers treat them. Children often are ashamed to bring up the subject; parents must. |
| • Enroll your child in a social-skills group in which children learn and practice skills in different situations. |
| • Model good relationships at home. Help siblings get along. |
| • Increase the social opportunities of all kids, but especially victimized ones. Invite other children, and groups of children, over to the house. Encourage sleepovers. This is your job; parents are social engineers. |
| • Enroll your child in classes or groups that develop competencies in activities that peers value. Even kids who don't love sports may like karate, tae kwon do, and similar activities. |
| • Shut off the TV; much programming reinforces the idea that aggression is the only way to deal with conflicts. |
| • Show empathy; instill in kids a sense of the distress that a victim experiences. |
| • Help your child come up with a set of clever comebacks to be used in the event of victimization by verbally abusive peers. |
| • See that kids in groups have plenty of things to do. Provide play materials. Buy a soccer ball. Bullying flourishes when kids are together and have nothing else to do. |
| • Do not tell or teach a kid to fight back. Fighting back is the worst defense. In most instances, victimized children really are weaker and smaller than the bully. Their fears of losing these fights may be quite real. Besides, not all bullying takes the form of physical aggression. Counteraggression to any form of bullying actually increases the likelihood of continued victimization. |
| • Do not expect kids to work it out on their own. Bullying is not simply a problem of individuals. Given the influence of the peer groups and reputation factors in maintaining the behavior of bullies and victims, it is extremely unrealistic to expect kids to alter the dynamics of bullying by themselves. |
| • Always intervene; adults have a crucial role to play in the socialization of children. Consistency counts; any time adults do not intervene they are essentially training others to solve problems through aggression. |
| • Intervene at the level of the group. Let all kids know bullying is not okay. Declare emphatically, "This is not acceptable behavior. You cannot do that here." |

(*continued*)

FIGURE 9.3 *(continued)*

| What Parents Can Do |
|---|
| • Talk to your child's teachers to find out what is normal behavior for children of that age group as well as to find out what the class atmosphere is like.<br>• Talk to other parents. Where there is one victimized child there are likely to be others.<br>• Get the school involved. At the very least, ask that the school make bullying off limits. A change in the atmosphere of the school is not only possible but also helpful in reducing bullying.<br>• Go to the school administration and demand that bullies be transferred to other classes or schools. Every child has the right to a safe school environment.<br>• If all else fails, see that your child is transferred to another school. The same child may thrive in a different school with a group of children having different values. |

## Parent Training

***Systemic Training for Effective Parenting (STEP).*** Dinkmeyer et al. (1997) developed this program in the form of a series of books and in-services for parents, students, and teachers. He followed the Dreikurs (1982) model of management, which focuses on students who have been unsuccessful in gaining social acceptance at home. This example of a confronting-contracting orientation described earlier also involves parents to redirect the child's misplaced goals.

Bullying is certainly one of the more serious outward manifestations of some of the student motivations for misbehavior that Dreikurs identifies. He categorizes these motivational factors as attention getting, power and control, revenge, and helplessness. Once the adult has identified the student's primary motive, the adult can use specific techniques or consequences that are considered effective to counter that causal behavior.

The particular way in which the adult responds to this identified student motivation is critical to alleviating some of the misbehavior. For example, a student whose primary motive for misbehaving centers on attention getting will repeatedly act in ways to become the center of attention. In this model, the teacher (as the acting adult) has a number of recommended levels of actions (depending on the degree of misbehavior), such as standing physically close to the student or moving the student's seat. Conversely, if this same student behaves properly, the teacher may use positive feedback by thanking the student after class.

The STEP model recommends similar but specific levels of adult behaviors depending on which motivating factor is causing the student misbehavior. These considerations need to be extended beyond parents and teachers to other faculty, administration, and student peers, depending on the seriousness of the misbehaviors. In-service training should incorporate representatives from all of these groups.

## Peer Mediation

The *peer mediation* model was designed as a practicum with the purpose of reducing incidents of harassment and increasing student sensitivity toward harassment behaviors (McMahon, 1995). The model applies conflict resolution and uses peer mediators (trained prior to sessions) to implement a series of group exercises. It also incorporates a pre and post self-assessment instrument for the participants, informational brochures for administrators and parents, and a variety of materials for group training sessions.

Outcomes of this practicum suggest formation of a student group that addresses issues of harassment on campus and follow-up data on effectiveness. They also typically include anonymous hot lines and other forms of communication for students. Some preliminary research findings on this model include a 42% decrease in reported incidents of harassments on campus and an increase in peer mediators' successful application of the concepts in their own lives (McMahon, 1995).

## Resources

*Conflict Resolution Education: Multiple Options for Contributing to Just and Democratic Peace* (Bickmore, 2002) focuses on the concept of how teachers can instruct students on conflict resolution within the context of the curriculum. Bickmore does this by citing methods of involving and incorporating students in real community issues and projects from the various disciplines of math, science, and literature. He makes the case that these types of scenarios with real community involvement have the potential to effect long-term positive change not possible with just in-service training. By involving students in situations in which the skills of decision making and conflict resolution are often applied, hopefully the student participants will learn strategies of nonviolent management of conflict that they can incorporate in their own lives. The manual contains a number of resources and examples for teachers of how to use this method of integrating conflict management into classroom applications.

*The Bullying Prevention Handbook: A Guide for Principals, Teachers, and Counselors* (Hoover & Oliver, 1997) serves as a resource for everyday intervention strategies for a wide range of educators in schools. These include specific approaches for educators in different roles, such as coaches, teachers, and administrators, that incorporate appropriate discussions and simulations within their context that can enhance a school-wide antibullying campaign. The handbook contains a resource guide, reading list, and models for discussion as well as action plans of solution-focused techniques for students.

*Behavioral Interventions: Creating a Safe Environment in Our Schools* (National Association of School Psychologists, 1997) includes chapter selections from a variety of leading experts on topics related to bullying and intervention techniques. This edited guide expands on concepts with the theme of applying a variety of practical experiences in schools that have proven successes related to interventions of bullying behavior. The practical and promising approaches include extensive strategies and references for teachers and administrators.

## *Putting It Into Practice:* Activity 9.4

In teams of preservice teachers, interview principals, assistant principals, and teachers, as well as other appropriate school personnel, at one site. The purpose of the interviews is to gain an insight into existing school-wide classroom management discipline practices, including bullying, that have been institutionalized within a school or district. More specifically, these interviews should address the actual school policies, programs and interventions, the rationale for the plan, and the effectiveness with which these administrators feel they have been implemented. From interviews and discussions, outline the overall perceived strengths and challenges of the school-wide plan.

Using your team's findings as a context, develop an audiovisual presentation (slides, pictures, digital film) that critically overviews the application of this school's policy. Classroom discussion will draw comparisons of the different policies at various sites. The final presentation of the activity will integrate Applying Technology: Activity 9.1.

## *Putting It Into Practice:* Activity 9.5

In this activity, the same teams as in Putting It Into Practice: Activity 9.4, at the same site, will now focus on observations of individual classroom teachers and the models they are actually using for classroom management. Your team should apply a reflective classroom observational technique. Observe a sample of teachers and record your findings related to classroom management.

As a second part of your on-site observation, observe students in an informal setting. The focus in this observation should be on how students (and any school ground supervisors, including teachers, security personnel, etc.) deal with conflict in an informal setting. Analysis of your team's findings should include:

1. management actions and issues of students in both formal and informal school settings;
2. an overall analysis of the comparison between the institutional policies and what the team actually observes within specific classrooms; and
3. an overview of any bullying behavior observed as well as reactions of bullies, victims, bystanders, and school personnel to the incidents. As in Activity 9.4, the final presentation of this activity will also integrate Applying Technology: Activity 9.1.

## *Applying Technology:* Activity 9.1

Use Putting It Into Practice: Activities 9.4 and 9.5 as the context for your audiovisual presentation related to the nature of the school-wide and individual teacher discipline policies. This presentation could take a variety of formats, including the use of PowerPoint, slides, overhead transparencies, digital film, or any combination of these, as long as it incorporates the context of the assignment.

## *Putting It Into Practice:* Activity 9.6

After having completed Putting It Into Practice: Activities 9.4 and 9.5, and Applying Technology: Activity 9.1, individually use the information and feedback to design and implement (during field experience) your own preliminary lesson plan addressing the specific ways you will attempt to introduce and then integrate classroom management policies into your own teaching practice. Present an overview of your initial lesson plan to the class to gain feedback and recommendations for rewrites. Implement this final revised plan in the beginning of your field experience. The final report should include reflections on the effective use of the plan as implemented, to be presented to the class for discussion and feedback.

## SECTION 4: CHAPTER SUMMARY AND REFLECTION

This chapter discussed a range of classroom management issues. Section 1 introduced models of classroom management, how they are classified, and what research informs us about effective practice.

Section 2 examined applications of classroom management beginning with strategies for dealing with behavior problems followed by an activity to practice strategies for the most common class disruptions. A specific case study illustrated how a model that integrates many of these concepts (compassionate discipline) can be implemented in difficult cases. The model emphasized gathering relevant information as well as informing and interacting with all individuals involved, before determining an action plan. Congruent with serious violent events in schools, we placed particular emphasis on a discussion of bullying. This section also covered methods to educate teachers and parents regarding identification of bullies and victims.

Section 3 focused on a school-wide response to bullies, which included school programs, parent training, and peer mediation. It also supplied additional resources. You were given the opportunity to apply knowledge gained from this chapter to field activities that explored school-wide discipline policies, teacher strategies for classroom management, and ways to integrate classroom management into your own lesson plans.

## *References*


Ahmad, Y., & Smith, P. K. (1994). Bullying in schools and the issues of sex differences. In J. Archer (Ed.), *Male violence* (pp. 35–48). London: Routledge.

Arroyo, A., & Selleck, G. (1989). *Loving our differences: Building successful relationships.* Virginia Beach: CBN Publishing.

Banks, R. (1997). Bullying in schools. *ERIC Digest* (EDO-PS-97-17).

Batsche, G. M., & Knoff, H. M. (1994). Bullies and their victims: Understanding a pervasive problem in schools. *School Psychological Review, 23*(2), 165–174.

Bickmore, K. (2002). Conflict resolution education: Multiple options for contributing to just and democratic peace. In W. Pammer & J. Killian (Eds.), *Handbook of conflict management* (pp. 10–15). New York: Marcel-Dekker Publishers.

Borich, G. (1998). *Observation skills for effective teaching.* Chicago: Merrill.

Brainard, E. (2001). Classroom management: Seventy-three suggestions for secondary school teachers. *Clearing House, 74*(4), 207–211.

Brendtro, L. K., Brokenleg, M., & Bockern, S. V. (2002). *Reclaiming youth at risk: Our hope for the future*. Bloomington, IN: National Education Service.

Brophy, J., & Good, T. (1986). Teacher behavior and student achievement. In M. C. Wittrock (Ed.), *Handbook of research on teaching* (3rd ed.) (pp. 17–35). New York: Macmillan.

Burden, P. (2000). *Powerful classroom management strategies*. Thousand Oaks, CA: Corwin Press.

Charach, A., Pepler, D., & Ziegler, S. (1995). Bullying at school—A Canadian perspective: A survey of problems and suggestions for intervention. *Education Canada, 35* (1), 12–18.

Council of Chief State School Officers (1992). *Model standards for beginning teacher licensing, assessment, and development: A resource for state dialogue*. Washington, DC: Author. www.ccsso.org/content/pdfs/corestrd.pdf

Curwin, R., & Mendler, A. (1988). *Discipline with dignity*. Alexandria, VA: Association for Supervision and Curriculum Development.

Dinkmeyer, D., Sr., Mckay, G., & Dinkmeyer, D., Jr. (1997). *The parent's handbook: Systematic training for effective parenting*. Circle Pines, MN: AGS.

Dreikurs, R. (1982). *Maintaining sanity in the classroom*. New York: Harper and Row.

Froyen, L. (1993). *Classroom management: The reflective teacher-leader* (2nd ed.). New York: Macmillan.

Glasser, W. (1992). *The quality school: Managing students without coercion* (2nd ed.). New York: HarperCollins.

Haberman, M. (1995). *Star teacher of children of poverty*. Indianapolis, IN: Kappa Delta Pi.

Hoover, J. H., & Oliver, R. (1997). *The bullying prevention handbook: A guide for principals, teachers, and counselors*. Bloomington, IN: National Education Service.

Johnson, S., & Johnson, C. (1986). *The one minute teacher*. New York: William Morrow.

Keating, J. (2001). The compassionate discipline model. Unpublished model.

LaFee, S. (2001, April 11). Without reason: Science hunts for biological clues to youth violence. *San Diego Union Tribune, Quest*, pp. D1–D4.

Lampert, J. (1998). Voices and visions: Adolescent girls' experiences as bullies, targets, and bystanders. *Dissertation Abstracts International, 58*(8A), 2986.

Marano, H. (1995, September–October). Big bad bully. *Psychology Today*, pp. 52–82.

Martin, N. (1997). Connecting instruction and management in a student-centered classroom. *Middle School Journal, 28*(4), 3–9.

McMahon, P. (1995). *Stemming harassment among middle school students through peer mediation and group activities*. Unpublish EdD practicum, Nora University.

Nansel, T. (2001). Bullying behaviors among U.S. youth. *Journal of the American Medical Association, 285*(16), 2094–2100.

National Association of School Psychologists (1997). *Behavioral interventions: Creating a safe environment in our schools*. Bethesda, MD: NASP.

Newman, D. (1999, December). The effectiveness of psycho educational intervention for classroom teachers aimed at reducing bullying behavior in middle school students. *Dissertation Abstracts International, 60*(5A), 1440.

Olweus, D. (1993). *Bullying at school: What we need to know and what we can do*. Cambridge, MA: Blackwell.

Smalley, G. (1992). *The key to your child's health*. Dallas: Word Publishing.

Stein, H. (2002, January 26). What kind of parent are you? *San Diego Union Tribune*, p. E4.

Terry, A. (1998). Teachers as targets of bullying by their pupils: A study to investigate incidence. *British Journal of Educational Psychology, 68*(2), 255–268.

Walton, M. (1986). *Deming management system*. New York: Putnam.

Wolfgang, C. (1995). *Solving discipline problems* (3rd ed.). New York: Wiley.

# Unit V

# Beyond the Classroom

# Chapter 10

# Collaboration Between Schools and Communities

**INTASC Principle 10:** The teacher fosters relationships with school colleagues, parents, and agencies in the larger community to support students' learning and well-being.

**Key Dispositions**

- The teacher values and appreciates the importance of all aspects of a child's experience.
- The teacher is willing to consult with other adults regarding the education and well being of his/her students.
- The teacher is willing to work with other professionals to improve the overall learning environment for students.

## Introduction to the Chapter

This chapter introduces strategies for collaboration between school and community. We have approached the topic from three specific directions: service-learning, parent involvement, and community involvement. Section 1 defines service-learning as a strategy that links service to the community to a specific discipline or disciplines that incorporate elements of reflection in an effort to instill lasting attitudes of caring for others. This has a number of benefits for the future teacher including a basis for a teacher–student interaction in a setting other than school; a real-world setting for incorporating and connecting concepts from the curriculum; experiencing an example of an "ethic of caring" as well as a way to become informed citizens; and a reflective-in-action process model that allows the connection of classroom theory to practice. This section discusses the broad support for the use of service-learning, citing national reform documents as well as a wide range of models on its possible implementation in the individual classroom. In addition to elements of service and curriculum connections, the discussion also suggests ways for teachers to incorporate career and career skills exploration opportunities. We also provide overviews of some examples of service-learning applications to the school curriculum.

Section 2 focuses on the important yet challenging aspect of involving parents in the education of their sons and daughters. It addresses several strategies to overcome obstacles. The section also highlights the importance of teacher–parent–student communication and monitoring including descriptions of several examples of communication methods. Also addressed is more direct involvement of parents at the school site, accompanied by descriptions of specific examples.

Section 3 delves into another level of participation—providing opportunities for parents, extended family, and community members to collaborate with teachers and school personnel on policy, curriculum, assessment, and other school matters. The ideas presented in this section represent more intimate involvement with a range of commitment and expertise, allowing participants to directly influence the educational process.

## Section 1: Service-Learning

Service-learning has been defined in a variety of ways. Initially linked to volunteerism, more recently its powerful connections to the curriculum have emerged and been added as a component; thus the service-learning concept has evolved in education. Kinsley and McPherson (1995) define service-learning as "a pedagogical model that intentionally integrates academic learning and relevant community service" (p. 21). The Department of Education at Hampton University adds that it also includes "providing students with opportunities to use newly acquired skills and knowledge in real life situations . . . and helps foster the development of caring for others" (Henry & White-Williams, 1998, p. 10). Service-learning has been identified as a process in which reflection is a critical component of the outcome, allowing future connections to learning (Kinsley & McPherson, 1995).

The Circle of Courage very closely aligns with the practice of incorporating service-learning into the classroom experience. Service-learning addresses most obviously the Generosity section of the Circle of Courage. The highest virtues in Native American culture are generosity and unselfishness, with a responsibility to consider the welfare of others in the community. Students have the opportunity to learn to become caring, responsible adults who give their help genuinely. Service-learning also addresses the section of the Circle of Courage representing Belonging through helping others and experiencing a sense of being part of the community. Relationships can be developed based on mutual trust and respect, providing motivation to live with a minimum of friction and a maximum of goodwill (Brendtro et al., 2002).

## Overview of Service-Learning

Experiences, such as service-learning, that promote awareness of community and its needs, can provide a variety of multidimensional benefits for the preparation of teachers, as well as long-term effects on students they will teach. Some of the potentially beneficial aspects of incorporating service-learning into teacher preparation programs include the following:

1. an experience that can give the preservice teacher a different perspective on the teacher–student interaction in a setting other than school (Root, 1994);
2. a real-world setting for incorporating and connecting concepts from the curriculum (Boyer, 1983; Cairn & Kielsmeier, 1991; Dewey, 1938);
3. a basis to assist the student in becoming an acceptable person who has an ethic of care (Noddings, 1988) as well as an informed citizen (Aronowitz & Giroux, 1985); and
4. a reflection-in-action process model that allows the connection of classroom theory to practice (Schon, 1987).

Broad support exists for the inclusion of school and student interaction with the community. Ernest Boyer (1983) in *High School: A Report on Secondary Education in America,* suggests that community service be a part of high school graduation requirements, and that a service component for all students would help build a sense of community and common purpose within a school. As early as 1938, John Dewey believed that the primary reason schools had problems organizing themselves as a natural social unit was because of the lack of the common and productive activity of community service. In *Second to None* (1992), the California Task Force suggested that schools fully integrate the community into the curriculum by exposing students to real-world problems.

***Examples of Service-Learning.*** As a prospective teacher you may understand philosophically the value of service-learning after reading and discussing the issues related to it but may not be sure how to implement it in diverse high school settings. A number of examples and models of service-learning can provide you as a preservice teacher with a basis to contemplate how to apply your own experiences to implementation and integration into high school classes (Cairn & Kielsmeier, 1991). Three general examples of ways that a teacher might include service-learning as part of the curriculum follow:

1. Granting service-learning credit to those high school students who want to participate in service-learning as an optional component, for extra credit or as a substitute for another assignment within a specific class.
2. Developing an elective course for those students who want to participate in a separate class devoted exclusively to service-learning projects of their choosing. Some schools have incorporated this as a graduation requirement. In such a course, the teacher acts as the adviser and the students receive release time to carry out projects in teams or as individuals.
3. Facilitating a classroom project (in which everyone participates as part of the class) for a major community involvement effort. Examples might include an environmental science class assisting in building a nature trail for the school district; a general biology class performing water analysis at beaches and recording weekly test results on a surfer web page; an interdisciplinary language arts and foreign language group of students publishing and distributing a newsletter for immigrants informing them about availability of educational, medical, and social services; or industrial arts and civics students planning, designing, and building ramps for the students with disabilities at a school site.

Individual high schools may offer a great variation in the ways they incorporate service-learning, depending on resources and teacher creativity. Appropriate experiences during teacher-training programs can inform preservice teachers of these variations, as well as address motivations, available resources, and mechanisms for applying service-learning in high schools.

Service-learning experiences can become a powerful learning tool, regardless of the models used. One way the teacher can accomplish this is to include a number of components in the experience. Besides the actual component of volunteering time and energy for others (service), the experience should consist of making a direct connection between the curriculum and the community service being performed (curriculum integration). The teacher integrates what students have learned in the course with their application of the knowledge and skills while performing a service to the community.

In addition, a third component embedded in most experiences in the community is career exploration; for example, providing the students with opportunities to explore careers in which they may be interested through shadowing, interviews, and interaction with professionals involved in the students' projects. To make the experiences meaningful to the student, as well as to the teacher, appropriate training and introductory activities should precede the actual experience. The teacher should structure assessments of the student experience and include both formative and summative components for evaluation. Examples of assessment may include (but not be limited to) student reflective journals, surveys (both before and after the experience), group presentations, and student interviews.

## Guidelines for Effectiveness

A number of groups and organizations have come up with recommended practices for teachers using service-learning. These include, for example, elements of high-quality

service-learning in *Building Support for Service Learning* (Addison-Jacobson & Hill, 1996). These authors suggest that the following elements are the most essential for successful service-learning: (1) enhancing and connecting academic knowledge and skills; (2) meeting a real need in the community; (3) student involvement in the planning; (4) reflection before, during, and after; (5) collaboration with all stakeholders; and (6) gathering data concerning the effectiveness of the service-learning program.

In 1995 the Maryland Student Service Alliance (MSSA) conducted one of the most expansive research-based studies including corresponding implications and recommendations on practices that make service-learning effective in high schools. Established as a resource for teachers in 1988 by the state of Maryland, its need was based on a service-learning requirement for all graduating high school students. As part of its mission, the MSSA has conducted extensive research through interviews, observations, and surveys on the effectiveness of various practices. The study selected 80 teachers to review and analyze these data and develop a document to assist teachers in the most effective ways to implement service-learning.

The final document, *Maryland Best Practices: An Improvement Guide for School-Based Service-Learning* (1995), reports the research findings. The document ranks (in order) the importance of essential components of service-learning as well as offers a variety of approaches to implementation. The seven best practices for school-based service-learning (Maryland Student Services Alliance, 1995) follow.

1. **Meet a recognized need in the community.** Teachers and students may define the need within a "community" narrowly (within their own school, for example) or broadly (within their state). The meaningful experience results in researching issues and having the courage to tackle real needs in a community.
2. **Achieve curricular objectives through service-learning by addressing standards.** The increased importance in connecting all learning to state or national standards allows service-learning to be a very effective mechanism to

accomplish curriculum objectives, because it provides relevancy and purpose to the learning. Students work collaboratively and apply new work skills and knowledge, facilitating a unifying force for many concepts and disciplines.

3. **Reflect throughout the service-learning experience.** The experience provides students with a way to process, debrief, and dialogue about their experiences and learning. The reflective process might involve opportunities such as reflective journals, conferencing with teachers, discussion time with other students, and final presentation forums. This allows for students to grow intellectually, personally, and socially.
4. **Develop student responsibility.** Students are most eager to participate in service-learning if they experience some ownership of the process. It is important to create an appropriate climate (depending on the developmental level) in which students, facilitated by the teacher, receive the opportunity to take on the responsibility of planning and implementing service-learning projects.
5. **Establish community partnerships.** Inviting community partners to help design and participate in service-learning adds value to the activities and encourages students to become more involved. It also provides an additional audience for student learning and performance beyond the teacher. By becoming involved with adults in real-world settings, students gain opportunities to explore career goals as well as establish potential longer term relationships.
6. **Plan ahead for service-learning.** By planning all the way through to the details, the project has a greater chance for maximum success and for providing benefits in all three areas of service, curriculum, and career exploration. It also provides a mechanism to develop, improve, or extend teacher–student or student–student collaboration processes as discussed in Chapter 6 on cooperative learning.
7. **Equip students with the knowledge and skills needed for service-learning.** Some skills may be novel and others may have been previously introduced in the classroom. In order for students to understand what is expected of them in the service-learning situation, teachers need to review the skills and practices they will use. Some might be as generic as good oral or written communication skills or as specific as how to tutor in reading. Discussion, simulation, and actual student practice may be the best way to prepare students up front. For example, in order to tutor reading effectively, a student tutor would need to understand some basic teaching practices as well as skill-building concepts for the teaching of reading. Of great benefit would be teacher training sessions prior to the experience as well as ongoing conferences with the tutors. This best practice also provides participants with experiences within a specific career modality, in this case teaching.

*A Closer Look*

**Instructional Resource I** provides a sample service-learning project.

***Levels of Approaches for Service-Learning.*** *Maryland Best Practices: An Improvement Guide for School-Based Service-Learning* (MSSA, 1995) defines and explains three different but increasingly complex levels of approaches for each best practice, as illustrated by Figure 10.1.

The different approaches teachers might implement in integrating service-learning projects into their curriculum would depend on the variety of teacher experience, student ability and experience, as well as the time constraints typically found in schools. For example, the first service-learning best practice (meet a

**FIGURE 10.1** The Maryland School-Based Service-Learning Best Practices and Related Approaches

1. Meet a Recognized Need in the Community:

| | |
|---|---|
| Approach 1 | Provide short-term assistance addressing a community need. |
| Approach 2 | Provide ongoing assistance addressing a community need. |
| Approach 3 | Work toward a lasting solution to a community problem. |

2. Achieve Curricular Objectives Through Service-Learning:

| | |
|---|---|
| Approach 1 | Incorporate service-learning into a unit. |
| Approach 2 | Use service-learning to unify the teaching of content and skills throughout the year. |
| Approach 3 | Teach content and/or skills in different disciplines using service-learning throughout the year. |

3. Reflect Throughout the Service-Learning Experience:

| | |
|---|---|
| Approach 1 | At the end of the experience, students contemplate their service-learning experience and receive response. |
| Approach 2 | Throughout the process, students contemplate their service-learning experience and receive response. |

4. Develop Student Responsibility:

| | |
|---|---|
| Approach 1 | Establish choices for students in how they implement the teacher-planned service-learning. |
| Approach 2 | Share responsibility with students for service-learning development and implementation. |
| Approach 3 | Facilitate student definition, coordination, and implementation of service-learning. |

5. Establish Community Partnerships:

| | |
|---|---|
| Approach 1 | A teacher consults with community partner for information and resources. |
| Approach 2 | Students interact with community partners. |
| Approach 3 | Students, teachers, and community partners collaborated as an action team. |

6. Plan Ahead for Service-Learning:

| | |
|---|---|
| Approach 1 | Plan service-learning independently. |
| Approach 2 | Collaborate with colleagues, students, and others to plan service-learning. |

7. Equip Students With Knowledge and Skills Needed for Service:

| | |
|---|---|
| Approach 1 | Equip students with knowledge and skills at the beginning of the experience. |
| Approach 2 | Equip students with knowledge and skills as needs arise or as the project changes. |

Note: From *Maryland Best Practices: An Improvement Guide for School-based Service-Learning* (p. 13), by Maryland Student Services Alliance, 1995, Baltimore: Maryland Department of Education.

recognized need in the community) suggests potentially three different levels of approaches for a teacher to take that vary in time, complexity, and level of experience required of students and teachers.

Illustrating approach 1 (provide short-term assistance addressing a community need), a Current Issues in Social Science class worked to identify a local social need through researching newspaper articles and other media for a potential project. They decided to assist a group of families whose homes had been burned. They raised and collected clothing, furniture, and money from the community, presenting it to the families. In this one-time short-term project, the class applied content skills of social studies such as social issues skills (communications), economics (raising monies and material goods), and group organizational skills.

As an example of approach 2 (provide ongoing assistance addressing a community need), a group of science students and their teacher decided to revitalize a stream behind their school. This neglected stream, full of litter, ran into a river, which in turn ran into the bay. The teacher received a grant to provide wood for bird and bat houses, plants for erosion control, mulch for trails, and water testing kits. She also received matching funds from the local community (MSSA, 1995). Students worked throughout the school year, spending one day each week on the project. Some of the outcomes included increased understanding of natural ecosystems and the impact humans can have on those systems; an education program for elementary students; water data for a city stream project; an outdoor classroom for other classes to utilize; and a visually cleaner environment. In addition, the teacher believed that after working on the project her students would be more likely to take on responsibility for public land in the future.

As an example of approach 3 (work toward a lasting solution to a community problem), a group of students in a high school journalism class organized a campaign against secondhand smoke in their county schools. They took a multidimensional approach by first investigating how ventilation systems spread secondhand smoke. Second, they gathered information on dangers of secondhand smoke. Third, the students posed a solution by recommending the prohibition of all smoking in any school building and presented this proposal to their county school board. When this failed to produce action, they contacted the media and the state school board and superintendent to make presentations. The students also extended their proposal to the Association of Athletics to ban all smoking at athletic events. Outcomes from the project included the banning of smoking in all schools and athletic events not only in their county but also throughout the state. The students had applied the content skills required of a journalist conducting research, writing editorials and participating in oral communication in a real-world situation, which had far-reaching and lasting consequences.

These approaches, illustrated by *Maryland Best Practices*, make it apparent that all students—regardless of experience, ability, or time constraints—can become involved and have meaningful service-learning experiences. Research findings from MSSA also suggest that initial success in short-term projects increases both students' and teachers' potential for success in more complex long-term projects (MSSA, 1995).

## Importance of Content Standards

Once again, we must emphasize the increased focus in today's educational system at the national, state, and local levels, on matching instruction to subject matter standards and incorporating accountability by assessing, either locally or through statewide tests, the achievement of those standards. Service-learning, if applied effectively as part of the curriculum, can be a very appropriate instructional tool to teach work skills and academic concepts (both basic and higher level), apply them in actual learning situations, and assess understanding of the concepts.

The Colorado Department of Education has linked its Goals 2000 content standards to service-learning activities. The following examples applying this linkage illustrate how content standards and service-learning can be integrated in very powerful ways.

For example, in physical science one of the standards addresses the importance of students' knowledge and understanding of common properties of matter, forms of energy, and interactions between the two (Education Commission of the States, 2000). One way this standard might be addressed in actual classroom practice would be to teach students how different common household appliances receive and use energy (electrical [AC and DC], fuel powered, solar, etc.) as well as determining the amount of energy they use in a specific time period. The service-learning application could be a classroom project involving selecting various businesses and/or homes and doing "energy surveys" for them that calculate individual and total energy. Students could use the data to make recommendations to the businesses or individual households for conservation measures.

Another example, taken from a foreign language standard, includes the ability of a student to read and derive meaning from a variety of materials written in a foreign language (Education Commission of the States, 2000). Foreign language students typically translate classroom text material to demonstrate this standard. A creative service-learning application might be for them to take an existing children's book written in English and translate it into the foreign language being studied (with input and feedback from the teacher and each other) and then reading the "translated" text to a group of elementary grade second-language students.

In both of these examples, the specific content is addressed and knowledge gained through typical classroom instructional lessons. Instead of typical assessment techniques, students are asked to apply that knowledge in the context of a community service-learning project. This technique not only informs the teacher and student about what was learned but also provides a benefit to the community from the student application.

From a practical and political perspective, funds to support service-learning are sometimes difficult to attain with the increased emphasis on accountability of student achievement through norm-referenced testing. Standardized tests do not usually capture the civic, social, academic, career, and personal outcomes from service-learning. Consequently, those teachers participating in service-learning need to collect qualitative and quantitative data about the effectiveness of their programs. This is a valuable application of action research, as discussed in Chapter 3, Assessment.

Recent research findings validate that effective service-learning programs help students acquire the academic skills and knowledge associated with state and national standards. In a 1998 report, "RPP International Evaluation of K–12 Service-Learning in California," students in more than 50% of the schools with high-quality service-learning showed moderate to strong gains on student achievement tests in language arts and/or reading, engagement in school, sense of educational accomplishment, and homework completion. The Center for Civic Education and Services at Florida State University found service-learning participation associated with higher scores on state tests of basic skills and higher grades in 83%

of schools using service-learning among 76% of participating students (Wisconsin Department of Public Instruction, 2000). Researchers at Brandeis University found that "well-designed" service-learning programs had a positive impact on student performance in 17 middle and high schools in the nationwide study. Positive outcomes included gains in attitudes toward school and improved grades in science, math, and overall GPA (Pickeral & Bray, 2000).

Studies suggest that if a teacher starts with the standards, integrates service-learning as a powerful way to meet those standards, and then designs authentic assessment techniques to effectively assess the outcomes, learning results can be shown. Several states are implementing such approaches to service-learning (Wisconsin Department of Public Instruction, 2000).

***School-to-Career Service-Learning.*** The school-to-career component of service-learning also functions as an effective means of aligning projects to content standards. The U.S. Secretary of Labor formed the Secretary's Commission on Achieving Necessary Skills (SCANS) (1990) with the purpose of examining the demands of the workplace to find out whether graduating students could meet these demands. The commission identified three foundation skills and five competencies needed for solid job performance, which are outlined in Figure 10.2. Service-learning can provide an entry platform to learn and apply these job skills and competencies.

**FIGURE 10.2** Foundation Skills and Competencies for the Workplace

| | **Foundation Skills** |
|---|---|
| Basic Skills | Reading, writing, arithmetic and mathematics, speaking, and listening |
| Thinking Skills | Thinking creatively, making decisions, solving problems, seeing things in the mind's eye, knowing how to learn, and the art of reasoning |
| Personal Qualities | Individual responsibility, self-esteem, sociability, self-management, and integrity |
| | **Competencies** |
| Resources | Allocates time (ranks tasks in order of importance), allocates money (computes cost of project), and allocates materials (acquiring, storing and distributing) |
| Interpersonal Skills | Participates as a member of a team, teaches others, serves customers, negotiates to reach a decision, works with people of diverse backgrounds and skill levels |
| Information | Acquires and evaluates information, organizes and maintains information (files), interprets or communicates information, uses computers to process information |
| Systems | Understands how organizational and technological systems work, monitors and corrects performance of systems and improves or designs systems |
| Technology | Chooses procedures, tools or equipment, applies technology to specific tasks, maintains and troubleshoots equipment |

Note: From *Identifying Necessary Skills,* by the Secretary's Commission on Achieving Necessary Skills (SCANS), 1990, Washington, DC: U.S. Department of Labor.

## *Putting It Into Practice:* Activity 10.1

Locate someone within your school (or where you will participate in a field experience) who already incorporates service-learning in the curriculum (preferably within your discipline). With your knowledge of service-learning (including *Maryland Best Practices*), interview the teacher and if possible observe the students in action during service-learning. From this interaction, you should be able to address the following elements or questions: (1) overview of the project; (2) whether the project integrated service, curriculum standards, and career explorations; (3) how it assessed students; (4) which elements of *Maryland Best Practices* it incorporated; (5) the overall effectiveness of the project from teacher and student perspectives; and (6) the overall strengths and weaknesses of the project and how would you change it. Present a report that addresses these findings from your experience.

## *Applying Technology:* Activity 10.1

Conduct an Internet search of web sites that could be used to create a resource list in support of service-learning. Use the National Technology Standards for High School Teachers (National Technology Standards) evaluation sheets for web sites to evaluate these sites in order to standardize the quality of those selected for use by the whole class. This resource list should include as a minimum: (1) sites that offer examples of how schools use service-learning, (2) print and video resources, (3) organizational resources, and (4) grant and other monetary sources for service-learning. After having completed this, you may create a compilation or master classroom resource that all can use as a resource for service-learning.

***Interdisciplinary Service-Learning.*** An interdisciplinary service-learning project designed by math, language arts, science, and social studies teachers provides an example of how content standards, work, job, and career-related skills can be integrated into the curriculum. This project, implemented throughout the school year, focused on community senior citizens (MSSA, 1995). Direct action (actual interaction with the seniors) took place in the language arts and social studies classes and indirect action in the science and math classes.

In language arts, students learned how to use a variety of communication skills that they would apply in working with the senior citizens. These included how to interview, ask good questions, listen, and organize findings in a written report (all SCANS related skills). In addition, students read to seniors, wrote poems and cards for them, and organized reports on interactions with them (content standard skills).

As part of the social studies course, students explored careers related to working with seniors by interviewing and shadowing personnel involved with the seniors such as nurses, doctors, caregivers, and social workers. They prepared visual charts to provide an overview of each career for a presentation within the classroom. In addition, they selected seniors to visit the class to talk about their life experiences from the perspective of historical events.

In their science course, students learned about the various physical and mental changes that occur during the aging process. They also discussed medications and other methods used to alleviate some of the discomforts of aging.

In the mathematics course, students collected data on physical disabilities of the aging, using statistics to calculate and graph the mode, mean, and range from their findings. They used this information to make a presentation in another class on the medical and social effects of aging (SCANS skill).

Many of these activities involved content-specific objectives such as the structure and process of writing poems or personally related experiences of serving in World War II, both of which were applicable to the Maryland School Performance Assessment Program. The state used an assessment tool to determine mastery of subject matter competency. Results of this curriculum suggested that students performed better on this test because it not only addressed standards but also utilized them in a situation that made learning come alive for students.

In addition, service-learning addresses such affective objectives as "caring for others" and working in a collaborative environment. Affective objectives apply not only to the student but also to the teacher and the community partner, as reflected in Figure 10.3, which lists the potential impact of service-learning on students, schools, teachers, and community partners (RPP International Evaluation, 1998).

***Reflective Practice.*** It is very important to provide students with opportunities to reflect on their experiences in both an ongoing (formative) as well as a final (summative) presentation (MSSA, 1995). This will help teachers assess whether students have mastered content standards. Teachers can gain valuable information

**FIGURE 10.3** Impact of Service-Learning on Participants

| **Impact on Students** |
|---|
| • Promotes positive effects on student learning<br>• Improves civic and social attitudes<br>• Develops personal and social responsibility toward work, school, and the community |
| **Impact on Schools and Teachers** |
| • Builds group cohesiveness among students<br>• Fosters mutual respect between students and teachers<br>• Improves overall school climate<br>• Contributes to achievement of school-wide educational and attitudinal goals<br>• Stimulates innovative instructional practices<br>• Promotes teacher collegiality and efforts to extend professionally |
| **Impact on Community Partners** |
| • Fosters positive change in the views of students and schools by the community<br>• Increases community support and involvement in schools<br>• Meets *real* community needs |

Note: From *Service-Learning Manual for K–12 Teachers,* RPP International Evaluation of K–12 Service-Learning in California: Phase II Final Report, 1998, Emeryville, CA: California Department of Education, Calserve Office.

Instructional Resource J provides a sample service-learning project reflection, written by a preservice teacher.

on how they might adapt the structure of the service-learning experience. Additional benefits from this process include opportunities for students to reflect on what they are learning and to learn from each other.

In practice this reflective process might take on the form of reflective journals, conferencing with teachers, discussion time with other students, and final presentation forums. The use of specific prompts has been suggested so that a structure to apply the reflections guides students and teachers (Henry & White-Williams, 1998; MSSA, 1995). These journals might provide the basis for discussion with teachers, final presentations to class, and overall assessment of the experience.

Terri Pickeral, project director for the Compact for Learning and Citizenship, Education Commission of the States (2000), summarizes the major premise of this section—that is, the importance of linking the curriculum (including career exploration) to service-learning. She reminds us:

> Deepening the quality and increasing the scope of Service-Learning in schools are essential, and standards may just be the ticket to help drive better integration of service, curriculum (and career exploration). Young people cannot afford to put their academic growth on hold for programs that are merely a sidebar or an outside activity that bears little relationship to the central activities of the school. Demonstrating success on academic standards has to become a top priority for Service-Learning. (Education Commission of the States, 2000)

## *Putting It Into Practice:* Activity 10.2

Identify people in your school or school district who have information about using service-learning in the classroom. Other initial resources might also include community service-learning organizations that act as intermediaries between the community and individuals. You may also want to use the resource list you developed in Applying Technology: Activity 10.1. Once you establish some potential community sites or organizations, contact them for ideas on potential projects for your students. This information can become a basis for you and your students to select projects. Use the following format to document your information.

1. Name of organization(s) or site(s):
2. Contact people (name, title, telephone #):

3. Address:
4. Overview of organization's mission or purpose:
5. Narrative of your experiences including any observations, interviews, and participatory activities (use back or attach if necessary):
6. Highlights:
   a. In what ways might this organization be supportive of incorporating service-learning into the school curriculum?
   b. What are the potential limitations or difficulties in working with this organization with your students? In what ways could you facilitate overcoming these limitations?
   c. How could you use this organization with your high school students for service-learning that would include elements from your content standards, service-learning, and career skills and exploration?
   d. If you have decided to start your own service-learning "organization" (which does not involve specific community organizations), explain how to implement it.

Using all the information collected from your exploration of the local community as well as the elements suggested in *Maryland Best Practices* in service-learning, design a service-learning lesson plan for your discipline that incorporates the use of the organization(s) you studied (or your own "organization") as the main focus of the lesson. This lesson plan should include how you will integrate the three critical aspects of service-learning discussed earlier (service, content standards, career skills, and exploration). This lesson plan should include all relevant components of a lesson plan such as (1) purpose and goals; (2) standards addressed; (3) cognitive, affective, and psychomotor and word objectives; (4) materials and resources; (5) scope and sequence of procedures and activities (matrix); (6) considerations for special needs students and any adaptations that might be appropriate; and (7) formative and summative assessments. An additional and valuable component may be the inclusion of an outline of how to use action research to evaluate the success of the project.

## *Applying Technology:* Activity 10.2

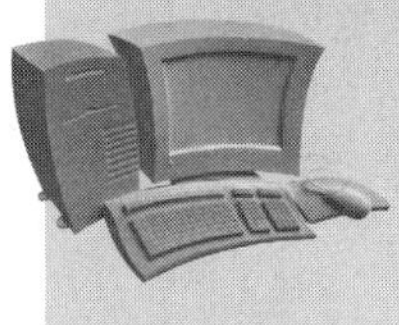

Use digital video and/or digital still photography to document your experiences in Putting It Into Practice: Activities 10.1 and 10.2, which explore potential or existing resources for using service-learning in the community or school. Incorporate the edited version of this in your presentation to the class, which should use PowerPoint or some other presentational tool that demonstrates your effective use of this technology.

## SECTION 2: PARENT INVOLVEMENT

The previous section focused on the interaction among the schools, teachers, and communities using service-learning with the integration of school-to-career, typically utilizing community businesses or organizations as the central focus. Another very important aspect of community involvement, often neglected or poorly implemented by high schools, is interaction with parents. They should, of course, be the specific community members who potentially have the most vested interest in involvement.

There is typically much less parental, family member, or guardian input in high schools when compared to elementary schools. Studies have cited a number of reasons for this lack of involvement between high schools and parents. The most common include (1) lack of desire by most students to want involvement of their parents; (2) lack of desire or time commitment by teachers to include parents; (3) school administrations' failure to provide leadership in support of a welcoming climate that establishes a range of involvement possibilities for parents; and (4) lack of parent comfort level in dealing with school personnel (Brian, 1994). Research findings on those high schools that actively seek parental involvement have seen many positive educational outcomes as a result of their efforts (Bauch & Goldring, 1993; Daniels, Bizar, & Zemelman, 2001; Eagle, 1989; Keith, Keith, Quirk, et al., 1998; Simon, 2001). These studies indicate higher grade point averages, higher attendance rates, lower dropout rates, and fewer referrals for disciplinary reasons as well as better preparedness for higher education. This section explores this very important aspect of community involvement (parent–teacher–school) by illustrating a range of strategies schools, teachers, and parents can initiate to seek opportunities for indirect or direct involvement of parents in high schools. When referring to parents in this section, the meaning may be applied to identify any parents, relatives/family members, or guardians of those students in the high school setting.

In today's society most families need two wage earners to hold full-time jobs. This may often restrict how much free time during school hours parents have available for interaction with teachers or schools. Consequently, if secondary schools are to actively engage parents, they will need to seek a range of ways to communicate to, interact with, and involve parents to ensure the majority have opportunities to be connected in some way appropriate to their family constraints. For example, scheduling a parent conference during the day may place hardship on some parents who may not be able to get release time from their jobs. Alternatives that accommodate working parents might be a phone conference, an early evening in-person conference, or a home visit.

Time demands and availability of teachers themselves also must be taken into consideration. Given the obvious time constraints of parents and teachers, schools must be very creative with these processes and at the very minimum provide parents and teachers a variety of opportunities and avenues for basic communication. Ideally, at least some interactions should occur in person at the actual school site with students, their work, and their teachers available for face-to-face interactions. These types of interactions may lead some parents to become more actively involved in the educational processes themselves. For purposes of this discussion, we group the range of types of involvement into three categories: (1) opportunities for teacher–parent–student communication; (2) opportunities for indirect involvement of parents in the educational processes at the school site; and (3) opportunities for direct involvement in the education processes for parents. Individual teachers can implement many of these examples whereas some are more systemic and will need administrative leadership and initiative. In addition, at least some might require teacher training by those familiar with the practice.

## Teacher–Parent–Student Communication

Too often parents have associated teacher communication with misbehaviors and other forms of negative issues with their son or daughter. Parents are likely to feel more comfortable collaborating with teachers on issues with their children if teachers initially place a greater emphasis on students' positive behavior and achievements (Blanchard, 2002). Teachers should place emphasis on how parents can collaborate in working with the teacher in reinforcing positive outcomes and redirecting challenging issues to encourage more positive outcomes. In addition, in many schools parents may primarily speak a different language than English. Therefore, it may be important to format communications in those languages so that all parents feel included. If the teacher does not know the language, interpreters may be available at the school site to assist. For example, some schools receive grants to provide interpreters at school sites making parents feel more welcome at schools at conferences and at whole school activities.

*Examples of Communication.*

1. **Email or web pages.** Teacher or school-developed sites offer information such as curriculum plans, syllabi, homework assignments (explanation and due dates), and grades as well as a basis for opportunities for communication between teacher and parent.
2. **Personal letters.** Letters sent home via students or mail delivery ensure those parents unable to access email would receive the same type of information. For example, a contract with students regarding classroom behavior signed by the parent could be sent electronically or in hard-copy letter format.
3. **Phone calls.** Teachers more than ever are giving out cell phone numbers and school numbers to parents to offer them opportunities to call them and leave messages. Conversely, teachers are communicating with parents via their cell phones.
4. **Teacher home visits.** Visiting the parent in the home is another option. Although time consuming to the teacher, it is a very powerful symbolic act. The teacher might offer this option to parents who are unable to visit the teacher during the school day. The teacher visiting the home of the student gets an opportunity to interact with parents in a less threatening environment for them and also gains a sense of where the student lives and the family environment.
5. **Homework connections for parents.** In order for students to be successful in school, they sometimes need to complete assignments at home. Encourage and inform parents through many of the avenues already described, such as parent–teacher conferences, emails, or newsletters, about the nature and importance of outside assignments (homework) and ways to provide a physical environment at home conducive to completing this homework. Parents also need to have access to information about alternative sites in the community that might provide computers, texts, and other educational assistance such as libraries, school facilities, or community centers. In addition, teachers should consider creating assignments that actively involve parents in assisting and collaborating with their sons and daughters.

   This type of assignment, in contrast to typical homework assignments, informs the parent of the curriculum, places value on parental knowledge, serves as a basis for the student to interact academically with the parent, and informs other students of "community knowledge." Even used occasionally, this strategy is a positive way for parents to interact indirectly with schools.
6. **Newsletters.** This could be an ongoing format that the teacher sends out to parents to highlight some of the activities and accomplishments in the classroom. It could also serve as a forum for announcements to parents of upcoming opportunities to encourage involvement. This general way to reach all parents gives a broader perspective of what the teacher and students are doing.

**Instructional Resource K** provides an example of a teacher-generated newsletter.

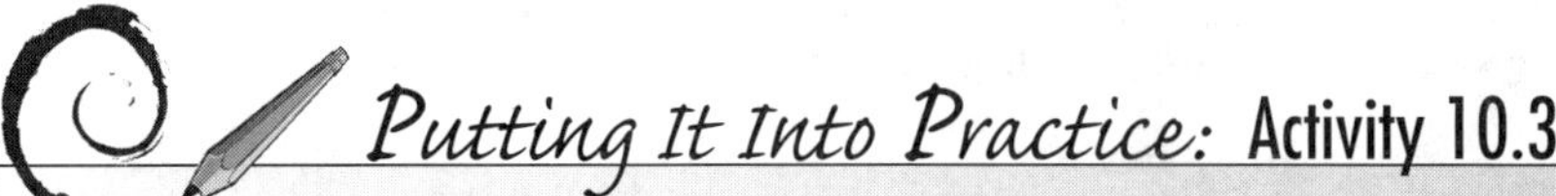

As a way to model basic communication and interaction with parents, design a letter or newsletter that you could send via email, web site, or hard copy. This would be different from your beginning-of-the-semester letter, because its purpose is to encourage ongoing parent communication. You may want to refer to Instructional Resource K for ideas.

## Parent Involvement at the School Site

The next level of involvement provides parents with opportunities to visit school sites and talk to school personnel, listen to presentations regarding school programs, view student work or presentations, and perhaps receive training/education related to their role as a high school parent. To ensure maximum participation in these activities, schools need to communicate the scheduling of times and locations (convenient for most parents to attend) well in advance of the event. In addition, it is advantageous to include parents as collaborators in the planning of these events. Furnishing food and refreshment, if possible, will also assist in presenting the image of a warm, positive social environment.

*Examples of On-Site Involvement.*

1. **Informational and interactive meetings of school organizations.** Successful school-wide programs such as AVID (Advantages via Individual Determination) have had great success not only in increasing academic achievement and college graduation rates of at-risk students but also in involving and informing parents. These programs hold regularly scheduled informational meetings with parents that outline the curriculum and time lines and encourage involvement in a variety of ways. Bilingual interpreters are available and parent involvement of students in AVID is generally much higher than in the general population.
2. **Parenting classes.** Classes made available at no cost to parents such as PET (Parent Effective Training) offer parents opportunities to collaborate with teachers on issues such as bullying, drug use, and general communication skills. They also provide the basis for opportunities for administrators, teachers, and parents to develop important social bonds in a more informal setting.
3. **Attendance at student presentations or performances at school.** These activities offer a variety of curricular and extracurricular opportunities whereby students give presentations or display their work. Many of these are open for parents to attend but schools should offer them at a range of times that maximize parent potential to attend. Some of these include science fairs, English fairs, art and music forums, student portfolio presentations, and student award ceremonies.

4. **Participation in formal parent-led organizations.** These may include Parent Teacher Associations (PTA) or Parent Teacher Organizations (PTO). The PTA, PTO, and other similar local organizations serve the purpose of providing a direct linkage between schools and parents. Just as importantly they support parents who may find it difficult to get involved in other more direct ways with schools. Typical activities may include fund-raising for curricular and extracurricular events, distribution of information on academic programs, avenues for input on curricular and extracurricular activities, and as a forum for informal interaction between the parents as well as between parents and school officials.
5. **Parent–teacher conferences.** Although conferences are typically held at school sites, alternatives might include conference calls or home visits. The important factor is to provide a way for any parent to participate. Adjustment of times and locations may be critical for inclusion of all parents. Sara Lightfoot (2003) suggests these face-to-face meetings are critical in establishing an initial parent–teacher rapport that will lay the foundation for a deeper understanding of the strengths and challenges of the overall education of their son or daughter. She suggests that the tone should be very positive and interactive, and include appropriate preparation by the teacher, availability of privacy, and enough time for both parents and teachers to illustrate their understanding of the student. She suggests parents and teachers encourage the use of specific examples or "storytelling" that assists in illustrating their unique perspective of the student. Lightfoot also maintains that in some cases, when deemed appropriate, students themselves should be present to offer their perspective and suggestions. These types of interpersonal interactions assist in establishing genuine trust and understanding of all parties and can lead to action plans to address potential challenges.

## SECTION 3: COMMUNITY INVOLVEMENT

Another level of involvement provides volunteers opportunities to collaborate with schools, teachers, or school personnel on policy, curriculum, assessment, and other school matters. The ideas presented in this section represent more intimate involvement with a full range of commitment and expertise.

### Volunteers in Education

Not all parents feel comfortable or capable of being involved directly in the education process as some of the following ideas would require training or mentoring, a longer time commitment than others, and in some cases additional expertise. Although some parents are pleased to be able to work directly to collaborate with schools, teachers, and school personnel, often siblings, aunts, uncles, grandparents, or other extended family and community members also have a great deal of interest in offering time and expertise.

#### *Examples of Volunteer Activities*

1. **Mentoring/internships.** Some parents and extended family have professional careers or positions that lend themselves well to becoming volunteer student mentors. In some cases, individual teachers have informally assigned interested volunteers as mentors for students interested in a particular career. In this way, students are able to gain experiences from mentors who are family members of

other students. Some schools have carefully designed mentoring programs that assign specific school personnel to coordinate volunteers and provide basic training in mentoring. Students benefit from the expertise these volunteers can offer from their perspective in the working community. Parents and family gain insight (and perhaps some empathy) in interacting with a high school student similar in age to their own.

2. **Team coaches.** A full range of extracurricular activities and competitions in virtually all subject areas requires teachers to be "coaches" or facilitators. Community volunteers, especially those who have a keen interest and perhaps expertise in a particular subject area, make excellent collaborators with the teacher. Since many of these activities are completed outside of school or at least outside the traditional school schedule, this may make it possible for many more volunteers to become involved. An example that illustrates involvement in an extracurricular program is called Odyssey of the Mind, or OM. The program actively encourages the use of a family member as coach/facilitator. This international, interdisciplinary problem-solving program requires the involvement of an adult (family member or teacher) with an emphasis on facilitation only. The adult's role is not to solve the problem but rather to facilitate the student team's solution to it. More specifically, in OM the adult's role may include assistance in facilitation of cooperative learning protocols, explaining and clarifying the problem, organizing meeting and location times, establishing task and completion schedules, training students how to brainstorm potential solutions to problems, and facilitation of student competitions. Teachers typically work closely to assist and train volunteers who are new to the program. Experienced coaches can ultimately take on more and more responsibilities with time.
3. **After-school project participation.** Another example that illustrates involvement in an academic collaboration yet involves much less commitment time than being an academic coach is called "Math, Science and Beyond." In this after-school program, K–12 volunteers attend periodic evenings whereby they collaborate with their students to work with themed-based, hands-on science and math experiential materials. This collaboration in learning involves formulating written responses to problems and interacting with their students and teachers to facilitate their answers. It also provides whole-group discussions of what has been learned and follow-up take-home materials. In this unique program all participants get a chance to think and learn together in solving science and math problems in a very informal setting. Research findings indicate a very positive response from all participants in this program in terms of the learning interaction that occurs and an increase in the use of hands-on materials by teachers during their regular classroom instruction.

## Direct Influence in the Educational Process

A deeper level of family and community involvement entails a direct influence in the educational process itself. Parents, extended family, and community members can be an excellent and much needed resource for teachers and administrators.

***Facilitators of Student Portfolio Presentations.*** As a facilitator of student portfolio presentations, volunteers can greatly assist teachers in evaluating and providing feedback to students on their work. This type of involvement also offers a model to understand alternative ways of evaluating student work from a firsthand perspective. This type of activity will require some recruiting by the teacher, training, and debriefing of the volunteers. Teachers note very positive multiple outcomes for students, volunteers, and teachers using this model.

### A Closer Look

**Instructional Resource L** provides an example of how this procedure is facilitated in a high school, which uses portfolios as a summative evaluative instrument.

***Community Members as Collaborators with Teachers.*** Some schools solicit community members to teach or present in areas of expertise during the regular school day. The range of this type of involvement might be a short-term commitment, such as a one-day presentation, to a longer-term commitment to the teaching process, to direct collaborative involvement such as assisting teachers with small group instruction in the class or during field trips. All of these typically require appropriate clearance through administrative procedures and some training or front-loading of classroom protocols between the teacher and volunteer.

An example that illustrates direct collaboration with the teacher would be a group of parents who volunteer as chaperones/facilitators on a field trip with the role of facilitating a small group in an observational study of animals at a local zoo. For effective implementation, the teacher would need to front-load information on logistics, use of any equipment such as digital video recorders, and background information equivalent to what was given to students on how to conduct animal studies. When volunteers act as group facilitators, they make a greater impact on the learning experience for students as compared to the typical role of field trip chaperones.

Some schools have encouraged longer-term teaching by parents or community members who have specific skills or knowledge that would serve as valuable experience for students as a minicourse or unit. An example of this type of more extensive involvement is illustrated by a school that included as one part of its mission the involvement of community and parents in a variety of ways. One outward sign of this is "the Friday School," which uses parents and community members to teach relevant minicourses as electives. Regular classroom teachers in this school use Fridays to meet in their teacher teams to collaborate on developing and evaluating curriculum, school policies, and classroom management issues. A couple of examples of courses offered by parent and community members included Problem-Solving Strategies, a hands-on, activity-based model with the goal of enhancing cooperative learning and problem-solving skills, culminating in a regional competition; and an Architectural Design course in which students assisted in the design and development of school buildings and landscaping for the future school site with a parent-architect.

Both of these examples benefited the school and the community in that they freed large blocks of time for teacher planning and incorporated rich world experiences for students with the use of community knowledge and professionals.

***Advisory Board Members.*** Some schools actively seek parent-led advisory boards. The parents, as members of these boards, take on many important roles such as advising the administration on issues related to curriculum, teacher hiring, and general school philosophy. Another example illustrates show a school uses this model to encourage more active involvement of parents and community. Under the guidelines of the Small Schools movement, which encourages active involvement of parents in schools (Levine, 2001), a high school established the following as part of its mission statement: "The family is the child's primary teacher . . . and that family involvement is essential to students' success at every age." This school "enrolls" families and fully engages them throughout the educational process (The Big Picture Company, 2000). Part of that engagement includes the Family Engagement Committee, which (1) recruits other volunteers as members to serve on student learning teams as facilitators and learning partners (pairing new members with veteran members); (2) establishes a solid and consistent communication system through a variety of formats including Family Net web-based information, emails, phone calls, home meetings, open houses, orientation nights, and rap sessions about adolescent issues; and (3) engages families in activities such as parent talent night, college workshops on financial aid, family night for community partners to meet with parents, and a year-end celebration.

Although the ideas presented here incorporate a wide range from simple to sophisticated methods of family and community involvement, evidence suggests that whatever can be accomplished, given your school and community climate, will improve overall student achievement.

## Applying Technology: Activity 10.3

Use any of the ideas or examples presented in this section on community involvement and incorporate the use of technology to design a community informational web page, group email, PowerPoint presentation, or any other technological application to increase community involvement. Demonstrate your final model to members of the class for feedback.

## SECTION 4: CHAPTER SUMMARY AND REFLECTION

This chapter covered a variety of strategies for school and community collaboration. Section 1 introduced research support for service-learning and a model for incorporating service-learning into the curriculum. It also described sample programs to illustrate powerful implementations of service-learning. Through the applications suggested in the Putting It Into Practice and Applying Technology activities, we provided opportunities to explore service-learning practice both through the eyes of the observer as well as firsthand as a practitioner of service-learning.

Research has also shown that in schools in which parents and family have a higher rate of participation the benefits are a higher academic achievement level, higher attendance rate, lower dropout rate, lower rate of disciplinary referrals, and better preparedness for higher education. Given this evidence, schools should consider carefully the importance of parent and community involvement in the educational process.

Section 2 explored ways to overcome some of the obstacles to increasing parent involvement at the school site. This section covered appropriate teacher training in parent involvement strategies, time for teacher–parent planning and reflection, and a systemic emphasis on a more positive, proactive, and constructive interaction between parents and teachers as priorities.

Section 3 emphasized the need to improve community involvement, providing strategies for administrators and teachers to work together to establish a philosophic disposition for schools and communities. These included suggestions for school volunteers in general as well as ways the community can have a direct influence in the educational process.

One of the intents of the chapter was to illustrate the main focus of the text, the Circle of Courage, highlighted by the practice of collaboration between school and community. Students benefit from opportunities to learn Mastery content in a real-world context; Belonging, through personally connecting to fellow classmates, teachers, and community members; Independence, by being involved in personal reflection, decision making, and problem solving; and Generosity, by showing concern for needy individuals and situations, and strengthening prosocial norms.

## References


Addison–Jacobson, J., & Hill, D. (1996). *Building support for service-learning*. Educational Leadership for Service-Learning (brochure). California ed.

Aronowitz, S., & Giroux, H. (1985). *Education under siege*. Westport, CT: Bergin & Garvey.

Batson, N. (n.d.). *Project SUCCESS: Creating change through community service* (brochure). Richland, MS: Corporation for National Service.

Bauch, P., & Goldring, E. B. (1993). Teacher work context and opportunities for parent involvement. In *High schools of choice: A view from the inside* (ERIC Issue: ED376169). Institute of Education. Retrieved October 7, 2002, from www.eric.ed.gov

Bickmore, K. (2002). Conflict resolution education: Multiple options for contributing to just and democratic peace. In W. Pammer & J. Killian (Eds.), *Handbook of conflict management* (pp. 10–15). New York: Marcel–Dekker Publishers.

The Big Picture Company (2000). *Learning through internships* (Book 1). Providence, RI: The Big Picture Company.

Blanchard, K. (2002). *Whale done!: The power of positive relationships*. New York: Free Press.

Boyer, E. (1983). *High school: A report on secondary education in America*. New York: Harper and Row.

Brannon, M. C. (1998). *Project SUCCESS: An inclusive service-learning curriculum for youth*. Washington, DC: United Cerebral Palsy Associations.

Brendtro, L. K., Brokenleg, M., & Bockern, S. V. (2002). *Reclaiming youth at risk: Our hope for the future*. Bloomington, IN: National Education Service.

Brian, D. (1994, April). *Parental involvement in high schools*. Paper presented at the Annual Meeting of the American Educational Research Association, New Orleans, LA.

Cairn, R., & Kielsmeier, J. (1991). *Growing hope: a sourcebook on integrating youth service into school curriculum*. Roseville, MN: National Youth Leadership Council.

California Task Force (1992). *Second to none*. Sacramento, CA: Department of Education.

Council of Chief State School Officers (1992). Model standards for beginning teacher licensing, assessment, and development: A resource for state dialogue. Washington, DC: Author. www.ccsso.org/content/pdfs/corestrd.pdf

Daniels, H., Bizar, M., & Zemelman, S. (2001). *Rethinking high school: Best practice in teaching, learning, and leadership*. Portsmouth, NH: Heinemann.

Dewey, J. (1938). *Experience and education*. Bloomington, MN: Kappa Delta Pi.

Eagle, E. (1989, March). *Socioeconomic status, family structure, and parental involvement: The correlates of achievement*. Paper presented at the Annual Meeting of the American Educational Research Association, San Francisco, CA.

Education Commission of the States (2000). Every student a citizen: Creating the democratic self. *Compact for Learning and Citizenship National Study Group on Citizenship in K–12 Schools*. Denver, CO: Education Commission of the States.

Farnan, N., & Baldwin, N. (1997). *School-to-career workbook for higher education*. San Diego: San Diego State University Press.

Henry, G., & White-Williams, S. (1998). *Expanding teacher education through service-learning handbook*. Hampton, VA: Hampton University Department of Education.

Keating, J. (1998). Models for the integration of service-learning and teacher education in learning with the community: Concepts and models for service-learning. In J. Erickson & J. B. Anderson (Eds.), *Teacher education*. (pp. 186–192). Washington, DC: American Association for Higher Education.

Keith, T. Z., Keith, P. B., Quirk, K. J., et al. (1998). Longitudinal effects of parent involvement on high school grades: Similarities and differences across gender and ethnic groups. *Journal of School Psychology, 36*(3), 335–363.

Kinsley, W., & McPherson, K. (1995). *Enriching the curriculum through service learning*. Alexandria, VA: Association for Supervision and Curriculum Development.

Levine, E. (2001). *One kid at a time: Big lessons from a small school*. New York: Teachers College Press.

Lightfoot, S. (2003). *The essential conversation: What parents and teachers can learn from each other*. New York: Random House.

Maryland Student Services Alliance (1995). *Maryland best practices: An improvement guide for school-based service-learning*. Baltimore: Maryland Department of Education.

Moon, M. S. (Ed.). (1994). *Making school and community recreation fun for everyone: Places and ways to integrate*. Baltimore: Brookes.

Noddings, N. (1988). An ethic of caring and its implications for instructional arrangements. *American Journal of Education 96*(2), 215–230.

Pickeral, T., & Bray, J. (2000, August). Service learning in an age of standards. *The School Administrator, 57*(7), 6–11.

Root, S. (1994). Service learning in teacher education: A third rationale. *Michigan Journal of Community Service Learning, 1*(1), 94–97.

RPP International evaluation of K–12 service-learning in California: Phase II final report. *Service-learning manual for K–12 teachers*. Emeryville, CA: California Department of Education Calserve Office.

Schon, D. (1987). *Educating the reflective practitioner.* San Francisco: Jossey-Bass.

Secretary's Commission on Achieving Necessary Skills (1990). *Identifying necessary skills.* Washington, DC: U.S. Department of Labor.

Simon, B. (2001). Family involvement in high school: Predictors and effects. *NASSP Bulletin, 85*(2), 8–19.

Superintendent's Service-Learning Task Force (1999). *Service-learning: Linking classrooms to communities.* Sacramento, CA: California Department of Education.

Thousand, J., Villa, R., & Nevin, A. (Eds.). *Creativity and collaborative learning: A practical guide to empowering students, teachers, and families in an inclusive, multicultural, and pluralistic society* (2nd ed.). Baltimore: Brookes.

Wisconsin Department of Public Instruction (2000). *Learning from experience: A collection of service-learning projects linking academic standards to curriculum*. Madison, WI: Wisconsin Department of Public Instruction.

# Chapter 11

# Professional Challenges

**INTASC Principle 9:** The teacher is a reflective practitioner who continually evaluates the effects of his/her choices and actions on others (students, parents, and other professionals in the learning community) and who actively seeks out opportunities to grow professionally.

**Key Dispositions**

- The teacher values critical thinking and self-directed learning as habits of mind.
- The teacher is committed to reflection, assessment, and learning as an ongoing process.
- The teacher is willing to give and receive help.
- The teacher is committed to seeking out, developing, and continually refining practices that address the individual needs of students.
- The teacher recognizes his/her professional responsibility for engaging in and supporting appropriate professional practices for self and colleagues.

## INTRODUCTION TO THE CHAPTER

The world of a classroom teacher is simultaneously as small as the single mind of an individual student and as large as the society in which the teacher functions. Today's teachers must develop the capacity to keep students as the focus of their work while coping with and responding to many external and internal factors that impact the classroom but have very little direct connection to the interaction of teacher and student. As you enter the teaching profession, the ability to balance all these factors and pressures will begin to define you as a professional.

Even with such challenges, powerful teachers all over the country successfully engage students from a broad range of backgrounds. By maintaining a strong professional foundation and focusing on each area depicted by the Circle of Courage (Brendtro et al., 2002), teachers can maintain a strong anchor to ground their practice. The skills, knowledge, and dispositions you have explored throughout this textbook will also help you be able to practice in an informed and ever-improving way. Once you enter into your first teaching position, you will begin to gain an emotional maturity and self-confidence through classroom experiences. These experiences will allow you to move your own practice forward on behalf of the students you teach.

Chapter 11 offers ideas on how each new teacher can become a self-renewing teacher who continues to establish and cultivate a classroom environment in which all students can learn. Section 1 examines strategies you can undertake to help sustain yourself in the profession. It explores how the development of your mission statement and an awareness of your professional stance can be effective guides as you weave your way through the first several years in the profession.

Section 2 identifies the need of all teachers to stay current with the profession as it evolves and as students entering schools change over the course of a professional career. Included in this section are examples of different ways teachers have adapted, both positively and negatively, to these needs and suggestions of strategies for successfully coping with change. Additionally, it presents ideas about working with colleagues and parents in a positive way.

The final section of Chapter 11 introduces the concept of culture as it applies to the educational community as well as examines why understanding it is important to achieving success in your work. Included in this section is an overview of the teacher evaluation process, with the intent of helping to demystify the process and allowing you to understand how you will be assessed in your first years. Finally, the cycle of the textbook closes with a discussion of the dispositions and attributes of a successful teacher that was initiated in Chapter 1.

## SECTION 1: PROFESSIONALISM

The many external factors beyond the control of a teacher can challenge a new professional's commitment and performance. Secondary teachers must consider complex societal issues as they address the needs of students. The range of issues creates part of the challenge to a teacher's work. For example, students now come from a variety of family configurations such as single-parent homes, blended families, same-gender parents, foster or other "guardianship" situations, as well as multigenerations living in one house. A student's living arrangements can be complex. In some cases, students may have two sets of parents whereas other students are "parentless," literally raising themselves.

Another well-researched factor is that high school students whose parents did not go to college tend to report lower educational expectations than their peers. This creates a cycle of underachievement and low aspirations that must be addressed. The use of the Circle of Courage model can help provide the needed support to encourage students to see the wide range of educational opportunities available to them. As they gain Mastery of skills and content and become connected to their schools and classrooms (Belonging), their own sense of Independence will enable them to see a future that may not have been modeled at home.

Sociological factors that affect classroom environments have also accelerated over the years, causing a significant impact on students. Use of drugs and alcohol can be a cause for lower motivation and impede learning. Gang affiliation as well as other cliques within school cultures can challenge a teacher's role in the classroom and student accountability. The many activities that compete for a student's time, such as television, video games and the Internet, can be distracters from time better spent used in study. Further, as noted in the previous chapter, infrequent parental involvement can preclude a strong partnership between parent and teacher when setting expectations for students.

In addition, new and veteran teachers are exposed every day to a school's established culture. A school culture that is positive, inclusive, and supportive for the professionals that work there will make your tasks easier. On the other hand, a culture in which complaints about students' abilities, ineffective administrators, and uncaring parents are predominant will force a new teacher to find "pockets of positive support" to stay motivated. When internal and external factors are added together, it is critical for teachers to maintain a keen awareness of their own beliefs that brought them into the profession.

### Professional Mission

If teachers are to maintain their sense of purpose, a personal mission that can guide practice over time and through challenges helps. While it is common for schools to create mission statements, it should also be common practice for individual teachers to develop and revisit their professional mission statements to help sustain their sense of purpose and commitment.

A professional mission statement is a concise and inspired description of why you, as an individual, have chosen to become a teacher and why you are teaching.

## *Putting It Into Practice:* Activity 11.1

Use your earlier work in Chapter 1 in which you identified your beliefs and philosophical foundation to help develop your personal professional mission statement. Your mission statement should be concise, focused on what you believe and what you hope to accomplish as a teacher. You may find it helpful to access the Franklin Covey Mission Builder web site at www.franklincovey.com/missionbuilder/index.html as a way to practice using words and sentences defining your inspiration and values. Once you have refined your mission statement, exchange it with two classmates and discuss common as well as differing elements.

It goes beyond family traditions: "All my relatives and my parents are teachers, so it seemed natural for me to be one, too." It does not focus on the "fringe benefits" of the profession: "The time off in the summer allows me to pursue my travel and recreational interests." Nor does it reflect sentiments such as "I tried the business world and it wasn't for me; teaching seemed like a good second choice."

A powerful professional mission statement reflects your deepest held teaching values. This concise, inspirational statement can help meet and sustain your focus and commitment despite the many challenges you will face in the profession and the criticisms of educators you will all too frequently hear or read. A personal mission can help you get through the heavy workloads and times when you feel underappreciated for the effort you expend. Your professional mission statement should guide and provide focus for your ongoing development as a teacher. By acting purposefully on your mission you will be able to make choices consistent with your own attitudes, behaviors, and beliefs.

## Professional Stance

It is not at all unusual for teachers to go through peaks and valleys during the course of their careers; these are expected in all careers and are a part of the profession. At the conclusion of some school years, you will have a deep sense of accomplishment; other times you might focus on all the things you could have done better and as a result have a sense of discouragement. It is easy to be motivated professionally when things are going well. The real test of your professionalism will come when the challenges seem to outweigh the successes. Certain strategies can help you retain your professionalism through the difficult times.

Reflect on your professional disposition. Some individuals have a strong educational foundation to guide their practice; understand and practice effective class management strategies; communicate effectively with students, colleagues, and parents; build connections and relationships with students; reflect continuously on their own work; model fairness and commitment; and, importantly, maintain a positive attitude.

By contrast, other individuals often fail to get their needs met; tend to act passively; fail to understand their own professional foundation; use their teacher authority to threaten as their primary class management tool; and as a result are unable to create supportive, collaborative environments. Some even go further and try to get their needs met at the expense of others. These teachers can be heard yelling and degrading students and, unfortunately, often physically and mentally abuse others.

Your professional disposition type will begin to develop from the moment you are hired for your first position. Whether you sustain your professionalism as positive and proactive, in contrast to negative and reactive, will depend greatly upon your preparation for the profession and on the mentors you choose. One of your first actions as a new teacher should be to seek out colleagues who exhibit the signs of being proactive teachers. Build relationships with them and try to learn how they have developed their procedures and ways of being in the classroom.

***Maintaining a Professional Stance.*** Maintaining your professional stance requires resiliency in the face of challenges. You will be more resilient if you work to ensure that your own physiological and safety needs, as well as your need to belong, are being met. If you begin to feel that you are in an unsafe environment, are ostracized or isolated from your colleagues, or that your authority is being challenged in a hostile way, you will be less capable of functioning in a professional manner. Maintain your own awareness about these issues so you do not slowly slip into a negative position. Address issues as they arise; do not let problems fester. Seek out advice from peers and mentors.

The first three years of teaching are considered particularly important to making certain your basic needs are met in a proactive and positive way. For example, it is common for new teachers to be given room assignments that require them to move from classroom to classroom, without a home base. This situation does not offer much in terms of fulfilling the basic needs we have discussed. How you decide to respond to this situation is crucial. Although a new teacher could begin to complain, this not a very professional response. Instead one might seek advice from a mentor and find a positive approach to overcoming the challenge. For example, if you are sharing classrooms and hope to maintain a sense of order in your work and life, perhaps you could acquire a cart, outfit it to your needs, and have a "moving desk." You could also, in an appropriate way, share your coping activities with your administrators so they realize you are responding in a professional way to whatever situations present themselves.

## Appropriate Interactions With Students

Adolescent students will inevitably have crushes on some of their teachers. It is the responsibility of the teacher to establish a barrier to inappropriate interactions, both for the emotional safety of the student as well as to preserve the teacher's professional reputation. The goal of the teacher is to build appropriate relationships. There is a definite difference between being friendly and wanting to become friend.

A teacher's career can be ruined by a single act of bad judgment. Social and romantic interaction with students is a clear example of bad judgment. The following suggested guidelines to working with adolescents can help you protect your professional reputation:

- Leave your classroom door open when students are visiting or studying in the classroom outside of regular class time.
- If you need to speak privately with a student, find a room that affords privacy but a window protects you from unfounded allegations of inappropriate behavior. Students in distress can be emotionally needy, which can lead to misunderstandings about the smallest show of sympathy on the part of a teacher.
- Avoid being in social settings with students, other than school activities such as sports events or dances that you are attending as a member of the school community or as a chaperone.

- Avoid sharing your personal life with your students. It is one thing for them to know your hobbies and the fact that you enjoy traveling during the summer. It is quite another for them to know the romantic details of a summer trip.
- Know when you are in over your head. High school students can get themselves into very adult problems. Should students seek you out for guidance on difficult personal problems, refer them to the appropriate expert. School counselors and administrators, as well as community agencies and faith-based organizations, have the training and expertise when it comes to many adolescent issues. Strike the balance between supporting students during a tough time (extending time on an assignment or not calling on a student in class for a period of time) and overreaching your knowledge or authority by becoming too involved in their problems.

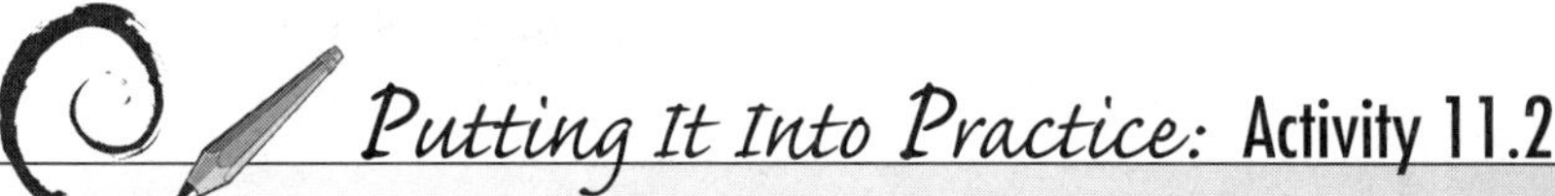


Based on the ideas discussed in Section 1, identify what you believe will be the three greatest challenges you will face in the first years of becoming a successful teacher. Develop ideas on how you will address each challenge. Once you have identified both challenges and strategies, meet in small groups of three or four to share your issues. The members of each group should listen for commonalities and help others extend these approaches to dealing with the identified challenges. If time permits, each small group should share the similar challenges and strategies with the entire class.

## SECTION 2: TIMES CHANGE

Each generation of students brings a new set of experiences and perspectives based upon the times in which they grow up. It is important for teachers to move with the times, adjusting their practices to the perspective and needs of the learners. Teachers who are unwilling or unable to make these adjustments can experience a loss of confidence, increased stress, frustration, and growing resentment.

Moving with the times does not mean abandoning your professional foundation or the academic standards and high expectations for students you have established. It means connecting with students in a way that makes sense to them. By striving to make this connection, teachers gain a higher probability of engaging students in a meaningful way and increasing their readiness to learn what the teacher has to offer.

### Adaptation to Today's Students

Sound research can assist teachers in understanding various predictable ways to respond to changes in the student population (McLaughlin & Talbert, 1993). Students in today's secondary classrooms are active, opinionated, and, to a degree, informed individuals. They may not be active in the way teachers would like; they may not yet possess the communication skills to share their opinions clearly; however, they likely are informed about the world in a way a teacher might easily dismiss.

**TABLE 11.1** *Domains of Adaptation*

| Pattern of Adaptation | Relations | Pedagogy | Content | Teacher Outcomes |
|---|---|---|---|---|
| Enforce traditional standards and tests | Teacher dominates: more rules and sanctions | Transmission teaching: more worksheets and memorization | Emphasis on traditional, fact-based learning | Burnout and cynicism |
| Lower expectations | Various: relax rules | Various | Watered-down subject matter | Disengagement |
| Change practices and group norms | Teacher facilitates: constructs learning | Active student role: cooperative understanding | Emphasis on conceptual understanding | Efficacy |

Note: From *Contexts That Matter for Teaching and Learning* (p. 61) by M. W. McLaughlin and J. Talbert, 1993, Stanford CA: Stanford University, Center for Research on the Context of Teaching. Reprinted by permission.

***Patterns of Adaptation.*** How a teacher adapts to the changing student population is important. For example, a teacher anxious about losing control of the classroom will demonstrate a tendency to create so many rules that students will inevitably violate several of them, just 10 minutes into the class period. This is the first pattern of adaptation identified in Table 11.1.

Over the course of a teaching career, all teachers will be faced with adapting to a changing professional environment. The following examples may help illustrate how teachers do or do not successfully adapt to new circumstances.

A veteran teacher with 27 years of experience was not satisfied with the school's referral slip that had five general infractions listed. This teacher had made her own referral slip on which she listed her 29 rules, ranging from "tardy" to "no pencil" to "disrespectful tone." Her area of passion was English literature, and when the revision of academic content standards included contemporary literature, she found the change appalling. Believing both that she had lost control of her subject matter and that this generation of students was arriving with little or no respect for her authority, she decided her only line of defense was to retain order by controlling her students' every action. This teacher had attempted to adapt to new standards and contemporary students by increasing control, diminishing student participation, and setting herself up as the all-knowing teacher expert. Her final years of teaching were filled with cynicism and resentment.

The next example, of a teacher who adapted to today's students by lowering expectations, exhibits the second pattern of adaptation found in Table 11.1. In his field of study, U.S. history, his primary instructional strategy was to "read the chapter, outline it, and answer the questions at the back of the chapter." His tests consisted of pages of multiple-choice questions that always included a few trick questions intended to trip up the students. Rarely did students in his classes engage in discussion or debate about the historical value of various events to the situations now facing the world.

Some students found his class to be a haven from any expectations at all. If they showed up and filled out the worksheets, they knew they could pass the U.S. history requirement. Toward the end of his career this teacher began using any video he could find to fill class time, even if it were not appropriate to the unit he was teaching. His only goal was to relieve his responsibility to teach students in a meaningful, engaging way. This teacher became a passive spectator, grateful for the few students who excelled in his class because they had found so little was expected.

Our final example illustrates the more successful pattern of adaptation to new generations of students, changing practices and group norms, also found in Table 11.1. A math and science teacher had spent each of his 11 years of teaching seeking out advice from his peers who seemed to get the best results from students. He stayed professionally current by subscribing to two professional journals, attending at least one content area professional development offering each year, and had even initiated an interdisciplinary teacher roundtable. At these monthly meetings teachers shared classroom management techniques, tips on efficient grading of papers, exemplary student work, and ideas for helping second-language learners fully participate in the classroom. He used the first week after school had ended in the spring to prepare for the new year while his ideas and recent experiences were fresh in his mind. While frustrated at times, the amount of satisfaction, collegiality, and student progress kept him on the cutting edge of teacher inquiry and practice. He liked his work more than when he had begun in the profession over a decade ago.

Teachers who are able to adapt in positive ways during their careers, connecting with students in a meaningful and productive way while staying true to their professional mission, adjust to new challenges each generation of students presents. By changing practices and group norms, teachers avoid burnout, cynicism, and disengagement, all of which can challenge a teacher's professionalism. Teachers who change with the times continue to be powerful in the classroom and can improve their practice in response to the learning needs of their students.

## Your Work Environment

Adapting to today's students by changing practices and setting new group norms is hard work, yet important if we wish to continue being effective in the classroom. The context in which a teacher adapts is crucial to success. Apart from the physical setting of the school, which is easily observable, less visible yet equally powerful elements exist within the environment in which a teacher teaches.

***Changing Environments.*** Psychological and philosophical context matter as much as the physical buildings and grounds. Lieberman and Miller (1999) have described the "new social realities of teaching," depicted in Table 11.2, which provides important ideas for successfully adapting to today's students.

The left-hand column describes elements of an isolated work environment in which a teacher operates alone behind a closed classroom door and decides how best

**TABLE 11.2** *The New Social Realities of Teaching*

| From | To |
|---|---|
| Individualism | Professional community |
| Teaching at the center | Learning at the center |
| Technical work | Inquiry into practice |
| Controlled work | Accountability |
| Managed work | Leadership |
| Classroom concerns | Whole-school concerns and beyond |
| A weak knowledge base | A broad knowledge base |

Note: From *Teachers: Transforming Their World and Their Work* (p. 24), by A. Lieberman and L. Miller, 1999, New York: Teachers College Press. Reprinted by permission.

to proceed. This model from decades ago was once believed to have served teachers well, when the world was a more disconnected and simpler place. Today, most question whether this was ever a good model of teaching practice.

The right-hand column of Table 11.2 describes elements of a working environment that presents the best opportunity for strengthening practice through collaboration, inclusion, and openness. This school culture finds itself much better suited to today's schools in which educational research continues to reveal more and more about how students learn. Students bring more knowledge with them into the classroom than ever before. The social forces outside the classroom help create student attitudes that must be considered in developing inclusive learning environments.

Teachers who either create for themselves or find they are trapped in the left-hand column school context are fighting an uphill battle in classrooms today. We believe your practice should focus on the right-hand column to establish inclusive, democratic, and relevant secondary classrooms, working in collaborative teacher teams.

## Collaborative Practice

Most new teachers, when joining a teaching staff, become members of already established teams. It is important to recognize that some teams are more functional than others, and the functionality of the team can have a significant impact on a new teacher. If the team tends to move toward the functional end of the continuum, the new teacher has another rich resource upon which to draw. New teachers will experience colleagues who have created cohesive and productive teams that consistently (1) exhibit trust in one another; (2) engage in open conversation around ideas; (3) commit to decisions and plans of action; (4) hold one another accountable for delivering against those plans; and (5) focus on the achievement of collective results.

Teams that tend to exist more toward the dysfunctional end of the continuum will often contribute to new teachers doubting their own abilities, which only discourages the newest members of the profession. These teams commonly exhibit (1) absence of trust, (2) fear of conflict, (3) lack of commitment, (4) avoidance of accountability, and (5) inattention to results (Lencioni, 2002).

In both types of teams, new teachers often have a hard time "finding their voice" during discussions. Typically they think their being the least experienced means they are the least capable of contributing to what they perceive as important conversations. Additionally, experienced teachers may unintentionally or intentionally diminish new teacher participation as they pursue their own line of thinking about these evolving issues. In order for new teachers to mature into the teaching profession, they must become engaged in issues that are important and become confident participants in these conversations.

At first, as a new member of the team, you may want to listen more than speak; however, once you understand the issues, your fresh ideas and new perspectives add value if an established team wants to keep up with the times. If you find yourself on a dysfunctional team, work not to get caught in the negative exchanges and find other colleagues who can help you resolve important teaching and learning issues you encounter.

## Cooperation with Parents

Unfair criticism can be a difficult challenge to teachers. As Parker Palmer (1998) has noted,

> Teachers make an easy target, for they are such a common species and so powerless to strike back. We blame teachers for being unable to cure socials ills that no one

knows how to treat; we insist that they instantly adopt whatever "solution" has most recently been concocted by our national panacea machine; and in the process, we demoralize, even paralyze, the very teachers who could help us find our way. (p. 3)

These unfair criticisms can trigger angry, defensive, and unprofessional responses from normally professional individuals. Criticism is particularly difficult when coming from parents, because teachers hope that parents will be their partners in helping all students learn. Yet, in this era of high expectations of teachers, parents can evoke strong reactions from teachers with unfair allegations.

***Communicating With Parents.*** Parental criticism of teachers often occurs in two areas: student discipline and communication between school and home. In order to decrease situations in which parents challenge a teacher's judgment of student behavior, teachers must have both a well-thought-out classroom management plan and a strong parent communication plan in place from day one of the school year. These should communicate commitments you are making to their students as well as classrooms expectations. You have explored strategies to accomplish both of these goals in previous chapters.

These must be communicated clearly to parents to avoid any misunderstandings and criticisms that might result from them. You must be proactive. Sending out an opening-of-the-year letter, similar to the one you developed in Chapter 8, effectively initiates the teacher–parent relationship. Remember, the primary purposes of the letter are to introduce yourself, outline the goals for the year, explain classroom policies and procedures, and describe how you assess student progress.

In communicating with parents, tone is as important as content. Be genuine and optimistic in all encounters with parents. Once you have made the initial contact, continue a concerted effort to make parents partners in the educational process. Provide parents with a clear, written explanation of academic and behavioral expectations and consequences. Do not surprise parents with changes in classroom or academic expectations; instead, keep them informed about anything that happens. Adjusting lesson plans to better meet student needs is one thing; changing course goals or major assignments is another. Return phone calls as quickly as possible; within 24 hours should be your goal. Always take the initiative to share good news as well as concerns.

## SECTION 3: THE PROFESSION

The first contract you sign will be a significant and exciting event. You will have worked hard to be credentialed and will be anxious to start teaching your own students. Effective contributions to student learning and the educational community as a whole will be your primary objectives. To accomplish this, you must understand the culture of the organization you are moving into, the way that your work will be formally evaluated, and the importance of continuing to be mindful of the teacher dispositions and attitudes that guide your behaviors as a teacher.

### School Culture

Understanding the *culture* of a school is critical to your success and that of your students. What does culture mean? Numerous definitions exist, but ultimately the culture of the school comes down to *what we believe* and *what we do* based on those beliefs. Culture has been defined as the social or normative glue that holds an organization together. It expresses the *values of social ideas and beliefs* that organization members come to share. Key elements of an organizational culture include values and ideals of the individuals who make up the organization; norms, expectations, and sanctions; and the ways actions within the organization are modeled (Smircich, 1983; Snowden & Gorton, 1998). These elements form the foundation for the behaviors of individuals and the group.

New teachers join organizations with an established culture. Although the ideal is for every school to have a positive culture, the fact is, not all do. But whether the culture is positive, negative, or something in between, you must understand the culture before you can either buy into it or change it.

***Classroom Culture.*** Your own classroom will have a culture that you create with your students, made up of these same elements. As you develop your classroom culture, you must think through each of these elements and create an environment in which you can do your best work and students can achieve. Ideas you explored in Chapter 8 can help you do this.

Your classroom is one part of the school, which is one part of the district, which is one part of larger entities such as county, state, and nation. Your school exists inside the cultures of these other entities, all of which have cultures of their own. As a teacher, you need to be aware of the larger picture so you understand the forces at play when decisions have to be made and actions do not accidentally violate an established value or norm.

Your ideals and values shape the norms by which the classroom runs, and will be the basis of your expectations for students and the consequences you impose when students do not meet expectations. The behaviors you model will influence students as much as or more than what you say. Your words and actions must be congruent in order to have the most positive impact on learning.

Of course, the best situation is being in a school with a culture that matches your own ideals. This may not always be the case, so there is a caveat: Being part of the culture does not mean buying in to negative aspects of the culture. Essentially, to know the culture of the school you must look, listen, and then reflect on what you see and hear. You must be sure you understand what is going on before you can influence others. As you learn, ask questions about how to do things and begin to ask why things are done that way. Over time, you will establish your presence in the school, and at that point you will be able to influence and change aspects of the culture to allow them to better serve students. Be patient during the process.

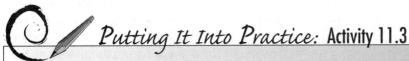

### *Putting It Into Practice:* Activity 11.3

Over the course of a month, clip 5 to 10 newspaper articles about a school in your community that you might be interested in joining as a teacher. If possible, visit the school and interview an administrator, teacher, counselor, and student. Write a description of the culture of the school based on the content of the articles and your interviews. You may have to read between the lines of articles that are critical of the school in order to make some "best guesses" about its values, beliefs, and expectations. Your interviews can help balance some of the media perceptions.

## *Putting It Into Practice:* Activity 11.4

To ready yourself to enter into a new school environment, you need to understand the educational culture of the community it serves. To accomplish this, prepare a paper that profiles your selected school, district, and community. The overall profile will be comprised of three miniprofiles: (1) the school, (2) the district, and (3) the city or community they serve. Each of the miniprofiles will include items from the following list, as well as any other information you believe affects the school and its culture.

1. *School:* brief history, community population it serves, number of students in the school, student and staff demographics, school and community connections, parental involvement, and specific specialized programs.
2. *District:* brief history, total budget, population it serves, number and types of schools, types of schedules, student demographics, community partnerships that are established, staff overview including administrative, certificated, and classified (with numbers and demographics), strategies for parental involvement and outreach efforts, and level of community support.
3. *City or community:* brief history, population, demographics, major occupations, average income, governmental organizations and services, service organizations, health organizations, major businesses, issues of importance currently facing the community, and level of community safety and pride.

Write a short paper describing the culture of the school, the district, and the city or community. Address whether the cultures intersect or diverge. To conclude the paper, provide a short rationale as to why the school you selected would or would not be one in which you are willing to begin your professional career.

## Evaluation Process for Teachers

All school districts in every state have a formal evaluation process in place. The process includes guidelines that determine how teachers will be evaluated and how they can gain permanent (tenure) status. Education laws and the collective bargaining agreements for each district typically describe these guidelines or rules. Although the details (specific time lines, forms, and number of classroom observations) may vary, the basic concepts underlying the process of gaining *permanent status* are fairly universal.

Teachers signing their first contract will have *probationary status*. This period typically lasts for 2 to 3 years depending on the state or district that is your employer. Once that period of time has passed, assuming the district has determined the teacher has performed the job at an acceptable level, the teacher gains certain permanent rights to the job. As a permanent employee you are guaranteed due process rights if there is ever any question of releasing you from your position. Though this occurs infrequently, it would serve you well to review the procedures in your district so that you understand your rights.

***Formal Evaluation Procedures.*** Schools supervise and evaluate probationary and permanent teachers on a regular basis. Probationary teachers generally receive more time and attention because a determination must be made as to whether to grant the individual permanency in the district. This is an important period in a new teacher's career.

A difference exists between supervision and evaluation and you need to understand the distinction. Supervision consists of the day-to-day interaction of a supervisor with a teacher. It includes encouragement, coaching, and, if needed, sanctions for unacceptable performance. Evaluation as a culminating event takes place at the end of an evaluation period. For new teachers that often means every year during their probationary period. At the end of each year, the administrative supervisor prepares, delivers, and discusses with the teacher a written evaluation, which is placed in the teacher's personnel file. For tenured or permanent teachers, a formal evaluation is generally completed every 2 years. A description of the five universal steps in the evaluation process follows:

1. **Setting of goals.** This takes place during a conference between the teacher and the administrator, usually a principal or assistant principal, and typically in the first month of the school year.
2. **Evidence/data gathering.** The supervisor usually does this through classroom observations. These may be a combination of both formal and informal classroom observations. The district collective bargaining agreement determines the number and type of observations. Other sources of evidence may include samples such as student work, professional portfolios, or assessment of student work through action research.
3. **Postobservation feedback.** This usually occurs immediately after a formal classroom observation, often both in writing and through a face-to-face conference.
4. **Concerns.** The administrator makes these known to the teacher and provides a plan with a time frame for improvement in the identified areas.
5. **A formal written evaluation.** At the end of the evaluation cycle, both teacher and administrator review and sign the formal evaluation. At this point the evaluation becomes part of the teacher's personnel file.

During the period of being a probationary employee, a teacher does not have the same rights to the job as do permanent employees. A district may choose to release that teacher "without cause." In other words, the school district does not have to prove that the teacher was unacceptable in order to terminate employment. However, as mentioned earlier, once a teacher gains tenure, termination of employment can take place only after due process. Due process includes a clear communication of the deficits in performance; assistance to remedy those deficits; adequate amount of time to remedy the deficits; and a fair assessment of improvement made by the teacher in the judgment of the evaluating administrator.

At the end of the probationary period, the evaluating administrator must make a determination as to whether to recommend the teacher as a tenured/permanent staff member of the district. Because of the importance of this decision, the administrator must be confident the teacher has demonstrated the capability of effectively helping students learn and being a positive member of the school community.

New teachers frequently make six mistakes that can jeopardize their chances of gaining permanency. These include the following.

1. Creating student dependency on the teacher. Make sure to assist students by guiding and coaching but not doing the work for the student. Keep in mind that high school students are not adults and need teachers to be direct and consistent in their working relationship with them. Find the balance between too much and not enough assistance so your administrator has confidence in your ability to help students become lifelong learners.

2. Creating too many rules and too few procedures. Your administrator needs to have confidence in your ability to establish and maintain a safe and productive learning environment. If you have created a "lock down" or "laissez-faire" classroom environment, your administrator will not gain that confidence.
3. Creating a reward system that is too extrinsic. If you are staying up nights tallying extra points or making trips to the bulk candy store for goodies, you are on the wrong track. Your administrator wants to see you bringing out the best in students, based upon the excitement of learning and respect for you and classmates.
4. Resorting to sarcasm, insults, yelling, and "serial" negative consequences.
5. "Laying hands" on students. Corporal punishment has no place in the school setting. Beyond the legality issues, use of physical force does not demonstrate sound educational limit setting. Using physical force to protect yourself, to protect other students, or to prevent students from hurting themselves is appropriate. The use of physical force for any other reason guarantees being relieved of duty.
6. Using instructional materials not approved for use. New teachers need to develop their plans within the curriculum guides adopted by the local school board. These guides determine the subject matter and specific content to be taught, as well as the approved instructional materials. If you follow the suggestions in Chapter 5, Unit and Lesson Plans, this will not be an issue of concern for you.

Avoiding common mistakes of new teachers, understanding the expectations your administrator and district have for you, following the sage advice of colleagues and mentors, and producing results with students will assure achieving tenure in the profession you have chosen. The strategies and concepts described throughout this textbook, if incorporated into your practice, will not only help you achieve permanent status but also allow you to emerge as a leader in your educational community.

### A Closer Look

Refer to Chapters 8 and 9 regarding classroom management.

### Putting It Into Practice: Activity 11.5

In most interviews for a teaching position the interviewer or panel will expect that you have read and understood not only the job description but also the background of the school to which you have applied to work.

Locate a job description for a teaching position that interests you. Review it, then write a reflective essay. Include what surprised you in the description, what questions you have, and any other observations you would make about the job description.

## Teacher Dispositions and Attributes

At this point you have worked through the entire textbook and hopefully have added to your teaching tool kit. The book has explored the professional knowledge and pedagogical skills that will help you become a successful and effective secondary teacher. These alone, however, will only get you part way to that goal. The ideas of modeling the dispositions presented throughout the book and the attributes of successful teachers described in Chapter 1 are the keys to reaching that ultimate goal.

***Dispositions and Attributes.*** At the beginning of each chapter we have presented you with the dispositions that align with the material that follows. The dispositions spell out the behaviors teachers must model continuously during their careers to both maximize the opportunity for students to learn and assist in ongoing professionalization. This important resource should guide your work. Keep the dispositions, as well as all the INTASC standard elements, in an easily accessible file, to review frequently.

The seven personal attributes you examined in Chapter 1, though targeting preservice teachers, can also be an important part of your professional files. These attributes form a quick checklist for a new teacher. The challenges you must confront in your first year can be mitigated if you constantly reflect on how well you believe you are modeling these behaviors every day. Keep in mind that getting a contract with a school is only the first step in establishing yourself in your chosen profession. You must demonstrate that the decision to hire you was a sound one.

***Final Thoughts.*** The overarching framework for this textbook, the Circle of Courage, can serve your professional endeavors well. If helping students achieve competence in each section of the Circle—Generosity, Belonging, Mastery, and Independence—guides a teacher's professional development, planning, instruction, and assessment, these efforts will be well rewarded.

We believe that your choice to enter the teaching profession is a bold one. This challenging and demanding occupation means that there will rarely be a day that doesn't excite and motivate you. Keep in mind as you move into the classroom, none of us have ever taught the perfect lesson or can say we never taught a lesson that didn't "crash and burn." Practice and experience will help you understand that issues with lessons do occur, yet, in a successful teacher's classroom, become more and more infrequent occurrences.

We are confident that the next generation of teachers—guided by your own strong professional foundation, ideas of what it is to be a powerful teacher (INTASC), and a willingness to remain professionally current—will serve all of our students well. We look forward to welcoming you as the newest colleagues to this wonderful profession.

## *Putting It Into Practice:* Activity 11.6

Retrieve the work you completed in Putting It Into Practice: Activity 1.5 from Chapter 1. Use the initial self-review from that activity and rerate yourself based on your current actions. Review the three growth areas you identified in that activity and evaluate the progress you have made in each. Give specific examples to show evidence of your growth and assess the effectiveness of the strategy you identified to help you meet each goal.

Now review your current self-assessment and identify three new growth areas at this stage of your professional preparation. Again, set target goals for each and detail specific strategies you will develop to meet your goals. This pattern of constant review and reflection on all aspects of your practice should become a regular activity in your professional life.

## SECTION 4: CHAPTER SUMMARY AND REFLECTION

Chapter 11 presented a range of information that new professionals will find useful to begin a teaching career. Section 1 explored issues of professionalism, various external societal factors that create challenges, as well as how school culture impacts the daily life of a teacher. It also covered strategies to assist you in maintaining a professional focus by developing your mission statement. Section 1 explored the idea of developing a professional stance and the importance, from the beginning of a career, to strive continuously to be positive in working with students and colleagues.

Section 2 set an expectation that teachers must continually adapt to changing times without abandoning professional standards. How a teacher adapts was a central issue of this section, which provided several examples of adaptation, both positive and negative. This section concluded with a discussion about strategies to adapt your practice in a positive way, ideas to collaborate with colleagues as the newest team member, as well as ideas for working with students' parents.

The concluding section described both school and community cultures and provided strategies to gather useful information about each. In addition, Section 3 briefly described the common elements in teacher evaluation systems. As noted in this section, every teacher will go through the evaluation process. You need to have a basic understanding of the system, how it is applied, and what you can expect in the first years of teaching. Section 3 concluded by revisiting issues introduced in Chapter 1: teacher dispositions and attributes of successful teachers. We have no doubt both are influential in making a difference between becoming a competent instructor or a powerful teacher. Our final thoughts are for you to set high standards for your work and to strive continuously to reach them.

## References


Brendtro, L. K., Brokenleg, M., & Bockern, S. V. (2002). *Reclaiming youth at risk: Our hope for the future*. Bloomington, IN: National Education Service.

Council of Chief State School Officers (1992). Model standards for beginning teacher licensing, assessment, and development: A resource for state dialogue. Washington, DC: Author. www.ccsso.org/content/pdfs/corestrd.pdf

Covey, S. (1990). *Seven habits of highly effective people*. New York: Simon & Schuster.

Jones, F. (1987). *Positive classroom discipline*. New York: McGraw-Hill.

Lencioni, P. (2002). *The five dysfunctions of a team*. San Francisco: Jossey-Bass.

Lieberman, A., & Miller, L. (1999). *Teachers: Transforming their world and their work*. New York: Teachers College Press.

Maslow, A. H., Frager, R., & Fadiman, J. (1987). *Motivation and personality* (3rd ed.). New York: Addison-Wesley.

McLaughlin, M. W., & Talbert, J. (1993). *Contexts that matter for teaching and learning*. Palo Alto: Stanford University, Context Center on Secondary School Teaching.

National Board for Professional Teaching Standards (1987). *What teachers should know and be able to do*. Washington, DC: National Board for Professional Teaching Standards.

Palmer, P. J. (1998). *The courage to teach: Exploring the inner landscape of a teacher's life*. San Francisco: Jossey-Bass.

Rosenberger, M. K. (1997). *Team leadership*. Lancaster, PA: Technomic.

Slavin, R. E. (1997). *Sand, bricks and seeds: School change strategies and readiness for reform*. Baltimore: Johns Hopkins University, Center for Research on the Education of Students Placed at Risk.

Smircich, L. (1983, September). Concepts of culture and organizational analysis. *Administrative Science Quarterly*, pp. 64–69.

Snowden, P. E., & Gorton, R. A. (1998). *School leadership and administration*. New York: McGraw-Hill.

Stone, S., Patton, B., & Heen, S. (1999). *Difficult conversations: How to talk about what matters most*. New York: Penguin Books.

# Instructional Resource A

## Interstate New Teacher Assessment and Support Consortium (INTASC) Standards

### PRINCIPLE 1

The teacher understands the central concepts, tools of inquiry, and structures of the discipline(s) he or she teaches and can create learning experiences that make these aspects of subject matter meaningful for students.

#### Knowledge

- The teacher understands major concepts, assumptions, debates, processes of inquiry, and ways of knowing that are central to the discipline(s) s/he teaches.
- The teacher understands how students' conceptual frameworks and their misconceptions for an area of knowledge can influence their learning.
- The teacher can relate his/her disciplinary knowledge to other subject areas.

#### Dispositions

- The teacher realizes that subject matter knowledge is not a fixed body of facts but is complex and ever-evolving. S/he seeks to keep abreast of new ideas and understandings in the field.
- The teacher appreciates multiple perspectives and conveys to learners how knowledge is developed from the vantage point of the knower.
- The teacher has enthusiasm for the discipline(s) s/he teaches and sees connections to everyday life.
- The teacher is committed to continuous learning and engages in professional discourse about subject matter knowledge and children's learning of the discipline.

#### Performances

- The teacher effectively uses multiple representations and explanations of disciplinary concepts that capture key ideas and link them to students' prior understandings.
- The teacher can represent and use differing viewpoints, theories, "ways of knowing," and methods of inquiry in his/her teaching of subject matter concepts.
- The teacher can evaluate teaching resources and curriculum materials for their comprehensiveness, accuracy, and usefulness for representing particular ideas and concepts.

- The teacher engages students in generating knowledge and testing hypotheses according to the methods of inquiry and standards of evidence used in the discipline.
- The teacher develops and uses curricula that encourage students to see, question, and interpret ideas from diverse perspectives.
- The teacher can create interdisciplinary learning experiences that allow students to integrate knowledge, skills, and methods of inquiry from several subject areas.

## PRINCIPLE 2

The teacher understands how children learn and develop, and can provide learning opportunities that support their intellectual, social and personal development.

### Knowledge

- The teacher understands how learning occurs—how students construct knowledge, acquire skills, and develop habits of mind—and knows how to use instructional strategies that promote student learning.
- The teacher understands that students' physical, social, emotional, moral, and cognitive development influence learning and knows how to address these factors when making instructional decisions.
- The teacher is aware of expected developmental progressions and ranges of individual variation within each domain (physical, social, emotional, moral, and cognitive), can identify levels of readiness in learning, and understands how development in any one domain may affect performance in others.

### Dispositions

- The teacher appreciates individual variation within each area of development, shows respect for the diverse talents of all learners, and is committed to help them develop self-confidence and competence.
- The teacher is disposed to use students' strengths as a basis for growth, and their errors as an opportunity for learning.

### Performances

- The teacher assesses individual and group performance in order to design instruction that meets learners' current needs in each domain (cognitive, social, emotional, moral, and physical) and that leads to the next level of development.
- The teacher stimulates student reflection on prior knowledge and links new ideas to already familiar ideas, making connections to students' experiences, providing opportunities for active engagement, manipulation, and testing of ideas and materials, and encouraging students to assume responsibility for shaping their learning tasks.
- The teacher accesses students' thinking and experiences as a basis for instructional activities by, for example, encouraging discussion, listening and responding to group interaction, and eliciting samples of student thinking orally and in writing.

## PRINCIPLE 3

The teacher understands how students differ in their approaches to learning and creates instructional opportunities that are adapted to diverse learners.

## Knowledge

- The teacher understands and can identify differences in approaches to learning and performance, including different learning styles, multiple intelligences, and performance modes, and can design instruction that helps use students' strengths as the basis for growth.
- The teacher knows about areas of exceptionality in learning—including learning disabilities, visual and perceptual difficulties, and special physical or mental challenges.
- The teacher knows about the process of second language acquisition and about strategies to support the learning of students whose first language is not English.
- The teacher understands how students' learning is influenced by individual experiences, talents, and prior learning, as well as language, culture, family, and community values.
- The teacher has a well-grounded framework for understanding cultural and community diversity and knows how to learn about and incorporate students' experiences, cultures, and community resources into instruction.

## Dispositions

- The teacher believes that all children can learn at high levels and persists in helping all children achieve success.
- The teacher appreciates and values human diversity, shows respect for students' varied talents and perspectives, and is committed to the pursuit of "individually configured excellence."
- The teacher respects students as individuals with differing personal and family backgrounds and various skills, talents, and interests.
- The teacher is sensitive to community and cultural norms.
- The teacher makes students feel valued for their potential as people, and helps them learn to value each other.

## Performances

- The teacher identifies and designs instruction appropriate to students' stages of development, learning styles, strengths, and needs.
- The teacher uses teaching approaches that are sensitive to the multiple experiences of learners and that address different learning and performance modes.
- The teacher makes appropriate provisions (in terms of time and circumstances for work, tasks assigned, communication and response modes) for individual students who have particular learning differences or needs.
- The teacher can identify when and how to access appropriate services or resources to meet exceptional learning needs.
- The teacher seeks to understand students' families, cultures, and communities, and uses this information as a basis for connecting instruction to students' experiences (e.g., drawing explicit connections between subject matter and community matters, making assignments that can be related to students' experiences and cultures).
- The teacher brings multiple perspectives to the discussion of subject matter, including attention to students' personal, family, and community experiences and cultural norms.
- The teacher creates a learning community in which individual differences are respected.

# PRINCIPLE 4

The teacher understands and uses a variety of instructional strategies to encourage students' development of critical thinking, problem solving, and performance skills.

## Knowledge

- The teacher understands the cognitive processes associated with various kinds of learning (e.g., critical and creative thinking, problem structuring and problem solving, invention, memorization and recall) and how these processes can be stimulated.
- The teacher understands principles and techniques, along with advantages and limitations, associated with various instructional strategies (e.g., cooperative learning, direct instruction, discovery learning, whole group discussion, independent study, interdisciplinary instruction).
- The teacher knows how to enhance learning through the use of a wide variety of materials as well as human and technological resources (e.g., computers, audio-visual technologies, videotapes and discs, local experts, primary documents and artifacts, texts, reference books, literature, and other print resources).

## Dispositions

- The teacher values the development of students' critical thinking, independent problem solving, and performance capabilities.
- The teacher values flexibility and reciprocity in the teaching process as necessary for adapting instruction to student responses, ideas, and needs.

## Performances

- The teacher carefully evaluates how to achieve learning goals, choosing alternative teaching strategies and materials to achieve different instructional purposes and to meet student needs (e.g., developmental stages, prior knowledge, learning styles, and interests).
- The teacher uses multiple teaching and learning strategies to engage students in active learning opportunities that promote the development of critical thinking, problem solving, and performance capabilities and that help students assume responsibility for identifying and using learning resources.
- The teacher constantly monitors and adjusts strategies in response to learner feedback.
- The teacher varies his or her role in the instructional process (e.g., instructor, facilitator, coach, audience) in relation to the content and purposes of instruction and the needs of students.
- The teacher develops a variety of clear, accurate presentations and representations of concepts, using alternative explanations to assist students' understanding and presenting diverse perspectives to encourage critical thinking.

# Principle 5

The teacher uses an understanding of individual and group motivation and behavior to create a learning environment that encourages positive social interaction, active engagement in learning, and self-motivation.

## Knowledge

- The teacher can use knowledge about human motivation and behavior drawn from the foundational sciences of psychology, anthropology, and sociology to develop strategies for organizing and supporting individual and group work.
- The teacher understands how social groups function and influence people, and how people influence groups. The teacher knows how to help people work productively and cooperatively with each other in complex social settings.

- The teacher understands the principles of effective classroom management and can use a range of strategies to promote positive relationships, cooperation, and purposeful learning in the classroom.
- The teacher recognizes factors and situations that are likely to promote or diminish intrinsic motivation, and knows how to help students become self-motivated.

## Dispositions

- The teacher takes responsibility for establishing a positive climate in the classroom and participates in maintaining such a climate in the school as a whole.
- The teacher understands how participation supports commitment, and is committed to the expression and use of democratic values in the classroom.
- The teacher values the role of students in promoting each other's learning and recognizes the importance of peer relationships in establishing a climate of learning.
- The teacher recognizes the value of intrinsic motivation to students' life-long growth and learning.
- The teacher is committed to the continuous development of individual students' abilities and considers how different motivational strategies are likely to encourage this development for each student.

## Performances

- The teacher creates a smoothly functioning learning community in which students assume responsibility for themselves and one another, participate in decision-making, work collaboratively and independently, and engage in purposeful learning activities.
- The teacher engages students in individual and cooperative learning activities that help them develop the motivation to achieve, by, for example, relating lessons to students' personal interests, allowing students to have choices in their learning, and leading students to ask questions and pursue problems that are meaningful to them.
- The teacher organizes, allocates, and manages the resources of time, space, activities, and attention to provide active and equitable engagement of students in productive tasks.
- The teacher maximizes the amount of class time spent in learning by creating expectations and processes for communication and behavior along with a physical setting conducive to classroom goals.
- The teacher helps the group to develop shared values and expectations for student interactions, academic discussions, and individual and group responsibility that create a positive classroom climate of openness, mutual respect, support, and inquiry.
- The teacher analyzes the classroom environment and makes decisions and adjustments to enhance social relationships, student motivation and engagement, and productive work.
- The teacher organizes, prepares students for, and monitors independent and group work that allows for full and varied participation of all individuals.

# PRINCIPLE 6

The teacher uses knowledge of effective verbal, nonverbal, and media communication techniques to foster active inquiry, collaboration, and supportive interaction in the classroom.

## Knowledge

- The teacher understands communication theory, language development, and the role of language in learning.

- The teacher understands how cultural and gender differences can affect communication in the classroom.
- The teacher recognizes the importance of nonverbal as well as verbal communication.
- The teacher knows about and can use effective verbal, nonverbal, and media communication techniques.

### Dispositions

- The teacher recognizes the power of language for fostering self-expression, identity development, and learning.
- The teacher values many ways in which people seek to communicate and encourages many modes of communication in the classroom. The teacher is a thoughtful and responsive listener.
- The teacher appreciates the cultural dimensions of communication, responds appropriately, and seeks to foster culturally sensitive communication by and among all students in the class.

### Performances

- The teacher models effective communication strategies in conveying ideas and information and in asking questions (e.g., monitoring the effects of messages, restating ideas and drawing connections, using visual, aural, and kinesthetic cues, being sensitive to nonverbal cues given and received).
- The teacher supports and expands learner expression in speaking, writing, and other media.
- The teacher knows how to ask questions and stimulate discussion in different ways for particular purposes, for example, probing for learner understanding, helping students articulate their ideas and thinking processes, promoting risk taking and problem-solving, facilitating factual recall, encouraging convergent and divergent thinking, stimulating curiosity, helping students to question.
- The teacher communicates in ways that demonstrate a sensitivity to cultural and gender differences (e.g., appropriate use of eye contact, interpretation of body language and verbal statements, acknowledgment of and responsiveness to different modes of communication and participation).
- The teacher knows how to use a variety of media communication tools, including audiovisual aids and computers, to enrich learning opportunities.

## PRINCIPLE 7

The teacher plans instruction based upon knowledge of subject matter, students, the community, and curriculum goals.

### Knowledge

- The teacher understands learning theory, subject matter, curriculum development, and student development and knows how to use this knowledge in planning instruction to meet curriculum goals.
- The teacher knows how to take contextual considerations (instructional materials, individual student interests, needs, and aptitudes, and community resources) into account in planning instruction that creates an effective bridge between curriculum goals and students' experiences.
- The teacher knows when and how to adjust plans based on student responses and other contingencies.

## Dispositions

- The teacher values both long-term and short-term planning.
- The teacher believes that plans must always be open to adjustment and revision based on student needs and changing circumstances.
- The teacher values planning as a collegial activity.

## Performances

- As an individual and a member of a team, the teacher selects and creates learning experiences that are appropriate for curriculum goals, relevant to learners, and based upon principles of effective instruction (e.g., that activate students' prior knowledge, anticipate preconceptions, encourage exploration and problem-solving, and build new skills on those previously acquired).
- The teacher plans for learning opportunities that recognize and address variation in learning styles and performance modes.
- The teacher creates lessons and activities that operate at multiple levels to meet the developmental and individual needs of diverse learners and help each progress.
- The teacher creates short-range and long-term plans that are linked to student needs and performance, and adapts the plans to ensure and capitalize on student progress and motivation.
- The teacher responds to unanticipated sources of input, evaluates plans in relation to short- and long-range goals, and systematically adjusts plans to meet student needs and enhance learning.

# PRINCIPLE 8

The teacher understands and uses formal and informal assessment strategies to evaluate and ensure the continuous intellectual, social, and physical development of the learner.

## Knowledge

- The teacher understands the characteristics, uses, advantages, and limitations of different types of assessments (e.g., criterion-referenced and norm-referenced instruments, traditional standardized and performance-based tests, observation systems, and assessments of student work) for evaluating how students learn, what they know and are able to do, and what kinds of experiences will support their further growth and development.
- The teacher knows how to select, construct, and use assessment strategies and instruments appropriate to the learning outcomes being evaluated and to other diagnostic purposes.
- The teacher understands measurement theory and assessment related issues, such as validity, reliability, bias, and scoring concerns.

## Dispositions

- The teacher values ongoing assessment as essential to the instructional process and recognizes that many different assessment strategies, accurately and systematically used, are necessary for monitoring and promoting student learning.
- The teacher is committed to using assessment to identify student strengths and promote student growth rather than to deny students access to learning opportunities.

## Performances

- The teacher appropriately uses a variety of formal and informal assessment techniques (e.g., observation, portfolios of student work, teacher-made tests, performance tasks,

projects, student self-assessments, peer assessment, and standardized tests) to enhance her or his knowledge of learners, evaluate students' progress and performances, and modify teaching and learning strategies.
- The teacher solicits and uses information about students' experiences, learning behavior, needs, and progress from parents, other colleagues, and the students themselves.
- The teacher uses assessment strategies to involve learners in self-assessment activities, to help them become aware of their strengths and needs, and to encourage them to set personal goals for learning.
- The teacher evaluates the effect of class activities on both individuals and the class as a whole, collecting information through observation of classroom interactions, questioning, and analysis of student work.
- The teacher monitors his or her own teaching strategies and behavior in relation to student success, modifying plans and instructional approaches accordingly.
- The teacher maintains useful records of student work and performance and can communicate student progress knowledgeably and responsibly, based on appropriate indicators, to students, parents, and other colleagues.

## PRINCIPLE 9

The teacher is a reflective practitioner who continually evaluates the effects of his/her choices and actions on others (students, parents, and other professionals in the learning community) and who actively seeks out opportunities to grow professionally.

### Knowledge

- The teacher understands methods of inquiry that provide him/her with a variety of self-assessment and problem-solving strategies for reflecting on his/her practice, its influences on students' growth and learning, and the complex interactions between them.
- The teacher is aware of major areas of research on teaching and of resources available for professional learning (e.g., professional literature, colleagues, professional associations, professional development activities).

### Dispositions

- The teacher values critical thinking and self-directed learning as habits of mind.
- The teacher is committed to reflection, assessment, and learning as an ongoing process.
- The teacher is willing to give and receive help.
- The teacher is committed to seeking out, developing, and continually refining practices that address the individual needs of students.
- The teacher recognizes his/her professional responsibility for engaging in and supporting appropriate professional practices for self and colleagues.

### Performances

- The teacher uses classroom observation, information about students, and research as sources for evaluating the outcomes of teaching and learning and as a basis for experimenting with, reflecting on, and revising practice.
- The teacher seeks out professional literature, colleagues, and other resources to support his/her own development as a learner and a teacher.
- The teacher draws upon professional colleagues within the school and other professional arenas as supports for reflection, problem-solving and new ideas, actively sharing experiences and seeking and giving feedback.

## PRINCIPLE 10

The teacher fosters relationships with school colleagues, parents, and agencies in the larger community to support students' learning and well-being.

### Knowledge

- The teacher understands schools as organizations within the larger community context and understands the operations of the relevant aspects of the system(s) within which s/he works.
- The teacher understands how factors in the students' environment outside of school (e.g., family circumstances, community environments, health and economic conditions) may influence students' life and learning.
- The teacher understands and implements laws related to students' rights and teacher responsibilities (e.g., for equal education, appropriate education for handicapped students, confidentiality, privacy, appropriate treatment of students, reporting in situations related to possible child abuse).

### Dispositions

- The teacher values and appreciates the importance of all aspects of a child's experience.
- The teacher is concerned about all aspects of a child's well being (cognitive, emotional, social, and physical), and is alert to signs of difficulties.
- The teacher is willing to consult with other adults regarding the education and well-being of his/her students.
- The teacher respects the privacy of students and confidentiality of information.
- The teacher is willing to work with other professionals to improve the overall learning environment for students.

### Performances

- The teacher participates in collegial activities designed to make the entire school a productive learning environment.
- The teacher makes links with the learners' other environments on behalf of students, by consulting with parents, counselors, teachers of other classes and activities within the schools, and professionals in other community agencies.
- The teacher can identify and use community resources to foster student learning.
- The teacher establishes respectful and productive relationships with parents and guardians from diverse home and community situations, and seeks to develop cooperative partnerships in support of student learning and well being.
- The teacher talks with and listens to the student, is sensitive and responsive to clues of distress, investigates situations, and seeks outside help as needed and appropriate to remedy problems.
- The teacher acts as an advocate for students.

---

The Interstate New Teacher Assessment and Support Consortium (INTASC) standards were developed by the Council of Chief State School Officers and member states. Copies may be downloaded from the Council's web site at http://www.ccsso.org.

Council of Chief State School Officers. (1992). Model Standards for beginning teacher licensing, assessment, and development: A resource for state dialogue. Washington, DC: Author. www.ccsso.org/content/pdfs/corestrd.pdf.

# Instructional Resource B

## Sample Individualized Literacy Preassessment

1. **Identify a student.** In an ideal situation you would have a classroom in which, after talking with the teacher and spending some time in the classroom, you select a student whom the classroom teacher recommends as someone having some difficulty with reading.

2. **Prewrite/prereflect.** Prewrite for a paragraph or two about the assumptions, questions, and expectations you have about your student and her or his school experience before you spend time with the student.

3. **Student interview.** Ask permission to gather some information about the student's school history and current interests. Sample interview topics:
   - Ask how many schools the student has attended.
   - Find out whether the student moved during the first three to four grades of elementary school.
   - Ask about the student's early memories of learning to read and write.
   - Ask how the student feels about school.
   - Try to discover how the student feels about his or her own literacy level.
   - Ask what subjects the student likes, dislikes, and why.
   - Find out whether English is the student's second language. If so, ask whether the student can read and write in both languages; ask which language friends and family use. Some students will be able to describe in which language they "think," and whether they still move in and out of two languages when learning in different content areas.
   - Ask about favorites: sports, music, activities, and so on.
   - Try to find out whether the student reads when he or she doesn't have to.
   - Remember to ask about family influences on the student's literacy. For example, does the student read at home? Does his or her family have lots of reading material around the house?

Use your own intuition and stop the questioning if your student seems to find all this too intrusive.

4. **Conduct an informal reading conference (Routman, 2000).** Keep a running record during the conference. Ask the student the following and record your observations:
   - *Bring me a book you can read pretty well.* This helps you determine whether the child is choosing and can choose "just right" books to read independently. Because students do the majority of reading independently, it is critical for them to choose appropriate books they can read and understand.
   - *Why did you choose this book?* This gives you insight into the self-selection process. Can the student self-select a book to read independently? What is the student's attitude about the book? Is this a favorite author or series? Did a peer recommend it? Did the student pick it because of the pictures or the length?

- *What's the reading level of this book for you?* Ask also: Is this book easy, "just right," or hard for you? How do you know? What does it mean if a book is "just right"? What kinds of books do good readers mostly read? Why is this a good book for you?
- *Tell me what the book is about so far.* If it is a chapter book or the student has read it before, this should help you determine whether the student can determine the main idea.
- *Read this part of the book for me.* Take notes as the child reads orally. Note miscues: Did the miscue make sense in the context? Did it change the meaning? Did the student self-correct? What is causing the miscues? Is it decoding? Is the book too hard? Note what strategies the student uses to make sense of text. Is the student self-monitoring? For example, does he or she stop when something doesn't make sense? Does the student reread or use other "fix-up" strategies? Does he or she attempt to figure out unknown vocabulary?
- *Tell me what you remember about what you just read.* Can the student talk about what he or she has read and tell the most important information? Sometimes students can decode the words accurately but can't say what the text was about. A retelling is one way to check for comprehension.
- *Let's look at how you did—what your strengths are and what you need to work on.* Discuss your observations/notes with the student. Be sure to state what the student has done well. Focus on meaning first. Together with the student, analyze the miscues and guide the student toward self-evaluation and self-correction where possible. For example, you might say, "Did it make sense when you said . . . ?" or "Do you know this part or chunk?" "Reread this part and tell me what happened."
- *How long should it take you to complete this book?* This gives you insight into the student's daily goal setting.
- *Let's set some goals for reading.* What will you do to help yourself the next time you read? These goals could include vocabulary strategies, chunking words, rereading sections that don't make sense, connecting to what is already known, choosing better "just right" books, summarizing.

5. **Content knowledge**
   - In actual practice it is very useful to determine the content knowledge of your students prior to beginning the unit of study.
   - Determine the major concepts that you want them to learn and develop a short answer (or multiple-choice) assessment.
   - You should, of course, let you students know that you will not formally grade them on it and that it is a way for you as the teacher to determine how to structure the unit. You might consider giving them credit for completing it to the best of their ability.
   - This preassessment of content might also serve as one of the summative or postunit assessments so that you and the students can see what content knowledge was gained.

6. **Writing analysis.** Collect two to three writing samples. If possible, get a range of samples—a journal entry, a piece that has been through the writing process, a nonfiction piece. If you cannot get writing samples, give the student a prompt and ask him or her to write for at least 10 minutes without stopping. The prompt could be about something you discovered in the interview or interest inventory. It must be something the student knows.

*Note: Use a pseudonym to keep your student anonymous. Black out all names that appear on the data, evidence, and student work you attach to the analysis.*

7. **Conducting your analysis**
   ***Introduction.*** Summarize all of the contextual information you've gathered from the student interview. Include age, grade, and any pertinent background information;

include what you know about this student's general attitudes toward school, sports, family, and other interests as well as specific attitudes about reading, writing. If your student expresses any strong likes or dislikes, include that information.

***Reading assessment.*** Summarize your findings from the informal reading conference. Include the title of the book and why the student chose the book. As the student reads orally, what errors did the running record evidence? During the oral reading, what teaching strategies did you use? For example, breaking words into parts, using onsets and rimes, read on and then come back to the difficult word. What strengths and weaknesses from your notes did you discuss with the reader? What goals did you and the student set for reading the next time? Your analysis is not that of a reading specialist; rather it is an informal set of conclusions based on close observation.

***Writing sample(s).*** Summarize your findings from the writing sample(s). Analyze your findings by looking for patterns and/or behaviors that are consistent or inconsistent with other information you know about this student. Is the writing level consistent with the reading level? Look for depth of ideas as well as "significant" syntax, spelling, and grammar errors. What kind of vocabulary does the student use in writing? Ask yourself what kind of ability, confidence, and interest this student has in writing.

***Instructional plan.*** Now that you have all this information about this student, what do you do with it? What would you do both for this student individually and for your whole group instruction to modify your instruction? Identify two specific strategies, one that comes from the goals you set with the student, and one that would both help this student as well as be used in whole class instruction.

***Reflection.*** Looking back on your original prewriting/prereflection, which assumptions held true and which did you have to struggle with in terms of disparities? What do your preliminary assumptions say about where you are as a teacher and what you need to focus on with future students? What implications does this experience have for you as a future teacher? What kind of "aha's" did you experience while completing this case study?

## Teacher Self-Assessment Rubric for Literacy Preassessment

Name: ______________________________ Date: ______________

| Criteria | Very Competent | Adequate Competence | Limited Competence | Resubmit with Revisions |
|---|---|---|---|---|
| The narrative includes an introductory paragraph(s) describing the reader and the book choice. | | | | |
| The narrative provides clear evidence of the teacher's (that's you) ability to record and analyze student errors. | | | | |
| The narrative provides clear evidence of the teacher's ability to use appropriate and varied teaching strategies during oral reading. | | | | |
| The narrative evidences the teacher's ability to engage him- or herself and the student in analytical conversation when discussing strengths and weaknesses and goal setting. | | | | |
| The analysis evidences an ability to describe, analyze, and evaluate student writing. | | | | |
| The analysis shows evidence of editing and proofreading final draft so that errors in spelling, punctuation, capitalization, and usage do not impede comprehension. | | | | |

Comments:

# Instructional Resource C

## Action Research Examples

### Action Research Project Report Example 1 Language Arts Tutoring

#### Problem Questions

1. How will 9th-grade students tutoring elementary school second-language learners affect the 9th graders' reading comprehension scores and their attitudes towards language arts, service-learning, and teaching as a career?
2. Will there be any significant differences between any of these variables for 9th graders who are second-language learners themselves and English only speakers?

#### Background Information

Research evidence suggests that service-learning projects may have greater positive effects on second-language participants than those students who are native language participants. Service-learning offers connections to real local community issues and opportunities for gains in personal self-esteem in second-language learners as possible causal agents or rationales for these differences.

Ninety 9th-grade students participated in this project; 30 were Honors English and 60 were regular English students. The project consisted of tutoring elementary students who were second-language learners for a minimum of 10 hours during a 10-week period. Based on data available prior to the tutoring experience, 55% of 9th-grade students were at or below reading levels for 9th grade; 57.7% of the student tutors were second-language learners.

#### Hypotheses

The 9th-grade students participating in the tutoring service-learning project will:

1. improve their own reading comprehension scores;
2. show positive gains in attitude toward participating in language arts as a subject, service-learning projects, and teaching as a career; and
3. show greater positive gains in each of the variables among student tutors who are second-language learners themselves when compared to English only speakers.

#### Experimental Design

Students received instructional strategies about effective tutoring techniques before and during the project. They were assigned local elementary students to tutor for a minimum of 10 hours over a 10-week period. The teacher held individual and group conferences with the tutors on a regular basis during this period. In addition, students received a grade based on a rubric for their participation in the project. The following data collection instruments and methods were used to evaluate outcomes from the project:

1. The use of the Stanford Reading Comprehension Test as a pre- and posttest measured any changes in reading comprehension.
2. A teacher-developed pre- and postsurvey was used to measure attitudes toward language arts as a subject, service-learning, and teaching as a career. (The survey is located in the table following the Data and Results section.)
3. The teacher reviewed personal student journal entries (using common prompts) documenting each tutoring session.
4. Teacher discussions and observations were also recorded.

## Data and Results

### *Reading Comprehension Test Results*

1. Of the 60 regular students in 9th grade, 47 improved an average of 2.6 grades in reading comprehension after 12 weeks of the tutoring project.
2. The students who had already scored at the top of the scale on the pretest, either at the 12th or 13th grade and consequently were not able to show any improvement, were not included in the statistical data.
3. Four students' scores decreased by an average of 0.3 grade. Nine students arrived during the project and consequently had no pretest scores. The greatest student improvement was a move from 5th-grade to 12th-grade reading level.
4. Of the 30 honors students, 20 were already scoring at the top of the chart, post high school, and could not improve. Five students improved an average of 2.5 grades. Three students' scores were identical and two students' scores dropped an average of 2.0 grades.
5. The comparison of boys and girls, Hispanic and non-Hispanic student scores revealed:
   19 Hispanic girls 6.2 + 2.1 = 8.3;
   10 Hispanic boys 5.9 + 2.93 = 8.83;
   13 non-Hispanic boys 7.87 + 2.17 = 10.04;
   11 non-Hispanic girls 7.2 + 2.85 = 10.05; and
   9 students transferred in during the project and did not take the pretest.
6. The ESL student scores showed:
   9 ESL girls 4.96 + 4.07 = 9.03;
   9 ESL boys 5.66 + 2.73 = 8.39; and
   1 ESL (Honors) 8.7 + 5.3 = 14.
   ESL students in this study were defined as students who have been enrolled in ESL classes during their school career.

***Changes in Attitude Results.*** A pre and post Likert scale survey was used to determine any changes in student attitudes related to language arts, service-learning, and teaching as a potential profession (see table).

On a scale of 1 to 5, 1 being low interest and 5 being high interest, students showed little change in attitude toward language arts. The average preproject score was 3.9. The postproject score was 4.1.

Students showed moderate gains in attitude toward service-learning. The average preexperience score was 3.5. The postproject score was 4.05.

Students showed moderate gains in attitude toward teaching as a profession. The average preexperience score was 3.1. The postproject score was 3.6. The highest scores were recorded by Hispanic girls, whose average score was 4.2.

## Conclusions and Implications

In conclusion, this service-learning project, involving peer tutoring in English, was highly successful in improving reading comprehension. Student tutors' reading comprehension scores improved more than 2.5 grade levels. There were gains among boys and girls in both Hispanic and non-Hispanic populations and in ESL and non-ESL populations, which supported hypothesis 1. The greatest gain was with ESL girls, whose reading comprehension scores improved 4.07 grade levels. This finding supports, in part, hypothesis 3, which predicted greater gains for some variables among ESL students.

These findings suggest that some moderate positive changes in attitudes occurred for all three variables. No significant differences were seen between ESL and non-ESL participants in the area of attitudes. Attitudes toward teaching as a career (hypothesis 2) did increase significantly among Hispanic female students (some ESL and non-ESL). Perhaps the relatively short time frame of the study was not long enough to further affect these attitudinal changes.

**Pre- and PostSurvey**
**Attitudes Toward Language Arts, Service-Learning, and Teaching as a Career**

I am using this survey to understand your attitude about several issues related to our tutoring project. Please write the number that corresponds *most closely* to your attitude or opinion.

The number:

(1) means no
(2) means a little; not very much
(3) means some
(4) means yes
(5) means yes a lot; very much

_________ 1. I like my language arts class.
_________ 2. I like reading.
_________ 3. I like helping people.
_________ 4. Someday I might like to be a teacher.
_________ 5. I feel confident being a tutor.
_________ 6. I am a good reader.
_________ 7. I feel confident and relaxed working with people who don't know much English.
_________ 8. I could teach other people how to be better readers.
_________ 9. I want to know more about being a teacher.
_________ 10. I want to know more about English, especially new vocabulary words.
_________ 11. I am motivated to be a better reader.
_________ 12. I like doing community service projects and getting credit in school.
_________ 13. I feel good about myself as a tutor.
_________ 14. Doing community service is a good way to learn.
_________ 15. I am a good student.

# Action Research Project Report Example 2
# Visiting Scientist

## Problem Question

Will 9th-grade students improve academically and develop more interest in science if they teach science to elementary students?

## Background Information

Discipline: Two classes of non–English Language Development (non-ELD) Life Science
Grade level: 9th grade

Reason for selection of project: Students would create a variety of methods of instruction in a fun and interactive way for younger students and improve their own understanding of the concept. In addition, students would have to share their work with elementary age students (service-learning).

Focus: Connections between curriculum and community, while also looking at achievement and attitudes of non-White students.

One of my main goals as a 9th-grade science teacher is to foster excitement and interest in science. I wanted to assess the attitudes and feelings of my students toward science before and after participating in a service-learning project, in this case peer teaching. Service-learning projects offer young people the opportunity to help others in their community, while providing a sense of accomplishment, give a different view of the world around them, create greater self-esteem, develop self-empowerment, create academic development, and practice civic responsibility. Resources for Youth states that 74% of teenagers say they do not volunteer because they do not know how to get involved, while 60% say they do not volunteer because no one has ever asked them to. Hopefully projects such as this will fuel the fire for continued community service.

## Hypotheses

1. My science students will increase their academic achievement in the class as a result of their participation in project Visiting Scientist.
2. My science students will increase their positive attitudes toward science as a result of their participation in project Visiting Scientist.
3. There will be a difference in the amount of achievement and attitude gain among my White (Caucasian) and non-White students.

## Experimental Design

The school in which this project was completed was Anytown High School. This traditional, comprehensive high school has 2,126 students enrolled, 83% of whom are White and 17% non-White (12% are Latino). This project was implemented with two of my 9th-grade life science classes, which have a group representative of the school ethnic numbers (86% White, 14% non-White).

Three weeks before the unit was to start my students filled out the preservice questionnaire. This questionnaire included questions about their attitudes toward science, activities they like to engage in, their current grade, their career choices, as well as whether they had ever done a service-learning project. At this time I also tried to contact the local elementary school for teachers willing to allow my class to present to theirs. I sent out a letter to the parents describing the project as well as how it was to be graded, with field trip permission forms so that students could leave campus. I also asked for parent volunteers to accompany us to and from the school.

The peer teaching project consisted of students, in groups of four, being assigned a particular classification of animal, plant, protist, or bacteria group. The students were then to research their group and collect a variety of resources to be used to create a fact sheet, from which they developed a fictional story with characters that would teach the reader about the class of animal, plant, protist, or bacteria. The story had to be entertaining, with many pictures, so that elementary students could understand it. The group also developed a game or quiz activity for the younger students to participate in that also taught about its animal, plant, protist, or bacteria. The students brought with them actual touchable examples of their animal, plant, protist, or bacteria (examples included live snakes, turtles, birds, lobsters, bacteria plates, seaweed, fruits, leaves, and preserved animals in jars). My students then worked on their projects for two and a half weeks. I allowed the groups to pick their own groups of four students so that students would be able to choose people they got along with and knew would help and collaborate on the project. I assigned to them which animal, plant, protist, or bacteria they would work on. I created checkpoints or dates that certain parts of the project had to be completed by. I also scheduled class time for students to go to the media center and computer lab to do research. I allowed for class time to work on the project each day, while still continuing with normal class time. Three days before the class was to present to the elementary students, they demonstrated their projects to each other, allowing time for peer feedback as well as my input. Students then had time to adjust projects before the presentation date. Students then presented their projects to the elementary students in several small groups. The elementary students gave feedback to the middle school students right after the projects. My students then had to write reflection papers on the process, implementation, and their feelings after they completed the projects. They filled out the postservice questionnaire two weeks later. I tallied up the results and wrote a reflection paper/conclusion on the project in the form of a question-and-answer format.

## Methodology

- Preservice questionnaire
- Postservice questionnaire
- Actual finished projects and observations on presentations
- Peer feedback (verbal)
- Elementary students' feedback (written and verbal)
- Parent feedback (verbal)
- Student reflection papers
- Teacher reflection

## Data and Results

1. Based on the pre/post attitudes toward science questionnaire and my personal observations, my students' attitudes toward science and their grades increased for my entire class and especially for my few non-White students. The following information for my entire class has non-White students' data in parentheses. Before the project, 14% (14%) of the class strongly disliked science, 22% (57%) disliked science, 36% (14%) neither liked nor disliked science, 22% (14%) liked science, and 6% (0%) strongly liked science. After the project, 0% (0%) strongly disliked science, 6% (0%) disliked science, 43% (57%) neither liked nor disliked science, 39% (29%) liked science, and 12% (14%) strongly liked science. In addition to the survey data, their reflective journals and discussions with other students suggested a very positive and empowering experience. Their most common responses from their reflections were: "This project was a lot of fun!" and "This was a very good learning experience for us and the children we tutored."
2. Their grades were as follows (non-White data in parentheses): before the project A—34% (14%), B—18% (0%), C—30% (57%), D—12% (29%), F—6% (0%). After the project the grades improved to A—72% (71%), B—16% (29%), C— 4% (0%), D—0% (0%), F—8% (0%).
3. Although all my students made significant gains in both achievement in and attitudes toward science, these gains were largest for White students in achievement in science and for non-White students in attitudes toward science. One possible explanation for these differences might be that non-White students typically do not have opportunities to take leadership roles in presenting to other students (thus greater gains). White students typically do better in tests of academic achievement in some cases due to better language proficiency required on tests.
4. Additional data, provided by the reflections and observations of the teacher, also supported gains in attitudes and achievement. Successes and challenges of the project and recommendations for future years are also noted.

## Conclusions and Implications

### *Successes*

- ✓ Overall attitudes toward class and science improved.
- ✓ Science grades improved.
- ✓ Students were excited to participate and present. They had fun and enjoyed themselves.
- ✓ They learned much about their subject matter, meeting my goals and expectations for learning.
- ✓ The children they were working with learned and were also excited about the subject matter.

### *Challenges: How They Were Addressed*

- ✓ It was difficult at first to find classes willing to accept our class for the day. The other teachers' schedules are packed with reading and mathematics block time, with little time for other activities. After asking the schools for volunteers in general announcements and getting zero responses, I asked my own students whether they had siblings in elementary classes and who their teachers were. I then called those teachers directly to ask their permission to come to their classes. This worked but one teacher was bitter about saying yes and the other teacher was very excited. Next year I think I will ask only 2nd-grade teachers because the curriculum aligns better.
- ✓ Another challenge was groups working productively with one another. I tried to solve this by letting the students choose their own groups, and telling them ahead of time that they needed to choose groups in which people got along with one another and were willing to work for the greater good of the group. Still some groups did not get along and were mad at a few members for not doing their share.

### *Professional Learning*

- ✓ I think doing service-learning projects in the classroom is extremely valuable and necessary. It is an overwhelmingly positive experience for everyone involved and makes learning fun and applicable to the real world.
- ✓ I could feel the excitement in the air when we were getting ready to make our presentations to the children at the elementary school. Students who were usually complacent and negative were excited and happy.
- ✓ I think this really shows kids how they can make a difference in the world around them as well as makes them feel more connected to the community.
- ✓ Hopefully this will lead the way for volunteerism and community service for these kids in the future.

### *Unexpected Benefits*

- ✓ Some students were much more excited about participating and learning during this project than any other time in class, and that made a world of difference in their attitudes toward this class and science.
- ✓ I think this project made the students feel important and empowered.
- ✓ Some students mentioned how they liked teaching others and might now consider a teaching profession. Others commented on how hard teaching is and that they think I have a really hard job.

### *Recommendations*

- ✓ Get in contact with an elementary school and particular teachers, hopefully within walking distance, early.
- ✓ Have students fill out a permission slip because they will be walking off campus.
- ✓ Have parent volunteers accompany you there and back again.

- ✓ Make time during class to check progress on the project. Have checkpoints that students should complete by certain times.
- ✓ Allow class time for students to demonstrate their projects to the whole class with feedback before the students present to the elementary children. That way they can fix or change aspects of their presentation to make it better for the younger kids. Feedback heard in class included: "You need to make the material more understandable to 2nd graders," "You need to edit your story and make it shorter, or clearer, or more about the animal group," and "You did a great job."
- ✓ Make the project worth many points so the students feel the importance of the project.
- ✓ Allow plenty of time for developing all parts of the project.
- ✓ Go to the computer lab or media center to allow time for students to research the project.
- ✓ Let the students grade each other on participation and work done in the class, because they know better than anybody who did the most work and the least.
- ✓ Make sure they write a reflection piece after they have finished the project so they process what they have done, and how their project has made or not made an impact on themselves and/or others.
- ✓ Have fun with this!

### *Student Growth*

- ✓ Empowerment of their own learning and the learning of others.
- ✓ Most of the class's grades improved.
- ✓ Their attitudes toward science improved.
- ✓ They developed a greater sense of community.
- ✓ They improved communication skills and writing skills.
- ✓ They learned a great deal about their subject matter.

### *Gains Students Made in Their Student Achievement Levels*

- ✓ The preservice questionnaire showed that 36% of students in my classes had a dislike of science before the project compared with only 6% after the project.
- ✓ Grades improved after the project. Before the project, the grade breakdown was as follows: A—34%, B—18%, C—30%, D—12%, F—6%. After the project, overall grades improved to A—72%, B—16%, C—4%, D—0%, and F—8%.

***Final Thoughts.*** I would recommend this project. This is just the beginning for me when it comes to the use of service-learning and action research. My classes as well as the ELD science class are going on a field trip to the beach to learn about the watershed, pollution, and tide pools. We will also be doing a beach cleanup and learning about various careers in the field of marine biology, the water district, and other water-related careers. I expect this trip to be equally successful in bolstering student achievement and attitudes toward science.

# Instructional Resource D

## Sample Unit Plans

### SAMPLE UNIT PLAN 1 NUCLEAR CHEMISTRY

**Step 1:** State the grade level(s), content area/class, and unit topic and length.
Grade level: 10th–12th grade
Content area: Chemistry
Unit topic: Nuclear Chemistry
Unit length: 7.5 days × 2-hour block

**Step 2:** Decide what key facts about your students you need to take into consideration as you plan.

*Student Characteristics*

- 27 students, 15 male and 12 female.
- Some students are college-bound.
- Most students are disengaged with the subject and lack internal motivation for studying chemistry. Nearly all students fail to see the usefulness of the subject outside of the classroom, so that the few students who are self-motivated are working hard only to get a passing grade.
- 2 ELLs.
- 0 IEP.
- Because few students have an interest in the subject itself, the focus of the classroom is social; students are talkative, gregarious, and eager to argue and discuss. Three or four students are quiet and withdrawn, including the two ELLs. Two students are high achievers; another three are not reaching their potential.
- Generally, students in the class seem comfortable with each other and with the classroom environment. Everyone's names are known and used by all students; each student has worked with every other student previously during the year; students have invested in their classroom's governance, with the result that students feel safer to share and make public mistakes in this classroom than in most of their other classes.

*Learning Needs and Considerations for Instruction*

- Engage interest of students by framing learning around real-life experiences and issues and by involving students in open-ended problem solving.
- Refer when appropriate to learning done in other classes, particularly social studies (historical examples) and biology.
- Prepare college-bound students for future courses by providing foundational learning that will establish schemata that may be filled in detail later.
- Provide students who may take extra exams (AP, SAT II, etc.) for college or who have special interests with supplemental resources.
- Encourage all students to pursue further (science) education and careers by showing them how their foundational knowledge has exciting implications for higher level science.
- Take care to provide foundational instruction with difficult concepts and vocabulary before the assigned reading, which will be particularly beneficial for ELL students; use

Specifically Designed Academic Instruction in English (SDAIE) strategies including advanced and graphic organizers, photographs, models, diagrams, and so forth.

- Engage students in cooperative learning to build models, solve problems, conduct research, and so on. Assign specific roles and tasks to each student member of the group to ensure that every student participates and contributes.
- Permit students to express their learning achievements in a variety of ways.
- Allow for student choice when possible to foster independent learning, self-governance, and a sense of control over their own education.

**Step 3:** Explain your rationale for this topic/unit.

The topic of nuclear chemistry gives students an opportunity to explore, form, and express their opinions about the use of nuclear technology, having become more informed on the pure and applied sciences and the related human issues involved when manipulating nuclear chemistry. Students will, hopefully, develop an appreciation for the profound social, economic, and political changes that so-called advancements in science may launch.

Students will also continue to learn to solve open-ended problems in cooperative small groups, a valuable skill in the workplace and in other real-life situations.

Finally, this topic will prepare students for state examinations, other standardized tests, and higher courses in the physical sciences.

**Step 4:** Identify both the specific goals and objectives for the unit (cognitive, affective, psychomotor, word) and how they align with state and district curriculum standards. Explain the critical concepts.

*Unit Goals*

(Cognitive = C; Affective = A; Psychomotor = P; Word = W)

After completing the unit, students will be able to:

1. Describe the composition of an atom's nucleus; name the subnuclear particles and their role in the nucleus; write the nuclide formula using chemical symbols, the atomic number $Z$, and the mass number $A$. (C and W)
2. Describe using formulas and words the three common types of radioactive decay ($\alpha$, $\beta$, $\gamma$). (C and W)
3. Define half-life in the vernacular and in scientific, technical jargon, and complete calculations using the half-life formula. (C and W)
4. Describe the nuclear changes that occur in fusion and fission reactions. (C)
5. Understand that nuclei may be transformed from one atom to another. (C)
6. Calculate the change in mass and energy of a nuclear reaction. (C)
7. List several of the effects of exposure to nuclear radiation. (C)
8. List several uses of nuclear reactions. (C)
9. Research in small cooperative groups one of the uses of nuclear reactions, synthesize information and opinions from several sources, and form a position for or against this particular use of nuclear energy. (A and C)
10. In groups, orally and visually present positive or negative arguments for this particular use of nuclear energy. (A and P)
11. Describe at least one way that manipulation of nuclear energy has initiated social, economic, and political changes in the world. (A and C)

*State Content Standards*

a. Nuclear processes are those in which an atomic nucleus changes, including radioactive decay of naturally occurring and human-made isotopes, nuclear fission, and nuclear fusion. As a basis for understanding this concept:

b. Students know protons and neutrons in the nucleus are held together by nuclear forces that overcome the electromagnetic repulsion between the protons.

c. Students know the energy release per gram of material is much larger in nuclear fusion or fission reaction than in chemical reactions. The change in mass (calculated by $E = mc^2$) is small but significant in nuclear reactions.

d. Students know some naturally occurring isotopes of elements are radioactive, as are isotopes formed in nuclear reactions.

e. Students know the three most common forms of radioactive decay (alpha, beta, and gamma) and know how the nucleus changes in each type of decay.
f. Students know alpha, beta, and gamma radiation produce different amounts and kinds of damage in matter and have different penetrations.
g. Students know how to calculate the amount of a radioactive substance remaining after an integral number of half-lives have passed.
h. Students know protons and neutrons have substructures and consist of particles called quarks.

**Step 5:** Assessments/evidence to demonstrate success of unit goals and attainment of benchmarks.

**(Summative = S; Formative = F)**

| Assessment | Objective Covered |
|---|---|
| Daily journal assignments (F) | 1–8, 11, a–g |
| Problem set (due at end of unit) (S) | 1–8, 11, a–g |
| Reading notes (due at end of unit) (S) | 1–8, 11, a–g |
| Mini-exam (S) | 1–8, 11, a–g |
| Observation (F) | 5, 9–11, g |
| End-of-unit reflection (S) | 10, 11 |
| Construction of clay models of atomic nuclei and radiation (F) | 1, 2, a, g |
| Allegorical cartoon (children's story, short story, video, skit, etc.) of nuclear fusion and fission (F) | 1, 4, d |
| Half-life activity (F) | 3, f |
| Research in small cooperative groups one of the uses of nuclear reactions, synthesize information and opinions from several sources, and form a position for or against this particular use of nuclear energy. (S) | 9 |
| In groups, orally and visually present positive or negative arguments for this particular use of nuclear energy. (S) | 10 |
| Student self-reflection (F) | 9, 10 |
| Reflective quick write (F) | 7–11 |

**Step 6:** Teaching and learning experiences; the knowledge, skills, and scaffolds students need to meet the expectations you have set.

*A. INTO.* To introduce the topic of nuclear chemistry and to assess what prior knowledge and attitudes the students have about it, I plan to engage my students in a gallery walk showcasing some of the more publicized episodes of nuclear chemistry in use from the twentieth century. I am interested to see whether students will make the connection between Bruce Banner, carbon dating, and the Manhattan Project. I am concerned that students will not have enough background knowledge to contribute to the gallery walk, so I will have words, pictures, and perhaps even brief articles or texts ready to go along with each of the pieces. If the students are too frustrated, and the lesson's outlook is bleak, I can add some background information or remind them of the instance, just so that they will know enough to be able to interact with the lesson. At the end of the period, we will spend 5 to 10 minutes as a class discussing the gallery walk, so that students may ask questions that they might have and so that the class can correct gross misinterpretations of the subjects (e.g., "Bikini atoll is where they make and tax swimwear"). I will not do complete and overwhelming follow-up on the elements of the gallery walk; we will refer to these subjects throughout the unit and will come back to these at the end of the unit via group research and position presentations. I will distribute the posters made at the beginning to the groups working on that topic for them to refer to and correct.

The gallery walk lesson should take 30 to 40 minutes, allowing time for students to spend a few minutes writing at several different stations and for students to read other students' contributions. It will take place during the second portion of a block period, the first half of which will be spent concluding the previous unit. At the end of the lesson, I will assign the unit's problem set and reading from the text. (Because I plan to make these assignments common to each unit, the students will understand already what is expected of them. The problem set is a collection of exercises from the text that will reflect calculations encountered on standardized tests and the end-of-unit exam. For the reading assigned, students are to take notes in any way that is meaningful and useful to them and store these in their notebooks. The intent of these two assignments is to promote development of reading skills, significant interaction with the text, and practice completing calculations using key concepts. The assignments also give students who are not good test takers an opportunity to succeed.)

B. *THROUGH.* See the unit calendar. The lessons are meant to be quick and brief, skimming over mere formulas while reinforcing major concepts (including vocabulary) and life application.

C. *BEYOND.* I will use three lessons to close the unit. We will spend the first half of the second-to-last period (5/26) taking a closed-book mini-exam students' ability to explain major concepts, use vocabulary properly, demonstrate appropriate symbol conventions, and manipulate formulas successfully that will assess. Although it is a low-level thinking assignment, the mini-exam will reflect exercises practiced daily in class and will reinforce behaviors demonstrated during standardized tests. The goal of this mini-exam is not to stump students but to emphasize basic, key scientific concepts that provide the foundation for higher thinking.

During the second half of this period (5/26), students will share their allegorical cartoons in peer groups of four or five students. Peer groups, given a detailed rubric, will evaluate each project based on its scientific accuracy, thoroughness, and creativity, and the outstanding projects from each group will be presented to the entire class (if time permits).

The final lesson of the unit (5/28) will consist of the groups' presentations of their findings and positions regarding the use of nuclear technology, past and present. Each presentation will last 5 to 10 minutes and must include scientific data, oral contributions from each member, and a visual element (PowerPoint, if available). Students will write self-evaluations at the end of their presentations regarding their contributions and participation in the groups. During the presentations, students will take notes on what their classmates say; students will use these in a reflective writing quick write at the end of the period in which they will evaluate positions for and against the use of nuclear technology. Students may also write about how their attitudes have changed or remained the same since the beginning of the unit. I would like to remain flexible during the following class period to respond, if necessary, to the content of these quick writes; students may be disturbed by some of the images presented or discussed in class or encountered during their research, and I want to be able to debrief with them as a class if necessary before moving on to the next unit. Possible topics for discussion might include depictions of nuclear reactions in pop culture and their (in)accuracy and journalistic purpose/bias.

**Step 7:** Materials and resources.

*Classroom Supplies*

Dry-erase markers/chalk
10 poster-size sheets
40 markers
Tape, staples, or pushpins
Overhead projector, transparencies, water-soluble pens
Plain white paper
Colored pencils and/or markers
Rulers

Index cards in three colors with nine different stickers on them
Clay in at least three colors
Wire

*Technology*

CD player and horizon-expanding mood music
Television and VCR
Computer with projector or TV display
Slide show (PowerPoint presentations) for "Effects of Radiation" and "Radiation in Astronomy"

*Media*

Textbooks in classroom
Archeology/anthropology and carbon dating video
"Atomic Cafe" video
Photographs:
- X-ray
- Marie Curie
- Manhattan Project staff
- Atomic explosion mushroom cloud
- Bomb shelter
- Radiation poisoning victims (PG-13)
- Radiation therapy patient
- Chernobyl disaster
- San Onofre power plant
- Radiation map from outer space

Diagram:
- Quarks (subnuclear structure)
- Nuclear structure

Articles:
- Radioactive markers in cancer therapies (*Scientific American*)
- Personal account of Hiroshima/Nagasaki bombing

Computer simulation of nuclear reactions (fusion, fission, and radiation)
Handouts:
- Unit syllabus and problem set
- Advanced organizer for archeology/anthropology and carbon dating video
- Advanced organizer for "Atomic Cafe" video
- Half-life activity
- Allegorical cartoon assignment description and rubric
- Group research presentation description and rubric
- Mini-exam
- Self-evaluation forms

Personnel:
- Guest speaker from San Onofre nuclear power plant

**Step 8:** Design lesson plans (samples available in Instructional Resource E).
**Step 9:** Self-assessment and reflection.

When I began this unit plan, I was not prepared for how much I would struggle and how much I would learn while completing it. I imagined that it would be a fun experience, which it was, with a lot of brainstorming and daydreaming about how my classroom would look and how my students would respond to different lessons, and I relished the enormity of the challenge. But I was surprised by how complicated the planning became. Just adding in a single objective halfway through forced me to move the calendar around, find new assessments, adjust the grading system, and tailor a new teaching method to the content. I was especially challenged to make the classroom student-centered, truly identifying with Joe's warning that "science teachers get so excited about their subject that they just want to tell their students all the secrets." What made this particularly difficult was that I had chosen a unit topic that was very theoretical and abstract, thinking that I had made a wise choice because it could be such a short unit. Unfortunately, no high school laboratory would be equipped to complete any sort of hands-on experiment with nuclear chemistry, so I was forced to find other ways to make the lessons hands-on and visual. I spent quite a bit of time trying to scaffold the readings for students. Relevance to the students was another element that consumed much of my attention and was sometimes a boon, sometimes a curse. Although students would recognize the atomic bomb's signature explosion, as I had predicted, only a few would really be interested in discovering how so much devastating energy could be produced from a single atom.

Despite these problems, and perhaps because of them, I am relatively satisfied with my unit plan as it exists today. Students have many opportunities to learn and to display their learning using different skills, including creativity; students must read, write, speak, and listen frequently and work together; a balance of authentic and traditional assessments exists; I have broken down long and tedious block days into manageable and quick-paced chunks; student learning relates to prior knowledge and real-life application, with an interdisciplinary bent; there are plenty of opportunities for students to teach each other and learn from each other, as well as to direct themselves at high and low levels; and I've incorporated elements of critical thinking and social activism.

I am sure, however, that there are weaknesses in the plans. I suspect, for example, that I have poorly estimated the amount of class time required to complete the activities and that I am overwhelming students with the sundry applications of nuclear technology. I am not sure whether I have enough means to assess student learning, and I fear that students will not be prepared for low-level-thinking tests. While teaching this unit, I would closely monitor formative assessments (i.e., daily journal entries) to check for student learning and modify my strategies appropriately; the summative mini-exam at the end of the instruction would also reveal whether or not students were adequately prepared for standardized exams. Reading the class's reflective quick writes on the concluding day would tell me what students were going to take away from the unit. In any case, I would most certainly ask an experienced teacher whose opinion I respect to review my unit plan before putting it into play, and I would ask that teacher to observe my class if possible so that I could have feedback from another educator. I am definitely looking forward to student teaching in the spring and am hoping that, if I am placed in a chemistry classroom, I can make use of at least part of this unit plan.

## Sample Unit Plan 2 *The Taming of the Shrew*

**Step 1:** State the grade level(s), content area/class, and unit topic and length.

Grade level: 10th grade

Content area: English/Language Arts

Unit topic: *The Taming of the Shrew*

Unit length: 11 block periods, 2 hours each; 22 total hours

**Step 2:** Decide what key facts about your students you need to take into consideration as you plan.

*Facts About the Learners*

- Number of students: 18 (9 girls, 9 boys)
- Number of ELLs: 5
- Number of IEPs: 0

*Student Characteristics*

- Approximately half of the students remain unengaged and nonparticipatory during class.
- Most of the students are fairly gregarious and enjoy group work.
- Two students display an intense desire to learn and are eager to participate, one showing more cognitive strengths, the other more affective.
- One of the ELLs, who is in a mainstream English class for the first time, never participates in class discussions and does not talk with his classmates but displays great attention to detail in drawing.
- A few students, one of them an ELL, display difficulty staying on task. One of these students has a tendency to disrupt neighboring classmates but also displays an energetic, theatrical, and creative personality.

*Learning Needs and Considerations for Instruction*

- Determine prior knowledge and applicable skills for reading and understanding Shakespeare; review where necessary.
- Give explicit direction for all activities, including objectives, expectations, and roles in group work. Speak clearly, model when appropriate, and point to visual prompts.
- Group students by abilities, partnering ELLs and those who struggle with those who have demonstrated high levels of skill and confidence in reading, writing, and group activities.
- Use SDAIE strategies including, but not limited to, advanced and graphic organizers, paraphrasing techniques, and other visual and audio assistance.
- Give extra one-on-one assistance to ELLs, especially the recently mainstreamed student.
- Connect to real-world experiences whenever possible.
- Allow for student voice and creativity as much as possible.
- Provide rubrics to help students understand specific expectations for writing and group assignments.
- Give options for further exploration and knowledge, such as books, articles, and Internet sites.

**Step 3:** Explain your rationale for this topic/unit.

*The Taming of the Shrew* provides challenging text for students to explore the nature and meaning(s) of sexism (including reverse sexism). By comparing and contrasting Elizabethan times to modern-day American cultures, the play serves as a vehicle to deconstruct societal roles of men and women according to status and gender. Through close examination of the relationships between Baptista, Kate, and Bianca (father and daughters) and the relationships between Kate and Petruchio, and Bianca and Lucentio (two couples), *The Taming of the Shrew* allows readers to discuss multiple perspectives on the ideas of love and power within the context of family and marriage. *The Taming of the Shrew* also provides students with a theatrical avenue to develop various reading, listening, and speaking strategies and to work cooperatively.

**Step 4:** Identify both the specific goals and objectives for the unit (cognitive, affective, psychomotor, word) and how they align with state and district curriculum standards. Explain the critical concepts.

*Unit Goals*

After completing *The Taming of the Shrew* unit, students *w*ill *b*e *a*ble *t*o (SWBAT):

1. Read in iambic pentameter.
2. Define sexism and give examples from Elizabethan England, the play itself, and current American society.
3. Compare and contrast status and gender roles between Elizabethan times and today.
4. Understand how love and motivation affect personal change.
5. Work in small, cooperative groups to interpret Shakespearean verse.
6. Role-play characters, offering and defending opinions representing different points of view.

*State Content Standards*

*The Taming of the Shrew* goals address the following state standards:

- Listening and Speaking Strategies §1.7 (Use visual aids to enhance the appeal and accuracy of presentations.)
- Literary Response and Analysis §3.3 (Analyze interactions between main and subordinate characters in a literary text and explain the way those interactions affect the plot.)
- Literary Response and Analysis §3.4 (Determine characters' traits by what the characters say about themselves in dialogue.)
- Literary Response and Analysis §3.5 (Compare works that express a universal theme.)
- Speaking Applications §2.1c (Describe with concrete sensory details the sights, sounds, and smells of a scene and the specific actions, movements, gestures, and feelings of characters.)
- Speaking Applications §2.1d (Pace the presentation of actions to accommodate time or mood changes.)
- Speaking Applications §2.2b (Convey information and ideas from primary and secondary sources accurately and coherently.)

- Reading Comprehension §2.5 (Extend ideas presented in primary or secondary sources through original analysis, evaluation, and elaboration.)

*District Standards*

- *The Taming of the Shrew* addresses the following district standards:
- Students will possess the skills necessary to succeed in and contribute to a global society, including thinking critically; connecting, integrating, and applying learning; and working in small groups.
- Students will listen, comprehend, respond, and interact effectively through spoken language and artistic expression.

**Step 5:** Assessments/evidence to demonstrate success of unit goals and attainment of benchmarks.

- Observation of participation in whole-class discussion will be used to assess goals 2, 3, 4, and 6 (formative).
- Observation of participation in dyads, triads, and small, cooperative groups will be used to assess goals 1–6 (formative).
- Observation of a Socratic seminar will be used to assess goals 2, 3, 4, and 6 (formative).
- Observation of in-class read-alouds will be used to assess goals 1 (formative and summative) and 6 (formative).
- Group presentations will be used to assess goals 2 (formative) and 5 (summative).
- Group-produced newspapers will be used to assess goals 2–6 (summative).
- Quick writes will be used to assess goals 2–4 (formative).
- Journal writing will be used to assess goals 2, 3, 4, and 6 (formative).
- Character diaries will be used to assess goals 4 and 6 (formative).
- Essays will be used to assess goals 2, 3, 4, and 6 (summative).
- Peer review will be used to assess goal 5 (summative).
- Student self-evaluations through quick writes (formative) and end-of-unit grading rubric (summative) will be used to assess goals 1–6.
- Student written evaluations of teacher and lessons will be used to assess the effectiveness and relevance of goals 1–6 (summative).

**Step 6:** Teaching and learning experiences; the knowledge, skills, and scaffolds students need to meet the expectations you have set.

A. *INTO.* An overview of introductory lesson plans follows.

To hook students, I will attempt to paint Shakespeare's language as a form of rap and Shakespeare's plays as the Hollywood movies of that day. I will attempt to pull students in through humor in the form of a cartoon. I want students to see Shakespeare as fun and funny from the very beginning; I want to catch the attention of those who view Shakespeare as boring. The first lesson will serve as an introduction to Shakespeare. It will assess and build on students' prior knowledge of Shakespeare through a KWL chart and group presentations. At the onset, students will become the "teachers" in these presentations and hopefully gain enough confidence through quick acquisition of expert knowledge to help cushion the possible frustration of having to "read" Shakespeare.

The second lesson will introduce *The Taming of the Shrew* and its possible themes. I will attempt to pull students into the unit's rationale by hooking them with a riddle. The riddle will get students to consider the ways in which society has influenced and biased their thinking toward men and women. A list-group-label activity will then build on this thinking and start to develop a conception of the term *sexism* and its meaning(s). Discussion of the book's title and cover illustration will further build on the idea of sexism and also relate to students' prior knowledge of the intricacies of relationships through a connection to their previous unit on *Waiting for the Rain.* The students seemed very interested in the characters of Tengo and Frikkie, two close friends violently torn apart by apartheid. Hopefully, in getting students to view *The Taming of the Shrew* as a similar work of literature, one that addresses both the passion and angst in human relationships, I will hook them into the play. The second lesson will finally introduce the play's plot and allow students the freedom to creatively envision the characters through completion of storyboards (just like in Hollywood).

B. THROUGH.

| | | **Wednesday 11/13**<br>*Introduction to Shakespeare*<br>• Cartoon<br>• KWL chart<br>• Group presentations<br>• QW: Interesting facts/questions | | **Friday 11/15**<br>*Introduction to Shrew and Sexism*<br>• Riddle<br>• List-group-label<br>• Compare/contrast *Shrew* to *Waiting for the Rain*<br>• Plot synopsis<br>• Character map<br>• HW: *Shrew* storyboards |
|---|---|---|---|---|
| | **Tuesday 11/19**<br>*Introduction to Role-Playing*<br>• Induction Scenes—audio and discussion<br>• Act 1, Scene 1—reading, video, and discussion<br>• Four Square Vocab<br>• HW: Journal write: Essay on the "perfect" relationship/ marriage | | **Thursday 11/21**<br>*Let's Bicker and Banter*<br>• Act 1, Scene 2—reading, video, and discussion<br>• Act 2—synopsis, video, and discussion<br>• "Shout-out" of Shakespearean insults<br>• HW: Kate's or Petruchio's diary: "Dear Diary, when I first met [insert name], I thought . . . because . . ." | |
| **Monday 11/25**<br>*For Better or Worse*<br>• Act 3, Scene 1—synopsis, video, and discussion<br>• Act 3, Scene 2—video, reading, and discussion<br>• Poetry Theater: Poems in Two Voices<br>• HW: Continuation of character diary: "Dear Diary, what happened at the wedding today made me feel . . . because . . ." | | **Wednesday 11/27**<br>*Oh, What a Tangled Web We Weave*<br>• Pretenders' song and lyrics: *Thin Line Between Love and Hate*<br>• Act 4, Scenes 1–5—video<br>• Model rewriting lines from previous acts into modern English<br>• Work in jigsaw groups for Act 4, Scenes 1–5: rewriting Shakespeare<br>• HW: Continue rewriting | | **Friday 11/29**<br>NO SCHOOL |

(continued)

(*continued*)

| | | | | |
|---|---|---|---|---|
| | **Tuesday 12/3**<br>*And Still We Weave*<br>• Alice Walker poem: "Gift"<br>• Continuation of group work for Act 4: rewriting Shakespeare<br>• Explanation of student newspaper and division into new groups<br>• Library computer lab: basic lesson in Word for creating text boxes and inserting images; work on newspaper<br>• HW: Continue rewriting | | **Thursday 12/5**<br>*The Taming of the Shrew*<br>• Shakespeare sonnet<br>• Jigsaw performances of Act 4 in modern English<br>• Peer review<br>• Discussion of Act 4: Connections to sexism<br>• Library computer lab for work on newspaper<br>• HW: Continuation of character diary: "Dear Diary, somehow things seem different now because . . ." | |
| **Monday 12/9**<br>*And They Lived Happily Ever After?*<br>• Act 5, Scene 1—synopsis, video, and discussion<br>• Act 5, Scene 2—reading and video<br>• QW: Interpretation of Kate's speech on a wife's duties to her husband<br>• Library computer lab for work on newspaper<br>• HW: Complete self-evaluation | | **Wednesday 12/11**<br>*I Am Woman, Hear Me Roar*<br>• *Moonlighting*'s "Atomic Shakespeare" video<br>• Compare/contrast to play<br>• Kate's speech on video and discussion<br>• Discussion: Is the play sexist?<br>• Handout of final essay choices and discussion of essay writing with note taking<br>• HW: Finish newspaper | | **Friday 12/13**<br>*Extra! Extra! Read All About It!*<br>• Final essay exam<br>• Group presentations of newspapers<br>• Transition to *The Lord of the Flies*<br>• Student evaluation of teacher and unit |

C. *BEYOND.* An overview of closing lesson plans follows.

To create closure for the unit, my last two lesson plans will focus on determining whether or not *The Taming of the Shrew* is a sexist play. In the second-to-last lesson, students will watch the "Atomic Shakespeare" episode of the television series *Moonlighting*, which is a modern take on *The Taming of the Shrew*. The episode showcases the witty banter between Kate and Petruchio with a great deal of slapstick humor and clever puns; the episode won awards for its screenwriting.

The last lesson plan will allow students to show what they have learned in this unit through a short-essay exam and presentation of their student newspapers. The lesson will begin with the short-essay exam. Students will be required to answer two out of four possible choices for response. We will have already fully developed two of the questions during class discussions and writing assignments throughout the course of the unit, and the other two questions will be geared toward those students who might want to attempt a more critical analysis of the play and more complex connections to both historical and modern life. Also, students will be allowed to use all notes, as well as quick writes, journal and diary writing, and handouts in forming responses.

Next the lesson will move on to student newspapers, such as *The Padua Gazette* or *The Globe*. Students will come up with newspaper titles and will have worked in cooperative groups, creating their newspapers over the course of four lessons using Microsoft Word and the Internet. The newspapers will be set during Elizabethan times, and students will take on the role of different characters from *The Taming of the Shrew* to serve as staff writers and editors. They will write sections and columns from the characters' perspectives, which will consist of at least the following items: headline news, editorials, horoscopes, classifieds, and comics. Students may include additional sections with approval. Stories may cover issues of concern in Padua, as well as more global events (no pun intended). Students may choose to compare Elizabethan England to its neighboring countries at the time, for example. I will encourage creativity.

*TRANSITION.* In discussing the conflicts between Kate and Petruchio over the course of the last two or three lessons, I will transition into the next unit, *The Lord of the Flies* (and grammar), by discussing how relationships shift and develop into new "creations" through motivation of character. For example, with the boys in *The Lord of the Flies*, roles change, moods change, and emotions get played out to the extreme. I will briefly connect *The Lord of the Flies* to the television show *Survivor*. I will also connect back to Tengo and Frikkie in *Waiting for the Rain.*

**Step 7:** Materials and resources.

*Main Text*

- Shakespeare, W. (1992). *The taming of the shrew.* (Eds. B. A. Mowat & P. Werstine.) The New Folger Library Edition. New York: Washington Square Press.

*Supplemental Texts*

- Dictionaries
- Newspapers
- Bernards, N., & O'Neill, T. (Eds.). (1989) *Male/female roles: Opposing viewpoints.* San Diego: Greenhaven Press.
- Doyle, J., & Lischner, R. (1999). *Shakespeare for dummies.* New York: Hungry Minds.
- Egendorf, L. K. (Ed.). (2000). *Elizabethan drama.* The Greenhaven Press Companion to Literary Movements and Genres. San Diego: Greenhaven Press.
- Epstein, N. (1993). *The friendly Shakespeare: A thoroughly painless guide to the best of the bard.* New York: Penguin Books.
- Fleischman, P. (1993). *Joyful noise: Poems for two voices.* New York: HarperCollins.
- Maurer, K., PhD. (2001). *Cliffs Notes Shakespeare's the taming of the shrew.* Foster City: IDG Books Worldwide.
- Mushat Frye, R. (1967). *Shakespeare's life and times: A pictorial record.* Princeton: Princeton University Press.
- Schoenbaum, S. (1979). *Shakespeare: The globe and the world.* New York: Oxford University Press in association with the Folger Shakespeare Library.

*Video*

- Atomic Shakespeare. (1986). *Moonlighting.* ABC/Circle Films.
- The taming of the shrew. (1976). *Great performances: Theater in America.* Thirteen/WNET.

*Audio*

- *The taming of the shrew.* (1998). Ark Angel Productions.
- The Pretenders. (1984). *Thin line between love and hate.* WEA Records Ltd.

*Poetry*

- Shakespeare sonnet

- Walker, A. (1973). Gift. *Revolutionary petunias and other poems.* New York: Harcourt Brace Jovanovich.

*Cartoon*

- Tennant, R. The 5th wave. www.the5thwave.com.

*Handouts*

- KWL Chart on William Shakespeare
- Shakespeare Jigsaw Excerpts with information and illustrations excerpted from the following authors: Doyle and Lischner, Egendorf, Epstein, Mushat Frye, and Schoenbaum
- Character Map from Cliffs Notes
- Four Square Vocabulary
- Shakespearean Insults
- Model diary entry
- Poems in Two Voices
- Pretenders' *Thin Line Between Love and Hate* lyrics
- Rewriting Shakespeare into Modern English
- Alice Walker's poem "Gift"
- Peer review form
- Student newspapers
- Model of short essay

*Overheads*

- Cartoon
- KWL Chart
- List-Group-Label
- Character Map
- *Shrew* storyboards and sample *Midsummer*'s storyboard
- Four Square Vocabulary
- Poem in Two Voices
- Peer review form
- Model of short essay

*Computer Resources*

- Microsoft Word (for creation of student newspapers)
- Google search engine (for creation of student newspapers)
- Internet sites:

  *For Lesson Plan*

  *Shrew Culture, Myths, Folklore, Stories and Poisonous Facts*. (2002). Retrieved November 5, 2002, from http://members.vienna.at/shrew/culture&myths.html.

  *For Optional Student Exploration*

  *Mr. William Shakespeare and the Internet*. (2002). Retrieved November 5, 2002, from http://shakespeare.palomar.edu

*Supplies*

- Art markers, pencils, colored pencils, poster paper (for presentations)
- Playing cards, colored sticks, student index cards (for class participation and grouping students)

**Step 8:** Design lesson plans (samples available in Instructional Resource E).

**Step 9:** Self-assessment and reflection.

In reflecting upon my unit plan, I think my initial efforts have produced a unit that can be successful in getting students interested and engaged in Shakespeare; however, it is difficult for me to clearly recognize the strengths and possible limitations at this point or the extent to which students will actually become interested and engaged. I know experience in the classroom with this unit will be the true test, but if I had to picture where my unit's strengths may lie, I think they might be in the variety of instruction, focus on discussion around characters and themes (as opposed to more of a focus on the facts of the plot and sequence of events), and use of SDAIE strategies. I have included activities that appeal to the various learning styles and multiple intelligences. For example, I am using both audio and videotapes to accompany in-class reading, and a range of activities to engage auditory, visual, and tactile learners, including reading out loud, performing scenes, using props, rewriting scenes, listening and connecting to music and poetry, and creating artwork and news pieces. I will offer further reading and Internet sites for exploration to meet the needs of high achievers.

In various group projects and activities, I will also pair high achievers with those who may struggle in order to better enhance all students' learning and their overall understanding of Shakespeare. In addition, I will pair those students who excel in the affective arena with those more introverted students in order to gently coax students into participating and hopefully increase their sense of achievement and boost their confidence. Finally, I also think my unit will meet the needs of ELLs through SDAIE strategies, such as modification, modeling, bridging, and contextualization, and will actively engage both the cognitive and affective spheres; however, only time and assessments will determine the degree of success and whether or not these two spheres have balanced out on my scale of social justice.

As far as my unit's limitations are concerned, I am sure there are many lurking in the murky waters beneath my surface efforts. I say surface efforts because I would estimate that it takes three or more years of trial and error before most of the kinks can be worked out of any unit plan. If I were to guess what my unit plan's limitations may be this first time around, I would have to say pacing and accurately hitting Vygotsky's zone of proximal development. Because I am actually student teaching this unit, I will have the luxury of testing both its limitations and its strengths in the near future, while the pains of planning are still fresh in my memory. I will evaluate the effectiveness of my lessons through daily conversations with my master teacher, self-notes written during class on my lesson plans, and reflections in writing; and I will evaluate my unit's overall effectiveness through student self-evaluations, teacher evaluations, and the end-of-the-unit essays and student newspapers.

In consideration of the aforementioned, I would determine where and what to change in my unit plan for the next time around. In the teacher evaluations, I will be certain to ask for student suggestions and feedback on ways I can improve. I will also periodically ask students whether they are enjoying the activities, whether the ideas and topics of discussion are making sense, and whether there is anything they can think of for me to add to or improve the lessons.

# Instructional Resource E

## Sample Lesson Plans

### SAMPLE LESSON PLAN 1 BUILD AN ANIMAL

Title: Build an Animal
Subject area: Science
Grade level: 10th grade

#### Lesson Goal

Inquiry is a focus of the lesson with the question: What characteristics does an animal need to be well suited to its environment? The students should gain understanding of how individual organisms adapt and relate to an environment. By picking a real biome and environment, the "animal" that the students create needs to match all of its life systems to a particular area.

#### Standards

Biological evolution, Interdependence of organisms, Behavior of organisms

#### Objectives

1. DESIGN a hypothetical animal that could live in a particular environment and CONSTRUCT a model of it.
2. CLASSIFY your animal into a phylum of animals.
3. INFER which anatomical structures and features would help the animal to survive in the environment.

#### Concept

The diversity of organisms on Earth is staggering. However, all organisms have an important characteristic, the ability to survive in a particular environment. In order to survive, each must have certain adaptations in terms of anatomy and behavior that are suited to the environment.

#### Materials Needed

Colored paper, string, colored clay, pins, straw, buttons, or other materials. Be creative in assembling your animal but DO NOT use materials that will spoil or bring ants.

#### Anticipatory Set

What is the strangest looking animal you have ever seen? How do you think it got that way? This project will give you a chance to go Mother Nature one better. Using the information you know about ecology and evolutionary adaptations, you are to create the strangest looking animal that ever "could" be on Earth. Be creative, let your imagination flow, and have fun.

## Procedures

1. Review information on biomes (land and water), classification of animals, and adaptations needed to survive in each environment.
2. Select an environment for your animal and decide what adaptations the animal would have and record it on a data record.
3. Decide what the animal would look like and sketch a picture of the animal.
4. Name the animal using proper genus and species format and classify it in a REAL (appropriate) phylum.
5. Describe the animal's behavior, including the way it obtains food, the kind of dwelling it lives in, reproduction, its defensive behavior, and how it moves and gets oxygen. Record all this information.
6. Use any materials to create a model of your animal. This is where you need to be creative! The stranger the animal the better as long as it lives in a real biome and has adaptations suited to that area.
7. Answer the analysis questions and write a conclusion. The model of the animal as well as the report is due in _____ weeks.
8. On the day you bring your animal to class, be prepared to write about another student's model and where it might live (see assessment 4).

Adaptations for students should be on a case-by-case basis. The important focus should be creating a hypothetical animal that could live in a real environment and be named in a real phylum.

Extensions for gifted students could include creating a story about the life of this animal and the future it may face.

## Assessment

### Short Paper

1. DESCRIBE the specific physical conditions that exist in your animal's environment including climate and land forms (temperature, wind, rain, soil, and sunshine).
2. For each of the conditions mentioned, describe a characteristic of your animal that makes it well suited to the environment.
3. State the characteristics that enable you to CLASSIFY the animal in the phylum you selected.
4. On the basis of what you saw when you looked at another student's animal model, formulate a HYPOTHESIS about the environment to which the animal is adapted. EXPLAIN your answer.

## Conclusion/Closure

Remember to summarize what environment your animal lives in and adaptations your animal has to help it exist.

## Assessment Based on Objectives

1. Points assigned to grading rubric may be as the teacher desires. Partial points for the construction of the animal and partial points for the report.
2. Design, construct, classify, and infer are the main objectives.

## Follow-Up

Utilizing independent practice, you are to create your animal and describe your biome on your own time. Remember no materials that will rot (fresh food) or draw ants. Do not copy another student's animal; each one must be unique.

## Reflections

In this particular case students will understand content knowledge related to adaptation and classification and then have to apply that knowledge to an "original" animal. Students would benefit from examples and models from former students because this "jump" to a higher order thinking skill may need scaffolding.

# Sample Lesson Plan 2 Applications of Nuclear Chemistry

Title: Applications of Nuclear Chemistry
Subject area: Chemistry
Grade level: 10th–11th grade

## Lesson Goal

Use a gallery walk model for students to develop the major concepts of nuclear chemistry and how they apply in the world.

## Standards

This lesson will provide background and foundational knowledge for state standards (California) in chemistry related to nuclear chemistry (11) a–g.

## Objectives

Upon completing this lesson, SWBAT:

- Relate each of 10 topics related to nuclear chemistry to their own personal experience or existing schemata.
- Know that each of the 10 topics discussed in the gallery walk are related to each other under the umbrella of nuclear chemistry.
- Identify at least three ways in which nuclear chemistry has made an impact on the "real world" (these might include both positive and negative impacts).

## Concept

The variety of ways that nuclear chemistry is applied (or has been applied) in both positive and negative ways.

## Materials Needed

- 10 poster-size sheets
- 40 markers (at least one per student)
- Photographs, diagrams, brief articles, or silent video of each of the 10 topics listed next
- CD player and mingling music

## Instructional Steps

### *Setup*

1. Before class starts, arrange 10 stations around the room at which a poster paper can be hung. (If there is enough white board space, this can be used in lieu of paper.) Also set up the CD player with mingle music.
2. While students are employed in the closure to the previous unit, unveil the photos of the 10 gallery stations: X-ray, Marie Curie, Manhattan Project staff, Atomic explosion mushroom cloud, Bomb shelter, Radiation poisoning victims (PG-13), Radiation therapy patient, Chernobyl disaster, San Onofre power plant, Radiation map from outer space. *10 min*

### *Into/Through*

3. Model free association thinking for and with students, brainstorming everything they know about a familiar image, such as George W. Bush or Mickey Mouse. Write down everything said aloud, without editing; call on students, several volunteers, and several quieter students, to collect their contributions while avoiding the auditory mayhem and inadvertent editing of "shout-out" answers. *5 min*
4. Pass out markers to students. Explain that they are to mill about—quietly enough that they can always hear the mingle music—until you stop the music. *2 min*
5. Begin the students' first run through the gallery walk by starting the music. Meanwhile, also wander around the room and make a mental note of students' egregious misunderstandings or lack of understanding. *10 min*
6. Stop the students, if necessary. Use this time to cross gross misinterpretations and to add extra information to the photos students seem to be "stuck on." Give verbal information, provide short articles, and so on as available. *5 min*
7. Allow students to continue. *7 min*

### *Beyond*

8. Stop students (by stopping music) and collect their markers as they go back to their seats. Have students look around the gallery; do they have any questions? What topic would they like to know more about? What is the common thread between the photos? *5 min*
9. Announce that the class is beginning a new unit on nuclear chemistry, which will relate to the issues and topics addressed in the gallery walk. Mention that, during the unit, the class will revisit these photographs to see how nuclear chemistry plays out in the world and the controversial issues associated with its use. Distribute the unit syllabus, with reading assignments and problem set. *3 min*

## Assessment

The teacher should assess informally as the students participate in the gallery walk and by a short discussion with the whole class.

*TOTAL 47 min*

## Reflections

In this type of lesson an introduction (or anticipatory set) to a unit is made whereby students will learn on a variety of levels. Students are actively involved and there is an emphasis on the audio-visual element to increase interest. Students not only are learning the content knowledge associated with nuclear chemistry but also are understanding how to apply it and are addressing a critical issue in science associated with the use and misuse of a science product from a social perspective.

# Instructional Resource F

## Examples of Cooperative Learning Projects

### Cooperative Learning Project Example 1
### Group Investigation: Solving an Energy Crisis

This is a case history of using technology in an 11th- and 12th-grade WebQuest project. In this interdisciplinary cooperative group project, students collaborated by using the Internet as their primary resource focus. The teacher directed the Internet search by providing students with selected powerful web sites. This type of student interaction with the Internet whereby the teacher guides the search is called a WebQuest. The teacher followed the group investigation model's six major stages of implementation for students as outlined by Sharan and Sharan (1992). The discussion about this example is in conjunction with these stages.

#### Stage I: Class Determines Subtopics and Organizes into Research Groups

During this stage, the teacher presented a broad problem to the whole class. In this case it related to the feasibility of using alternative forms of energy in southern California. Students had previously studied nonrenewable forms of energy and the impact of those sources on the environment. This project asked them to compare these to alternative forms.

The teacher had three main objectives for student teams in this project: (1) work in teams using the Internet to evaluate various forms of energy for use in southern California; (2) design, build, and explain a device that would use this form of energy; and (3) present the research results to a panel and the class using PowerPoint. All of these objectives were embedded in the problem posed by the teacher-created letter from a mythical energy company called Midwest Energy.

***Step One.*** The problem was posed in the form of a letter in which Midwest Energy was looking for a feasibility study on utilizing some form of alternative energy in southern California. The central question was, What form of alternative energy, in the form of a product, is most appropriate for southern California? Students had to consider these factors, though not in any particular order: cost to consumer versus production costs, environmental impact, production, and maintenance costs.

The teacher stimulated interest in the problem by a discussion of the impact of the energy cost spikes and blackouts in southern California, which triggered a renewed interest in alternative energy sources. Students brainstormed all the potential forms of alternative energy and self-selected into interest groups.

***Step Two.*** The teacher placed students into interest group teams of four to six, who brainstormed all the things they already knew about a particular form of alternative energy and all the things they believed they would need to know in order to solve the problem. They restated the problem by clarifying exactly what Midwest Energy wanted them to present, which finished product (and alternative energy source) they would produce, and what the necessary tasks were for the solutions.

***Step Three.*** Students created subtopics from questions that more clearly defined the task, such as (related to the product that will use the alternative energy source): What materials will we need to construct our product? What are the dimensions? What will it do? How much energy will it use? Who will the consumers be? What will be the cost to the consumer?

***Step Four.*** Students negotiated who would do what tasks and the time frame to finish it. They based the final determination on interest and skill in that area. Sometimes students paired up to work within the group on similar issues. At times the teacher had to facilitate the negotiation of tasks in the groups to ensure that the determination of roles included elements of equity and fairness. In this project the teacher brainstormed with the whole class, and by consensus it was determined that roles be assigned by expertise: (1) historian/culture expert (researched how this form of energy is being used in other parts of the country or world); (2) local expert (researched the suitability for use in this part of the country); (3) environmentalist (researched potential impact on local environment); (4) engineer (researched and designed a device that will use this energy source); and (5) market/media artist (designed a PowerPoint presentation that included reasons to select this device and alternative source, costs/profit margins, marketability, description/blueprint, and advertising potential).

## Stage II: Groups Plan Investigations

During this stage the teacher encouraged the groups to develop a task form (or group planning form) that clearly defined the tasks; listed individuals, noting who would be responsible to complete each of the tasks; and spelled out when it would be completed and what resources would be needed to complete the task. The teacher asked questions (as opposed to giving criticism or giving solutions) to stimulate or redirect students' thinking as suggested by Sharan and Sharan (1992). In this project the teacher had each team share the proposed plan from its task sheet with the whole class. This provided additional feedback for possible adaptations to each team's plan.

## Stage III: Groups Carry Out Their Investigations

The teacher listed specific Internet sites to explore as part of the WebQuest. The students, of course, were not limited to just these sites, nor to the Internet as the sole resource. Books, research journals, videos, experts in a variety of areas, and many other sources provided information in solving the problem.

The teacher's role was critical in facilitating ideas for possible sources of information and assisting students in how to organize the information, such as the use of outlines, graphic organizers, charts, summary statements, and diagrams. The teacher also asked students to document which sites they visited or resources they looked at and the value of each.

Teams and the whole class met regularly to share findings, ask questions, and assist each other in their tasks. The teacher built in some daily formative assessment (in progress checks) for an intermediate grade evaluation. This assisted students in making appropriate adjustments to their investigations and motivated them to stay on task. For example, they received intermediate grades on blueprints, logs, and task sheet completion forms.

## TABLE F.1 Assessment Rubric–Group Investigation Alternative Energy Sources WebQuest

| Activity | Level 4 Exemplary | Level 3 Very Good | Level 2 Satisfactory | Level 1 Minimal |
|---|---|---|---|---|
| 1. Use of technology | Uses Internet time exceptionally well. Makes extensive log notes about web sites that were useful. Locates several new resources in addition to those that were provided. | Uses Internet time well. Makes adequate log notes about web sites that were useful. Locates some new resources in addition to those that were provided. All records are well organized. | Internet log contains complete notes about web sites visited. All records are kept neatly. | Time on Internet is spent on task. Internet log is completed. |
| 2. Completion of individual task | Takes responsibility for whole project. Makes sure that individual task is coordinated with the whole. Shares own progress with others. Shows faultless quality of work. Completes all tasks within the time frame set by the class. Has excellent organization. | Helps others see how each contributes to the entire project. Shows work of high quality. Completes tasks within the time frame set by the class. Level of organization facilitates the work of others in the class. | Clearly sees how assigned task contributes to the whole. Work may have errors that are corrected by consulting with others. Level of organization does not interfere with the tasks of others. | Is aware of how assigned individual task fits in with the whole. Completes work in a timely manner. Does not hinder the work of others in the class. |
| 3. Teamwork | Provides vital leadership to the team. Gives and receives suggestions and/or help to/from other team members. Maintains a positive attitude. Contributes significantly to development and evaluation of finished product(s). | Helps to organize and facilitate the team. Encourages others. Stays on task. Meets deadlines. Contributes somewhat to development and evaluation of finished product(s). | Participates in discussions during development and evaluation of finished product(s). | Works well in group. Contributes to group effort. Does not try to take over group or do all the work alone. Observes development and evaluation of finished product(s). |
| 4. Journal entries | All assigned journal questions have complete and thoughtful responses. Documents original thoughts and/or questions many times. | More than half of the assigned journal questions have complete and/or thoughtful responses. There are some original entries. | Less than half of the assigned journal questions have complete or thoughtful responses. There are few original entries. | Brings journal to class daily and uses class journal time for journal writing. |

### Stage IV: Groups Plan Their Presentations

The presentation, in this case, was via PowerPoint (with backup hard copies) including oral input from each group member. In preparing for this, individual members needed to take an active role in the preparation of their parts of the PowerPoint as well as the oral presentation to the class. The team also had to consider time constraints and allotting time for questions from the audience as well as from Midwest Energy (invited energy experts).

### Stage V: Groups Make Their Presentations

The teacher believed that the appropriate formative evaluation of each team and its individual members helped ensure the success of the final presentations. It was also important to have an "active audience" during the presentations. Motivators ensured that students listened, learned, and asked good questions. In this case each member of the class received some general prompts as guides to evaluate the presentations. They were to ask at least one question and later write a short position paper outlining the pros and cons of each device and alternative source of energy. A teacher might also, as an alternative, give a written exam on the material presented or require reflective journals.

### Stage VI: Teacher and Students Evaluate Their Projects

The teacher used a set of rubrics to evaluate four areas related to processes used in the project including use of technology, completion of individual tasks, teamwork, and journal entries (see Table F.1). In addition, the teacher had individual members of the teams self-evaluate their groups using the same rubric. The position papers assisted in evaluating the content knowledge they had gained about alternative energy sources, and the rubric in Table F.1 evaluated the cooperative group processes that were utilized. By using a variety of formative and summative assessments, the teacher was able to assign individual as well as group grades for each team. This combination of assessments was well matched to the original three objectives. Based on these assessments as well as informal input from the expert panel, the teacher made adjustments to the time schedule and added a commercial as a requirement (one team presented a creative commercial in its presentation) for future alternative energy projects.

## Cooperative Learning Project Example 2
## Learning Together: Film Class

Film Class was an interdisciplinary, cooperative learning project that incorporated the learning together method of cooperative learning designed by Johnson and Johnson (1994). This educational program intended to teach the basic artistic and technical elements of creating video. The prime targets of Film Class were secondary students who ordinarily did not have access to the skills and tools of contemporary media. Financial poverty, limited command of English, and cultural or geographic isolation were some factors that limited opportunity for them. Their academic skills were considered low, and they generally had little confidence in their own ability to communicate.

The teacher believed the lives of students, particularly Hispanic students, were seldom reflected in the mass media, except perhaps in stereotypes, and that Film Class could help them begin the long process of taking control of the portrayal of their own experiences and cultures. These young people had stories to tell: Film Class gave them the vehicle to tell it. Additional outcomes targeted in this experience were enhanced skills in literacy in the areas of written and oral communication, and technical–digital skills (filming and editing), as well as the successful integration of the Johnson and Johnson model of cooperative learning.

Film Class as a collaboration brought together unskilled secondary students, and both high school and preservice teachers with at least a beginning level of training in camera operation and editing or performance. Teachers assessed the objectives of the Film Class, listed next, through various means. Data indicated all were successfully achieved. The process consisted of approximately 6 weeks of cooperative teamwork. The processes utilized included story development, scriptwriting, storyboarding, performance (acting and directing), camera operation, computerized editing, and marketing. Each team of five to seven persons ended up with a number of final products including a 5-minute edited video, script, film trailer, radio ad, movie poster, and product merchandise.

## Objectives

1. Students will demonstrate improved language arts skills through the integration of listening, speaking, reading, and writing processes.
2. Students will report increased self-esteem through achievement of a multitask goal that culminates in a film festival including parent involvement.
3. Students will demonstrate development of creative higher order thinking skills.
4. Students will demonstrate increased cooperative, collaborative organizational skills as a result of using the learning together method.
5. Students will demonstrate the technical skills in using digital video technology (including filming and editing).
6. Parent–teacher–student interaction will be increased.
7. Collaborative experiences with preservice teacher mentors will be increased.

The learning together method recommends utilizing four essential elements into each cooperative learning project (Johnson, Johnson, & Holubec, 1994b). Film Class incorporated these successfully in the following manner.

***Positive Interdependence.*** Each member of the team was responsible to write, storyboard, direct, film, and edit one scene. The scenes had to go together to produce a coherent film. Much collaboration, interaction, and feedback existed between students on each of these processes. To ensure this, daily team meetings and weekly class-wide "dailies" gave student teams time to share their intermediate products for feedback.

***Individual and Group Accountability.*** Because each member of the team was responsible for the elements of the film previously described, the teacher had a basis and rubric to evaluate individual students. Group accountability was evaluated on the overall quality of the final products: film, trailer, poster, merchandise. Students evaluated the quality of team products also. On the basis of the evaluations, the teacher presented Film Class awards to outstanding teams and individuals in different categories.

***Face-to-Face Interaction.*** Teams met on a daily basis (dailies) to provide input to all team members as they proceeded through the process of writing, storyboarding, filming, editing, and marketing. In addition, class-wide dailies provided time for teams to receive feedback on these products from other teams.

***Interpersonal and Small Group Skills.*** Simultaneously, students in cooperative teams learned academic subject matter and the skills required for the project (task work) and the small group skills (teamwork). The latter included effective leadership, trust building, communication, and conflict management. Prior to the project, students were involved in the five interactive simulations that model these small group skills. In addition, teachers continually reinforced these through discussions and small group interactions.

Teams met daily to discuss issues related to tasks as well as with teamwork. The teacher led a final "focus group" to discuss issues, questions, and concerns in both of these processes.

The students filled out a group processing survey that self-evaluated their group processing skills. Findings from the three groups of Film Class that have been implemented indicated significant growth in all areas of cooperative learning as a result of participation.

## Cooperative Learning Project Example 3
## Complex Instruction: Mousetrap Mobile Races

This project describes the complex instruction model as it was used with a class of primarily Navajo Indians participating in a remedial physical science class. The project, Mousetrap Mobile Races, was an interdisciplinary, cooperative learning project.

To initiate the project, the teacher organized students into heterogeneous teams based on observed skills used in shorter tasks. These observed skills included leadership, the use of oral and written language, technical skills or engineering, and collaborative or small group skills. Student were allowed to self-select tasks they believed were best suited to their talents. The teacher undertook some facilitation of these decisions when the team reached an impasse.

The teacher placed a major emphasis on learning science concepts through the inductive approach, deriving science concepts from experiences with hands-on materials. During the project, the teacher directed student teams to (1) document all stages of discovery in written and oral format (group accountability); (2) clarify the problem; (3) gather information; (4) form a hypothesis; (5) design and test models; (6) gather data based on experiments; and (7) form conclusions. The use of task sheets identified individual tasks for each student for individual accountability.

The teacher evaluated these individual tasks throughout the project (formative assessment) and then assessed the final presentation (summative assessment). The final presentation consisted of two parts: (1) Each student team tested the effectiveness of its products (mousetrap mobile racer) as it competed against other entries through a course; and (2) presentations that included the integration of a skit matching the theme of the project. For example, one team, dressed as race car drivers, produced an announcer voice-over, with appropriate music, describing how its mousetrap mobile was faring as it competed on the course.

The project afforded bilingual Navajo students multiple opportunities to (1) learn science concepts and their applications; (2) apply and improve written, reading, and oral academic language skills; and (3) improve small group skills. These were assessed through a variety of formative and summative means including individual tasks, application of research articles, written reports, performance competitions, presentations, and self-evaluation of group process skills.

Details of the Mousetrap Mobile Races project in full follow.

### Problem

Using a standard mousetrap, construct a vehicle that will be able to traverse three different courses, described next, in 10 minutes or less.

### Objectives

Student teams will be able to:

1. identify and apply the principles of motion and energy to a mousetrap mobile and demonstrate these principles in a competitive performance;
2. create a skit using a variety of interdisciplinary skills appropriate to the theme of the project;

3. demonstrate a variety of academic language arts skills; and
4. demonstrate cooperative learning skills.

## Topic

Motion/energy/engineering (physics)

## Materials Needed

Standard mousetrap, wheels, rubber bands, balsa sheets, Styrofoam, and other materials as determined by student or teachers

## Resources

To be determined by student and teacher; might include Internet and print resources

## Time Frame

Approximately 10 class periods (45 minutes each)

## Student Grouping

Teams of three to five students

## Directions/Rules/Limitations

1. The total cost may not exceed $10, not counting the materials supplied by the teacher.
2. The maximum length of the vehicle is not to exceed 12 inches and the maximum height is not to exceed 12 inches.
3. Only one standard mousetrap (supplied) may be used, although modifications are allowed. This provides the only source of energy for the vehicle. In the performance competition, the team may set the trap as many times as necessary but may trigger it only with a pencil.
4. Three courses will be set up near each other. The vehicles must complete the courses in this order:
   a. The first course consists of a flat track 25 feet long and 5 feet wide. The vehicle must start behind the starting line and pass the finish line (multiple triggers are allowed but time consuming). If the vehicle goes out of the side area, the team must place it back onto the course approximately where the car exited (with a penalty of 10 points for each violation). When the vehicle finishes this course, the team must calculate the average velocity (for all triggers) over this course and present this to the judges as part of its score. The team then carries the vehicle to the second course.
   b. The second course consists of a short box ramp with an angle of approximately 15 degrees and a length of 3 feet. The team places the vehicle on the ramp with the back supported by a small lip. The vehicle must traverse up the ramp and jump onto the floor across 10 feet more of flat floor to the finish (multiple triggers are allowed but time consuming). The team then carries the vehicle to the third course.

c. The third course consists of four rectangular spaces outlined by tape on the floor, each consisting of 10-foot lengths and 5-foot widths. Each part of these four rectangles is a subcourse and has some obstacles or targets to navigate through in this order:
   - Section 1 has three balloons with bonus point values of 5, 10, and 25 for breaking them, depending on their size (smaller balloons have larger point values). Once the vehicle has hit the wall and/or a balloon, the team moves it to section 2.
   - Section 2 has two small (bowling-pin type) obstacles approximately 1 foot apart in the center section of the course. To receive full points for this course, the vehicle must go between pins without touching (10-point penalty) and *stop* before hitting the wall but after passing the pins (25-point bonus).
   - Section 3 has no obstacles but the vehicle must be triggered and go backward through the entire course.
   - Section 4 has a piece of thick carpet covering a 2-foot strip (2 feet long by 5 feet wide) approximately in the middle of the 10-foot length of this course. The vehicle has to navigate across this different terrain to the finish line. The total time for the three courses (A, B, and C) is recorded when the vehicle crosses the final finish line.

## Scoring

1. The vehicle finishes each course and subcourse (20 points each × 6) = 120 points.
2. The vehicle finishes/completes a course using only one trigger (10 points each × 6) = 60 points.
3. Correct calculation and representation of the average velocity on the first course = 10 points.
4. Total time for *completion* of the courses: 8:00–10:00 minutes = 20 points; 6:00–7:59 minutes = 25 points; 4:00–5:59 minutes = 30 points; 2:00–3:59 minutes = 35 points; less than 2:00 minutes = 50 points. (No points are given for completion if time elapses before the completion of all of the courses.)
5. Balloon pops in section 1 = 5/15/25 points (depending on size of balloon).
6. Vehicle is able to stop in the proper location in section 2 = 25 points.
7. Creativity and appearance of the vehicle = 0 to 25 points.
8. Written team report and group process evaluation (includes elements of formative and summative assessments) = 100 points.

## Penalties

These are subtracted from total score for performance and style.

1. Out of bounds (side) of any course = deduct 10 points each occurrence.
2. Hitting a single pin = deduct 10 points each occurrence.
3. Exceeds height or length limits = deduct 25 points each.
4. Exceeds cost limit = deduct 50 points.
5. Failure to use pencil to trigger = deduct 25 points each.
6. Poor sportsmanship (as determined by judges) = deduct 5 to 50 points.

## Presentation

The performance should be connected to the theme of the problem, may be presented any time during the 10 minutes, and must include all of the team members.

1. Correct use of five key terms and their concepts (as determined by teacher or students) in proper context, as related to the laws of motion and energy, during the style presentation = 0 to 20 points.
2. Creativity of the style presentation = 0 to 20 points.
3. Appearance and performance of at least one of the characters in the presentation = 0 to 20 points.
4. Finished sketch/blueprint of the vehicle appropriately displayed during the competition = 0 to 20 points.
5. Appropriate match of music, dance, or artistic backdrops (original preferred) to the theme of the problem = 0 to 20 points.

# Instructional Resource G

## Sample Interdisciplinary Thematic Unit

| | |
|---|---|
| Camille: | English Preservice Teacher |
| Larry: | Social Science Teacher |
| Gina: | Science Preservice Teacher |

Hillside High School

### Table of Contents

## Working Theme/Rationale

Based on the relative location of the college campus and the nearby Blue Lake community (a senior citizen planned community), we feel it is important for our student body to be educated with regard to the relationship between two extremely different communities. For this reason, each member of the team will develop his or her own discipline around the dynamics of community. Camille will develop the literature/language arts (English) component focusing on intergenerational relationships. Larry will develop the social science component focusing on community and community relationships. Gina will develop the environmental science component focusing on the ecological relationship between humans and the environment.

The ITU will be taught to a group of 11th-grade students and will consist of 13 days of instruction. Although it is important to incorporate established standards into this unit, we also feel that it is vital to expose our students to community neighbors and locations that might not be familiar to them.

## Standards

In order to ensure that our students are educated to meet the expectations set forth by the state of California, we plan to incorporate standards from each of our disciplines as follows:

### Literature/Language Arts

#### *Reading Standards*

*Reading Comprehension*

*2.6:* Critique the power, validity, and truthfulness of arguments set forth in public documents; their appeal both to friendly and hostile audiences; and the extent to which the arguments anticipate and address reader concerns and counterclaims.

*Literary Response and Analysis*

*3.2:* Analyze the way in which the theme or meaning of a selection represents a view or comment on life, using textual evidence to support the claim.

*3.7:* Analyze recognized works of world literature from a variety of authors:

b. Relate literary works and authors to major themes and issues of their eras.

#### *Writing Standards*

*Writing Strategies*

*1.6:* Develop presentations by using clear research questions and creative and critical research strategies.

*1.7:* Use systematic strategies to organize and record information.

*1.9:* Revise text to highlight the individual voice, improve sentence variety and style, and enhance subtlety of meaning and tone in ways that are consistent with the purpose, audience, and genre.

*Writing Applications*

*2.3:* Write reflective compositions:

a. Explore the significance of personal experiences, events, conditions, or concerns by using rhetorical strategies.

### *Written and Oral English Language Conventions Standards*

*1.1:* Demonstrate control of grammar, diction, and paragraph and sentence structure and an understanding of English usage.
*1.2:* Produce legible work that shows accurate spelling and correct punctuation and capitalization.
*1.3:* Reflect appropriate manuscript requirements in writing.

### *Listening and Speaking Standards*

*Listening and Speaking Strategies*

*1.1:* Recognize strategies used by the media to inform, persuade, entertain, and transmit culture (i.e., perpetuation of stereotypes).
*1.6:* Use logical, ethical, and emotional appeals that enhance a specific tone and purpose.
*1.7:* Use appropriate rehearsal strategies to pay attention to performance details, achieve command of text, and create skillful artistic staging.
*1.8:* Use effective and interesting language, including:
   a. Informal expressions for effect.
   b. Standard American English for clarity.
*1.10:* Evaluate when to use different kinds of effects to create effective productions.

*Speaking Applications*

*2.3:* Deliver oral presentations to literature:
   a. Demonstrate a comprehensive understanding of the significant ideas of literary works.
   b. Analyze the imagery, language, universal themes, and unique aspects of the text through the use of rhetorical strategies.
   c. Support important ideas and viewpoints through accurate and detailed references to the text or to other works.

## Social Science

### *Standards*

*11.8:* Students analyze the economic boom and social transformation of post–World War II America.
*11.11:* Students analyze the major social problems and domestic policy issues in contemporary American society.
*12.2:* Students evaluate and take and defend positions on the scope and limits of rights and obligations as democratic citizens.
*12.3:* Students evaluate and take and defend positions on what the fundamental values and principles of civil society are.
*12.7:* Students analyze and compare the powers and procedures of the national, state, tribal, and local governments.

## Environmental Science

### *Standards*

*6:* Stability in an ecosystem is a balance between competing effects.
*6a:* Students know biodiversity is the sum total of different kinds of organisms and is affected by alterations of habitats.
*6b:* Students know how to analyze changes in an ecosystem resulting from changes in climate, human activity, introduction of nonnative species, or changes in population size.

*6c:* Students know how fluctuations in population size in an ecosystem are determined by the relative rates of birth, immigration, emigration, and death.
*6d:* Students know how water, carbon, and nitrogen cycle between abiotic resources and organic matter in the ecosystem and how oxygen cycles through photosynthesis and respiration.

## Behavioral Objectives and Assessments

Behavioral objectives are observable objectives, which teachers can measure using a variety of assessment strategies. This matrix is a compilation of the various objectives we will cover and the assessment strategies we will use to measure them.

| Objectives | Goal 1 | Goal 2 | Goal 3 | Assessment |
|---|---|---|---|---|
| COGNITIVE | To **break down** text and other data and **identify** key points that can be **applied** to situations and used to **formulate** educated opinions. | To **analyze** the relationship between the communities of Blue Lake and Hillside High School (HHS). | To **develop** a sense of who the residents of Blue Lake are. | • Technology-based product to illustrate the interrelationship between HHS and the senior community.<br>• Unit notebooks and/or journals that will include research, writing assignments, as well as other components.<br>• Individual and group self-assessments at end of unit. |
| AFFECTIVE | Students will demonstrate **cooperation** with each other during group activities. | Students will share and **report** on the findings of various research activities. | Students will **recognize** the value of differing perspectives and opinions. | *The above listed assessment will include components that will address all three types of objectives. |
| PSYCHOMOTOR | Students will **obtain** physical evidence of ecological change/evolution. | Students will **build** a portfolio of assignments during this unit (teachers will determine what assignments will be included in the portfolio). Students will **design** and **create** a visual representation of the Blue Lake community. | Students will **describe** their relationship to/with the community of Blue Lake before and after the unit in a quick-write format. | *See previous statement for assessment rationale. |

## Scope and Sequence Matrix

This matrix is a visual representation of the specific activities that each individual discipline will cover. To ensure that we are all connected to our theme, we have developed daily themes that tie into the overall theme of the ITU.

| Daily Themes | Coordinated Activities | Literature/ Langage Arts | Social Studies | Environmental Science |
|---|---|---|---|---|
| ***DAY 1*** INTRODUCTION | | Read *The Lorax*. Have students focus on the intergenerational relationships between the characters. (**Interior monologue**) Also, discuss the environmental factor of the book. **Standards:** Reading: 3.2 L&S: 2.3a, b | Students will brainstorm what they know about their community and what is known about the senior community. In addition, students will debate the meaning of "community" and its relative importance to society. | Read *The Lorax*. Have students focus on the ecological relationships between the environment and how people affect it. Have students write a journal entry. |
| ***DAY 2*** FOUNDATION BUILDING | | Discuss society's perceptions of "youth" and "elderly" persons. (**KWL**) Media and periodical portrayals. (**Quick write**) **Standards:** Reading: 2.6 L&S: 1.1 Writing: 2.3a | Students will choose one aspect of "community" that is important to them and write a short journal entry communicating their view. In addition, students will begin to brainstorm for information on the senior community in preparation for field trip. | Divide students into groups and jigsaw ecology concepts as a refresher. Make posters and present to the class. Topics are:<br>• population growth<br>• im/emigration<br>• competition<br>• biodiversity<br>• water quality |
| ***DAY 3*** FIELD TRIP | The combined content areas will travel a short distance to the senior community to gain perspective on the ecological and sociological aspects of the community. | Students will spend the day researching the activities enjoyed by the residents of the senior community. Students may also interview residents to gain a personal account of the lifestyle of the senior community residents. | Students will spend a set part of the day exploring Blue Lake from a perspective of what social indicators exist to join Blue Lake with and divide it from their community. | Students will take a guided tour of the lake and take note of animals and plants seen. When possible collect a sample or draw a picture of the species. |

(*continued*)

(*continued*)

| Daily Themes | Coordinated Activities | Literature/ Langage Arts | Social Studies | Environmental Science |
|---|---|---|---|---|
| ***DAY 4*** REFLECTION OF THE EXPERIENCE | | (**Venn diagram**) Based on the information gathered on their trip, students will create two Venn diagrams comparing and contrasting Blue Lake and HHS populations and students' perceptions of the population of Blue Lake and the actual population of Blue Lake. **Standards:** Reading: 2.6 Read students Chief Joseph's speech on the environment. (**Quick write**) **Standards:** L&S: 1.1 | Students will discuss expectations versus realities after the field trip and write a reflective journal entry on what they saw as their most important discovery during the field trip. | Reflection: Differences and similarities between Blue Lake and Hillside. Students will also identify the species seen on the tour and research species that are native to the area. |
| ***DAY 5*** WHERE DO WE COME FROM: PAST MEETS PRESENT | | *The Joy Luck Club*. (**SSR**) Focus on the intergenerational relationships. **Standards:** Reading: 3.7b | Students will hear guest speaker from Blue Lake and ask pointed questions constructed prior to hearing speaker. | Immigrating/-emigrating species. Make a time line around the room and illustrate with pictures and captions when ecological events took place in the area. |
| ***DAY 6*** INTRO OF PROJECT AND ASSIGNMENT OF GROUPS | Explain project to students who will present the following topics through a PowerPoint presentation, video diary, or collages. Students will be divided into groups to cover the following topic in each discipline: population, beliefs and values 40 years ago, beliefs and values today, development of Blue Lake community. | Project—Give students a handout with required assignments for **portfolio.** Go over **portfolio** with them and explain **gallery walks** and **presentation** of final research project (video). Project topic: Is the relationship between Blue Lake and HHS positive or negative? | Project—In collaboration with the teaching team, students will be divided into cooperative groups to research and create a technologically based presentation on the interrelationship between Blue Lake and the community, which the high school represents. | Project—Give students handout with instruction, expectations, and rubric. Go over project with students, then model a presentation. Divide into groups to cover topics that emphasize ecology: effects of population growth, environmental values 40 years ago, environmental values today, development of Blue Lake community, effect of building the lake. |

(*continued*)

(continued)

| Daily Themes | Coordinated Activities | Literature/ Langage Arts | Social Studies | Environmental Science |
|---|---|---|---|---|
| ***DAY 7*** RESEARCH DAY | Directed research concerning interrelationships, focusing on individual disciplines | Students pick teams (no more than five, no fewer than three students per team). Intergenerational relationships. (**Jigsaw**) *The Joy Luck Club*. If time allows, **tableau.** **Standards:** L&S: 2.3a, b, c | Community relationships focused on physical characteristics | Ecological relationships |
| ***DAY 8*** RESEARCH DAY | Directed research concerning interrelationships, focusing on individual disciplines | Intergenerational relationships (**Gallery walk**) | Community relationships focused on physical characteristics | Ecological relationships |
| ***DAY 9*** CONSULTATION AND PROGRESS CHECK | Confer with each group and make sure they are on track. Troubleshoot any problems. | Student–teacher consultations. Consultations will help students gauge where they stand in regard to their final project and presentations thereof (**Gallery walks**), as well as their portfolios. | Midproject consultations whereby students and teachers will discuss projects and make necessary adjustments as well as gauge progress | Hold group conferences. Provide tutorials for PowerPoint and other technologies, as needed. |
| ***DAY 10*** RESEARCH DAY | Directed research concerning interrelationships, focusing on individual disciplines | Intergenerational relationships. Go over what assignments need to be included in **portfolios.** Use checklists. Research project revisions. **Standards:** WOLC: 1.1–1.3 | Community relationships focused on physical characteristics | Ecological relationships |
| ***DAY 11*** FINALIZING PROJECT/CATCH UP | Directed research concerning interrelationships, focusing on individual disciplines | Intergenerational relationships | Community relationships focused on physical characteristics | Ecological relationships |

(continued)

(*continued*)

| Daily Themes | Coordinated Activities | Literature/ Langage Arts | Social Studies | Environmental Science |
|---|---|---|---|---|
| ***DAY 12*** PRESENTATIONS | | Student teams will present their projects. After projects, students will participate in a **gallery walk.** After this activity, students will engage in a **discussion. Standards:** L&S: 1.6, 1.7, 1.8a, b | | Students will present their group projects. They will also evaluate other student presentations. |
| ***DAY 13*** SELF-ASSESSMENTS AND CLOSURE | | Students will write a **reflective journal** on the topic of the relationship between Blue Lake community and Hillside High School: What did you learn from your research? From this unit? How have your perceptions changed based on your first **quick write?** Students will turn in **portfolios** (including the **reflective journal**). Brief teacher discussion on the connection among the various subjects and the theme of the unit. **Standards:** Writing: 1.6, 1.7, 1.9 | | Students will evaluate their own work and the work of group members. Students will also write a reflection: Ecologically, has the relationship between Blue Lake community and Hillside been beneficial? |

## SDAIE Justification

Specially Designed Academic Instruction in English, commonly known as SDAIE, incorporates a myriad of techniques that help second-language learners succeed in school. Although most commonly associated with English language development (ELD) programs, SDAIE techniques will help all students succeed in school.

## Literature/Language Arts

| Day and Theme | Activity | SDAIE Justification |
|---|---|---|
| ***DAY 1***<br>INTRODUCTION | Read *The Lorax*. Have students write an **interior monologue** on a specific character (Once-ler, Lorax, boy). Group discussions, focusing on intergenerational relationships. | Students will listen to a story by Dr. Seuss, which has an easy-to-follow story line and abundant illustrations. I will explain and **model** how to do an **interior monologue.** Students will activate (**bridge**) prior knowledge regarding intergenerational relationships that they may have experienced with older family members, neighbors, etc. |
| ***DAY 2***<br>FOUNDATION BUILDING | Students will fill out a **KWL** grid regarding society's perceptions of youth and elderly peoples using media and periodicals. Class discussion and **quick write.** | I will explain the purpose of a **KWL** grid and show students how to fill it out. This activity also **bridges** their previous knowledge of "old" people and helps them take a good look at themselves as "young" people. |
| ***DAY 3***<br>FIELD TRIP | Students will take a guided tour of the Blue Lake community center and surrounding areas. Students will note the activities the residents of Blue Lake enjoy. Also, students may interview residents (if resident volunteers are available). | With their firsthand knowledge of Blue Lake's residents' lifestyles, students will be able to determine the similarities and differences of their own thoughts (from the previous day's **quick write**) and the media portrayal of youth and elderly persons. This will help their reflections. |
| ***DAY 4***<br>REFLECTION OF THE EXPERIENCE | Students will complete two **Venn diagrams.** | Students' **schemas** will be actively engaged. They will begin to make explicit connections between what they know (or "think" they know) and what they are learning. |

# Lesson Plan Example for Social Science

Title: Introduction to ITU
Subject: U.S. History
Grade: 11th grade
Context within unit (week/day of instruction): Day 1
Time (block/single period): 50-minute single period

## Purpose

The purpose of this lesson is to introduce the ITU and to specifically challenge students to look at historical concepts through the lens of reality and their present world. Standard(s): 11.11

## Objectives

***Cognitive.*** Students will work individually and in groups to identify important elements of what "community" means and to formulate educated opinions of the importance of the concept of community relative to society.

*Psychomotor.* Students will use the brainstorming activity to help form their description of what community means to them. In addition, students will begin the process of building a unit notebook, which will include different elements including contributions from the day's first activities.

*Affective.* Students will work in cooperative groups that will debate the relative importance of community in present society.

### Procedures

*Activity 1.* Students will take part in an open discussion relating to the concept of community. Using a visual prompt and shared interpretation as an anticipatory set, students will discuss what community means. Further, utilizing a graphic organizer, students will begin to see that community is a concept open to many different interpretations.

*Activity 2.* After the discussion, the teacher will pair students, who will engage in a "think-pair-share" activity in which they ponder the importance of community in today's society. The instructor's prompt provides the basis of this activity: Does community exist in today's society? Why or why not? In addition, it is hoped that differing opinions will arise and that a lively debate will ensue.

### Closure

Review/preview will take up the last few minutes of class, in which the next lesson is set up. In addition, this time will remind the class of the unit's theme and the approaching project.

### Assessment

The teaching team has chosen three important assessment elements that will run through the entire unit. Specifically for the first lesson, students will begin to build a unit notebook, to hold many of the unit's writing activities and other miscellaneous paperwork.

## Action Research

This culminating activity not only would serve as an assessment tool regarding the success of the ITU but also would allow students to become more involved in the Blue Lake community. It is our hope, by including a community service component to this ITU, that the relationship between Hillside High School and the Blue Lake community would be more amicable.

### Problem

Friction and distrust exist between the Blue Lake and the Hillside High School communities.

### Information

Traditionally there has always been a cultural gap between the youth and the elderly of the United States; however, after talking to residents of the Blue Lake community and reading a newsletter, we discovered the negative views they had of the Hillside High School population. We read an article that detailed acts of vandalism that had taken place in the Blue Lake community by suspected Hillside High School students. Due to this speculation, a large amount of distrust and lack of communication exist between the two groups. Several meetings have taken place between school administrators, the sheriff, and Blue Lake residents to find resolution for the events. The students, who are perceived to be the perpetrators of these actions, have not been involved in these meetings. As a result of such lack of communication, the students do not know who the residents of Blue Lake community truly are and vice versa.

## Hypothesis

An interdisciplinary thematic unit (ITU) focusing on the relationships between the two communities will promote understanding between the two groups and reduce the current friction. This unit will also promote critical thinking skills so students can form and support educated opinions regarding the relationship between Blue Lake and Hillside High School.

## Experimental Design

Three preservice teachers from the local university have designed an ITU to examine the relationship between the two communities and to promote critical thinking about current community issues. The unit consists of 13 days of instruction and the three preservice teachers will teach it in an academy. A detailed outline of the unit is presented in the previous pages. Three forms of assessment will be used to triangulate the effectiveness of the unit.

## Data/Results

Data will be collected from three assessment tools and one optional project.

***Journals/Notebooks.*** The teacher will ask students to keep a notebook during the course of the ITU, which will contain all of the quick writes, activities, and research they have done. It will be collected at the end of the ITU and graded. If the ITU is a success, we should be able to see the students' opinions and knowledge grow from generalizations to educated opinions that they are able to support.

***Presentation.*** The students will create a presentation using a form of technology of their choice, on a topic they have become experts on. They will be able to present both sides of a community issue and then express their personal views, supported by research.

***Self-Assessment.*** For their final assignment in the unit, students will reflect on the experiences they have had and evaluate what they have learned. If the unit is successful, students will be able to express what they have learned and how their views have changed.

***Community Service.*** This assignment will be extra credit. Part of our goal is to have students make a connection with the Blue Lake community and hopefully reduce the current friction. For this optional assignment, students would write a proposal detailing an existing need in the Blue Lake community and how they would alleviate it. Students would then volunteer 20 hours of community service. The number of students who attempt the project and interviews of both the students and the residents will measure the success of this component. The interviews would examine each group's attitudes toward the other.

## Conclusion

The ITU will be measured by examining how attitudes and opinions have changed about the community and the issues it is facing. If opinions and attitudes have changed that reflect a positive attitude about the Blue Lake community, and friction between the two groups has decreased, we will consider the ITU a success. It is then up to the school to examine its goals and values to determine whether all students should participate in the ITU.

# Instructional Resource H

## Basics for the Compassionate Discipline Model

A. Teacher has conference/interview with the individual student to determine issues and needs.

B. Teacher/facilitator meets with the interested parties (parent/guardian, principal, counselor) to discuss student issues and needs and to define problem and propose action plan.

C. Minitraining is implemented with the team: discussion of parenting management styles that lead to potential child response (Stein, 2002).

   1. **Permissive:** allows children to do what they want; cannot say no; showers with presents and privileges.
      **Child's response:** loses initiative and spontaneity, has tantrums and ignores rights of others, and as adolescent adults tend to hate work, easily distractible, impatient, and tyrannical with others.
   2. **Neglectful/hands off:** often preoccupied with other things; may know what child does but accepts it as just part of the learning process of life.
      **Child's response:** resistance to authority, loneliness, lacks sense of right and wrong, and as adolescent adults tend not to want to get involved or assist others, tend to avoid controversial issues or commitments.
   3. **Authoritative, military type:** in command—tells you, demands, takes authority, no choices allowed.
      **Child's response:** docile obedience, active rebellion, passive resistance (daydreaming, forgetting), and as adolescent adults tend to bully or push others relentlessly and/or refuse to comply with rules and regulations.
   4. **Democratic/loving and firm:** meets needs of the child by developing a relationship through talking and listening of mutually acceptable set of rules and consequences.
      **Child's response:** feels security of love and acceptance, not afraid to try and fail, positive attitude, willing to help, share, contribute to and cooperate with others. As adolescent adults tend to also be democratic, caring, and honest with their peers and family members.

D. Discussion of the four levels of motivation

   1. **Me Stage** (preschool): I want what I want and I want it now! These needs include food, attention, objects.
   2. **Pleasing Adults Stage** (K–6): more social, will do what you want. Good time to teach values: exhibits nonrebellious behavior, will do chores, wants to spend time with teachers, wants acceptance for actions, wants to learn, raises hand to respond, is compliant.
   3. **Pleasing Peers Stage** (grades 7–12): wants to do what peers want. Exhibits more rebellious behavior, testing earlier values, challenges authority. Clothing, music, and other cultural contexts match peers, not desires of teachers or parents. Primary reason for joining gangs or other social contexts in school—sports, clubs, and so on.
   4. **Serving Others Stage** (post high school): goes to college, gets a steady job, marries, has children, involved in cultural and socially acceptable service to the community.

E. Use the elements of the compassionate discipline model to design and sign the social contract (this included a left-hand side on which the disruptive student had listed his student-centered short, intermediate, and long-term goals (25–50) and a right-hand side that listed the rules and consequences, values, and responsibilities (at home and at school). After another discussion with this student, this was finalized and signed by all parties.
F. Teacher meets with the other members of the class (without the disruptive student being present) to explain the social contract, the purpose, and to request their assistance in helping the target student meet his or her goals. This might include a small in-service with them that uses some simulations on how to praise this student when he or she acts appropriately as well as how to respond assertively and appropriately to inappropriate behavior. This step is considered a very important and appropriate social/interactive learning opportunity for the other students; one that is critical in dealing with the implementation of this plan. It will give them some of the skills to apply to any future similar incident with which they might be confronted.
G. Implementation of the social contract by all parties by consistently praising and rewarding positive behavior, clarifying expectations, and assigning consequences for negative behavior (both at home and at school).
H. Periodically revisiting the social contract with the student and the other interested parties and making appropriate modifications when necessary.

# Instructional Resource I

## Sample Service-Learning Project

### JUSTIFICATION

My main goal for wishing to implement a service-learning project in my class of English language learners (ELLs) was to help them to gain confidence in their abilities to communicate in English so that they can begin to take an active role in their education and the community. I teach a high school English language development (ELD) class of students at the transition level. In short, this means that my students can understand and compose oral communication fluently. At the end of the year, my students either graduate or enter regular mainstream classes. Whereas most of the students experience success in the ELD program and pass the district reading and writing proficiency with ease, students entering the mainstream English classes at the school typically are not successful. Most teachers blame this on the fact the mainstreamed ELLs seem to be content to sit quietly and fail. They do not ask for help, get makeup assignments, or participate in group activities if they do not know their group members. Thus, my goal was to help my students to become more active learners and community members.

Based on published data on the effects of service-learning, I was certain that the successful implementation of a project in my ELD classrooms would help my students to develop the confidence and communication skills needed for them to become and feel a part of the school community.

### SAMPLE

The school in which this project was completed is located in southern California and had the following makeup as of 2000:

Enrollment: 2,681
White (non-Hispanic): 1,269 (52.67%)
Non-White: 1,412 (47.33%) (1,167, or 43.5%, of the school is Latino)
LEP (limited English proficient): 530
FEP (fluent English proficient): 370
ELD class enrollment: 155

It is obvious from these numbers that the successful integration of non-English-speaking students into the community and the campus could have major implications. For the implementation of this service-learning project, I used my ELD-IV class. The class had 26 students at the end of the year. Twenty-three of the students were from Mexico and one each from Vietnam, Morocco, and Serbia. The students were in grades 9–12 and had been in the country anywhere from between 8 months and 5 years. Only 15 of the students in the class at the beginning of the year were in the class at the end of the year. Most of those who left the class moved to other districts or went back to Mexico; the ones who joined the class either were moved up from ELD-III or moved into the district from another. Because I had given an attitudinal pretest at the beginning of the year, I used only the data from the 15 students who had been in the class all year.

## Methods

During the last 6 weeks of the school year, I was given a curriculum on writing problem-solution essays designed by the Project Write Institute. Included in the curriculum packet was a component entitled "Students as Problem Solvers." This was easily adapted into a service-learning unit, which I used to try to help my students to improve their self-confidence and communication skills.

The project had the students form groups and choose a problem within their community that needed to be solved. The students were then to go into the community to investigate the causes, effects, and possible solutions for the problem. The final phase of the project, which I did not implement, has the students go into the community to gain support for solving the problem.

I decided to use problems that the students determined existed at the high school. In order to determine these problems, my class identified ten problems that they had seen at the high school, and then they conducted a survey of other classes to determine the top five problems on campus. After these were determined, the class divided themselves into five groups; each group was then assigned one of each of the problems. As a group, students were required to conduct interviews about the problem, write letters to the student government, make a poster, and write presentations to give to other classes about the problems studied. As individuals the students had to write essays and give an oral presentation.

In order to measure the success of the project based on my goals, I conducted attitudinal surveys at the beginning and end of the project, which I compared to their attitudes at the beginning of the school year. Additionally, I analyzed student reflections written during the project, I observed them carefully during the project, and I used my informal analysis of their essays to measure their written academic achievement.

## Data and Observations

I broke the data into three categories: student attitudes about their communication skills, student attitudes about their place in the school, and teacher observations of student achievement. I had hoped that all three of these categories would show that student skills and attitudes had improved.

### Student Attitudes—Communication Skills

The four questions on a survey measured student attitudes on their skills. The students were asked to rate their attitudes based on a five-point Likert scale of 5 = Always, 4 = Almost always, 3 = Sometimes, 2 = Almost never, and 1 = Never. The mean of each question was determined for the pretest and posttest ratings, and a *t*-test was performed for students' pretest and posttest scores to determine whether or not attitudes had significantly changed after the service-learning project. The results of the analyses can be seen here:

| Question | Mean (Pre/Post) | *t*-test |
|---|---|---|
| I feel comfortable speaking in front of class. | 2.87/3.07 | 0.26 |
| If I do not understand something, I ask for help. | 4.20/4.27 | 0.42 |
| I would feel comfortable starting a conversation with a stranger. | 2.60/2.87 | 0.17 |
| I am good at communicating with others. | 3.27/3.80 | 0.52 |

As the data show, although all of the means increased, none of the results showed significant increases. In the student reflections after the project had been assigned, five students indicated their concern at the prospect of having to give an oral presentation. No students mentioned any concern with having to conduct interviews or surveys.

## Student Attitudes–Place in School

In order to determine student attitudes about their perceived place in the school, students were asked rate their attitudes to six statements based on a five-point Likert scale of 5 = Always, 4 = Almost always, 3 = Sometimes, 2 = Almost never, and 1 = Never. Students were tested at the beginning of the service-learning project and about 4 weeks later at the end of the project. As with the previous data, the mean of each question was determined for the pretest and posttest ratings, and a *t*-test was performed for students' pretest and posttest scores to determine whether or not attitudes had significantly changed after the service-learning project. The results of the analyses can be seen here:

| Question | Mean (Pre/Post) | *t*-test |
|---|---|---|
| I like school. | 4.07/4.27 | 0.23 |
| This is a good school. | 4.00/4.00 | 0.61 |
| I am an important part of this school. | 3.27/3.60 | 0.91 |
| I can make a difference at this school. | 2.93/3.40 | 0.82 |
| Students at this school are friendly. | 3.27/3.07 | 0.32 |
| I am proud of this school. | 4.27/4.13 | 0.30 |

As with the student attitudes toward communication skills, the data do not show that there was a significant difference in student attitudes after the service-learning project had been completed. Interestingly, the means on the last two questions dropped slightly and that of the second question stayed exactly the same. In the reflections completed at the beginning of the project, 11 of the 15 students thought that their efforts would lead to solving the problem, whereas in the final reflections only 7 thought that they could help to solve the problems.

## Teacher Observations–Student Achievement

While the student rankings of their own attitudes show little growth, my judgment based on my informal observations leads me to believe that they did make significant increases in their skills and attitudes. First of all, there were the student reactions as they left and then came back from doing interviews around campus with adults in the administrative offices, other teachers, and campus supervisors. As each group of students left, they were nervous and arguing about which one of them would do the questioning. When they returned, they were smiling and bragging about how nice everyone was, and they were anxious to place the new information they had gained on their posters.

There was also the integration of students into groups. My three non-Spanish speakers had always been somewhat leery of outsiders in the classroom. This was partially because of the Spanish speakers' tendency to switch into Spanish either when discussing things they had difficulty expressing in English or when they were discussing personal matters. My Moroccan and Vietnamese students, both boys, dealt with the problem by forcibly saying, "English, please," but my Serbian student, a girl of a higher social status and education level than the rest of the class, would simply withdraw into a book or her own work. She always preferred to work alone and would do as little as possible when made to work in a group. During the last week of the project, I saw a remarkable change in my Serbian student's attitude and behavior. She was laughing with the other members of her group. She was giving instructions and taking directions from the other group members. Beyond the changing of the group dynamics, was the fact that the other two seniors in her group had convinced her to participate in the graduation ceremony. Even more incredible was the fact that all five of my graduating seniors decided to go to Grad Nite—an all-night party for seniors after graduation. Only weeks before none of them had wanted to go, especially my Serbian student who had thought it was a stupid idea.

The most remarkable change was in the emotions of those graduating seniors on the day they had to give their oral presentations. While the underclassmen were presenting to our class, I sent the seniors into regular, mainstream English classes to give their presentations. Before they left my room, they were begging me to change my mind. But off they went into the symbolic "real world" of regular English. When they returned, all but one of the six seniors (the one who had not earned enough credits to graduate) were ecstatic. They were saying how nice the other classes were, how they could not believe that they had been so nervous, and that they were so proud of themselves. The one who was not talking had not given his presentation, and interestingly enough, he was the student who had ranked his posttest attitudes toward his place in school as one, or "never"—meaning that he never liked school, was not proud of the school, and so on. This had been an extreme change in attitude, because at his pretest he had ranked most of the statements as "sometimes" or better.

Overall, most of the students appeared to have had a positive experience and their final problem-solution essays proved it. They were the best essays they had written all year. Their ideas were clearly articulated and the information they had gained from their interviews made their explanations more complete.

## Conclusions

Although there is no quantitative data to support that the service-learning project increased my students' attitudes about their communication skills or their places in the school, my qualitative observations prove otherwise. Whether or not they solved the five problems they investigated, my students took an active role on the campus—many of them for the first time ever. Only one of the students in my class played sports at the school, and only five were members of clubs on campus. Most never voted in student elections and only one of them went to the prom. In short, they go to school and that is it; they are not a part of the school community.

Participating in this project had several observable benefits for my students. All of them, even the minorities in the class, worked well in the groups. Additionally, all the groups experienced success during their interviews, and all but one of the students doing presentations accomplished the task and felt good about it. My graduating seniors decided to participate in graduation and all the parties after it. The entire environment of the class had changed. The students had a purpose, and it was related to the real world. Instead of calculating percentages because a textbook said to, they were calculating percentages to determine what students felt were the most important problems at the school. They were checking and double-checking each other's work. They were making plans to solve problems that affected them and their peers. They were writing papers with a purpose. Suddenly, things became real to them.

## Implications

This was the first time that I had taught the problem-solution essay using the Project Write Institute curriculum, and it was the first time I had tried to implement a service-learning project. Obviously, I need to do some things differently in the future. First of all, it might be more useful to use student reflections and teacher observations to assess students' communication skills and their place in the classroom and at the school. It seems as though student attitudes might not have been the best measure of the success of the project. Finally, the project needs to be started at the beginning of the year so that the students could more actively bring their efforts into the school community.

There were additional benefits to the school that I had not expected and thus did not measure. For example, the office personnel and teachers that my students had interviewed were very intrigued by the project and my students. They were thrilled that students would ask them about problems on campus. Additionally, they were pleased to see ELLs taking an active interest in the school. In the same way, the students in the classes my students presented to were also impressed by both the courage and the skill of students who were relatively new to the country and the school. I am sure that if the project were to be completed and the posters hung around campus, letters written to the student government, and the announcements made during the daily bulletin, that the effects of my students' project on the school community would have been more obvious. These effects, and the attention they would have brought my students, would probably have changed my students' attitudes toward their place in the school in a more dramatic way.

---

Used with permission of Kathy Salvatori (2001).

# Instructional Resource J

## *Preservice Teacher Reflection on Service-Learning*

### Implementation

I had planned to implement a service-learning project at the beginning of the school year with the hopes of having it continue into the second semester. The original plan had been to take my class of English language learners across the street to a retirement home. The purpose of this plan was twofold. First of all, we would be providing a service to the elderly by offering them companionship. Second, and more importantly to me, was the fact that I would be taking my students who are at the "transition" level of their development (which means that they will be in regular classes with no support next year) into the real world and helping them to develop self-confidence and communication skills. Unfortunately, I encountered an administration that was less than supportive. Due to less than stellar test scores, my curriculum was changed at the last moment. It was made clear to me that I was to teach in a "back to the basics" way—which meant no frills like service-learning. No amount of research-based argumentation could sway my administration. Luckily, during the last 8 weeks of school, I was presented with a new unit from the Project Write Institute. This is a district-supported curriculum, so when I saw that the unit included a service-learning section, I seized the opportunity to use it. The unit focused on writing a problem-solution essay by doing community research and activities in order to determine the causes, effects, and possible solutions to problems. I saw that this unit offered to fulfill the most important of my goals, that is, helping to build the self-esteem and confidence of my students in reference to their English skills. The other purpose, providing a service to the community, would come in a more discrete way than originally planned. So, in the end, I was able to implement about 4 weeks of what would have been a very effective 8-week project. The way it was done was different than I had planned, but the outcome was very positive.

### Successes

My greatest successes were those that resulted from the release of responsibility from me to the students. Each group of problem solvers had its own project management team responsible for the different projects within the overall assignment. All I had to do was monitor their progress and introduce each new assignment. I was thrilled to see that the minorities within my classroom—the Serbian, Vietnamese, and Moroccan students—had finally taken an active role with my Spanish speakers. Because they had taken such an active role, the Spanish speakers had less of a tendency to slip back into Spanish during group discussions. All of my successes were directly related to the students, unless, of course, you count the fact that I was able to do a service-learning project when it had been so heavily discouraged.

## Challenges

My greatest challenge was the administration. I was able to address this challenge by using a district-mandated curriculum to implement the project. In this way, I was able to go against the system by using the system against itself. Because more packaged curricula are including service-learning components, and more districts are requiring community service as a graduation requirement, I believe that it will be easier for teachers in the future to gain the support of their administrations.

## Role of Administration

I am a little biased, or perhaps I am an idealist, but I think that the district and administration should support a teacher's efforts in the classroom. Although I do believe that a school's administration should take somewhat of a "watchdog" approach to what teachers are doing, I also believe that administrators and district curriculum personnel need to stay current on educational research and curriculum so that when a teacher wants to implement a new strategy, the administration not only will understand what the teacher is attempting to do but also should know what to expect—field trips, access to technology, community contacts, and so on.

## What I've Learned

I learned a few things from this experience; first of all, I was reminded of how much students can do when given a chance. It is easy for teachers to let themselves believe that if students are going to succeed, teachers must maintain control and lead students every step of the way. This project reinforced for me the importance of giving students responsibility and keeping expectations high. The papers and discussions that resulted from this unit were by far the best they had done all year. Personally, I learned that where there is a will, there is a way, and there are ways to beat the system by using the system itself.

## Benefits

The most unexpected benefits were in the social interactions that took place involving my students.

a. As I mentioned earlier, my three non-Spanish speakers took a more active role in the class and became integral parts of their problem-solving groups. The most marked improvement was in my Serbian student. Not only did she speak a different language, but she was also of a different social class than most of my other students. She was highly educated, as were her parents. She was also completely separated from her family, living with a distant relative. She had been in a kind of self-imposed isolation throughout the school year. She would work with other students in the class when asked, but she preferred to work alone. Although she was in the classroom early every day with other students, she rarely socialized with them. When students would start speaking in Spanish, she would give a look of disdain and continue her work in isolation. But by the end of this unit, she was laughing with the other girls in her group, who had convinced her to participate in the graduation ceremony. And, by graduation night, she had decided to go to Grad Nite—a celebration for graduating seniors that only two weeks before she had thought was a stupid idea. Overall, all the students worked well in groups together, and those who did not pull their fair share, were reprimanded by the other members of the group and assigned "makeup" work in order to be allowed to continue to be in the group. (This plan was devised by the students not me. It worked very well. In the end, only two students were given a grade of C by their peers when it came to participation.)

b. Yet another benefit came from my seniors giving their presentations in regular classes. Besides the feeling of accomplishment that my students gained, the students in the regular classes also gained a new appreciation for the skills of the ELD (English language development) students. They enjoyed the presentations, were intrigued by and agreed with the subject matter, and appreciated the courage that it had taken for my students to get in front of the classes.

c. My students also went to the front office and spoke with administrators, secretaries, counselors, and campus supervisors to conduct interviews. From that point forward, I was inundated with inquiries and comments about my students. Everyone thought they were polite and pleasant and could not wait to hear the results of their investigations. It seems that the office personnel rarely had dealings with English language learners and were anxious to hear from them again.

## Recommendations

When this project is done again, I recommend that the following changes be made:

a. Implement the project over an 8-week period so that the results can be shared more completely with the community.

b. Start the project earlier in the year so that the groups could continue to work on solving the problems yearlong if they wished.

c. Involve the student government and administration to really try to solve the problems.

d. Take a lot of photos and videos to share with other teachers, the community, and the district in order to promote the use of service-learning with English language learners.

e. Brag in the faculty lounge.

## Student Gains

My students gained many things, but the top three are as follows:

a. Their essays were the best they had written all year. They were able to clearly and effectively communicate their ideas. They also were able to integrate their ideas with those of their peers and adults, which means their papers were also more elaborate and complete.

b. The seniors felt an immense sense of accomplishment after completing their presentations to other classes. They came back smiling and hugging each other and me—all this only 15 minutes after they had been almost in tears at the thought of giving their presentations. They were proud of themselves and said they would definitely do it again. Then, my underclassmen started asking when they could go and give their own presentations. They were ready to experience what the seniors had experienced. (Unfortunately, there was no time for this to happen, but they did feel some of the same things as they conducted interviews—although it was nothing as intense as what the seniors had felt.)

c. Although the full benefits to the community would be realized when this project could be completed in its entirety, there were many small benefits to the community of San Marcos High School. First of all, the students in regular classes who heard my senior students' presentations were made aware of the existence of ELLs and gained an appreciation of their abilities. The office personnel were touched by my students interviewing them and excited by the fact that there were students on campus who were concerned with problems at the high school. They felt honored that the students were asking for their advice.

# Instructional Resource K

## Sample Newsletter

Know Your Writes
Volume 1
Ms. Evans' Junior English Class
September 2003


**In This Volume:**



WELCOME

### Greetings and Hello!

Let me tell you a little bit about myself. I grew up in a small Ohio town named after the Ottawa Indians and attended a high school of roughly 600 students. I earned a bachelor's degree in English from Bowling Green State University in Bowling Green, Ohio. After college, I moved to Washington, D.C., and worked as an editor for several years. After moving to San Diego, I worked as a business development coordinator and also as a paralegal. I earned my teaching credential from California State University, San Marcos.

### What do you have to say? FREEDOM of SPEECH

As young adults and adults alike, we are lucky to live in a society that values our right to express ideas and opinions. In this class, we will focus on what it means to think critically and how to communicate clearly, effectively, and respectfully.

We will play with words, brainstorm ideas, formulate opinions, and examine text and facts in a variety of ways, producing narratives, essays, reports, reflective journals, projects, presentations, business pieces, and student portfolios. We will also explore American literature from various cultural and historical perspectives, including new and interesting voices. You will work individually, in pairs, and in small, cooperative groups. So tell me, what topics interest you? Do you have a complaint to share with the principal or the president? Would you like to spend some time exploring future careers? We can do that! Everyone has good ideas. Let me hear from you!

### Class BILL of "WRITES"

Each student is entitled to:

I. Be respected
II. Think critically
III. Ask questions
IV. Share opinions
V. Discuss ideas and concerns
VI. Choose topics of interest
VII. Quest for knowledge
VIII. Be creative
IX. Receive positive feedback, support, and guidance; and...
X. **SUCCEED!**

### Aiming High

Our class Mission Statement: Change is possible. It is a process to live by, not an end in itself. Our mission is to transform the world into a better, more just, more peaceful place by what we say and how we say it. Each of you deserves such a world and can help bring about change every day.

My expectations of each of you: You will demonstrate a positive attitude toward learning and achieving personal goals. You will come to class on time and be prepared to participate. You will be respectful and responsible in words and actions. You will thoughtfully complete all assignments on time. And you will work cooperatively with your peers and seek help whenever needed. We are here for each other.

You can expect to earn grades based on your commitment to the above, your quality of work, demonstration of progress, and self-evaluations. The majority of your work will be assessed using rubrics, provided in class. Exams will consist of an essay format, allowing for choice in response. Class participation will also count as part of your grade.

### To Get in Touch:

**Call me**
555-555-5555

**Write me**
The Greatest High School
1234 Open Road
Freedom, CA 99999

**Find our class on the Web**
Class Web page: www.ghs.edu/evans
Teacher e-mail: tevans@ghs.edu

## Do It the Write Way

**SUCCESS**—How can you succeed in this world? Some people think making connections is the answer, while others put their faith in money alone, but there is a way to achieve both. Two key words can help you build and maintain relationships while proving to employers that you are worth the paycheck—effective communication.

In this class, students will learn to communicate effectively through writing; they will learn to "do it the write way." Along this path, there are six key steps to...to follow? No, to venture on! **1.** Be inquisitive—question the possibilities and be open to not necessarily finding concrete answers, but more questions. **2.** Be page-turners—look up your topic in books and read, read, read. **3.** Be techno-trekkers—surf the Internet to find further information. **4.** Be investigative reporters—talk to people and seek opinions, new points of view. **5.** Be critical thinkers—explore the dark recesses of those caves we call brains and shed some light on where the information has taken you. **6.** Be writers every step of the way. Then polish your words until they shine!

But beware because plagiarism is a crime in this class. Any evidence of stealing the words or ideas of others is punishable by a failing grade for assignments and possibly for the quarter and final grade.

## Calling All Parents

There will be a number of opportunities for parents to participate in class activities. At the beginning of the year, you will reflect on your reading, writing, and verbal skills. You will examine past achievements, including those areas where you might struggle or specific skills you want to sharpen. Then you will come up with two or three goals to work on throughout the year. In setting these goals, you will discuss your thoughts with a parent or guardian.

Parents will also be participating in a book chat with you. You will share one of your chosen SSR books with a parent or guardian. The purpose is to create an open and active dialogue about a work of literature that interests you.

At the end of the year, parents will also be invited and encouraged to attend a Student Conference, organized and hosted by you. It will give you an opportunity to showcase your portfolios and discuss what you have learned and the goals you have achieved.

I will periodically communicate with parents throughout the year via e-mail, phone calls, and/or arranged meetings to discuss your achievements and any concerns. I welcome you to attend any meetings.

**THOMAS EDISON**

q u o t e s

"Opportunity is missed by most people because it is dressed in overalls and looks like work."

Genius

Inspiration
Perspiration

c o r n e r

"I have not failed. I've just found 10,000 ways that won't work."

# Instructional Resource L

## *Example for Involving Volunteers in Student Portfolio Presentations*

For early June portfolio presentations, we began the process of recruiting in late April. We needed 55 volunteers to cover our 6 periods (each period a 2-hour block) of portfolio presentations. Three of the periods involved one class each; three involved two classes presenting together. We planned so that groups contained 4 to 5 students and 1 volunteer. Once our phone calls and personal inquiries led to a list of potential volunteers, we invited each person on the list using this letter:

Dear __________ [person's name]:

Our students and we invite you to join us on either __________ or __________ [day, month], when they will present their final portfolios. These will be the culmination of their work this year in __________ [class].

Your role would be to facilitate a group of four to five students and to provide feedback on the presentations. Students will share their portfolios with one adult and a small group of their peers, focusing on their learning more than on the individual pieces. We hope that many students will choose to read a few short selections from their work. We doubt that you would need to do much facilitating, beyond asking who wants to go next. However, you could feel free to ask questions of any presenter and to encourage the other students to do so also.

The purposes of this activity include:

- Providing students with an opportunity to practice presenting themselves and their strengths orally, in a professional context.
- Celebrating their achievements publicly.
- Showing people they respect what they have accomplished this year.
- Demonstrating, to interested members of the education community, the power of portfolios.

You do not need to be an English teacher (or a teacher) to be part of this activity. The goals are to help the students discuss their work and to provide a serious audience for them.

If you would like to join us, please let us know by leaving a message at __________ [phone number] or by returning the slip below, via FAX or mail.

Thank you for your willingness to consider helping us.

Sincerely,

__________ [teacher name] and __________ [teacher name]

*******************************************************************************************

NAME: ______________________________________________

I'd like to be involved. I am available: __________ [period time] __________ [period time] __________anytime.

I'd prefer to work with: __________ sophomores __________ seniors __________either.

As we received responses to our invitations, we created a grid for each period, keeping track of the facilitators' names and preferences (date, time, and grade level). We had learned from previous experience with last-minute cancellations that we should have one or two extra facilitators for each period. This gave us the cushion we needed in an emergency "no show." We asked these extra facilitators if they would be willing to be on standby or to participate in a group with another facilitator—a partnership. When we had a partnership facilitator situation, we made sure that the students involved would be comfortable presenting to two adults.

Knowing that regular communication with volunteers is essential to reducing problems, we sent a follow-up letter to volunteers after they had confirmed their involvement with us. We used this letter as an opportunity to further define our expectations for the portfolio presentations and to help cement the facilitators' understanding of the thinking behind the presentations:

Dear __________ [volunteer's name]:

Thank you for agreeing to help with our portfolio presentations. We hope that this activity will be enjoyable and beneficial for us all. We are excited that the students have this opportunity to share the fruits of their labors. They have worked diligently all year and have accomplished some fine work.

Your role will be to facilitate and respond to their presentations. Each student will introduce her/himself and then present her/his portfolio to the small group, focusing on her/his learning more than on the individual pieces. These portfolios will contain materials selected by the students to represent their achievements in specific areas. We hope that many students will choose to read selections from their work.

After the first student presents, each member of the group will give oral feedback on both the presentation and the portfolio. We'll have some guidelines for you the day of the presentations. When all members of the group have responded, the next student will begin.

We doubt that you will need to do much facilitating, beyond asking who wants to go next. However, do feel free to ask questions of any presenter and to encourage the other students to do so. If a student gets stuck, feel free to ask questions such as:

1. What was the most challenging assignment for you? What made it challenging? How did you deal with that challenge? What was the outcome?
2. What are you proudest of? Why?
3. What assignment did you learn the most from? Why? What did you learn?
4. Reviewing your work as a whole, what do you plan to focus on in future English classes?
5. Is there anything that you accomplished this year that surprises you? What? Why does it surprise you?
6. What assignment was the easiest for you? Why? What does that suggest about you?

Again, thank you for giving your time and energy to this project. The students and we appreciate it a great deal. Please meet us in __________ [location] at __________ [time] on __________ [day], __________ [date]. You will be working with a group of four to five students. We look forward to seeing you there.

Sincerely,

__________ [name] and __________ [name]

After confirming our volunteers and their day and class period, we shared the list of volunteers with our students (just those people scheduled for those students' class period). We invited students to choose the person to whom they would like to present. Some students chose former teachers, wanting to visit with them and to share how far they had come in their learning. Other students chose parents of friends as an opportunity to reveal a new side of themselves to an adult they were already close to. Others chose people from the community with whom they shared a common interest. For example, students interested in pursuing writing as a career and/or college major often chose professional writers as their facilitators. We placed students who did not have a preference as we thought best. Without being dictatorial, we strove to create fairly heterogeneous groups rather than ones comprised entirely of friends. To maximize the learning, students must present and listen to others who are not as familiar to them as their closest friends. To create such groups can sometimes take tact to persuade students who have arranged themselves in comfortable groups of friends to switch groups. However, when we remind students of the goals of presenting, they adapt to solutions that work more productively.

To establish a relaxed yet professional atmosphere for our students and community volunteers, we reserved the media center for our presentations. Using this location allowed groups to sit around large tables rather than be separated by desks; it set a different tone by removing students from the traditional classroom environment and offered more space so that classes of different grade levels could participate together. Combining the sophomore and senior classes, even without much direct interaction between the two groups of students, added to the special feeling and helped validate the experience.

To further the ambiance, we served bagels and pastries. Individuals ate and chatted briefly before we officially began presentations, or they snacked during short breaks between presentations. We found that food plays a critical role in changing the paradigm of school for students and in relaxing all of the participants. The first year we bought dozens of bagels ourselves, incurring the cost personally. The second year we had an ambitious student call a variety of local bagel and pastry shops. They were happy to donate food for our event—we had more than we could eat in two days!

Presentation-day morning has been marked with anxious anticipation and last-minute details. Prior to participants' arrival, we set up a table with napkins and baskets of food, arranged the tables and chairs into appropriate groups, and placed the following on each table:

- A computer-generated name tent printed with the facilitator's name in big bold letters with students' names printed underneath—each individual group had its own name tent. These tents simplify seating arrangements as people arrive at staggered times.
- Blank stick-on name tags that individuals fill in as they arrive.
- A small box of different-colored markers (for the name tags).
- Blank paper and a few pens (in case anyone wants to take notes).
- An instruction sheet that recaps the oral instructions given in the contact letters and at the beginning of the presentations (to follow).
- Enough half-sheets of suggested response questions for each group member (to follow).

Before students shared their work, we spent a few minutes introducing ourselves as the teachers to the large group and establishing our goals for the period. We thanked the volunteers for joining us and asked each to stand, introduce him or herself, and share why he or she chose to participate as a facilitator. We explained the time frames for each presentation (and the need for a timekeeper) and the general presentation instructions, reminding them that they had a written copy at each table to refer to as they went along. The instruction sheet looked like this:

Welcome and thank you for being part of our students' presentations of their final English portfolios. A possible scenario for the groups is as follows:

1. All members of the group introduce themselves.
2. Students agree upon the order in which they will present.
3. The first student presents his or her portfolio to the group, focusing on his or her learning more than on the individual pieces. Listeners might take notes during the presentation, to help them give more specific and thorough feedback afterward. *(One of the listeners should volunteer to watch the time so no one student uses more than a fair share of the time.)*

4. After each student presents, each other member of the group offers oral feedback on both the presentation and the portfolio. Each presentation should take 15 to 20 minutes and responses about 5 minutes.
5. After all the members of the group have responded to the first student's presentation and portfolio, the next student will begin (return to 3).
6. When all presentations are complete, please encourage the group to discuss what they have learned individually and as a whole from the portfolio presentations.

Please feel free to ask questions of any presenter and to encourage other students to do so. If a student gets stuck, you might ask questions such as:

- What was the most challenging assignment for you? What made it challenging? How did you deal with that challenge? What was the outcome?
- What are you proudest of? Why?
- What assignment(s) did you learn the most from? Why? What did you learn?
- Reviewing your work as a whole, what do you plan to focus on in future English classes or language arts projects?
- Is there anything that you accomplished this year that surprises you? What? Why does it surprise you?
- What assignment was the easiest for you? Why? What does that suggest about you?

Thank you for giving your time and energy to this project.

The suggested response questions handout looked like this:

Response Questions

- What impressed or interested you most about the presentation and/or the portfolio? Why?
- What surprised you? Why?
- What did you want to know more about? Why?
- What do you see as the presenter's major accomplishment(s) this semester or year?
- How did the presentation help you understand what the portfolio shows?
- What might the presenter do differently next time (or in a similar situation)?

Using our suggestions as a foundation, the facilitators brought their own enthusiasm and interests to the process, and students valued their involvement. Brooke appreciated that a facilitator took "notes on what [they] found interesting about a student's portfolio. Not only does this give the student some feedback and make them feel good, it also makes [the facilitator] seem like [they] are interested in what [the student has] to say." Another student said, "It is important to have an evaluator who recognizes how important these portfolios are to us. It is much more fun, and much easier, to present to a lively, interested, responsive audience. An evaluator that gives feedback is definitely appreciated." A common theme expressed among students is a need for specific and constructive feedback. Stephen suggested, "that everyone should give more suggestions and comments to the person presenting [i.e., prior to the presentation, ask all group members to think of something that they would like to comment on to the presenter]. This would help get everything running and the atmosphere to relax a little bit. Second, make sure to comment when you like something—my evaluator did and it made a big difference."

# Name Index

# Subject Index